Critical Dialogues in Southeast Asian Studies

CHARLES KEYES, VICENTE RAFAEL, AND LAURIE J. SEARS,
SERIES EDITORS

Critical Dialogues in Southeast Asian Studies

This series offers perspectives in Southeast Asian Studies that stem from reconsideration of the relationships among scholars, texts, archives, field sites, and subject matter. Volumes in the series feature inquiries into historiography, critical ethnography, colonialism and postcolonialism, nationalism and ethnicity, gender and sexuality, science and technology, politics and society, and literature, drama, and film. A common vision of the series is a belief that area studies scholarship sheds light on shifting contexts and contests over forms of knowing and modes of action that inform cultural politics and shape histories of modernity.

Imagined Ancestries of Vietnamese Communism:
Ton Duc Thang and the Politics of History and Memory
by Christoph Giebel

Beginning to Remember: The Past in the Indonesian Present
edited by Mary S. Zurbuchen

Seditious Histories: Contesting Thai and Southeast Asian Pasts
by Craig J. Reynolds

Knowing Southeast Asian Subjects
edited by Laurie J. Sears

Making Fields of Merit: Buddhist Female Ascetics and
Gendered Orders in Thailand
Monica Lindberg Falk

Love, Passion and Patriotism: Sexuality and the Philippine
Propaganda Movement, 1882–1892
Raquel A.G. Reyes

Love, Passion and Patriotism

Sexuality and the Philippine Propaganda Movement, 1882–1892

Raquel A.G. Reyes

NUS PRESS
Singapore

in association with

UNIVERSITY OF WASHINGTON PRESS
Seattle

© 2008 NUS Press
Printed in Singapore

All rights reserved. This book, or parts thereof, may not be reproduced in any form or by any means, electronic or mechanical, including photocopying, recording or any information storage and retrieval system now known or to be invented, without written permission from the Publisher.

Published simultaneously in Singapore and the United States of America.

NUS Press
National University of Singapore
AS3-01-02, 3 Arts Link
Singapore 117569
Website: http://www.nus.edu.sg/npu

ISBN 978-0-295-98805-4

University of Washington Press
P.O. Box 50096
Seattle, WA 98145-5096, USA
www.washington.edu/uwpress

Library of Congress Cataloging-in-Publication Data

Reyes, Raquel A.G.
  Love, passion, and patriotism: sexuality and the Philippine Propaganda Movement, 1882–1892/Raquel A.G. Reyes. – 1st ed.
    p. cm. – (Critical dialogues in Southeast Asian studies)
  Includes bibliographical references and index.
  ISBN 978-0-295-98805-4 (pbk.: alk. paper)
  1. Philippines—History—1812–1898. 2. Propaganda—Philippines—History—19th century. 3. Sex—Philippines—History—19th century. 4. Philippine literature—19th century—History and criticism. 5. Sex in literature. I. Title.

DS675.R47 2008
306.709599'09034—dc22   2007051779

Cover photo: Rizal visiting Paz Pardo de Tavera and Juan Luna
(Pardo de Tavera Collection, Rizal Library, Ateneo de Manila University)

The paper used in this publication is acid-free and 90 percent recycled from at least 50 percent post-consumer waste. It meets the minimum requirements of American National Standard for Information Sciences—Permanence of Paper for Printed Library Materials, ANSI Z39.48–1984.

For

Ruben Varías Reyes and Neria Gesmundo Reyes

Contents

List of Illustrations   ix

Preface   xi

Introduction   xvii

1. **The Sensual Scene: Love and Courtship in Urbane Manila**

The City and European Civilities	1
City Folk and the Experience of Romance	11
The Rules of Urbanidad and the Affirmation of Bourgeois Sexuality	20
Manila Society and Bourgeois Honor	26

2. **Encountering *La Parisienne*: Juan Luna and the Challenge of Modern Femininity**

Painting *La Parisienne*	39
Defining the Modern Woman	43
Journeying to Modern Life	49
Ilustrados and the Allure of Paris	53
Parisian Chic	59
"Monsieur Wants to Kill Madame"	67

3. **Antonio Luna's *Impresiones*: The Anatomy of *Amor Propio***

Disenchantment	84
A Question of Honor	91
Sport and Sartorial Subversion	94
Vulgarity	101
Entering the Contact Zone	103
"Does she love me?"	108

4. Friar Immorality and Female Religiosity in the Ilustrado Imagination

Eradicating the Human Poison	117
Sex and the Sacerdotes	121
The Ignorance of the Masses	128
Sleeping with the Enemy: The Culpability of Women	133
Supplanting the Friars: Bourgeois Men and the Path to Redemption	139

5. Pathological Visions: Rizal, Female Sexuality and the Sickness of Society

Truth in Science	154
Chengoy's Gossip and "The Eastern Question"	162
Mad, Bad and Hysterical: Female Sexuality in *Noli me tangere*	167
Rizal's Patria	177
Sculpting the Sensual	180

6. Silencing the Flesh: Rizal's Erasure of Female Sexual Pleasure

Sex and Civilization	198
Footnoting Fornication: Rizal's Annotations of Antonio de Morga's *Sucesos de las Islas Filipinas*	206
A Lexical Detour: Defining Desire in Serrano Laktaw's *Diccionario*	217
The Elusiveness of Virtue	222
Sex Education	225
Brotherly Advice	230

Conclusion	254
Biographical Appendix	260
Bibliography	275
Index	296

List of Illustrations

1. José Rizal, Marcelo H. del Pilar and Mariano Ponce, c. 1890 — xv
2. Antonio Luna, Eduardo de Lete and Marcelo H. del Pilar, c. 1890 — xv
3. Juan Luna in his *atelier* with Eduardo de Lete, José Rizal and Felix Pardo de Tavera, c. 1889 — xvi
4. Antonio Luna, c. 1890 — xvi
5. Map of Intramuros and Binondo, 1901 — 6
6. Juan Luna, *La Parisienne*, c. 1886 — 41
7. Juan Luna, *Una Chula I*, c. 1885 — 44
8. Juan Luna, *Una Chula II*, c. 1885 — 44
9. Map of Paris, c. 1890 — 55
10. Juan Luna, *Parisian Life*, c. 1892 — 57
11. Juan Luna, *Parisian Life*, c. 1892 (detail) — 57
12. *Matrimonio Luna*, 8 December 1886 — 62
13. Juan Luna, *Una Dama Francesa*, c. 1890 — 62
14. Juan Luna, Portrait of Paz Pardo de Tavera in hat, 1886 — 62
15. Photograph of Paz Pardo de Tavera, Juliana Gorricho and Juan Luna (with face scribbled out) — 64
16. Photograph portrait of Paz Pardo de Tavera — 64
17. Juan Luna, *En sueños de amor*, c. 1886 — 68

18. Juan Luna, Portrait of woman holding rosary, c. 1890 — 68

19. Juan Luna, *Odalisque*, c. 1886 — 69

20. Juan Luna, Study for *Odalisque*, c. 1886 — 70

21. Juan Luna, *Luling castigado por su Mama*, c. 1892 — 72

22. Ilustrados in Madrid, c. 1890 — 96

23. Juan Luna, José Rizal and Valentin Ventura, c. 1886 — 98

24. Juan Luna, self portrait, 1886 — 99

25. José Rizal, *The Triumph of Science over Death*, or *Scientia*, 1890 — 181

26. José Rizal, *The Victory of Death over Life*, 1890 — 181

27. José Rizal, *Reclining Nude*, 1890 — 182

Preface

This book explores the manifold, oftentimes contradictory, ways in which sex suffused the patriotic discourse of the young men who first shaped a Filipino national identity. The study focuses on selected works by four renowned Filipino patriots — literary pieces by José Rizal (1861–96), Marcelo H. del Pilar (1850–96) and Antonio Luna (1866–99) and paintings by Juan Luna (1857–99).[1] These works are assessed in the context of their authors' backgrounds, their academic training, their travels overseas and their relationships with women.

Plaques commemorating the historical presence of these remarkable Filipinos can be found in London, Paris, Madrid, Barcelona, Ghent and other European cities. These plaques are on the houses and hotels where they stayed, in cafés where they gathered, and on university buildings, libraries and museums where they studied. José Rizal, the Philippines' most important national hero, has the singular distinction of having a garden square named after him in Paris, and a monument erected in his honor in Madrid.

These markers attest to the exceptionally wide range of interests and activities that preoccupied the ilustrado Filipinos: they moved through the turmoil of city crowds with energy and alertness, young men at the height of their powers. But they reacted to urban modernity differently than the Baudelairean *flâneur* and *dilettante*. They scrutinized Europe's treasures, traditions, learning, women and the cosmopolitan modernity that so profoundly captured their imaginations.

By 1896 the most prominent propagandistas were dead. Marcelo H. del Pilar and Graciano López Jaena both died from tuberculosis in Spain, impoverished. Rizal was executed by a firing squad in Manila after being found guilty of treason to Spain. The death of the brothers Antonio and Juan Luna followed three years later; the first by assassination, the latter by a heart attack. Cast by history in the sacral light of patriotic sacrifice, the deaths of these men have swept aside the vicissitudes of their lives, erased the private, the sexual and the everyday.

This book offers a new interpretation of the propagandistas' patriotic project by discerning coherence between their patriotic aspirations and the complex dynamics of their lives in Europe. I do not argue there to be a causal relationship between the propagandistas' political aims and their sexual attitudes and behavior. This book springs from my conviction that a focus on the humanity of the propagandistas is a fruitful means of understanding their ideals, their labors, and their desire to be modern. I show how they found Europe to be intellectually, imaginatively and libidinally stimulating as well as a source of anxiety and disenchantment.

It is opportune here to note that the propagandistas mainly wrote in Spanish, but several were proficient too in other languages. Rizal believed that man multiplied himself by "the number of languages he possesses and speaks, and prolongs and renews his life in proportion to the number of places he visits."[2] Rizal was a polyglot and few could rival his command of languages; nevertheless some learnt to speak French and English, most spoke and wrote in Tagalog and a few liked to shift between two languages in their informal correspondence.[3] As we shall see, Rizal often switched from writing in Spanish to Tagalog, occasionally sprinkled his German letters with Spanish and French words, and wrote to his younger relatives in the Philippines in English. This linguistic switching sometimes held significant connotations. A shift from Spanish to Tagalog in Rizal's letters for example, signalled a need for a deeper level of confidentiality and privacy that was mutually shared and understood amongst the compatriots. The sources have been translated to reflect this linguistic fluidity and highlight the importance the propagandistas placed on being able to move through different linguistic terrain.

I was extremely fortunate to have the support of several institutions and people who in various ways contributed to the research and writing of this book. I wish to thank the British Arts and Humanities Research Board for providing financial support throughout the life of this project. I was also a grateful recipient of generous travel grants from the British Academy and the University of London which enabled me to undertake crucial research in Manila, Chicago, Paris and Madrid.

I deeply appreciate the assistance given to me by the staff of several libraries and archives. In particular, I warmly thank Mercie Servida at the López Museum, Frank Puzon at the Pardo de Tavera Room, Rizal Library in the Ateneo de Manila University, the staffs at the Philippine National Museum, the Bangko Sentral ng Pilipinas and the Metropolitan

Museum; in Paris the staff at the Musée et Archives de la Préfecture de Police and the Archives de Paris. Thanks are also due to Ramon Villegas who was kind enough to take me through some of his collection.

I owe special debts of gratitude to those people who carefully read every page of the manuscript and forced me to sharpen my thoughts with their perspicacious comments. At the School of Oriental and African Studies, University of London, William Radice, friend and mentor, rescued me in so many ways. I am deeply grateful for his enthusiasm, intellectual generosity and patient guidance. David Smyth shared his expertise in Southeast Asian literature and was always supportive. Jo Labanyi, at New York University, inspires me with her intellectual rigor and tireless energy. I am always grateful for the assiduous eye she casts over my work and for her warm encouragement. At the University of Washington, Vicente Rafael, at a very early stage in my research, steered me, albeit unwittingly, into writing this book. As will be evident in the pages that follow, I have in many ways drawn upon his insights and expertise. I cannot thank him enough for his marvellous scholarship, his advice, support and kindness.

Talks in front of students and faculty at the University of the Philippines were very helpful in developing and clarifying my thoughts. Many thanks go to Carolyn Sobritchea, Raul Pertierra, Rosario de los Santos. I also thank Megan Thomas whom I met, serendipitously, while researching in Manila. Ambeth Ocampo, Vivencio Jose and Maria Luisa Camagay shared with me their deep knowledge of Philippine history. Santiago (Jak) Pilar's keen expertise is truly admirable, I thank him for all his help and his warm comradeship. Armando Malay, Jr. was supportive well beyond my time at the Asian Center at the University of the Philippines where he was Dean during my affiliation as a research fellow in 2000–2001.

Several descendants of the propagandistas welcomed me into their homes, recalled precious memories and made my research in Manila richly memorable. Asunción López Bantug, grandniece of José Rizal, the late Mita Pardo de Tavera and Mara Pardo de Tavera, descendants of Trinidad Pardo de Tavera, bore my questions with good grace and generous hospitality, sharing with me their insights on their illustrious ancestors and supplying me with photographs. I thank Paul Kratoska at NUS Press for having faith in this work and Lena Qua for her patient editing. In the final stages of bringing the manuscript to press, I also received much appreciated assistance from the Royal Netherlands Institute for the Study of Southeast Asia and the Caribbean (KITLV) in Leiden. Peter Boomgaard was particularly inspiring.

Certain people, however, are responsible for my survival in the process of writing this book. I am deeply grateful to Taghred Elsanhouri, Jennifer Josef, Montira Rato and my wonderful aunts Tita Didi and Tita Aida Malabo in Chicago who provided me with a home while I worked at the Newberry Library. In London, Jim Richardson's friendship and good humor made my labors much more pleasurable. He has helped me in ways that I could not begin to detail. My family know just how much they contribute to my life and work. I thank my brother Richard for all his support and encouragement; my daughter Gaïa, who spent the first years of her life with me in museums, libraries and lectures. For their belief in me and their unstinting support and love, I thank my parents Ruben Varías Reyes and Neria Gesmundo Reyes, to whom I dedicate this book.

Raquel Reyes
London/Madrid/Paris

Notes

[1] Photographs of the principal propagandistas discussed in this study are reproduced as Figs. 1 to 4. These photographs have been selected to highlight the men's youthfulness, comportment and sartorial style.
[2] José Rizal, "Los Viajes," *La Solidaridad* 1: 7 (15 May 1889): 159.
[3] In this book I look at sources written in Tagalog, French, German and Spanish, and unless otherwise stated the translations are my own.

Fig. 1 José Rizal, Marcelo H. del Pilar and Mariano Ponce, c. 1890 (Ramon Villegas Collection)

Fig. 2 Antonio Luna, Eduardo de Lete and Marcelo H. del Pilar, c. 1890 (Filipiniana Division, Main Library, University of the Philippines, Diliman)

Fig. 3 Juan Luna in his *atelier* with Eduardo de Lete, José Rizal and Felix Pardo de Tavera, c.1889
(Filipiniana Section, Philippine National Library)

Fig. 4 Antonio Luna, c.1890
(Filipiniana Division, Main Library, University of the Philippines, Diliman)

Introduction

Avengers of Filipino Honor

José Panganiban had got himself into trouble. Whilst studying medicine in Barcelona, he had been having an affair with a married Spanish woman and had been caught. He had made the mistake of writing her a piquant letter and leaving some papers in her keeping. The woman's husband had discovered this incriminating evidence and had gone searching for the rogue. The Filipino succeeded in evading him for a while by hiding out at the house of a compatriot, but his luck ran out when the cuckolded husband spotted him strolling one Saturday night in the Plaza de Cataluña. The husband and another man then gave Panganiban a vicious beating. The Filipino defended himself bravely, even managing to knock one of his assailants down, but a heavy blow to the head bloodied him and sent him reeling, bringing the skirmish to an end.[1]

Much to the relief of the Filipino community in Spain, this episode did not reach the courts. His friends, however, still fretted over his romantic recklessness, of which this episode was but the latest example. Writing from Barcelona, a worried Mariano Ponce briefed José Rizal on the situation: "What we want is to retrieve the papers and separate the adulterers. We are keeping this affair a secret; I am only telling you about it so that you will know of our misfortune."[2] The matter did soon find a resolution, but a sad one. Less than two months later, José Panganiban lost his long battle against tuberculosis and died aged just 27.[3]

Love affairs with European women were by no means unusual amongst the students and other Filipino expatriates, and were just as intensely discussed as the strategies, successes and setbacks of the political campaign. Indeed, an affair of the heart was treated as hot news. At the root of Ponce's anxiety about Panganiban's discovered affair lay the desire to protect the integrity of the patriotic cause in Spain and maintain the good name of the community. Sexual misdeeds that turned into scandals were considered no less damaging than internecine faction fights and personal squabbles. Each threatened the reputation of the Filipinos and the credibility of their campaign. Sexual discretion and careful concealment were vital. But adventures with European women were also applauded as affirmations of Filipino manliness and patriotic honor. Tales of experimentation, exploration and conquest animated the young men's gossip and camaraderie, and the need for discretion nourished a semi-conspiratorial sense of solidarity amongst the scattered expatriates.

José Panganiban was greatly mourned by his compatriots. Passionate, gifted and hardworking, he was recognized as a great loss to both the campaign and the nation's future. Rizal had once called him a man "very necessary to our cause."[4] In his eulogy to Panganiban, though, his friend and fellow patriot Graciano López Jaena did not dwell on his achievements or contributions to the movement. Desiring to elevate and memorialize the young man's life, he focused instead on the young Filipino's sense of honor. Panganiban's dangerous romantic dalliances, López Jaena believed, reflected his wider ambition to live a life of passion, courage and patriotic conviction. Like most young men, Panganiban dreamed of achieving renown, glory, applause and distinction. His talents, extolled López Jaena, would have helped set the nation on the path to prosperity and redemption had his life not been so cruelly cut short. He then recalled what his friend had once asked him: "When I die, put this epitaph on my tomb: 'Here lies the avenger of Filipino honour.'"[5]

These words, López Jaena admitted, had been spoken in jest. Fornication could not always be excused or dignified on the grounds of patriotic honor, and to pretend otherwise would have been both spurious and invidious. Sometimes, fornication was simply fornication. The fact remains, however, that the link Panganiban and his friend López Jaena both drew between manliness and patriotism exemplified a new way of thinking for Filipinos. Rather than trivialize Panganiban's bravado and bluster, López Jaena discerned in the exultant epitaph an undercurrent of solemnity and a wish to be remembered in a specific way. Panganiban had struggled to assert what Spanish prejudices and insults had denied Filipino men — the recognition of their worth in society, a respect for their manhood and an understanding of their humanity. His sexual adventuring was seen not as a stain on his character but as a matter for pride, comparable with professional distinction or political achievement. Panganiban's sexual recklessness had thus found legitimation: "Your misdeeds, your frailties," López Jaena assured the shade of his departed friend, "are justified and kindly regarded in our unfortunate country."[6]

This perception of Panganiban's affair appears to exemplify Foucault's insight into how sex and its experiences came to be affiliated with the lustre and exaltedness of political causes in the nineteenth century.[7] But certain forms of love could also be associated with notions of progress and a new type of identity that could be defined as both patriotic and modern. In his analysis of incipient nationalist sentiments in late 1920s and 1930s Indonesia, James Siegel has argued how only a certain love, a love linked to selflessness and to the struggle for progress, a love wrapped in idealism, might also be an expression of modernity. Such a love was above all "moral" and here lay its power. As Siegel writes, only love distinguished by selflessness could be deemed true and legitimate and had the potency and power to "compel recognition of desire transformed into idealism.... At that time this meant not independence and not equality. It meant rather the possibility of having a certain identity."[8]

Panganiban's sexual desire, as Lopez Jaena pictured it, is properly moral because it is directed towards recovering the dignity of the Filipino people. Lopez Jaena's words indicate an attitude that went beyond merely wanting to vindicate his friend. Panganiban's sexuality was recognized as being a key element in his identity as a man of honor and Filipino patriot. A sexual identity that embodied patriotic love and a commitment to the advancement of one's country distinguished a self that was new and transformed. This was a profoundly different and new recognition of a Filipino identity. To have this identity was to feel love and passion with great seriousness. It marked one as progressive and modern.

Scholars have recognized that the scope of the propaganda movement extended beyond the narrow political arena into a wide-ranging exploration of Philippine history, languages and cultures aimed at engendering a sense of national consciousness, identity and community. Very little scholarly attention, though, has been given to how, within the process of fostering a new national identity, the propagandists sought to delineate an ideal, distinctively Filipino model of social behavior. This entailed stipulating criteria of sexual identity and standards for sexual behavior to which men and women needed to conform for the sake of the country and its progress. The following study aims to describe and illustrate the ways in which sexuality was central to the shaping of a social and national identity. The control and regulation of male and female bodies and their particular sexual natures, it is contended, was crucial to the propagandistas' creation of a Filipino national consciousness and their understanding of modernity.

The Propaganda Movement

In the narrow political sense the propaganda movement ended in failure. Spain never acceded to its demands for the Philippines to be granted the same status as the provinces of the Peninsula, with representatives in the Cortes; for Filipinos to be granted the same rights as Spanish citizens; for the power of the friar religious orders to be curtailed; and for fundamental liberal reforms. When the campaign collapsed in the mid-1890s, it was already torn apart by internal disunity and starved of funds. In the broader, longer-term view, however, the *ilustrado* (enlightened) propagandistas left an intellectual and cultural legacy that helped shape Philippine nationalism and Philippine society throughout the next century.[9] In art, poetry, prose, journalism, speeches and scholarly essays on history, language and folklore, the propagandistas were the first to craft a specific nationalist vocabulary and to create a body of work that signaled, for the first time, a self-conscious effort to speak of a common heritage and a common destiny, to depict a particular, authentic and recognizably Filipino character and identity.

This emergence of a national consciousness is the central theme explored by the American Jesuit historian John Schumacher, whose studies of the propaganda movement and its illustrious *laborantes* are by far the most detailed yet written.[10] Schumacher's scrupulously researched works examine not only the ideas, organization, campaign methods and activities of the early nationalists but also their material and ideological contexts. In Schumacher's analysis, the propagandistas' consciousness of a specifically Filipino identity is narrowly restricted to the ways in which they imagined Filipinos to possess a common origin and destiny and to be equal to their Spanish colonizers. This political conception of nationality was asserted and made manifest in their literary and artistic accomplishments. In this view, one that dominates traditional historiography, the construction of a national identity and its meanings finds broad explanation in the ambitions awakened amongst the elite by growing overseas trade and contact with the currents of European liberalism.

There is a great deal to be lost in taking this limited, partial view. The exclusive attention given to the propagandistas' political campaign strikingly neglects to describe the rich texture of their everyday human life; the illuminations brought by such experiences as homesickness and lovesickness; the terrors of tedium, loneliness, physical illness, financial debt; the anger that an insult arouses; the degree of passion that sexual jealousies stoke; and the intimacies, consequences, pursuits and pleasures of sex.

A few historians, more recently, have endeavored to portray the Philippines' national heroes in a more human light by recounting details that hagiographies have liked to avoid.[11] Hitherto ignored aspects of the propagandistas' lives in Europe such as their grooming, their duelling and womanising do indeed make provocative, even titillating reading, dramatizing historical lives which conventional history writing has made hollow and lifeless. Yet there remains a need to understand how duelling, sexual affairs, attention to clothing and appearance, the appeal to reason, the insistence on politeness, cleanliness and a healthy physique contributed to the imaging of a national identity. Racist colonial ideology and the identities it imposed, for example, animated a range of reactions amongst the propagandistas who sought to resist and combat its emasculating effects through displays of manliness. To charges of puerility, cowardice, effeminacy, savagery, laziness, filth and barbarism, they vigorously responded with exhibitions of manly courage and honor, meticulous sartorial style and intellectual achievement. This book pursues a particular strand of enquiry in relation to the propagandistas' conceptions of a Filipino identity. It aims to show how aspects of the sensual, macho stylishness and scientific interests became deeply embedded in the propagandistas' patriotic endeavors and influenced their notions of sexual difference.

Trying to imagine how nineteenth-century Filipino bourgeois men regarded sex and sexual categories is a problematic undertaking. Many of the works I look at have not customarily been seen as having a significant sexual content. To some scholars, the importance of these works lies in what they tell us about the political and social vision of the founding fathers of the Philippine nation. "Reading sex" into these documents, as common parlance might describe my focus, may be seen by such scholars as highlighting what is either thought to be trivial or, worse, thought to be absent. This is an easy accusation to make. But it is a charge that can only be supported if one takes the view that the propagandistas lived lives cleansed of the quotidian and insulated from sexual passions — lives, in other words, of singular and undeflected political purpose. This is a fallacious view. Sex ripples through their works in humorous innuendo, or in withering blasts of criticism of Church hypocrisy or didactic moralizing. Memoirs may subtly describe a youthful, ludic moment; loquacious letters record an exchange of opinions about sex, recall the sharing of a private joke, or a discreet discussion of a sexual dilemma.

Sex, however, does more than give flavor and color to the propagandistas' works and correspondence. It was an integral part of their experience of Europe, their understanding of the sexual nature of women and of themselves as men. Rather than ignoring or dismissing sex, we are duty bound to ponder the specific weight of its meaning within the complexity of the propagandistas' daily lives. The approach taken then becomes important.

Recent decades have seen an increase in academic studies that explore the gendering of national imaginaries. In his groundbreaking study *Imagined Communities,* Benedict Anderson has asserted that "in the modern world everyone can, should, will 'have' a nationality, as he or she 'has' a gender."[12] Though the point was left unelaborated, the idea that national identity and gender are relational and contiguous has struck a chord amongst scholars attempting to map the terrain of passionate patriotism and the political dynamics of nationhood.[13] This terrain is marked both by bloodshed and bonds between men, for the ties that are imagined to bind the modern nation into a community are deep and fraternal, inciting great loyalty and eliciting sacrifice that "[make] it possible, over the past two centuries, for so many millions of people, not so much to kill, as willingly to die for such limited imaginings."[14] Anne McClintock has emphasized how "all nationalisms are gendered, all are invented and all are dangerous ... in the sense that they represent relations to political power and the technologies of violence."[15]

While the nation privileges ties between men, women have historically figured as effective symbols and metaphors of and for the nation.[16] Indeed, as some scholars argue, it is often the widespread dissemination of images of gendered bodies produced within nationalist and revolutionary cultures that send out the most powerful political and social messages. Joan Landes has examined how representations of women prevalent in French popular imagery did much to "visualize the nation," work to articulate and promote French republicanism and define collective ideals. Yet, within this brave, new "*la Patrie*" being forged by French eighteenth-century revolutionaries, where the private and domestic was given equal importance to the public and political realm, participation and access to privileges in the new nation would always be different for men and women. Man's enjoyment of citizenship and universal rights, his essential identity as a national subject, hinged upon the requirement for men and women to play entirely different roles and to take entirely unequal positions in society.[17] For early French republicans, writes Landes, "possessing *la Patrie*" turned on a paradox: under the new nation, the status of women was to be elevated; women were to be possessed by men, honored, cherished and protected by men, respected and consulted on important issues, but were never to be granted the same liberties as men. Following George Mosse, Landes reveals how certain codes of conduct, attitudes to sexuality, manners and morals became inextricably linked to modern nationalism. "Sex, it happens, mattered a great deal," writes Landes, "and so did morality":

> In both arenas [sex and morality], women were expected to behave differently from the way men did. What is more, good behaviour was not just a private matter; private morality was intimately tied to public virtue and state interest. Unhampered sexuality was seen as a threat to the republican body politic, and women's unlicensed sexuality and untempered enthusiasms were thought to imperil state and civil order.[18]

Landes' insight is useful to the present study which aims to tease out the intimate connections between the emergence and development of nationalism and the crucial changes in attitudes towards morality, in ideas of sexual and social propriety, in social respectability and civic virtues, in conceptions of public life and that of private life and domesticity.

Southeast Asian nationalist historiographies have particularly tended to exclude the perspectives of certain marginalized groups in their construction of a nation's history. Women especially, and until recently, remained markedly absent in national stories. Southeast Asian feminist historians, acutely aware of the absence of women within nationalist male-dominated meta-narratives, have endeavored to redress the balance by researching and publishing works devoted to biographies of outstanding women in the nation's history. In the Philippines and elsewhere, the effort to include an array of notable women and their sacrifices for the nation is actively promoted by governments who sponsor a range of prizes — in poetry, painting, and biographical writing — especially during national celebrations, for works that focus on the nation's heroines.[19] But if recognition of female participation within nationalist histories has become more widespread, women's histories, as Barbara Watson Andaya pointedly notes, continue to be treated as supplementary, as interruptions in nationalist narratives, typically inserted into accepted nationalist themes that privilege the activities of men — revolutionary and nationalist campaigns, struggles for freedom against colonial oppression and the awakening of nationalist consciousness. Serving only to "'modify' standard accounts of how new nations were made" the effort to incorporate women has done little to disturb the "hegemony of the national epic" and change the way in which national history is written.[20] Questions concerning women and their relationships with men are markedly elided and "in the majority of cases, those who have earned a part in the nation's drama have done so by demonstrating their success in 'male-like' roles."[21]

Studies on late nineteenth-century Philippine nationalism have long dominated Philippine historiography. But unsurprisingly, it is conspicuous that works investigating the relationship between the emergence of Filipino nationalism, gender, sexuality and the lives of the ilustrado-propagandistas in Europe in the late nineteenth century are so few and scattered.[22]

The temptation to interpret the propagandistas' understanding of sexual difference with twenty-first-century empathy has unfortunately marked attempts to confront the interdependence of masculinity and the formation of a Philippine national identity in the late nineteenth century. "If ... in trying to rebut Spanish challenges to Philippine masculinity they failed to question the very premises of the challenge," Norman Owen writes, "it can be forgiven."[23] This type of anachronistic judgement, however well meant, teaches us nothing about the historical moment in which these intellectuals lived.

Drawing on a careful and more nuanced examination of visual and textual sources, Vicente Rafael has approached nineteenth-century ilustrado imaginings of nationhood by investigating gendered representations of the nation found in Rizal's writings, or as Rafael puts it "textualised embodiments of the motherland," and photographic images of the ilustrados, the studiously dignified and reserved images of "photographed bodies of male patriots." For Rafael, the ilustrado love of country produced a patriotic discourse filled with oedipal tension and conflict. Equally animated by hostility and jealousy towards Spanish friars and the power they wielded in the colony over money and women, as well as the anxious and urgent desire to displace clerical authority with their own, ilustrado love fused filial duty toward the mother, both real and figurative, and toward country:

> Equating love of nation with love of mother idealised the former in terms of the latter. Thus could sacrifice and loss appear necessary and reasonable: by acting as their protectors, sons could reciprocate the affections of mothers, real or imagined.[24]

Sexuality and sexual categories, we now know, possess histories. They are neither static nor fixed, universal biological givens but cultural constructs, moulded by time and place.[25] Part of this book's project is to reveal the propagandistas' aspirations to sexual modernity by showing how, as members of the nineteenth-century Filipino elite, they took over and embodied the codes of honor and comportment of the European noble gentleman whilst simultaneously linking them to chivalrous patriotism, national progress and modernity. I will also show how the propagandistas' conception of sexual identity was imbricated in European medical and scientific thinking, which believed sexuality to be deeply rooted in the biological structures of individuals.

My reading of the propagandistas' art and literature tacks between such varied sources as their diaries, memoirs, reminiscences and personal correspondence; their social milieu and the overall European cultural and intellectual context in which they lived and produced their works. No one has previously attempted to situate the propagandistas' patriotic aspirations wholly within the pressures and complications of their everyday lives in Europe, and their encounter with European cultural and scientific thinking. Nor has anyone hitherto delineated the manner in which the propagandistas' patriotism was subsumed by their desire for modernity, a condition to which contradictory sexual attitudes were intrinsic.[26]

Encountering Europe

The propagandistas spent their prime years in Europe. Not one of the principal men who figure in this study spent less than 8 years on the continent: Juan Luna lived there for a period of 17 years, from 1877 to 1893, and his younger brother Antonio for 8 years, from 1885 to 1893. Graciano López Jaena lived in Barcelona from 1882 until his death in 1896 and Marcelo H. del Pilar lived in Spain from 1888 until he too died there from tuberculosis in 1896. José Rizal spent 8 years in Europe in total, staying first from 1882 to 1887 and then from 1888 to 1891.

In an important sense, they considered Europe, and not just one country within it, as their living place. They had the time and the means to travel widely. Financially dependent on their families in the Philippines, they could enjoy the luxury of pursuing their own interests, their only obligation being to study for the professions.[27] Rizal, the most restless of all, lived at different times in five countries — Belgium, France, England and Germany as well as Spain. Filipino travelers received hospitality and assistance from networks of friends, relatives, political sympathizers and fellow freemasons. In London, ilustrado Filipinos gravitated to the large home of the wealthy lawyer, the old political reformer Antonio Regidor, and in Paris they found a welcome in the houses of the Pardo de Tavera family.

The propagandistas were prolific in their fields and possessed fine, inquiring minds. They were intellectual innovators, pursuing interests that encompassed a wide and disparate field of disciplines — philology, botany, history, art, law, engineering and the biomedical sciences. Indeed, living in Europe and travelling to multiple European capitals fuelled their exuberant intellectual cosmopolitanism. To paraphrase Resil Mojares, no decade was as "productive and consequential" for Philippine intellectual history as the 1880s.[28] With the aid of new technological inventions — telegraphic cable systems, expanded railway networks and postal services — they themselves and their country were brought into contact with some of the most exciting political, scientific and literary developments to have occurred in nineteenth-century Europe. This contact held intriguing possibilities of communication, to colonial society and importantly beyond it. For the ilustrados, the foreign, to paraphrase Vicente Rafael's memorable phrase, carried this important promise.[29]

As students and expatriates, the ilustrados were also at a good vantage point from which to judge the culture and society of a Europe which then seemed to be in the throes of panic about sex and gender. The 1880s and 1890s, in the words of one contemporary writer, were decades of "sexual anarchy."[30] In London, for example, women not only competed with men for gainful employment but also, as the diary of Amy Levy details, frequented women's clubs and smoking rooms and toiled in the Reading Room of the British Museum.[31] By the end of the nineteenth century, the image of the sexually independent New Woman who seemed to challenge male supremacy in art, the professions and the home had become a familiar figure all over Europe.

In England, scandals and debate raised the levels of public awareness about sexuality. From 1885 to 1889, the most significant debates on the question of sexuality occurred in the meetings of the Men and Women's Club where Olive Schreiner and Eleanor Marx were members. Rizal was in London when these discussions were at their most heated, and when the newspapers were filled with homosexual scandals and Jack the Ripper's gruesome murders of East End prostitutes, a climate of sexual crises he remarked upon in *La Solidaridad*.[32] When Juan Luna was living in Paris, the prostitutes in the streets inspired artists but alarmed public health officials. In 1889 one doctor estimated the figure to be well over 100,000, feeding fears over the social circulation of vice and perceptions of an uncontrollable "invasion."[33] The ilustrado Filipinos noticed how European women moved freely and easily in public spaces — in streets, museums, galleries, shops and cafés, and on boats and trains. Prostitutes and the commerce in flesh exerted both a libidinal and sociological interest to the propagandistas. Rizal even took note of the dubious advertisements for female housekeepers, maids and companions in German newspapers, which asked applicants to present themselves at specified railway stations in Holland, France and England.[34]

If this wider European cultural context is considered, we can see how the propagandist desire to define a Filipino sexual identity and behavior fell in step with European cultural anxieties and scientific debates over human sexuality. Medicine during the course of the nineteenth century was preoccupied with the pathological aspects of human sexuality and those training to be physicians amongst the propagandistas would encounter for the first time the study of hysteria, masturbation, prostitution and its attendant venereal diseases as sexual problems. Medical students and specialists in Paris in the 1880s were invited to scrutinise hysterical symptoms in female patients at Jean Martin Charcot's celebrated neurology clinic at the Salpetrière asylum. The clinical evidence from these investigations was utilized to develop a technical language and classificatory systems to describe hysteria as much as to find a treatment and cure.

The physiological foundation of sexual difference was explicitly spelled out in a profusion of sex manuals, both scientific and pseudo-scientific. The Spanish physician Pedro Felipe Monlau, for example, writing in his popular guide for married couples *Higiene del Matrimonio*, could not have been clearer about the natural attributes of the male: "ardent, proud, robust, generous, hairy (*velludo*), daring and dominant." *El sexo masculino*, in the Spanish doctor's view, was physically destined for an active life and possessed elevated mental faculties. The creation of man, or indeed woman, he counselled, began at conception. He recommended women wishing to conceive a son to be active and bathe in seas and rivers; they were to eat a good strong diet of succulent meats and shellfish, and to drink several daily glasses of a potent aphrodisiac, a red wine tonic spiced with ginger, cinnamon and musk. For women wishing to conceive a daughter, on the other hand, Monlau prescribed a regime of inactivity, of domesticity and stillness. They were to drink white wine accompanied by the roasted and finely ground liver and testicles of a suckling pig.[35] Science contended that women were the weaker sex because of their biological functions. Women possessed smaller bones, skulls, arms and hands; were smaller in stature, their skin whiter, and their blood vessels finer. Since their nature was dominated by emotions and delicate sensibilities, women were biologically unsuitable for the institutions of learning, incapable of great discoveries and the composition of epic poetry. Their destiny lay in the delights of the family and of love.[36]

Male individual corporeal confidence and the possession of courage and virility, the propagandistas widely agreed, expressed itself in a robust physicality, European male attire, facial hair, displays of manliness within public life, in sports such as fencing and pistol practice, in sexual affairs with women. The conceptualization of a vigorous masculinity drew a web of connections linking patriotism and the well-being of the country with the medical idea that spermatic expenditures be carefully regulated; with the belief that non-reproductive forms of sexuality — such as lesbianism — should be shunned; and non-reproductive forms of sexual practices — such as sodomy — be abhorred and treated with disgust. The Filipina, on the other hand, was believed by the propagandistas to possess inherent qualities of tenderness, sweetness, gentleness, docility and passivity, attributes they saw as the appropriate, natural and biologically-ordained complement to the sexual identity of men.

"Love, Passion and Patriotism"

This book examines how the propagandistas wanted Filipino sexual behavior and codes to embody their ideals of patriotic love, modernity and progress. The zigging and zagging procedure that characterizes my approach aims to reflect the several intellectual and cultural contexts that marked the ilustrado experience of Europe. It is an approach that strives towards an articulation of the past through the kind of historical materialism that Walter Benjamin has described as seizing hold of an image or memory that "flashes up at the instant when it can be recognised."[37] The chapters in this book are organized and structured around such moments of recognition and illumination. As each of the chapters will show, moral reform of the sexual character of Filipino men and women was believed to be crucial to the well-being of the country. However, the changes the propagandistas sought to make in the sexual nature of Filipino women which, they believed, had become corrupted and fouled by colonialism and modern cosmopolitanism, finds contradiction in their attitudes towards European women. As we shall see, if the unconstrained and brazen sexuality of European women was a keen source of libidinal attraction for the ilustrados, a similar display in their female compatriots generated disgust, fear and loathing.

Chapter 1 begins the story in Manila and discusses meanings of love in the context of political and cultural changes that were occurring in the modernizing city. Manila would always act as anchor and reference point for the propagandistas, the place where they first migrated from their provincial homes and were taught as adolescents the sexual codes that constituted *urbanidad*.

In Chapter 2, the focus moves to Europe and centers upon the differing effects of European modernity on the propagandistas' notions of femininity and masculinity. Whilst modernity was seen as a positive force for the development of a man's intellectual and social character, it was seen as having an opposite, corrupting impact upon the sexual nature of the Filipino woman. Through a detailed study of selected paintings by Juan Luna examined in the context of his artistic and domestic life in Paris, the chapter aims to highlight a dramatic moment of sexual crisis, Luna's escalating conflict with his wife, whom he accused of a legion of crimes. She was, he perceived, altogether too modern and worldly, grievously disrespectful of his *amor propio* or manly pride, and finally adulterous.

Examining the highly valorized manly attribute of *amor propio* more closely, Chapter 3 demonstrates how the bodies and sexuality of the male ilustrados and their expressions of sociability reflected their bourgeois status. The chapter describes the development and affirmation of a distinctive code of male sexual behavior as it came to be expressed in writings, love affairs and incitements to duelling of Antonio Luna, and more generally, in the personal comportment, dress and bodily gestures of the propagandistas.

The final three chapters attend to the differing strategies the propagandistas adopted to reform the sexual nature of their female compatriots. The fourth chapter highlights the propagandistas' attack on the supposed sexual depravity of the Spanish friars and on the ignorance, religiosity and submissiveness that made many Filipino women complicit in perpetuating the "monastic supremacy." This chapter will show how the effort to purge Filipino women of their religious vices by encouraging them to study and educate themselves was directly rooted in an anxiety towards female sexuality and the propagandistas' own interests in discrediting the moral authority of the Spanish friars and replacing religious power with the secular, bourgeois enlightened moral authority of their own.

That female sexuality posed a danger to progress and the country's liberty is discussed in Chapter 5, which situates Rizal's representations of the force of female sexual desire within his application of medical metaphors and scientific discourse. Rizal depicts native female sexual identity as volatile, unstable and anarchic, as a striking pathological symptom of a society in decline. Rizal's medical diagnosis of deviant female sexuality is here seen in parallel with his libidinal attraction to the sexualized European woman.

The sixth chapter, "Silencing the Flesh," pursues the issue of female sexual nature and moves towards a fuller discussion of how Rizal and the propagandistas linked female sexuality with the levels of civilization a society had attained. The chapter discusses the ways in which Rizal embraced the notion then prevalent in western medical and social thinking that female passionlessness was a measure of civilized society. Rizal, it is shown, was disinclined to pass on his medical knowledge regarding female sexuality to bourgeois Filipinas, even to his own sisters. He preferred instead to moralize, handing down injunctions to make it clear that female sexual pleasure and desire had no place in a society that claimed to be civilized, modern and free.

If patriotic motherhood, the rearing of future sons of the country remained women's special responsibility, men had to display courage, virility, honor and chivalric patriotism. As the conclusion shows, the propagandistas' conception of a Filipino identity turned upon cherished ideas of masculinity and femininity that strengthened the ideology of separate spheres, equating love and passion with patriotism and duty to one's country.

Notes

1. Mariano Ponce (Barcelona) to José Rizal, 24 June 1890, in *Cartas entre Rizal y sus colegas de la propaganda, 1889–1896* (Manila: Comisión Nacional del Centenario de José Rizal, 1961), p. 554.
2. Ibid.
3. Graciano López Jaena, *Speeches, Articles and Letters*. Translated and annotated by Encarnación Alzona. Edited and with additional annotations by Teodoro A. Agoncillo (Manila: National Historical Commission, 1974), f.p. 52.
4. José Rizal (Paris) to Mariano Ponce, 1 July 1889 in *Cartas*, p. 397.
5. Graciano López Jaena, "A Pepe Panganiban: Aquí yace el vengador del honor Filipino (meditación)," in *Discursos y artículos varios* [1891]. Nueva Edición revisada y adicionada con escritos no incluidos en la primera (Manila: Bureau of Printing, 1951), p. 56.
6. Ibid.
7. Michel Foucault, *The History of Sexuality*, vol. 1, trans. Robert Hurley (London: Penguin Books, 1990), p. 103.
8. James T. Siegel, *Fetish, Recognition, Revolution* (Princeton, New Jersey: Princeton University Press, 1997), p. 146.
9. The literature on this subject is vast. See for example Cesar Adib Majul, *The Political and Constitutional Ideas of the Philippine Revolution* (Quezon City: University of the Philippines Press, 1996); Cesar Adib Majul, "Principales, ilustrados, intellectuals and the original concept of a Filipino national community," *Asian Studies* 15 (April, August, Dec, 1977): 1–20; Jonathan Fast and Jim Richardson, *Roots of Dependency: political and economic revolution in 19th century Philippines* (Quezon City: Foundation for Nationalist Studies, 1979); Floro C. Quibuyen, *A Nation Aborted: Rizal, American hegemony and Philippine nationalism* (Quezon City: Ateneo de Manila University

Press, 1999); Elmer A. Ordoñez, *The Philippine Revolution and Beyond*, 2 Vols. (Manila: Philippine Centennial Commission, National Commission for Culture and the Arts, 1998). Nineteenth-century *ilustrado* nationalism has recently been approached through the lenses of race and racial science by Filomeno V. Aguilar, Jr., "Tracing Origins: Ilustrado nationalism and the racial science of migration waves," *The Journal of Asian Studies* 64, no. 3 (August 2005): 605–37.

[10] John N. Schumacher, SJ, *The Propaganda Movement, 1880–1895: The creation of a Filipino consciousness, the making of the Revolution* (Quezon City: Ateneo de Manila University Press, 1997); and John N. Schumacher SJ, *The Making of a Nation: essays on nineteenth-century Filipino nationalism* (Quezon City: Ateneo de Manila University Press, 1991).

[11] In a long series of anecdotal vignettes, Ambeth Ocampo has focused on generally ignored aspects of the propagandistas' lives in Europe such as their grooming, duelling and womanizing. See for instance Ambeth Ocampo, *Rizal without the Overcoat* (Manila: Anvil Publishing, 1998), rev. ed. and also his *Luna's Moustache*, with an introduction by Vicente Rafael (Manila: Anvil Publishing, 1997). For the most recent effort to confront the diverse and conflicting political ideas and personal motivations of the propagandistas see Alfredo Roces, *Adios, Patria Adorada: the Filipino as ilustrado, the ilustrado as Filipino* (Manila: De La Salle University Press, 2006).

[12] Benedict Anderson, *Imagined Communities: Reflections on the origin and spread of nationalism* (London: Verso, 1991), rev. ed., p. 5.

[13] A good survey of this literature is given in the "Introduction" in *Nationalisms and Sexualities*, ed. Andrew Parker, Mary Russo, Doris Sommer and Patricia Yaeger (London: Routledge, 1992), pp. 1–18.

[14] Anderson, *Imagined Communities*, p. 6.

[15] Anne McClintock, *Imperial Leather: race, gender and sexuality in the colonial contest* (New York and London: Routledge, 1995), p. 352.

[16] Nira Yuval Davis and Floya Anthias tersely summarize five ways in which nationhood implicated women, cited in Anne McClintock, ibid., p. 355. Conceptions of a Filipino national identity in relation to gendered images of the nation during the Philippine Revolution against Spain, 1896–98, and the Philippine-American War, 1898–1902 have recently been touched upon by Reynaldo Ileto, "Mother Spain, Uncle Sam, and the construction of Filipino national identity" in *Imperios y Naciones en el Pacífico: la formación de una colonia: Filipinas*, ed. Ma.Dolores Elizalde, Josep M. Fradera and Luis Alonso, vol. 1 (Madrid: AEEP Consejo Superior de Investigaciones Científicas, 2001), pp. 119–31.

[17] Joan Landes, *Visualizing the Nation: Gender, representation, and revolution in eighteenth-century France* (Ithaca and London: Cornell University Press, 2001), p. 135.

[18] Ibid., p. 5.

[19] See for example Vim Nadera, *Mujer Indigena: isang pamatbat ng pagbabagong-anyo* (Quezon City: Philippine Centennial Commission, University of the Philippines Press, 2000), winner of the Centennial Literary Prize, 1898–1998; Elmer Ordoñez, *Toward*

the First Asian Republic: Papers from the Jakarta International Conference on the Centenary of the Philippine Revolution and the First Asian Republic (Quezon City: Philippine Centennial Commission, 1998).

20 See the important scholarship by Barbara Watson Andaya on women, gender and Southeast Asian history. Barbara Watson Andaya, ed., *Other Pasts: women, gender and history in early modern Southeast Asia* (Honolulu: Center for Southeast Asian Studies, University of Hawai'i Press, 2000), pp. 4–5; also Carolyn Brewer and Anne-Marie Medcalf, *Researching the Fragments: histories of women in the Asian context* (Quezon City: New Day Publishers, 2000).

21 Barbara Watson Andaya, *The Flaming Womb: repositioning women in early modern Southeast Asia* (Honolulu: University of Hawai'i Press, 2006), p. 3.

22 The few studies that have focused on the intertwined links between gender, sexuality and early Filipino nationalism importantly examine the literary undertakings of the propagandistas, particularly José Rizal, but also Antonio Luna. See especially, Vicente Rafael, "Language, Identity, and Gender in Rizal's *Noli*," *Review of Indonesian and Malaysian Affairs* 18 (Winter 1984): 110–40; selected essays in Vicente Rafael, *The Promise of the Foreign: nationalism and the technics of translation in the Spanish Philippines* (Durham and London: Duke University Press, 2005); Alma Jill Dizon, "Beyond the Melodramatic Vision: national identity and the novels of José Rizal," unpublished PhD diss., Yale University, 1996; and Benedict Anderson's analysis of translation and Rizal's use of language and humor in the *Noli me Tangere* in Benedict Anderson, *The Spectre of Comparisons: nationalism, Southeast Asia and the world* (London and New York: Verso, 1998).

23 Norman Owen, "Masculinity and National Identity in the 19th century Philippines," *Illes y Imperis* 2 (1999): 23–47.

24 Vicente Rafael, "Nationalism, Imagery and the Filipino Intelligentsia," in *Discrepant Histories: translocal essays on Filipino cultures* (Manila: Anvil Publishing Inc., 1995), pp. 140–41.

25 Studies on the contemporary construction of sexuality and identity in Indonesia provide productive comparisons. See especially Suzanne April Brenner, *The Domestication of Desire: women, wealth and modernity in Java* (Princeton, New Jersey: Princeton University Press, 1998); Laurie J. Sears, ed., *Fantasizing the Feminine in Indonesia* (Durham: Duke University Press, 1996); and Tom Boellstorff, *The Gay Archipelago: Sexuality and nation in Indonesia* (Princeton and Oxford: Princeton University Press, 2005).

26 For studies that examine gender and sexuality in mid-twentieth-century Philippine revolutionary culture and masculinity and the building of a national armed force in the Philippines, see respectively, Vina Albero Lanzona, "Gender, Sex, Family, and Revolution: Women in the Huk Rebellion in the Philippines, 1942–1956," unpublished PhD diss., The University of Wisconsin-Madison, 2000; and Alfred W. McCoy, *Closer than Brothers: Manhood at the Philippine military academy* (New Haven, Conn.: Yale University Press, 1999) and Alfred W. McCoy, "Colonialism and the Cult of Masculinity," in *Imperios y Naciones en el Pacífico: la formación de una colonia: Filipinas*, ed. Ma. Dolores Elizalde, Josep M. Fradera and Luis Alonso, vol. 1 (2001), pp. 149–77.

27. Alejandro Roces, *Felix Resurrección Hidalgo and the Generation of 1872* (Manila: Eugenio López Foundation, 1995), p. 123.
28. Resil Mojares stresses the importance of this period for Philippine intellectual history by connecting the activities of the ilustrados in Europe to a broader "Filipino Enlightenment" that spanned from the late eighteenth century to the end of the nineteenth century. Resil Mojares, *Brains of the Nation: Pedro Paterno, T.H. Pardo de Tavera, Isabelo de los Reyes and the production of modern knowledge* (Quezon City: Ateneo de Manila University Press, 2006), p. 451.
29. Rafael, *The Promise of the Foreign*. See also Benedict Anderson, *Under Three Flags: Anarchism and the Anti-Colonial Imagination* (London and New York: Verso, 2005); Rudolf Mrazek, *Engineers of Happy Land: Technology and nationalism in a colony* (Princeton and Oxford: Princeton University Press, 2002).
30. George Gissing quoted in Elaine Showalter, *Sexual Anarchy: gender and culture at the fin de siècle* (London: Virago Press, 1992), p. 3.
31. Linda Hunt Beckman, *Amy Levy: her life and letters* (Athens: Ohio University Press, 2000), p. 81.
32. José Rizal in *La Solidaridad* 2: 30 (30 April 1890): 195.
33. Alain Corbin, *Women for Hire: prostitution and sexuality in France after 1850*, trans. Alan Sheridan (Cambridge, Mass.: Harvard University Press, 1990), p. 22.
34. José Rizal, *Diarios y Memorias por José Rizal* (Manila: Comisión Nacional del Centenario de José Rizal, 1961), pp. 163–4.
35. Dr. D. Pedro Felipe Monlau, *Higiene del Matrimonio, ó el libro de los casados en el cual se dan las reglas e instrucciones necesarias para conservar la salud de los esposos, asegurar la paz conyugal y educar bien a la familia*, Cuarto edicion (Paris: Librería de Garnier Hermanos, 1883), pp. 25–7.
36. Ibid., pp. 14–7.
37. Walter Benjamin, *Illuminations*. With an introduction by Hannah Arendt, trans. Harry Zohn (London: Fontana, 1992), p. 247.

1
The Sensual Scene: Love and Courtship in Urbane Manila

The City and European Civilities

This story opens in Manila in 1869, a place and time electrified by currents of progress and notions of freedom. In the air was a palpable feeling of hope. Liberal officials arriving from Spain were lending their voices to the cry for reforms and "modern liberties" already raised by the discontented *hijos del país* — the Philippine-born Spaniards. Manila welcomed a new Governor General, Carlos María de la Torre, a man appointed by the anti-clerical liberals who had brought Spain to revolution in 1868. Preceded by his liberal reputation, De la Torre immediately enjoyed the support of the Comisión de Filipinos[1] who flamboyantly paid court to the highest official in the land by honoring him with a serenade one balmy July night at the central plaza of Santa Potenciana.[2] De la Torre seemed personable and approachable, eschewing the formality and protocol of his office by walking amongst the people unescorted and casually wearing a native straw hat. Even more famously, he and his mistress, Señora María Gil y Montes de Sanchiz, welcomed the Comisión de Filipinos to intimate evening receptions (*intima tertulia*) at Malacañang Palace.[3]

Married to a colonel in the artillery, Doña María de Sanchiz was a writer and poet who scandalized Manila high society with her open support of the Filipino cause. Dubbed insultingly *"La Madre de los Filipinos"* and the subject of much malicious whispering amongst conservative officials, Doña de Sanchiz was the Comisión's most unconventional yet powerful ally. After the serenade, the Comisión's members were invited to a *buffet* with the Governor at which the Señora personally served them refreshments, honored them with a toasting speech and regaled them with readings of her poetry.[4] Two months later, on 21 September 1869, the

Filipinos once again enjoyed her lavish attention. To commemorate the 1868 Revolution in Spain, the Comisión participated in a magnificent banquet at the Palace which featured natives with banners, music and lanterns led by Father José Burgos. In a gesture evocative of the women of the French revolution, Doña María made her glorious entrance wearing scarves and sashes of red, the color of revolution. To the delight of the Filipinos present, there could be no mistaking the political meaning of the apparel of the Governor's Señora. Guests at the grand occasion looked agape at the ribbons bearing the exhortation "*Viva el pueblo soberano!*" decorating her hair, and other ribbons tied around her collar in the manner of a cravat upon which were written "*Viva la Libertad!*" and "*Viva el General de la Torre!*"[5]

It was not to last. Three years later, in January 1872, native troops garrisoned in the port of Cavite mutinied and killed their Spanish officers. Rumors of a general uprising had been in the air for some months and it seemed that the Cavite conspiracy had been simmering quietly below the surface throughout De La Torre's term of office. The plan was both audacious and deadly: native troops were to assassinate Spanish soldiers at the barracks, native orderlies and servants were to kill their superiors, the Captain General was to be murdered by his native body guard, and any other friars and Spaniards would also be immediately put to death. What actually occurred, at least from the point of view of the Spanish authorities, was little more than a skirmish easily quelled. From the perspective of the conspirators, the episode was a disaster. Greatly dependent on the element of surprise and careful timing for the success of the plan, the native conspirators could not foresee they would be betrayed by one of their own — a Tagalog woman in love with a Spanish sergeant who was in charge of the native regiment. Overlooked in historical accounts of the Cavite mutiny, the following episode places love at the heart of the events.

On that fateful afternoon of 20 January, she had consented to renew sexual relations with the Spanish sergeant and entreated him not to leave her in the evening. Insisting he should return to the barracks and to his duty she, fearing for the Spaniard's life, revealed what was to take place. She led him to a window and explained the significance of the scene below:

> Do you see those women on their knees praying before an image surrounded by burning candles? Well, they are praying to the Virgin

that the massacre of all the Spaniards, which is to take place tonight, may be crowned with success, and if you go to the barracks you will also be killed.[6]

Treachery and betrayal was the consequence of the Tagalog woman's misplaced loyalties and sexual desire. "Love," reflected the Spanish historian José Montero y Vidal, "has played the principal part in the failure of nearly all the conspiracies in the Philippines."[7] Though localized and short-lived, the mutiny set in motion a crashing wave of repression. The movement for reforms was brutally subdued, hundreds of Filipino liberals being sent into exile and three Filipino priests, including Father José Burgos, being publicly executed by garrote. Their bodies were dumped into an unmarked common grave in Paco cemetery while the city reverberated with the sombre tolling of Church bells.[8]

This was the turbulent climate that the youthful José Rizal, Marcelo H. del Pilar and the brothers Juan and Antonio Luna encountered in Manila and in which many of their older relatives became embroiled. But aside from shaping their political sentiments, the experience of Manila had a profound and abiding impact on their cultural tenets and their perceptions of the outside world. At this place and time, as privileged college and university students, these young men first lived away from home, began to discover their vocations, fell in love, and learnt a little more about life. In June 1872, five months after the Cavite Mutiny, the 11-year-old José Rizal went up to Manila from his home province of Laguna to sit the entrance exams for the Ateneo Municipal. Like other young men of his social class, Rizal was embarking on a long period of student life and residence in the capital city before leaving the Philippines for further study in Europe. At about the same time, Del Pilar, older than Rizal by 11 years, was temporarily interrupting his law studies at the University of Santo Tomas and working in a minor bureaucratic post somewhere in the city. Living on Calle de Barraca in the commercial district of Binondo, meanwhile, were the parents of Juan and Antonio Luna. The elder brother, Juan, was away taking an apprenticeship as a sea pilot, but in 1874 he abandoned that career and returned to Manila to embark on an eight-year fine arts course at the Academia de Dibujo y Pintura on Calle del Cabildo in Intramuros. His brother Antonio Luna was but a boy of six in 1872, living with his merchant parents in Binondo, being tutored privately and trying to memorize the catechism from the *Doctrina Cristiana*.[9]

This Manila of the 1870s in which Rizal, Del Pilar and the Luna brothers lived was a dynamic, burgeoning city, very different in atmosphere from the Manila that had existed a century earlier. Although it was one of the principal trading ports in South East Asia, the colonial capital was then still closed to all non-Spanish westerners. From the 1790s onwards the activities of the Real Compañía de Filipinas allowed a trickle of foreigners to penetrate the prohibitions, but those who entered were at first numerically too few and their visits too fleeting for their cultural influence to be anything but superficial. Spain's restrictive trade policy had effectively insulated *las islas Filipinas* from the rest of the world. The liberalization policies Spain began to adopt after the Napoleonic wars, however, drew this mercantile exclusivism to an end. The port of Manila was opened formally to the ships of all nations and permission was granted to non-Spanish westerners to settle in the city.[10]

With the lifting of all restrictions by 1835, local elites and Chinese mestizos who were able to quickly and smoothly shift to cash crop cultivation, raising such crops as sugar, cotton, pepper and añil (indigo), found important new sources of support in the British and American trading houses that established themselves in Manila a decade or so earlier.[11] Scholars have examined the crucial impact of foreign capital on the economy of the colonial city, the vital role it played in strengthening the colony's *principalia* (native elites), through the stimulation of commercial agriculture and domestic commerce, and how it wrought far reaching changes in the terms of land ownership and the management of land throughout the archipelago.[12]

This turnabout in colonial economic policy heralded not just a new commercial prosperity. Global trade, the spread of capitalism and monetization, much like colonialism, brought on tremendous social and economic transformations — from intensifying the commodification of labor, irrevocably altering traditional concepts of reciprocal indebtedness, honor and shame, to the commodification of sexual desire as libidinal interests were penetrated by the cash nexus.[13] Prostitution, and the figure of the prostitute, that figure of modernity *par excellence*, became an integral part of city life.[14] To demographic historians, the story is familiar: the rise of urban centers coupled with the fast growth of an agricultural export economy had simultaneously encouraged the migration of job seeking rural poor and landless to cities. Manila presented an attractive destination for young women from the provinces looking for work, easily obtaining regular cash wage work in the cigar factories, as domestic servants, seamstresses, washer women and street vendors.[15] Prostitution provided an easy route to augment a meager income. While some women who became prostitutes did so as a result of coercion and threats of violence,[16] others entered the trade by choice, lured by the promise of quick money perhaps after hearing talk amongst other working women.[17] For the first time, prostitution no longer existed on the periphery, confined to military troops, sailors and foreigners who purchased sex from a "few wayward women." Sex was purchasable in brothels, the streets, opium dens and private homes of assignation.

Intensified global trade signaled the beginnings of cosmopolitanism and an unprecedented influx of news, stories, fashions, styles, trends, luxury goods and foods from the west. These foreign intrusions affected every aspect of the life of Manila's *alta sociedad*: their diet, dress and interior décor, their social interactions, their manners, the way they passed time in leisure and even their bodily habits, deportment and gestures. Causing major changes in the emergent Filipino elite's self-consciousness and their relationship with the outside world, western influences were embraced, but at the same time domesticated through the ideals of courtesy, good manners and *urbanidad*. Subtly and insidiously, urbanidad redefined ways in which men and women interacted with each other, reconstructed sexual relations and transformed notions of love. These processes took impetus from Manila itself, a city that was unfolding and expanding, and was being conceived by its inhabitants in new ways.[18]

Surprised by the strikingly European style of what he called the "better class of houses in Manila," Sir John Bowring, the British governor of Hong Kong, detailed the lavish interiors of mestizo-owned mansions:

> The apartments, as suited to a tropical climate, are large, and many European fashions have been introduced: the walls are covered with painted paper, many lamps hung from the ceiling, Chinese screens, porcelain jars with natural or artificial flowers, mirrors, tables, sofas, chairs, such as are seen in European capitals; but the large rooms have not the appearance of being crowded with superfluous furniture....[19]

Foreigners, Spaniards and mestizos resided in outlying pueblos close to Manila such as Tondo and Malabon, affluent towns that prospered not by farming, but by a variety of industries: textile weaving that included cottons and silks; and the production of salt and sugar, tiles, bricks and

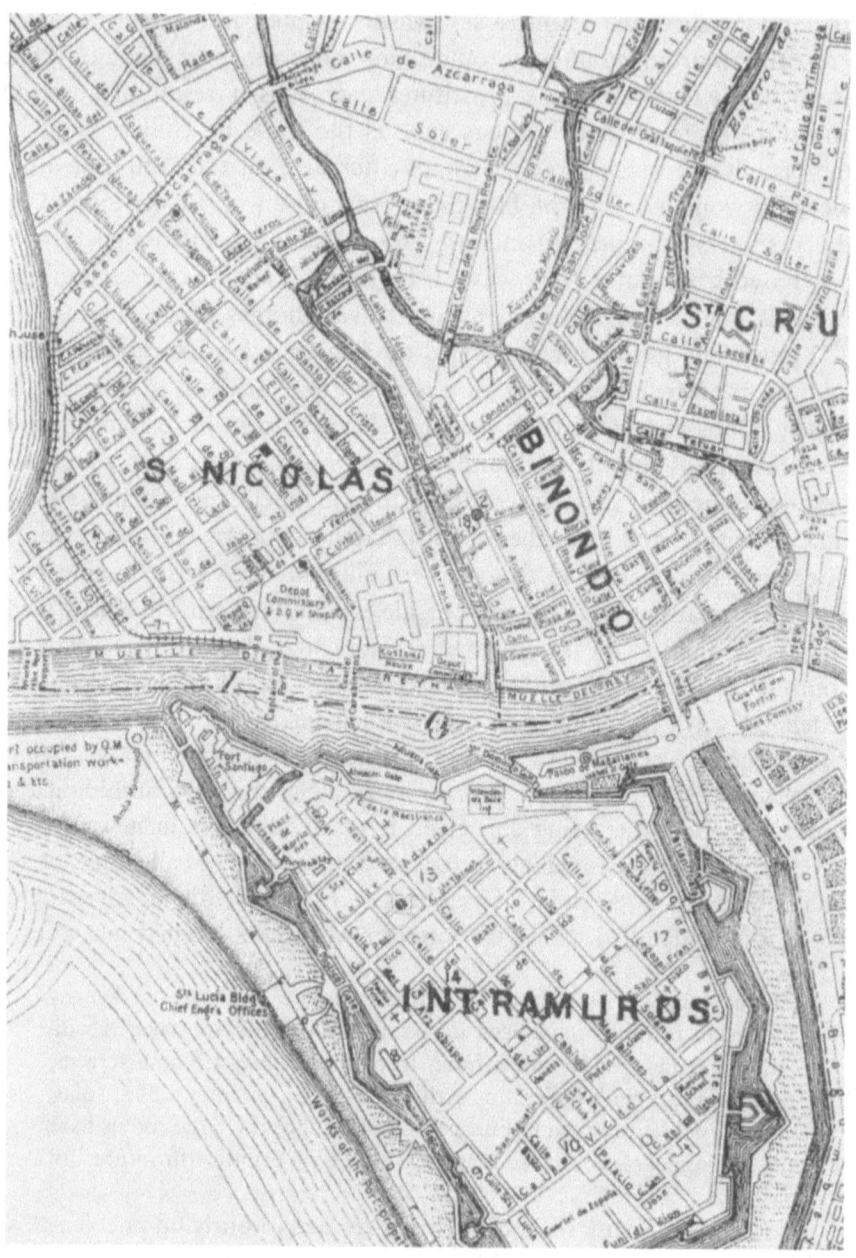

Fig. 5 Map of Intramuros and Binondo, 1901
[*A Pronouncing gazetteer and geographical dictionary of the Philippine Islands* (Washington: U.S. Government Printing Office, 1902)]

jars. But at the heart of Manila's new urbanism lay Binondo, situated directly across the Pasig from Intramuros. The district manifested neither planning, poetry nor majestic style, but it pulsed with life and dynamism. Formerly a modest settlement which had existed primarily to service Intramuros, Binondo had boomed to become in effect the economic capital of the colony, a place of trade and money from which the poor had mostly been ejected, their nipa huts demolished to make room for the *bodegas*, offices and homes of the wealthy traders, merchants and ship owners.[20]

Binondo was the center of urban industriousness and life. Here, as O.D.Corpuz describes, were the tobacco factories; as well as 800 shops that sold European, Asian and domestic fabrics; gun and cannon, church bells, cauldrons and stirring rods and candleholders were forged in the city's foundries and by its ironmongers; soaps and edible oils were made in six oil mills, and here too, worked the cream of the city's artisans — musicians, artists, scribes, clerks, jewelers, sculptors, shoemakers, tailors, silversmiths and watchmakers.[21] Slaughter houses in Manila supplied beef to the tables of the wealthy, as demand for it rose in tune to the changing tastes of rich cosmopolitan Filipinos who were turning beef consumption into a "mark of class."[22] This was true also for opium consumption. Officially prohibited to non-Chinese, opium was widely used by well-heeled Filipinos who, with wealthy Chinese, patronized the "private," more luxuriously furnished, dens established especially for those with status. By 1898, there were 190 dens in Manila alone selling 130 tons of opium.[23] For fine dining, dressing, accommodations and therapeutic treatments, lux could be found in the exclusive street of Escolta where there was a Parisian-style restaurant, an English hotel that boasted superior rooms and, thanks to new indoor plumbing, a *baño de ducha*. There were "award-winning" bespoke German hat-makers whose clientele, it was claimed, were the highest officials of the land; and German and English pharmacies or *boticas*, purveyors of a vast range of fine perfumes, toiletries, surgical equipment and even electromechanical devices for the body.[24]

Visiting the capital in 1879, the French scientist Alfred Marche noticed how time could be marked by the life that appeared on the streets:

> In the morning, at the first hour, one sees the *lecheras* (milkmaids) passing, running with their vessels on the head; then come the *zacateros*,

peddlers of *zacates*, small bundles of grass for the horses; finally appear the Chinese barbers who are at the same time hairdressers, cleaners of nose and ears, and then the ice cream peddlers, who go running on the streets shouting: "*Sorbete! Sorbete!*"[25]

Male western eyes were titillated by the exquisite transparency and delicate embroidery of finely woven native textiles like the *piña* worn on female bodies. Women wore the most ostentatiously colored and striped silks, satins and shawls of costly taste; their delicate feet were impractically shod in tiny velvet slippers, heels and the tips of fingernails were seen to be polished and tinged in vivid carmine. Female westerners like Anna D'Almeida commented at length on the native propensity to superstition, noting small, curious details adorning women's dress such as the charms or scapulars that hung from their necks after having been sprinkled by a priest with holy water to "increase their magic effect."[26] Moreover, as was also noticed, women regularly went about town "corsetless," walking coquettishly with an undulating swing, with their long, lustrous, perfumed hair falling abundant and loose down to their ankles, and with a thick smoking cigar wedged between their lips.

Through the shop fronts could be seen the sweaty industriousness of cabinet makers, tin and coppersmiths, blacksmiths, tanners, dyers, carpenters, barbers and cobblers; on stalls and pavements petty traders set out their wares; and everywhere the peddlers scurried, hawking anything from bouquets to fried food to lottery tickets. Whilst the old city had a quiet, even sepulchral air, Binondo was a market place, full of chaos and cacophony. The variegated exotica of its streets and waterways belonged indisputably to an Asian city. And the district did not just look like the Orient; it also smelled like the Orient. Smell could establish for European visitors, but most especially for the natives, the ways Manila had drawn its lines of demarcation, the functions of its parts and their intermingling and separation, or essentially, how its inhabitants perceived it as a city. Binondo smelt awful. Into the esteros poured effluent and filth, contributing to the permanent putrid stew of vegetable matter that lay in a fetid sludge at the bottom that swirled to the oily iridescent surface with the passing of each *casco* and *banca*. "Manila is another Venice and ... at low tide, these canals are as ill smelling as in Venice," commented Alfred Marche.[27] The rainy season stirred the dusty streets into a stinking ooze, multiplied the stagnant puddles that gathered in the cracks and holes of the roads, and caused the putrescent waters of the esteros to flood. Dean Worcester's comments on the state of the Intramuros moat in 1887 could be applied to the perennial state of the city's dysfunctional drainage system: "it is undoubtedly a menace to the health of the city; yet the authorities fear to disturb it lest they breed a pestilence."[28]

The Spanish intellectual Sinibaldo de Mas, on his visit to the colony, discerned the far more subtle but equally penetrating smell of insolence arising from Spain's colonial subjects. As de Mas opined, he had more than a few times suffered the "noisy emanations of an outpouring" released by utterly unapologetic natives who liked to voice their displeasure towards European authority by emitting farts that were memorable for their noise and atrocious smell.[29] To the Russian writer Ivan Goncharov the people reeked: "We tried to avert our faces from the many shops which already smelt too much of the Chinese," he wrote.[30] If Goncharov had been more charitable, he could have observed that the Chinese and the Chinese mestizos could claim a large part of the credit for Binondo's sweet smell of commercial success. Concentrated in three main streets in Binondo's centre — Calle Nueva, Calle del Rosario and most especially Calle Escolta — were the Chinese-owned general stores, or "bazaars," that sought to satisfy the new elite's appetite for things western. Crammed with every imaginable imported luxury, bazaars like those of Chua Farruco and Mariano Velasco Chua Chengco indicated the extent of the mania for European opulent living and style.[31] A number of western entrepreneurs also opened stores that profited from the local anxiety to appear fashionable. German hat-makers and tailors, for example, had a subtle influence on local fashions. With their attractive colored silk linings and hand-sewn gold labels, German hats locally made in Binondo were a particularly prized item. In their Escolta stores, German tailors stocked only the finest quality European fabrics and sought to attract the upmarket "respectable public" by claiming to cut gentlemen's suits following the "newest fashions of Paris, London and Germany." It was in these European-owned emporia that many young ilustrados equipped themselves with suitably fashionable wardrobes before leaving the Philippines to take up their studies in Europe in the 1880s and 1890s.[32]

For the European visitor to Manila, the clutter found inside an Escolta bazaar could be a disconcerting confrontation with a bewildering array of the familiar. As Goncharov discovered, here was all of bourgeois Europe piled in a little room of a shop:

> We found ourselves in a European shop in which such eclecticism reigned that nothing would have enabled you to say straight off what the proprietor's main line of business was. Two or three dining room clocks were standing about with a box of gloves, several cases of wine and a piano; materials laid out, gold chains hung down and bookstands, handsome tables, cupboards and couches clustered together in a heap....[33]

The bazaars of the Escolta, Calles Nueva and Rosario were not merely purveyors of foreign fripperies upon which money was carelessly frittered. The "conveniences and luxuries" that filled these shops articulated the concept of gracious bourgeois living being sought by the Manileño elite and reflected the new urbane temperament in which recreation, display and European fashions served as the essential elements. Indeed, as Henry T. Ellis noticed during a visit to Manila in 1856, all that was necessary for the fashionable home could be found in the Escolta stores including "pictures of the Saints, with very rosy cheeks, and of the Virgin, dressed in the latest and gayest Parisian mode."[34]

Holy images of *santos* with Europeanized features and a flashy Virgin Mary took the English visitor by surprise, but the fact that such objects took pride of place in the shrines of wealthy Christian homes was evidence that Europe was neither remote nor alien. For some western visitors, similarly, the sight of Manila's urbane inhabitants appeared like unwanted interruptions within a text emphasizing the strange. Goncharov, like many other foreigners, ultimately found the European flavor of Manila urban life disappointing. "I myself expected something more," he wrote, deflated. "But what? Perhaps a brighter and more vivid colour scheme, more poetic reveries and a little more of a life unknown to us Europeans — of a life with its own customs."[35] In their desire to highlight difference, European visitors tended to be dismissive of the bourgeois Manila elite and their adoption of European style. Describing Manila elite society in 1880, the conservative Spanish historian Wenceslao Retana was pointedly denigrating:

> As we may say, and here it is said discreetly, Manila high society needed a mentor, in view of its backwardness: using and even abusing circumlocutions, omissions and euphemisms, one affirms that Manila, in 1880, was a nascent society, lacking in intelligent good taste.[36]

As it appeared to commentators like Retana, the "great problem" afflicting educated Manila society was its lack of intellectual and social sophistication. Parochialism characterized the life of the colonial city: by following the fashions of Europe, native elites had only succeeded in poor imitation, showing little more than artificiality and affectation. But, "new fashion, new theatricality, and new nationalism emerged at the same time," comments Rudolf Mrazek in relation to the early twentieth century newly-born native "dandy" of the Dutch Indies — the disturbingly modern native who dressed in a Western way, in trousers, shoes, jacket, tie, hat and moustache. Like the fashionable Filipino who preceded him, the Indonesian dandy was flagrant, dazzling, absurdly neat and imagined, at least in literature, to be "penetrating Dutch houses and penetrating Dutch women."[37] Retana's anathematizing judgments were missing the disturbing modernity of the Filipino dandy, missing the meanings that transactions with the foreign generated, and were failing to interpret the density of signals arising from the special overcrowded space of the city.

City Folk and the Experience of Romance

As we have seen, urbanidad in the context of cosmopolitan city life involved the calculated display of the dress and manners of the European elite. Yet this did not simply mean aping the wealthy European. Urbanidad was marked by a knowledge of the foreign. The pursuit to acquire the material accoutrements of European bourgeois culture obviously supposed wealth but it also meant style and social polish. Urbanidad was a fashionable and desirable standard that showed a concern for refinement and sophistication. For city folk, urbanidad symbolized a turning away from rusticity towards sophistication, an idea that had its roots in eighteenth-century Spain, as Carmen Martin Gaite has shown.[38] Urbanidad displayed an ease with the complexities of urban life — a state of being city folk associated with the self-confident elite. Urbanidad was fundamental to city life: it set down the procedures for social interaction and determined how love was recognized in the city.

Serving to illustrate this point is the play *La Filipina elegante y el Negrito amante* (*The Elegant Filipina and the Amorous Negrito*). Within this comical one-act farce or *sainete* written by the nineteenth-century poet and playwright Francisco Baltazar,[39] there occurs a dialogue between two street-sweepers named Uban and Kapitan Toming, the latter being an Aeta tribesman from the mountains. Short, curly haired and dark skinned, Toming the *Negrito amante* believes the only way he can win the love of Menangge, a pretentious Tagalog girl of a small country-town, is to discard his tribal loin cloth, the *bahag*, and wear the clothes of the Spanish elite. As Baltazar's sainete unfolds, the audience laughs at the Aeta's audacious act of vestimentary transgressiveness and the blatant use of European clothes as a new courtship stratagem. In true theatrical spirit, the comedy turns on costume as cultural sign drawing on the symbolic power of the European coat for its fetishistic focus. Precisely what the coat represented was crucial. It was neither an iconographic index to Spanish imperialism, nor a cunning means of deception. Instead, the coat was a symbol of urbanity, and wearing it expressed a desire to appear urbane, rather than simply a wish to imitate the Spanish.

The opening scene is a dung-filled town plaza and Kapitan Toming has just made his spectacular entrance wearing a *levita*, a stylish long European frock coat.

Toming: I am Kapitang Toming, the Aeta dandy and lover. Just take a look at me! Am I not elegant?

Uban: (Laughs) Ha ha, ha hay! How funny the *levita* looks on that small negrito fool.

Toming: *Baya!* How stupid you are, even if you are from the town! Do you know why I am wearing these fine clothes?

Uban: Well, what is the reason then?

Toming: I am madly in love!

Uban: What a fool is this mountain black!

Toming: A black man in love is just like a Tagalog in love!

Uban: Well, even if you are bursting with love from head to foot, you still look ridiculous in that suit of yours!

Toming: I am now Spanish in form and fashion; Spanish enough, Uban, to be loved by the beautiful Menangge. When I courted her in my *bahag*, she would not as much as look at me even when I brought her a present. Then I put on a Tagalog mestizo's clothes (*damit-mestisong tagalog*), and donned a wig, but she would still have none of me. Next I put on the shirt and pants of a Chinaman (*baro't salawal insik*) and brought her a gift of wax, but she took no interest. At last I put on the clothes of a brave Balanggingi muslim (*morong Balanggigi*) but still I could make no impression. Now let us see if she will love me in this *levita*, for today I look more like a Spaniard than an Aeta.

As an Aeta, Kapitan Toming was a member of the most disenfranchised and marginalized of the indigenous minority groups within Philippine society, his stature and skin color bearing the imprint of social stigmatization. Merely by sight, the Aeta's physical appearance renders the various clothes he tries on — costumes and styles representative of racial and caste categories in colonial society — anomalous, literally unsuitable. In what is essentially a performance of cultural illegibility, his cocky strut and proclamations of elegance provokes laughter, the humor sustained by race and class prejudice. But there is another aspect to the comedy. "Now let us see if she will love me in this levita, for today I look more like a Spaniard than an Aeta," says the amorous Negrito. By donning the dress of the Spanish elite, Kapitan Toming, an Aeta street-sweeper, the lowliest member of colonial society, believes he can locate himself into a different world and persona, imagining that the coat endows him with the necessary sophistication to win the heart of his lady-love. Thus the operations of the farce: the coat is thought to unlock urbane society by providing access to a language that by political, social and cultural definition excluded a street sweeping Aeta.

Just as the coat was unable to change his appearance, neither could it eliminate the inelegance of his words, nor avert their rustic and uncouth dull wit. For a town girl like Menanggue, Love is recognized only in the artful forms of "oaths, lies, and jokes" and nourished by "a fond glance" and "a mischievous wink." To behave in any other way was to be rustic. Unacquainted with this way of speaking, Kapitan Toming, the amorous hero from the hills, suffers a bucolic betrayal. But there was a final twist to what appears to be Kapitan Toming's doomed efforts at courtship. Songs intersperse the dialogue. In response to each rejection, the ardent Kapitan Toming serenades her with a *kundiman*. Known as the "love song of the Tagalog"[40] the kundiman is typically written in three-four time whose rhythm and melody is "erotic and gloomy," giving "consolation to anguished hearts. Sentimental words are matched with sad music ... to soften stubborn hearts."[41] Following the lugubrious conventions of the kundiman, Kapitan Toming expresses the depths of his grief at her rejections in song, with all the despair and melancholy of a romantic lover. The kundiman weaves its spell, and Kapitan Toming's persistence reaps its reward. At long last, Menanggue accepts his suit.

In the nineteenth century, opposing and contradictory forces were shaping the nature of love and the practices associated with it. Influencing the amorous behavior of city folk was the notion of romantic love. Modeled on the conventions of courtly love in the medieval and Renaissance traditions, romantic love glorified passion. Feelings were as ungovernable as hurricanes or smoldering volcanoes. Plunged in sentimental excess, heroic lovers suffered inconsolably over love that was unfulfilled and tragic. Such were the romantic exaggerations of self-conscious native poets who, in striving for urbanity and respectability, decorated Tagalog poetry with classical rhetoric and fanciful allusions to Spanish love ballads and Greek and Roman epics.[42]

Indigenous romance writers heightened the "profane" within their creative adaptations and interpretations of imported metrical romances by giving prominence to the passions of chivalry, gallantry and heterosexual love in the *awit* and *corridos* whose popularity peaked in the nineteenth century.[43] The *teatro tagalo* flourished on its productions of *comedías* and *moro-moros* where native playwrights indulged their local audience in long, extravagant verse plays in which Christian and Moorish princes and princesses declared their love and fought battles in recognizably native sentiments and local settings. The system of love illustrated by these types of popular literature was steeped in clichés. The most common individual motif was love at first sight — heroes glimpsed beautiful maidens fleetingly as they rode by in carriages. The preferred settings for love scenes remained in gardens and featured swoonings, convoluted sentimental speeches, separations and reunions. Religious didacticism infused the language of passion and love scenes were exploited for their edifying lessons or examples; the central tenets of Catholic doctrine were highlighted whenever there was a chance, courtship followed conventional patterns with men soliciting and women bestowing love, and the ideal marriage was inevitably monogamous and sanctified in proper church ceremonies. Heroes and heroines were devoutly religious, devoted to saints and the Virgin; and the representation of romance heroines always conformed to extreme physical beauty, maidenly purity and chaste innocence.

In her analysis of the "romance mode" in nineteenth-century Philippine literature, Soledad Reyes identifies the educational role of romance. "As a civilizing construct", Reyes writes, "the romance propagated the code of chivalry and lauded ideals of gentility. Love, which was a major theme, created in its wake a codified system of behavior revolving around the agony undergone by lovers."[44] Romance in the *awit* and *corrido* refracted reality, constructing an ideal world in which the complexities of reality were simplified and framed by a comprehensible design that could be easily discerned by the reader. There was also a subversive element in the depictions of courtly love, whereby love without compromise, individual exploits and fantasies of female domination served to undermine entrenched hierarchies of feudal society.

Representations of romantic love as popularized in the awits and corridos and performed in the teatro tagalo ironically found its strongest critics amongst the ilustrados who, writing in the latter half of the nineteenth century from the capitals of Europe, dismissed the use of centuries old clichés and metaphors, archaic language and far fetched hyperbole.[45] More fundamentally, attacking the foreign elements found in the metrical romances, Rizal took a dim view of the amorous, adventurous romantic heroines who seemed to him remote and far removed from indigenous symbols of femininity:

> What are those princesses doing who go into battles, exchange strokes and two-handed blows with the sword; do battles with princes and roam alone through mountains and valleys seduced by the *tikbalang?* In our customs we love sweetness and tenderness in a woman — and we would be fearful to clasp a damsel's hands which are reeking with blood, even if this were the blood of an infidel or a giant.... Would it not be a thousand times better for us to depict our own customs in order to correct our vices and defects and commend the good qualities?[46]

But it was not the falsified, fanciful or foreign derived plots that lay at the core of Rizal's contention. Rather, Rizal's indictment of the sentimental excesses of metrical romances is here shown to rest on the inappropriate behavior of the female heroines. Pointedly, women should not do battle with infidel and giant, nor should they allow their hands to become stained with blood or scandalously wander alone in wildernesses laying themselves vulnerable to the tikbalang, the grotesque and lascivious giant satyr of Philippine popular mythology. Embracing European bourgeois respectabilities, members of the Hispanized elite recoiled from an overly passionate female sexuality that threatened to overturn the discipline of the masculine order.

The notion of romantic love contained within awit poetry gripped the erotic imagination of the general native populace, and was pursued in the performance of religious or social rituals that occurred throughout the city's main thoroughfares, on its streets and central plazas. Principal streets were the sites for the numerous fiestas, feast days for patron saints and religious processions that combined secular amusements with the show of piety. Here, the positive, idealized visions of woman in romantic love seamlessly joined with religious symbolism, finding a place in the cult of the Virgin Mary, whose popularity increased in the period.[47] Amorous young women wishing to find a lover or recover one who strayed, prayed to St. Anthony of Padua the advocate of lost and found while the image was paraded on the saint's feast day on 13 June.[48] Local notions of romantic love also found elaboration in street games. Main plazas on feast days held *torneos*, tournaments, or were decorated for the *juego de anillo*. In this game, reminiscent of medieval jousts, young men mounted on horseback and bearing a wooden lance rode through an arch of bamboo and palms from which were suspended rings hanging by colored ribbons. Using the tips of their lances, the young men endeavored to pluck a ring as they passed through the arch, returning the ring to its female owner identified by the color of the ribbon. As in the jousting tournaments of a medieval court, the male players were rewarded for their skill with tributes from the woman they adored from afar.[49]

But the fiesta, as Reinhard Wendt has shown, also provided the opportunity for spontaneity and the expression of informal and self determined modes of behavior.[50] Indeed, according to John Bowring's observations in 1859, the most serious of all celebrations in the Catholic calendar, the Lenten Passion, brought forth all manner of illicit assignations, especially under the cover of darkness:

They are fond of religious dramas, especially of one in Tagal representing the passion and death of Christ; but these religious representations and gatherings give rise to scandal and abuse, and the birth of many illegitimate children. The priests have generally prohibited these exhibitions at night, and sometimes disperse them, whip in hand; at other times the singers are denounced, and get flogged for their pains — or pleasures.[51]

Amongst the urban masses the notion of romantic love perhaps represented erotic aspirations rather than the strictly followed norm. But notions of romantic love certainly began to permeate the popular consciousness and became blended with older beliefs and practices which, despite priestly admonishments and chastisements, had persisted from pre-Spanish times. Men and women continued to consult the *Golo*, "witch doctors of love" (*hechizo de amores*), who concocted the *gayuma*, potions made from herbs and roots or spells that would induce feelings of love.[52] Special chants, *oraciónes*, a mixture of Latin and Spanish words sewn on a piece of cloth or embossed on metal were obtained by amorous male lovers and worn discreetly on their body as a charm to conquer the heart of women (*para conquistar el corazón de las mujeres*).[53] In the act of lovemaking the faculty of smell was particularly important. Lovers ascertained the state of each other's affections by the odour of their bodies. They gifted one another with recently worn intimate garments "impregnated with the passion of their owner" that was kept until the scent had faded. Sinibaldo de Mas reported that natives indicated sexual interest by wrinkling their noses at the desired and continued to kiss by rubbing noses although they had learnt from the Spaniards to accomplish the act with their lips.[54] Natives, it seemed, selected only what suited them. An exasperated priest remarked how the word "horn" (*cuernos*) with the sexual connotations Europeans had given to it, was freely adopted by the lower strata of society who used the equivalent Tagalog word *sungay* to mean all manner of perversions and corruptions.[55] The indios, priests were concerned, were coupling sinfully and indecorously, flagrantly disregarding the "proper mode of courting" as laid down by the Church. Jean Mallat was likewise horrified to learn that virginity in women was not as valued as the widespread romantic image of chaste maidens pretended. "Husbands," he observed:

cared little to find in their wives that flower so precious in the eyes of Europeans, they even considered themselves very lucky when a former suitor had spared them the effort or the expense, we say the expense, for there were men whose profession was to deflower the *dalagas* and who were paid for it, unless however an old woman had performed this during the young woman's childhood an operation consisting in breaking the hymen.[56]

Filtered through a combination of religious language and Catholic doctrine found in the awits and corridos, the notion of romantic love spread to the lower classes of native society who were far from insensible to the delicacy of its sentiments and the complexity of its emotional adventures. Although drawn from traditional and foreign sources, romantic love as indigenized by playwrights and poets captivated the popular imagination and presented a new, idealized experience of love and courtship for natives who continued adhering to and practising more deeply rooted and ancient amorous strategies that existed alongside romance. This folk experience of love was part of the fabric of Manila's culture; it surrounded the young ilustrados as they studied in the city and helped shape their perception of erotic life.

In his first year at the Ateneo, the young Rizal boarded at Calle Carballo in Binondo at a small house situated at the point where the Estero de Santa Cruz made a loop before flowing under the wide Calle Gandara that crossed Santa Cruz. Here flourished street-walking prostitution and it is unlikely that the observant Rizal would have missed that fact.[57] The street-walking prostitute was of course not confined to Calle Gandara. The Paseo de Azcarraga, a few selected streets in San Nicolas, the Plaza de Calderón de la Barca in Binondo, and the Calzada de Iris in Quiapo were also areas in which they plied their trade, not far from the rich shopping streets of Calles, Escolta, Rosario and Nueva.[58]

By most accounts, Manila prostitutes were also less glamorous, less flamboyant. They were rural, socially disadvantaged women whose average age was 16, migrants to the city and "truly powerless, utterly without standing or prospects for advancement in life."[59] Part of the Manila underworld, prostitution was the dark side of carnal love in the city. Spanish doctors were alarmed at the rapidly worsening problem of venereal diseases (particularly syphilis) caused principally, they claimed, by the increase in unregulated prostitution. Dr Cornelio Mapa y Belmonte, for instance, blamed poverty, lack of education and the "seduction" of uneducated pubescent girls by older, depraved women also given to the vice.⁶⁰

Official *reglamentos* distinguish between four categories of prostitutes: street-walkers; those who operated from prostitution houses run by *amas* or *amos* (mistresses or masters); those who visited clients in their own homes; and those who received clients at their private residence. Involving women of non-Filipino origin — Spaniards, Americans, and English — who lived at more salubrious addresses, this fourth category implicates men and women from the powerful and wealthier upper classes and suggests that a more refined and concealed mode of prostitution was in place.⁶¹

Secondly, the definition of prostitution might be seen as somewhat fluid in the Philippine cultural context. As narrowly defined in the Reglamento of 1897, the *mujer pública* was one who regularly engaged in the flesh trade. Her Spanish legal names — *prostituta, vagamunda, indocumentada* — gave an equally limited description and reflected a wandering person of no fixed abode and unregistered to pay the *cedula*.⁶² Outside such legal strictures, the practice of concubinage or the *querida* relationship in which financial support was provided in return for intimate companionship outside of marriage was a common and socially condoned domestic arrangement that blurred the definitional distinction between concubinary relations and serial prostitution. Concubinage displayed the class and racial power of the colonial order. In their relations with unmarried local women, many Spanish men blithely applied the maxim "fornication is no sin," freely entering into any number of concubinary relations with women whom they expected to remain monogamous yet were often abandoned with mixed-blood children at the end of the Spaniard's tour of duty in the colony.⁶³

As Daniel Doeppers highlights, it was especially common for European and Chinese men to maintain concubines because of the shortage of women in the city from their own ethnic backgrounds, but it was also commonplace for Filipinos to keep a *querida* (mistress) and a second family in conjunction with a "legitimate" wife and household. Among the Tagalog lower classes, such arrangements did not stigmatize Filipino women nor did estrangement from family and social networks automatically result, despite the observance of Catholic teachings.

Correspondingly, prostitutes were not as a rule ostracized by their communities nor was prostitution viewed as an obstacle to future marriage ties. Indeed, the Tagalog euphemism for prostitutes — *kalapating mababang lumilipad* (low flying doves) — mirrors this attitude.[64]

This relaxed view was reflected in official policy. Despite concern over the spread of venereal diseases, Manila's public authorities were generally tolerant towards the city's prostitutes. In this respect, officials were simply following the view long entrenched in Spanish society that prostitution served to protect the institution of marriage; it was "a necessary evil" that needed to be organized, regulated and restricted to its own ghetto.[65] Prohibiting public solicitation in streets, entrances and balconies of homes aimed to protect public morals and maintain public decorum.

The Rules of Urbanidad and the Affirmation of Bourgeois Sexuality

Ilustrado criticism of popular lower class culture was borne out from the messy reality of Manila's culturally hybrid urban environment where people of all classes lived together, maintained a range of sexual arrangements and followed fluid, sometimes conflicting forms of desire. There was a need for the new middle classes to assert the moral high ground, to secure bourgeois morality and ensure the triumph of bourgeois culture. But this effort antedated the ilustrados' work in Europe. Urbanidad represented a bourgeois way of life where its display — whether bodily or in the determined pursuit to acquire material trappings — distinguished the person of property, propriety and social polish. Yet urbanidad was also a discourse that advocated the end of the romantic nature of love and the imposition instead of discipline and self-restraint. It linked prescriptions of personal conduct to the management of sexuality and a wider ordering of life that affirmed and cultivated a bourgeois self — politically subjugated and controlled by Church and state.

To begin with, social appearances were an obligatory but also risky business carrying the potential of committing innumerable social slipups. Urbanidad as it was set out in books of conduct was an ideal code of behavior brought to bear on almost every aspect of social life. The *Nuevo manual de urbanidad*, a popular book of conduct concerned with courtesy, decorum and etiquette for the refined gentleman, stipulated that urbanidad formed the "fundamental basis of decorum or decency and the preservation of duties in every action and circumstance in life."[66] In this work, a highly detailed and specific set of injunctions guided a gentleman in the ways he ought to conduct himself at all levels of social interaction. Beginning with his duties, moral and religious, to the family and the state, the manual went on to provide instructions on proper behavior during "regular communications," from visiting and conversing to the writing of letters. Just as there were instructions on how to conduct oneself at weddings and baptisms, the significant occasions of life, equally emphasized was how to behave in a decorous manner during important leisure activities such as the evening *paseo*, mealtimes, and at evening receptions and balls.

In the formalization of conduct and comportment, the dictates of urbanidad expressed the new values of the Christianized and Hispanized emergent bourgeoisie: decency, respectability and civility. Such was the importance placed on urbanidad that its "rules" appeared on the curriculum for primary education as set forth by the 1863 Royal Decree.[67] Taught alongside the compulsory subjects of "Christian doctrine" and "notions of morality," "rules of urbanity" or "good manners" formed part of the daily schedule of classroom lessons and was allocated half an hour in the afternoon of every week day before the school day ended.[68] Although removed from the 1871 curriculum as a separate taught subject, the "rules of urbanity" continued to be taught with other subjects at both primary and secondary levels (the latter, "*segunda enseñanza*," being instituted by Royal Decree in 1871).[69]

Studying at the Jesuit-run Ateneo Municipal, a school that generally attracted children from wealthy mestizo and Spanish families, the young José Rizal and Antonio Luna would have been required to learn the principles of "good conduct and deportment" from the first year. Present throughout the academic program offered at the Ateneo for boys from the ages of seven to twelve years old, the rules of urbanity took their place amongst the critical subjects of reading and writing, Spanish grammar, arithmetic and the sciences.[70] Marcelo H. del Pilar at the Colegio de San Juan de Letran, similarly, followed the curriculum of Grammar or Latinity which taught boys from 11 to 16 the principles of urbanidad with Christian doctrine, Latin grammar, poetry and "elements of rhetoric."[71]

Children were introduced to urbanidad at an early age through "primers."[72] Specifically designed to be read by young children of native middle class society, Esteban Paluzie y Cantalozella's little book of urbanidad, for example, was also published in Tagalog and explicitly emphasized respect and obedience. Within its pages, perfect for small hands, children learnt that urbanidad constituted "courtesy, politeness and attention to good deportment in society (*cortesanía, comedimiento, atención y buen modo de portamos en la sociedad*)." The cultivation of personal hygiene, a clean and neat appearance and good conduct was impressed upon young children as values required by society, and whose display was especially important when in front of those whom one owed a duty towards, such as priests, teachers, elders and government authorities.[73]

Like the *vidas* (works chronicling the lives of saints), *corridos*, the *Pasyon* and *novenas* (books of prayers and spiritual exercises), books of conduct are characterized by their intensely moralizing purpose. They explicitly conflated good breeding and behavior with obedience to the Catholic faith. Reflecting a commonly shared knowledge,[74] the book of conduct assumed a unified readership living together within an established Christianized community, the *parroquia*, held together with mutual interests and concerns.[75] Described by the Philippine literary historian Resil Mojares as "anatomies of conduct," these books took for their subject matter the ordinary and everyday life of the native parroquia but focused on "mental attitudes" rather than characterization, in which human characters held a "non-narrative purpose functioning mainly as mouthpieces of the ideas they represent."[76] As such, books of conduct disseminated an important message aimed at moulding the middle class native into an obedient, conservative subject of the Spanish empire: "The good Catholic was also the perfect colonial."[77]

Exemplifying the prescriptive text in Tagalog, the "Filipino proto-novel"[78] *Urbana at Feliza* by the Filipino secular priest Modesto de Castro delineated a moral program for the new native middle classes. Born in the province of Laguna in 1819, Modesto de Castro was educated at Manila's Colegio de San José and, after serving as a parish priest, became rector of Manila Cathedral.[79] Characterizing his works was a concern for social protocol, the "custom and ceremony" of urbanidad that urged the observance of smooth interpersonal relations within a hierarchical society governed by religion and state. Of the works that survive, *Urbana at Feliza* was his most popular with its use of contemporary language, depiction of characters and local customs.[80] Written in the epistolary style, *Urbana at Feliza* centres on the correspondence between Urbana, who is studying at a religious school for women in Manila, and her younger sister Feliza who remains at home in the provincial town of Paombong, Bulacan. While Feliza's letters constitute little more than requests for her sister's advice and counsel, Urbana is positioned as her sister's role model and writes letters that repeatedly speak of religious duties, Christian devotion and the social behavior she is learning at school.

The author focuses on two occasions in life, a family death and a marriage, that provide De Castro with the opportunity to convey his message. In matrimony, the prelate advises, it is necessary always to temper desire with decorum. About midway through the book, Feliza asks her sister Urbana for advice about marrying a man named Amadeo from the same town. Urbana's reply is mediated by a priest furnishing Feliza with a set of commandments (*kahatulan*) for a "harmonious marriage."[81] Over and above all else, moderation is impressed as the virtue that should govern the relationship of marriage, as it must in all other kinds of relationships. Love (*pag-ibig*), defined as a "precious golden chain," must never be excessive.[82] Here, love is referred to only within the bounds of marriage and treated as a duty to one's spouse and children; love is an element required to maintain domestic peace and stability, to ensure the endurance of the marriage and for the purpose of procreation. Contrary to romantic love with its celebrations of mystery and ecstasy, the married couple should only be "lovers of tranquility." Ideal love, according to the rules of urbanidad, should avoid passion, its dangers and incitements to feelings of jealousy or lust.[83] Metaphorical links to hygiene and "cleanliness" (*kalinisan*) depicted sex in terms of purity that determined all acts of togetherness (*pagsasasma*). Just as the passion of jealousy could plunge souls into hellish torment, lustful lovemaking, likened to the raging seas, was equated with blasphemy:

> In your togetherness always be pure.... The waves in the sea are vicious, roaring with rage, but upon reaching the shore they quiet down and do not trespass the line wrought by God. It is the same with husband and wife; there is a rule to follow that must not be overstepped so that purity will not be harmed. Remember that God is holy, Jesus Christ is holy, and that matrimony is holy; you must therefore strive hard to keep your union and conduct holy.[84]

Moderate and seemly partnerships depended on the regulation of female sexuality and the acknowledgement of male authority within the family. Fundamentally, De Castro's moral guidebook figured a woman's submissiveness, passivity and obedience as God ordained: Woman had not been taken from the head of the man "because she was not designated to be master who will command men."[85] The suitable wife should neither be beautiful, for that would provoke the desires of other men and her husband would not be able to sleep at night from anxiety, nor should she be richer or of a higher social class than her husband. Congratulating Feliza on dressing modestly, Urbana enjoins women in general to imitate the habits of a local fish:

> ... To show curves, to dress immodestly, a woman who does not take care in the way she moves, flaunts her body to the whole world. There is a fish called *pesmulier*. They say this fish has breasts and wide fins. If the fisherman catches this fish, it will immediately cover its breast with its fins (*caraca-raca ay ibinababa ang palicpic at itinataquip sa dibdib at nang di maquita*). This is a nice example to women![86]

The biblically-defined Woman of Virtue — modest, patient, God fearing, forbearing and long-suffering[87] — also fulfilled the requirements of bourgeois domesticity:

> King Solomon sought and praised the virtuous woman not the beautiful one so that she can be safely trusted with her husband's heart ... her industriousness is not towards the acquisition of jewelry and its extravagant display which is not appropriate to her, but to take care of the household, to seek wool and flax and weave them for the benefit of her husband, children and not to eat the bread of idleness.[88]

It was a woman's duty to assume a nurturing role, and since she was entrusted with the physical and moral care of the bodies of husband and children, then it followed that in her hands lay the well-being of the body politic. As concepts of femininity were tied to a wife's duties towards her husband and family, so essential dispositions of bourgeois manliness were linked to instructions in how a husband should treat his wife. On advising Amadeo in his role as a husband, the priest explicitly prescribes bourgeois gender roles and a division of labor within the household conforming to the middle class moral economy:

You Amadeo do not forget it is your duty to earn a living, as head you are charged to feed your wife and future children. You Feliza should save what Amadeo earns and take care of the household, avoid extravagance so that you will not be impoverished. You Amadeo do not forget your calmness (*catahimican*) so that [you] will not be a cause for suspicion by Feliza who may think you are being unfaithful (*pinag lililohan*). You Feliza do not leave the house without permission from Amadeo so that you will not be suspected of unfaithfulness. You are both like a garden with a key where no one may enter save the owners.[89]

Yet if the domestic domain operated as the primary site in which bourgeois morality could be secured, it was also here that it could be dangerously undone. The Woman of Sin in this respect was posited as the scourge of society. Her negative traits were legion: she was a gambler, a drunkard, lazy, extravagant as to cause the penury of her husband and children, immodest and talkative. As this type of woman was the most common, according to De Castro, men are enjoined to caution, and to be especially wary of the attractive woman:

There are women whose appearance is pleasing and attractive (*nakagigiliw*), they have cheerful demeanors and when socializing with other people appear to show a beautiful inner spirit (*sa pakikipagkapwa-tao ay kagandahang loob ang ipinakikita*), but once you offend her, she will immediately show her true self. With eyes glaring, her mouth ringing like a big church bell, she will shower you with an endless insulting tirade that sound like the cackles of an old hen. From her mouth spits obscenities like fire in the air. To what can we compare these women except to hornets that swarm and sting, to vipers with deadly poison?[90]

If the proper behavior for a young man was characterized by "order," "decorum" and "moderation" in all aspects of social interaction, a young woman was judged by her sexual purity. She needed to take care in all her bodily movements — in the way she walked in the street, in the use of her eyes and her hands and in the manner she wore her clothes.[91] The woman who failed to control her actions and her desires fell prey to lust. Sexual recklessness defined the sinful woman whose unconstrained approach to love destroyed her honor (*puri*) and the reputation of her family and caused her community to gossip:

In time, after numerous dalliances, her honour is shattered, her family's reputation is tarnished while the townsfolk tattle, but the most painful is the damage to the souls (*kaluluwa*) of these pitiful young women (*dalaga*) and the many people who sinned because of the example set by them. Who will God blame for these sins but negligent parents?[92]

Marriage signaled the end of a woman's independent life. By marrying she conformed to a sexual and moral criteria restricted to service — to her family, husband and community. In granting her blessing to Feliza's marriage, Urbana warns that marriage is characterized by hardship, its success dependent on a woman's self-abnegation:

If you Feliza, can endure hardships, can embrace the heavy cross borne by a woman with a husband, then accept these heavy burdens. If you do not possess all the virtues of the woman sought by King Solomon and praised by the Holy Spirit, then try your best to follow the counsels. My advice is to accept the Holy Sacrament of Matrimony.[93]

The prescriptive effort of books of conduct was directed to ensuring that bourgeois values would lie at the hegemonic core of middle class culture and that a middle class moral milieu would define what was normal and respectable in civil life.

Manila Society and Bourgeois Honor

In practice the rules of urbanidad were malleable. Marked by a co-existence between native and European manners and mores, Manila elite society seemed to embody a set of fundamental tensions between passion on the one hand and religious morality on the other that tempered romanticism. These were the features of a hybridized society whose members lived by melding cultures, values and tastes.[94] Operating carefully along lines of modification, adaptation, selection, the appearance of urbanity involved an exhibition of finely tuned skills in manipulating the signs of ethnicity, age, sex, and nuances of class as well as negotiations between local custom and Europeanness. Christine Doran's study of the lifestyles of Spanish and mestiza elite women identifies a particular "mixed mestizo culture" arising from a process of acculturation and physical adjustment to the tropics. Such women, Doran suggests, were especially open to adopting local Filipino customs and habits in their daily lives.[95] But the creation of a "nativized" bourgeois habit and its apparent disregard of European social protocols by elite women did not indicate a failed effort to live up to the standards of European bourgeois civility. Sustained by wealth, privilege and female dependency, the indolent bourgeois domesticity cultivated by colonial elite women was tied to European ideas of leisure and gendered notions of domestic arrangements that were contingent upon the presence of domestic help. For elite women, adoptions of "native customs" were only permissible and practised in privacy, during the long, hot daytime hours when social callers were not expected and only native servants were present. In public, elite women affirmed the superiority of European manners and mores (and by implication Europeanness), by following the behavioral and sartorial regulations prescribed by the cultural repertoire of bourgeois leisure activities.

Prominent amongst the daily pleasures was the evening stroll on the *calzada*. An opportunity for ostentatious display and gossip, the promenade was also the scene of flirtation and matchmaking. Who was who, who was there, who was with whom were the burning questions whispered discreetly by men and women as they ambled or sat in a slowly rolling carriage in the ritual of the paseo. Every evening the paseo offered the excitement of encounters with propriety merely heightening the thrill. As European waltzes played in the background, the public spectacle of the paseo concealed the intimacies of courtship and lovemaking. Casual glances, innocuous smiles, the slight brush of a hand were little acts pregnant with meaning and obtained eloquent responses of silence, blushes or their combination to indicate unease. Within the ritualized atmosphere of the meeting and mixing, these were signs that carried possibilities of love, hinted at courtship, and were understood as suggestive gestures of desire or at the very least, interest.[96]

Away from the street, the architecture of the new stone houses of the elite provided the most propitious setting for the courtship rituals of the bourgeoisie. In the early evening before the departure for the paseo or promenade, young women dressed to sit at the grand windows of the *sala*, the drawing room, or the wide and spacious *caida*, the reception room. Sitting at windows overlooking the street, glances or greetings would be exchanged with men who passed below.[97] Writing in his journal, the young Rizal reminisced on an adolescent love that unfolded in these evening gatherings. On visits that occurred in the presence of a chaperone, Rizal's exchanges were filled with the uncertainty and agonies of a juvenile infatuation:

> ... My aunts returned and we continued our conversation. The subject turned to trifles. It is true that during the conversation our eyes met, and the most intense glances full of a loving melancholical expression came to enslave my soul forever.[98]

Romanticism permeated the pattern of amorous behavior of the bourgeoisie. Flowers, handkerchiefs, fruit and canes served as a refined means of secret communication between unofficial lovers circumventing the presence of a chaperone. An open fan held across the bosom or closed and pressed chastely to the chest were coy signs of modesty. These Spanish customs of love served to forge notions of femininity and female sexuality that was conspicuously passive and inarticulate. Rizal's infatuation for a thirteen year old "K" is marked by glances that were "terrible for their sweetness and expressiveness." In his youth, Rizal conducted such intimate exchanges in settings that were only appropriate to and in line with bourgeois culture — the landings of grand staircases, at window seats, within carriages, outdoor patios. Such amorous sentiments and settings of bourgeois romantic love were always remembered: the most important love scene in Rizal's first novel was not only set in the *azotea*, the open patio of balustrades and tiles decorously overflowing with potted plants of fragrant flowers and herbs but repeated the flowery gestures of romance:

> What were those two souls saying who were communicating in the language of the eyes, more perfectly than with the lips, a language given by the soul so that sound does not disturb the ecstasy of feeling ... to a query of love by a glance, brilliant or veiled, the word has no answer: only the smile, the kiss or the sigh.[99]

While ilustrado men enthusiastically depicted women as submissive and wordless in love, equally there was a recognition that such feminine behavior resulted from a deficient education. In the nineteenth century the social attributes and accomplishments of bourgeois daughters reflected the academic instruction available to young women at schools. While the educational decrees of 1863 promoted primary and secondary education for girls as well as boys, it was not possible for young women to progress to the top colleges or the colony's sole university, Santo Tomas. Teaching, however, was regarded as a suitable career for women and the "normal course" taught at the Municipal school for girls in

Manila to prepare women for a teaching profession represented the highest academic instruction available to women.[100] In school the curriculum for girls was much less academic than for boys. At the popular La Concordia which had the largest enrolment of girls in Manila in 1880, and where Rizal's sisters attended, what was emphasized was vocal music, learning the piano and harp, and "industrial work" which entailed "elementary notions of domestic hygiene," needlework, embroidery and the "cutting and sewing of men's shirts."[101]

As early as his teenage years, Rizal had realized the consequences of this deficient education. Recalling an awkward moment with a sweetheart, he writes:

> We knew each other very well, but the education that the sisters of her college gave her made her excessively timid and bashful, so much so that I refrained from using the least ambiguous word.... To entertain her during the trip I asked her about her college, her friends, and her hopes or illusions. She answered me in monosyllables and I noted that she had forgotten half of Tagalog if not all of it.[102]

Within elite circles, the accomplishments of women were recognized in the domestic domain, a fact highlighted during special occasions. As an excess of sumptuous food and flamboyant décor were marks of social status during fiestas, young women were tasked to show off their skills in the preparation of opulent fiesta fare. Skill in ornate pastry making, confections, and knowledge of French cuisine were amongst the attributes considered desirable in young bourgeois women and the daughter responsible for the table setting was publicly congratulated, thus gaining introductions to potential suitors.[103] Daughters were also expected to demonstrate their accomplishment and eligibility by playing the harp or piano for the gathered guests, or by singing. In front of the shrine to the Virgin Mary placed before the *sala*, a daughter would sing a *loa* exalting the image, or accompanied by a guitar or harp would sing a kundiman whose lyrics sorrowfully told of the miseries of married life.[104]

At fiestas young men sought the object of their desire at night-time processions that signaled the end of the *novena* or nine day prayers. The second Sunday of December 1886 was a particularly memorable night for the young Antonio Luna. It was the first day of the fiesta of Sampaloc and the last night before his departure for Europe. As he was to recall, his only poignant memory of that fiesta night rested in a vision of feminine perfection, the image of the young woman with whom he had danced in "a measured Boston" at a party and had left with "flushed cheeks, breathing hard."[105]

From this inventory of intimacy, the amorous behavior of the Hispanized bourgeoisie is clearly defined by sex: women were expected to show a retiring refinement, coyness and passivity. Since the signs of love were so confusing, women could only respond with blushes, breathlessness and meaningful glances. In contrast, men were expected to pursue their desires by taking the initiative and to show an essential disposition of manliness characterized by courtly gallantry and chivalry. Even within the private, secret arena of an amorous romance, considerations of honor still governed.

Honor, in this respect, represented a particular form of pride. According to Bartolomé Bennassar, the passion of honor was the quality that most defined the Spanish people. Finding its roots in the Castilian code of the Partidas of the thirteenth century, the Hispanic code of honor was defined by the reputation a man had acquired "by virtue of his rank, his high deeds, or his valor" and emphasized that public insults dishonored a man. Personal action and social position were its motivations and "*honor, honra, honradamente, honrado, honroso, amor propio*" constituted its vocabulary. [106] Valorized by public display, honor required witnesses; gender specific, the display of honor could be distinguished between the sexes, as Bennassar wrote:

> [for a man is defined by his] reputation, which he must defend at the risk of his life; if he cannot, all is lost. The honor of a girl resides in her virginity, that of a married woman in her fidelity.... Some traits of honor, such as its association with a married woman's fidelity or a girl's virginity, remained unchanged. Here the honor of the whole family — and this was as true of the king as of the peasant — was involved.[107]

To the urbane new bourgeoisie, keen to assert their elite status through gentility, respectability and sophistication, these features of the Hispanic code of honor were especially attractive. The political, social and spatial changes that were transforming Manila in the nineteenth century impacted upon the consciousness of its urban inhabitants at the most quotidian level. Changes in the way indios dressed, ate, walked, built and furnished their homes, experienced and articulated desire became the foundation of a new consciousness. The bourgeois elite was cultivating a new sense of selfhood that found expression in the hybridized systems of love and patterns of amorous behavior that were being practiced in the urban landscape. Here, notions of romantic love as refracted through the lenses of Catholic dogma and medieval tradition interwove with the process of forging concepts of masculinity and femininity. How the encounter with modern femininity imperiled ilustrado male identity and challenged the cherished idea of male honor is the subject of the next chapter.

Notes

1. According to Montero y Vidal, the Comisión de Filipinos was composed of "various *Españoles filipinos* (Philippine-born Spaniards), Chinese mestizos, native clergy, students from the municipal suburbs of Santa Cruz, Quiapo and Sampaloc." José Montero y Vidal, *Historia General de Filipinas desde el descubrimiento de dichas islas hasta nuestros días*, vol. 3 (Madrid: Tello, 1895), p. 503.
2. *El Porvenir Filipino*, 14 July 1869.
3. Montero y Vidal dwelt indelicately on the intimacy of their relationship, remarking how when Doña María stayed with the Governor, she was "honored" in Malacanang Palace as if she was "the owner of the house (*dueña de la casa*)." No less scandalously, "while her husband who had been marching was taken ill at a house of Recollect priests at Imus, she stayed in Manila assisting the [Governor] General with her counsel and attentive care." Montero y Vidal, *Historia General*, vol. 3, p. 500.
4. *Diario de Manila*, 13 July 1869.
5. Montero y Vidal, *Historia General*, vol. 3, p. 511.
6. José Montero y Vidal, quoted in John R.M. Taylor, *Philippine Insurrection against the United States: a compilation of documents*. With an introduction by Renato Constantino (Pasay City: Eugenio Lopez Foundation, 1971), vol. 1, p. 44.
7. Ibid.
8. Ricketts (Manila) to Lord Granville, 10 March 1872 (PRO/FO 72/1322) reproduced in Horacio de la Costa, S.J., *Readings in Philippine History* (Manila: Bookmark, 1965), p. 157.
9. Santiago Albano Pilar, *Juan Luna: The Filipino as painter* (Manila: Eugenio Lopez Foundation, 1980), pp. 36–7; José Rizal, *Reminiscences and Travels of José Rizal (1878–96)* (Manila: José Rizal Centennial Commission, 1961), p. 13; Vivencio José, *The Rise and Fall of Antonio Luna* (Metro Manila: Solar, 1986), p. 45; Fidel Villarroel OP, *Marcelo H. del Pilar at the University of Santo Tomas* (Manila: University of Santo Tomas, 1997), p. 34; John N. Schumacher SJ, *The Propaganda Movement, 1880–1895: the creation of a Filipino consciousness, the making of the Revolution* (Quezon City: Ateneo de Manila University Press, 1997), p. 106.

10. Benito J. Legarda, Jr., *After the Galleons: foreign trade, economic change and entrepreneurship in the nineteenth century Philippines* (Manila: Ateneo de Manila University Press, 1999), esp. pp. 94–100.
11. O.D. Corpuz, *An Economic History of the Philippines* (Quezon City: University of the Philippines Press, 1997), pp. 106–8; German Pacheco Troconis, "El añil commercial en Filipinas: surgimiento, consolidación y ocaso, 1773-1876," in *Illes I Imperis*, no. 6 (2002): 101–23; for an analysis of Spain's neo-mercantilist policies and their consequences to foreign capital in the late nineteenth century, see Wigan Salazar, "British and German passivity in the face of the Spanish neo-mercantilist resurgence in the Philippines, c. 1883–1898," *Itinerario* 21, no. 2 (1997): 125–47.
12. See especially the important essays in Alfred W. McCoy and Ed C. Jesus, *Philippine Social History: global trade and local transformations* (Manila and Sydney: Asian Studies Association of Australia in cooperation with Ateneo de Manila University Press and George Allen and Unwin Australia, 1982).
13. I have in mind here Georg Simmel's concept of economic exchange as a form of social interaction. Georg Simmel, *The Philosophy of Money*, trans. Tom Bottomore and ed. David Frisby (London: Routledge, 2004).
14. Walter Benjamin, *Illuminations*. With an introduction by Hannah Arendt (London: Fontana Press, 1992), esp. pp. 152–68.
15. Interestingly, the principal cigar factory was located in a convent in Binondo which the Dominicans provided rent-free. In the 1850s, this monopoly factory employed between 8,000 to 9,000 workers, all of whom were women. See O.D. Corpuz, *An Economic History of the Philippines*, p. 121. Also Daniel F. Doeppers, "Migration to Manila: changing gender representation, migration field and urban structure," in *Population and History: the demographic origins of the modern Philippines*, ed. Daniel F. Doeppers and Peter Xenos (Metro Manila: Ateneo de Manila University Press, 1998), pp. 139–79; and Daniel F. Doeppers, *Manila 1900–1941: social change in a late colonial metropolis* (Manila: Ateneo de Manila University Press, 1984).
16. Ken de Bevoise, *Agents of Apocalypse: epidemic disease in the colonial Philippines* (Princeton, New Jersey: Princeton University Press, 1995), esp. pp. 69–73; also Greg Bankoff, "Servant-master Conflicts in Manila in the late Nineteenth Century," *Philippine Studies* 40 (1992): 281.
17. De Bevoise, *Agents of Apocalypse*, p. 75.
18. See Fig. 5. This is an enlarged section of a map compiled by the Office of the Chief Engineer, Division of the Philippines, and dated 12 November 1901. It has been used here because of the clarity with which the principal streets are marked, but some features — such as the railway line — post-date the period covered in this chapter. It should also be noted that the area marked S. Nicolas was administratively part of Binondo until 1894. The original version of this map is inserted in United States War Department, Bureau of Insular Affairs, *A Pronouncing Gazetteer and Geographical Dictionary of the Philippine Islands* (Washington: Government Printing Office, 1902), f.p. 184.

19 A Visit to the Philippine Islands by Sir John Bowring, LLD., FRS., Late Governor of Hong Kong, H.B.M.'s Plenipotentiary in China, Honorary Member of the Sociedad Economica de las Filipinas, etc. etc. (London: Smith, Elder & Co., 1859), p. 17.
20 Xavier Huetz de Lemps, "Shifts in the meaning of 'Manila'," in *Old Ties and New Solidarities: studies on Filipino communities*, ed. Charles J.H. MacDonald and Guillermo M. Pesigan (Metro Manila: Ateneo de Manila University Press, 2000), p. 227.
21 Corpuz, *An Economic History of the Philippines*, p. 125.
22 According to Daniel Doeppers, the annual slaughter of cattle in the city was a remarkably high 17–18,000 heads between 1879–80 and 20–21,000 during the period 1884–86. See Daniel Doeppers, "Beef consumption and regional cattle husbandry systems in the Philippines, 1850–1940," in *Smallholders and Stockbreeders: Histories of foodcrop and livestock farming in Southeast Asia*, ed. Peter Boomgaard and David Henley (Leiden: KITLV Press, 2006), pp. 307–24.
23 Edgar Wickberg, *The Chinese in Philippine life, 1850–1898* (Quezon City: Ateneo de Manila University Press, 2000), p. 118; Alfred W. McCoy, *The Politics of Heroin* (New York: Lawrence Hill Books, 1991). A not entirely dissimilar situation could be found in neighboring colonial Indonesia in the same period. See James R. Rush, *Opium to Java: Revenue Farming and Chinese Enterprise in Colonial Indonesia, 1860–1910* (Ithaca and London: Cornell University Press, 1990).
24 *Anuario Filipino para 1877 pr D. Ramon Gonzalez Segunda Edicion del Manual del Viajero en Filipinas* (Manila: Establecimiento tipografico de Plana y Ca., 1877); *Guia Oficial de Filipinas 1890* (Manila: Tipo-Litografica de Chofre y Compa., 1890) and 1898 edition (Manila: Secretaria del Gobierno General, 1898). Unfortunately, the adverts give little detail of what these *máquinas eléctricas* were used for.
25 Alfred Marche, *Luzon and Palawan* [1879], translated from the French by Carmen Ojeda and Jovita Castro (Manila: The Filipiniana Book Guild, 1970), p. 83.
26 Anna D'Almeida, *A Lady's visit to Manilla and Japan* (London: Hurst and Blackett, 1863), p. 24.
27 Marche, *Luzon and Palawan*, p. 31.
28 Dean C. Worcester, *The Philippine Islands and their people: A record of personal observation and experience, with a short summary of the more important facts in the history of the Archipelago* (New York: The Macmillan Co., 1898), p. 40.
29 *Informe Secreto de Sinibaldo de Mas Informe sobre el estado de las Islas Filipinas en 1842*. III. Spanish original with an English translation by Dr. Carlos Botor; rev. by Alfonso Felix, Jr.; and an introduction and notes by Juan Palazon (Manila: Historical Conservation Society, 1963), p. 160.
30 Ivan Goncharov, "The Voyage of the Frigate 'Pallada'," in *Travel Accounts of the Islands* (Manila: Filipiniana Book Guild, 1974), pp. 161–2.
31 Edgar Wickberg, *The Chinese in Philippine Life, 1850–1898* (New Haven and London: Yale University Press, 1965), pp. 107–8.
32 Wigan Salazar, "German Economic Involvement in the Philippines, 1871–1918," unpublished PhD dissertation, School of Oriental and African Studies, University of London, 2000, p. 177.

33 Goncharov, "The Voyage of the Frigate 'Pallada'," p. 161.
34 Henry T. Ellis, R.N., *Hongkong to Manilla and the Lakes of Luzon, in the Philippine Islands, in the year 1856* (London: Smith, Elder and Co., 1859), p. 69.
35 Goncharov, "The Voyage of the Frigate 'Pallada'," p. 213.
36 W.E. Retana, *Aparato bibliográfico de la Historia General de Filipinas*, vol. 3 (Madrid: Imp. de la Sucesora de M. Minuesa de los Rios, 1906), p. 1588.
37 Rudolf Mrazek, *Engineers of Happy Land*, p. 145.
38 Tracing the concept of rusticity as a negative quality to elite attitudes in eighteenth-century Spain, Carmen Martin Gaite writes: "Rusticity, as a concept opposed to decency, referred, above all, to an inelegant and untidy appearance. In this sense few eras upheld as strongly as did the eighteenth century the adage that clothes make the man, as if refinement in dress automatically eliminated grossness and dull wit. Pains were taken to affirm that the new fashions called to revolutionize outer appearances as well as the traditional codes in human relations, averted all discomposure or brusqueness." In Carmen Martin Gaite, *Love Customs in Eighteenth Century Spain*, trans. María G. Tomsich (Berkeley: University of California Press, 1991), p. 46.
39 Francisco Baltazar, "La india elegante y el negrito amante." Sayneteng wikang Tagalog na sinulat sa tula ni Francisco Baltazar at nilapatan ng tugtugin ni Gregoria San José [Udyong, Bataan, 1855], pp. 1–16. Unpublished manuscript, Philippine National Library.
40 Manuel Walls y Merino, *La música popular de Filipinas* (Madrid: Imp. de M.G.Hernandez, 1892), p. xix.
41 Antonio J. Molina, "The Sentiments of Kundiman," in *Filipino Heritage: the making of a nation*, vol. 8 (Manila: Lahing Pilipino, 1978), p. 2026.
42 See Bienvenido L. Lumbera, *Tagalog poetry 1570–1898: tradition and influences in its development* (Quezon City: Ateneo de Manila University Press, 1986), p. 87.
43 Damiana L. Eugenio, *Awit and Corrido: Philippine metrical romances* (Quezon City: University of the Philippines Press, 1987), pp. xxxvi–viii.
44 Soledad Reyes, "The Romance Mode in Philippine Popular Literature," *Philippine Studies* 32 (1984): 168.
45 See for example José Rizal, "Barrantes y el teatro tagalo," *La Solidaridad* 1: 9 (15 June 1889): 201. This and subsequent citations from *La Solidaridad* are taken from the Spanish-English parallel text version with translations by Guadalupe Fores-Ganzon (Quezon City: University of Philippines Press, 1967; republished Pasig City: Fundación Santiago, 1995–96).
46 José Rizal, *Noli me tangere* [1887], trans. Ma. Soledad Lacson-Locsin, ed. Raul L. Locsin (Manila: Bookmark, 1996), pp. 157–8.
47 Robert R. Reed, "The Antipolo Pilgrimage: Hispanic origins, Filipino transformation and contemporary religious tourism," in *Converging Interests: traders, travelers and tourists in Southeast Asia*, ed. Jill Forshee with Christina Fink and Sandra Cate (Berkeley: University of California Press, 1999), p. 151.
48 Nick Joaquin, *Almanac for Manileños* (Manila: Mr & Ms Públications, 1979), p. 36.

49 Encarnacion Alzona, *The Filipino woman: her social, economic and political status 1565–1937* (Manila: Benipayo Press, 1938), p. 46.
50 Reinhard Wendt, "Philippine Fiesta and Colonial Culture," *Philippine Studies* 46 (1998): 10.
51 Bowring, *A Visit to the Philippine Islands*, p. 137.
52 Listed in Ferdinand Blumentritt, *Diccionario Mitológico de Filipinas* [1895], reproduced in W.E. Retana, *Archivo del bibliófilo filipino*, vol. 3 (Madrid: Imprenta de la Viuda de M. Minuesa de los Rios, 1896), p. 335.
53 W.E. Retana, *Supersticiónes de los Indios Filipinos: un libro de aniterias* (Madrid: Vda de M. de los Rios, 1894), p. 24.
54 Sinibaldo de Mas y Sanz, *Informe sobre el estado de las Islas Filipinas en 1842*, vol. 3 (Madrid: s.n., 1843), reproduced in Emma H. Blair and James A. Robertson, eds., *The Philippine Islands, 1493–1898*, vol. 52 (Cleveland, Ohio: A. H. Clark, 1909), p. 31.
55 Pedro Serrano Laktaw, *Diccionario Tagalo-Hispano* (Manila: Estab. Tipografía "La Opinion," 1889), p. 1220.
56 Jean Mallat, *The Philippines: history, geography, customs, agriculture, industry and commerce of the Spanish colonies in Oceania* [1846], trans. Pura Santillan-Castrence in collaboration with Lina S. Castrence (Manila: National Historical Institute, 1983), p. 39.
57 Ma. Luisa Camagay, *Working Women of Manila in the 19th century* (Quezon City: University of the Philippines Press and the University Center for Women's Studies, 1995), p. 109.
58 Ibid. See also Greg Bankoff, "Households of Ill-repute: rape, prostitution and marriage in the 19th century Philippines," *Pilipinas* 17 (1991): 35–49.
59 Ken de Bevoise, *Agents of Apocalypse: epidemic disease in colonial Philippines* (Princeton: Princeton University Press, 1995), p. 75.
60 Cited in De Bevoise, *Agents of Apocalypse*, p. 73. The social historian's picture of prostitution must however be treated with some caution. A reliance on court record sources has inevitably portrayed a situation in which prostitution almost exclusively involved members of the native working classes, or the near destitute and desperate, those members of society most likely to get arrested and penalized and therefore to appear in archival records.
61 Camagay, *Working Women*, p. 110.
62 Ibid., pp. 112–5. The cedula was an official document designating the racial identity of its bearer, which determined tax liability and also served as an internal passport.
63 Charles Boxer, *Mary and Misogyny: women in Iberian expansion overseas 1415–1815: some facts, fancies and personalities* (London: Duckworth, 1975), p. 127.
64 Daniel Doeppers, "Migration to Manila: changing gender representation, migration field and urban structure," in *Population and History: the demographic origins of the modern Philippines*, ed. Daniel F. Doeppers and Peter Xenos (Metro Manila: Ateneo de Manila University Press, 1998), p. 145; Camagay, *Working Women*, p. 106.

65 Bartolomé Bennassar, *The Spanish Character: attitudes and mentalities from the sixteenth to the nineteenth century*, translated with a preface by Benjamin Keen [originally published as *L'Homme Espagnol: attitudes et mentalités du XVIe au XIX siècle* (Berkeley: University of California Press, 1975), p. 192.

66 *Nuevo manual de urbanidad, cortesania, decoro y etiqueta o el hombre fino contiene todas las reglas del arte de presentarse en el mundo segun las practices que la civilizacion ha introducido en todos los casos que occurren en la sociedad, como son visitas convites, reunions filarmonicas, matrimonies, duelos y lutos, &c., con un tratado sobre el arte cisoria* (Madrid: s.n., 1880).

67 As Bazaco notes, "rules of courtesy" appeared in the curriculum of the Superior school as late as 1894 being taught to children in the first and second years. Evergisto Bazaco, *History of Education in the Philippines* (Manila: University of Santo Tomas, 1953), p. 223.

68 Ibid., p. 245.

69 Daniel Grifol y Aliaga, *La Instrucción Primaria en Filipinas* (Manila: Tipo-Litografía de Chofre y Comp., 1894), pp. 409–10. *Manual de la Infancia para las clases de enseñanza primaria* (Manila: Imprenta y Litografía de M. Perez (hijo), 1893), a Jesuit textbook, contains a section on urbanidad among lessons on geography, grammar, history and other subjects. Cited in Retana, *Aparato bibliográfico*, vol. 3, p. 1274.

70 José Arcilla, SJ, "Ateneo de Manila: problems and policies, 1859–1939," in *Jesuit Educational Tradition: the Philippine experience*, ed. Raul J. Bonoan and James A. O'Donell (Quezon City: Ateneo de Manila University Press, 1988), pp. 32–3.

71 Villarroel, *Marcelo H. Del Pilar*, p. 14.

72 *Tratadito de urbanidad, adaptado para los niños en Visaya-Cebuano*, Cebuano translation by Carlos Arpon (Manila: Colegio de Santo Tomas, 1894) was, for example, a little book of urbanidad especially adapted for Visayan-Cebuano children.

73 Esteban Paluzie, *Diutay nga talamdan sang Urbanidad nga maayo sa mga cabataan* (Manila: Imprenta Amigos del País, 1884), presumably translated from Esteban Paluzie y Cantalozella, *Tratatido de urbanidad para los niños (diminuto)* (Barcelona: Paluzie, 1842). Another edition was published in 1886 by the Binondo-based Imprenta y Litografia de M. Perez (hijo). Retana, *Aparato bibliográfico*, vol. 2, pp. 994–5.

74 As Soledad Reyes argues in the case of Modesto de Castro's *Urbana at Felisa*, despite the lack of evidence to show who actually bought books of conduct an "analysis of the text is bound to show that its very composition could not have been possible if no distinct middle class had been formed, perhaps not as numerous nor as powerful as they would have wanted to be, but nonetheless, a concrete aggrupation of people with similar interests and goals." Soledad Reyes, "Urbana at Felisa," *Philippine Studies* 47 (1999): 8.

75 The Cebuano book of manners, for instance, the *Lagda sa pagca maligdon sa tauong Bisay*, was published in at least five editions, in 1734, 1746, 1850, 1865 and 1893. The 1865 edition was published in Binondo by the Imprenta de M. Sanchez y Cia. Written specifically for the "Visayan people" (*tauong Bisaya*) it is described

by Mojares as "a collection of maxims setting down detailed, specific injunctions as to how a good Christian must conduct himself from the time he rises in the morning until the time he retires at night. The reader is also instructed on moral vigilance in avoiding occasions of sin, which include dances and the *comedia*." Resil Mojares, *The Origins and Rise of the Filipino novel: a generic study of the novel until 1940* (Quezon City: University of the Philippines Press, 1998), p. 76.

76 Mojares, *The Origins and Rise of the Filipino Novel*, p. 76.
77 Ibid.
78 Ibid., p. 77.
79 Modesto de Castro, *Pagsusulatan nang dalauang binibini na si Urbana at ni Feliza na nagtuturo ng mabuting kaugalian) (Letters between two sisters Urbana and Feliza that teach good manners)*, ed. Romulo P. Baquiran, Jr. (Manila: Sentro ng Wikang Filipino, Sistemang Unibersidad ng Pilipinas at National Commission for Culture and the Arts, 1996), p. x.
80 First published under the title *Pagsusulatan ni Urbana at ni Feliza na pagcacaalaman nang magandang asal na ucol sa pagharap sa capoua tao* in 1864. The book underwent numerous editions and translations into other Filipino languages.
81 De Castro, *Urbana at Feliza*, p. 141.
82 Ibid., p. 57.
83 Ibid., p. 141.
84 Ibid., p. 163.
85 Ibid., p. 159.
86 Ibid., p. 66.
87 Ma. Teresa H. Wright, "Woman's Place as defined in ten Nineteenth Century Books of Conduct," unpublished MA dissertation, Ateneo de Manila University, 1990, p. 115.
88 De Castro, *Urbana at Feliza*, p. 145.
89 Ibid., p. 162.
90 Ibid., p. 149.
91 How Filipino women should behave was the principal subject of interest in magazines for elite women such as *El Bello Sexo*. Despite advertising itself as a magazine of art, literature and science, the staple articles carried by *El Bello Sexo* focused on married women's domestic obligations, female virtue, the proper arrangement of the boudoir, and instructions on hygiene and clothing. See for example *El Bello Sexo: semanario ilustrado del literatura, bellas artes, ciencias y conocimientos útiles, dedicado exclusivamente a la mujer*, Año. I, Num. 6 [ca. 1891].
92 De Castro, *Urbana at Feliza*, p. 154.
93 Ibid., p. 151.
94 Lilia Hernandez Chung, *Facts in Fiction: a study of peninsular prose fiction, 1859–1897* (Manila: De La Salle University Press, 1998), pp. 147–8.
95 Christine Doran, "Spanish and Mestizo Women of Manila," *Philippine Studies* 41, no. 3 (1993): 285.
96 Rizal, *Noli me tangere*, p. 378.
97 Fernando Zialcita and Martin Tinio, Jr., *Philippine Ancestral Houses, 1810–1930* (Manila: GCF Books, 1980), pp. 95–102.

[98] Rizal, *Diarios y Memorias*, vol. 1, p. 22.
[99] In the *Noli*, chapter 7 is entitled "Idyll in the Azotea," p. 56.
[100] Alzona, *The Filipino Woman*, p. 31.
[101] Bazaco, *History of Education*, p. 224.
[102] Rizal, *Diarios y Memorias*, vol. 1, p. 26.
[103] Felice Prudente Sta. María, "Leisure Time in Old Manila," *Kasaysayan: The Story of the Filipino People*, vol. 4 (Manila: Asia Publishing, 1998), pp. 12–3.
[104] A popular song of the 1870s, "*Paalam sa pagkadalaga*" for instance was a gloomy tune that bade "farewell to maidenhood." Damiana Eugenio, ed., *The Folk Songs* (Manila: De la Salle University Press, 1996), p. 415 (Philippine Folk Literature series, vol. 3).
[105] Taga-Ilog (Antonio Luna), "*Un beso en Filipinas*," *La Solidaridad* 2: 35 (15 July 1890): 473.
[106] Bennassar, *The Spanish Character*, pp. 213–7.
[107] Ibid., p. 213.

2

Encountering *La Parisienne*: Juan Luna and the Challenge of Modern Femininity

Painting *La Parisienne*

From 1884 until 1893 the Filipino painter Juan Luna lived in Paris. It was the most fruitful period of his artistic career, and a time in which his prodigious production was distinguished by a plethora of images that depicted the Modern Woman. The theme interested the young artist almost to the point of obsession. Not only did he complete numerous oil paintings of Parisian women, he also filled several sketchbooks with life studies in pencil, pen and ink and wash.

Little documentation survives to help explain the intention lying behind Luna's tenacious artistic interest, or to establish that his works were commissioned, entered into exhibitions, or even to indicate how they were received. While the works had enough ready appeal for Luna to sell them commercially outside of exhibitions, "like potatoes at the market," as he wryly joked, nothing is known about the buyers.[1] Given the scant documentary evidence, it is perhaps unsurprising that the paintings have barely been described, let alone analyzed, within the existing literature on Philippine art history. But these diverse representations of the women of the Paris bars, boulevards and cafés hold nevertheless a unique historical interest, because unlike any other artworks or writings by a nineteenth-century Filipino, they explore a manifestation of modern femininity which exerted a profound hold on the ilustrado imagination. The paintings provide a transparent and vivid record of the fantasies, fascination and contempt of a male Filipino's encounter with the novel sexual fashions and customs of *belle époque* Paris.

This chapter offers a detailed reading of Luna's representations of the Modern Woman and examines them from a variety of perspectives. First, the pictures will be situated in the context of a range of attempts to invent and define a pictorial imagery of the Modern Woman in nineteenth-century France, a subject that was associated with pressing contemporary social and moral issues concerning prostitution and women of "low morals" in Paris. Secondly, the pictures will be considered in the context of Luna's artistic ambitions in Europe and the significance of his move to Paris. His journey from Philippine provincial origins to Manila and thence to Rome, Madrid and finally Paris was seen by the propagandistas as integral to his artistic achievement as a Filipino and the transition to modern life. Just why this was perceived to be vital will be seen, thirdly, in the light of the ilustrado experience of Paris. Despite the fact that the Modern Woman, especially the figure of the prostitute, was generally absent in ilustrado accounts of Paris, we shall see that Luna's paintings redressed this striking occlusion, betraying the ambivalent, double-edged interest this aspect of modernity held for the ilustrados. Lastly, Luna's images will be examined in relation to the artist's private life, and in particular to the horrific *crime passionnel* he committed in September 1892, when he shot dead his wife and mother-in-law.

Throughout his time in Paris, Juan Luna did not involve himself directly in the political or journalistic activities of the reform movement, but through his friendships and acquaintances he was very much at the dynamic core of the movement, and because of his reputation as an artist his support was hugely valued. In 1884 his *Spoliarium*, an immense painting depicting the appalling gore of slain gladiators, was awarded the gold medal at the Exposición Nacional de Bellas Artes in Spain. The fame that flowed from this signal triumph and from later successes helped win attention, respect and sympathy for the Filipino reform movement, as Rizal grasped in his *brindis* speech toasting Luna's achievement. Luna brought to the campaign his celebrity status and influential contacts; and many of his major works in the historical genre came to be used, as he intended, to reinforce the reform movement's message of Filipino equality. His art was patronized by Spanish royalty, and in later years his royal connections would stand him in good stead. In 1893 they aided his defence when he was on trial for the double murder, and in 1896 they would be called upon again to expedite the release of himself

Fig. 6 Juan Luna, *La Parisienne*, c.1886
[From Santiago Albano Pilar, *Juan Luna: the Filipino as Painter* (Pasig City: Lopez Memorial Museum, 1980)]

and his brother from incarceration when both were implicated in the Philippine revolution against Spain. Despite his slaughter of his wife and mother-in-law, his reputation ensured that his honor and dignity remained intact, and in 1899 Luna would be appointed as a diplomatic envoy for the newly proclaimed Philippine republic.

But all this lay in the future. In 1886, with his newfound fame as a painter, Luna was enjoying life in Paris. He had just married the wealthy Filipino-Spanish *mestiza* Paz Pardo de Tavera, the younger sister of the noted Philippine scholar and reformist Trinidad H. Pardo de Tavera, and had completed *El Pacto de Sangre* (The Blood Compact), a major commission undertaken for the Ayuntamiento of Manila that depicted the sixteenth-century moment of alliance between the Spanish explorer Legazpi and the native chieftain Sikatuna. A smaller canvas completed that same year, *La Parisienne* (Fig. 6), marked several beginnings of Juan Luna's new life in Paris. It signaled his interest in the everyday scenes and images of Parisian modern life, an important shift that eventually drew to an end his devotion to grand scale historical canvases, of which *El Pacto de Sangre* was one of the last, and developed the intimate attention he would increasingly give to interpreting modern femininity.

La Parisienne is a bust portrait of a woman painted against a background of vivid scarlet and lurid ochre. The image is a strong, sudden shock of a much too worldly woman in garish abstract space, starkly stripped from the usual contexts of conventional domesticity in which women were often formally portrayed. Defined not so much by the details of "feminine" adornment as by brusque pigment, tones and textures, Luna's application of paint revels in picturing a dubious and dangerous corporeality. First the signs of her scandalous sex are present: her lips are a parody — a fierce red stain so pronounced as to be fictional in their fleshly fullness. Her skin would offend academic aesthetic expectations that demanded a woman's skin be healthy and sensual, an orchestration of pale porcelain and pearly alabaster flesh tones. Here, Luna's *La Parisienne* is intentionally pictured in a state of dissolution. Tints of yellow and red shading imprint on her flesh the livid marks of corruption, fatigue and filth. Walter Benjamin thought Baudelaire had captured this look, a look that only a city dweller beset by loneliness could understand, for it was a face that revealed the "stigmata which life in a metropolis inflicts upon life." Baudelaire's *La Parisienne* appears sister to Luna's creation:

> ... She resembled the type of the fiery and yet pale Parisian woman, the woman who is not used to fresh air and has been affected by living among the masses and possibly in an atmosphere of vice, the kind that can be recognised by a certain glance which seems unsteady if there is no rouge on her cheeks.[2]

Alain Corbin has observed how the prostitute was widely perceived by conservative policy-makers as having a corporeal connection with putrefaction. By assuring the elimination of excess sperm, a prostitute functioned as society's sewer, and was literally thought of as putrid, her body acting as a drain through which filth flowed: "As putrid body and emunctory/sewer," Corbin writes, "the prostitute maintains complex relations with the corpse in the symbolic imagination of the times."[3] She smelled and looked like death. Bearing the signs of her immoral nature and corrupted physicality, the revealed skin of Luna's image suggests not only moral rot, but rot itself. This was the undisguised effect of modernity, Luna seems to be saying. It produced a kind of hard-edged, threatening, malnourished malevolence. Significantly, the type or a category of urban woman to whom Luna gave the generic title "La Parisienne" was a prostitute. Modernity, for Luna, was epitomized in the dangerous image of the prostitute, a mercenary figure whose unwholesome, rapacious sexuality entrapped and caused the downfall of men.

Luna dedicated the painting to "*mi amigo Ferrer*," who was almost certainly the young Spanish anarchist Francisco Ferrer y Guardia. Luna may have meant his gift as a chilling, sobering reminder of dangerous women. Ferrer, exiled in Paris in 1886 with the republican radical Manuel Ruiz Zorilla, later narrowly escaped murder at the hands of his own wife, who tried to shoot him in a Paris street.[4]

Defining the Modern Woman

The eroticized attentiveness Luna gave to painting the transgressive, sexually independent woman had found earlier expression in his series of striking and commercially lucrative portraits of the lower class, "*barrio-bajo*" (poor district) women of Madrid known as *chulas*. Also conceived of as a type, Luna's chulas are the visual embodiment of a Mediterranean femininity whose mythic qualities were encapsulated by Rizal: "The beautiful women of the black eyes, deep and ardent, with their mantillas and fans, always gracious, always full of fire, of love, of jealousy, and sometimes of vengeance."[5] But in Rizal's opinion this vision was idealized, classicized and allegorized. It could only come, he remarked, from nostalgia; an idea imaginable when "one is in a country covered with snow."[6] The reality, he observed in Madrid, was earthier, more sordid: "it is indeed shocking that in many places (women) intercept men and they are not the ugly ones either."[7]

Luna's *Chula* studies blend the myth with the reality, depicting single, isolated figures removed from any given context but strongly resonant in associations. In the portrait *Una Chula I* (Fig. 7), the woman turns her head in a directly flirtatious address. She looks back at the viewer mischievously, enticingly, her head at a coquettish tilt and her expression clichéd in its complicity; her face, body and bosom collectively constituting a playful, beckoning pose of sexual promise.

With a similarly daring, brazen sensuality, the woman in *Una Chula II* (Fig. 8), sits squarely with arms resting on the chair, almost mannishly, exuding an air of sexual confidence and worldliness. She is smoking,

Fig. 7 Juan Luna, *Una Chula I*, c.1885
[From Santiago Albano Pilar, *Juan Luna: the Filipino as Painter* (Pasig City: Lopez Memorial Museum, 1980)]

Fig. 8 Juan Luna, *Una Chula II*, c.1885
[From Santiago Albano Pilar, *Juan Luna: the Filipino as Painter* (Pasig City: Lopez Memorial Museum, 1980)]

an obvious sign of fast living and an inclination towards transgressive behavior. The evocative, lit cigarette is held flirtatiously between two fingers, its suggestive burning tip echoes her painted red lips, a slight smile provocatively playing upon them. Her unashamedly bold gaze does more than implicate the viewer; it is a compelling invitation.

In these two paintings the indecency of the two women is fixed and blatant. But, unlike the image of *La Parisienne*, the sexually confident and morally questionable women presented in the *Chula* series possess an unmistakable attractiveness. The proletarian passion the women represent speaks comfortably of a spontaneous sexual spiritedness that inspires libidinal confidence in the male viewer. Lacking sophistication, what they offer is something impulsive and thus more wholesome. Little wonder, then, that Luna's *Chula* paintings sold successfully to various commercial firms in Madrid, Paris and to wealthy friends.[8]

Bearing the common title *Chula*, the images are of well-known working class types. Their salty coarseness captures the distinctive charm of the chula; a familiar delectation shared around in male company like a rude in-joke: "... And well, the *chulas* painted by Luna are the real *chulas* ... who stupefy;" writes Graciano López Jaena with a barely concealed nudge and wink. "They are the free and easy chulas ... with all their witticism, their facetiousness, and their strut. From (Luna's) palette emerged those chulas who should be seen to be admired."[9] Felix Roxas, writing in his memoirs, affirms López Jaena's depiction of working class women's low morals, recalling the sexual delights promised by certain excursions:

> As a student in Madrid, I lived among the proletariat. The three daughters of my landlady worked as seamstresses.... Sometimes they would organise a party.... I never missed such engagements.... At the picnic site, and by affinity, each girl would find her partner, while their mothers would busy themselves preparing the food. In all that hustle and bustle, there were always opportunities to slip away and inspect wooded areas, shady trails, etc., from where the girls would return somewhat tired and rosy-faced from their exertions.[10]

Roxas continues his narrative of these sexual forays: "The couples that had 'compromised' themselves sought privacy from the others, and those couples who returned as they had come, returned discouraged." For Roxas, these illicit sexual trysts in which single students like himself could freely indulge without the expectation of a serious commitment left charming memories: "Oh, those blessed years, so happily lived!"[11]

In comparison to the sexual idylls promised by the Spanish chulas, the professional stare of the prostitute depicted in *La Parisienne* breathes grimness, the title itself conjuring up the spurious, unclassifiable and enigmatic. That she is a woman of the Paris lower depths is in some ways beside the point. The image can be seen more powerfully as a confrontation with the detestable, corrupt and disturbingly modern.

How then was the Modern Woman being defined and imagined? Boldly seductive, sexually independent, and dangerous, the *fin-de-siècle* Modern Woman was an important figure whose image, as the French historian Michelle Perrot has traced, had become widespread throughout the major capitals of Europe. The Modern Woman took "root in new definitions of public and private spheres and sex roles, in a new vision of the couple, and in individualized love relationships, all of which were seen as markers of modern times."[12] Dangerous because of the threat her modernity seemed to pose, the *fin-de-siècle* Modern Woman rebelled against society's view that marriage was a woman's only avenue to fulfilment; she obtained an education, freely chose to live alone or accepted no restrictions on how to live or whom to love; and she challenged male supremacy in art, the professions and the home. The bourgeois "New Woman" of London, Elaine Showalter discovers, was perceived as an "anarchic figure who threatened to turn the world upside down and to be on top in a wild carnival of social and sexual misrule."[13]

In France, and specifically in *belle époque* Paris, the Modern Woman took shape in the image of *La Parisienne*. This iconic figure, in the words of art historian Tamar Garb, embodied "a commodified femininity, one which was packaged to create an alluring, eroticized spectacle centering on the fetishized, fashionable body and flirtatious address of the female figure."[14] For writers, moralists, journalists and social critics alike, *La Parisienne* symbolized the essence of contemporary French Womanhood, a femininity that flourished in the soil of the social and cultural expectations and assumptions formed out of nineteenth-century gender ideology. An emblem too of modern consumerism, the Parisian Woman was a product of purchasing power. Her femininity was fashioned by the boutique chic, which could now be bought in the new department stores of Paris, the *grands magasins de nouveautés*.[15] Further, she was a creation dependent on new sartorial styles, the rituals of an elaborate toilette and the tightly laced rigors of modern corsetry.[16] The desirability of Modern Woman was thus dependent on her transformation — brought about by a careful, private process involving the powdering, ornamenting and sculpting of the female figure.[17]

Juan Luna's attempt to depict Parisian women can be situated in relation to a history of pictorial precedents that portrayed modern, Parisian Womanhood within this prevailing, commodified system of representation of the female body. The subject of intense male fascination, this Modern Woman, created by culture, artifice and the nineteenth-century public imagination, generated endless speculation, specular scrutiny and sexual fantasy in Paris culture and art. Proliferating in the contemporary popular press, the imagery of Parisian Womanhood from the *grisette* to the *lorette* and the *cocotte* constituted a large and familiar, public iconography of female seducers who, while not clearly categorized as prostitutes, were women understood to be engaged in the sex trade.[18]

The Impressionists, in particular, depicted urban femininity in a manner that proclaimed the iconic, sexualized Paris Woman as the quintessential emblem of metropolitan modern life.[19] Contributing to, if not personifying, the enchantments of the modern city, according to the male imagination, Parisian Woman was frequently invoked by popular image-makers as possessing a tantalizingly elusive *je ne sais quoi* quality. Her only defining requirement was the possession of a mythical, mysterious, erotically compelling feminine allure, which Luna's *pompier* (or conventional) contemporaries aimed to capture.[20] Rather than portraying and celebrating the elusive allure of the Parisienne, as for instance James Tissot's highly publicized narrative canvases sought to do, Luna's images brought to the surface the ways in which a woman's nature became corroded and debased by modern life.[21]

Luna's habit of writing short descriptive notes on his models, complete with their names and addresses, to accompany his sketches,[22] shows a methodical pre-occupation with classifying and categorizing facial and physical characteristics. Reading like an index file, his system of labelling reveals a classificatory mentality that had its origins in Johann Kaspar Lavater's influential system of codifying human nature through a reading of a person's external, physical signs. This tendency towards a taxonomic scrutiny of the human face, the attempt to systematically find "clues" to a person's character by looking at their physical characteristics, created a catalogue of stock characters within the pages of Luna's notebooks in the vein of the *physiologie* genre, an iconic and textual elaboration of the societal roles and manners of mid-nineteenth-century Parisian types.[23] Mme. Perre of rue Coustou, for example, is seen as "large looking" and like a "female butcher," while a favorite model, Mademoiselle Angela Duche of rue de Gergovie, carried the following flattering description beside her sketch: "supremely distinguished looking, pinkish white skin, body and shape of beautiful proportions, model No. 1."[24] Luna was concerned with the *effects* of modernity upon a woman's nature, and wanted to portray in paint how those effects were legible upon her face, her dress and her outward bearing. The superficial surface of Modern Woman's public appearance, he believed, tellingly disclosed her manners and moral character. Rather than simply imitating realist painters such as Tissot, Luna's iconographic renditions effected a *coup de force* not only by depicting but also by interpreting modern French femininity. Luna thus laid his own claims to representing the French fantasy.

Luna's paintings show the contemporary spiritedness of his artistic experimentation — his bravura and competitiveness — in the culture capital of the world.[25] Comprising mainly small canvases, studies and sketches, these works reflect the fervent and stirring effect the Paris art scene had on the young Filipino painter.[26] Luna thrived in the vivid atmosphere of high artistic activity and vital social climate of the urban metropolis, and his art connected closely to current Parisian themes and techniques. In later years, the attention Juan Luna gave to the "humble and disinherited" of the Paris streets in pictures such as *Les Ignorés* (1889–90) injected into his paintings a sense of class-consciousness.

For Luna, social realism was an expression of a moral sensibility. He visited his local iron foundry for the experience of choking for a few hours on the finely milled coal dust the workers were forced to breathe everyday. He wrote asking Rizal to suggest books that would inspire his mind in picturing the wretched, a subject he thought worthy of an eight-metre canvas:

> I am reading *Le Socialisme Contemporain* by E. de Laveleye which is a compilation of the theories of Karl Marx, Lassalle, etc; ... but what I would like is a book which stresses the miseries of our contemporary society, a kind of *Divine Comedy*, a Dante who would take a walk through the shops where one can hardly breathe and where he would see men, children and women in the most wretched condition imaginable.[27]

Luna declared his new allegiance to social realism to his friend, the Manila journalist Javier Gómez de la Serna, a vigilant watcher of the painter's progress:

> It's not a vulgar or iconoclastic realism. On the contrary, it's a sublime reality in a new form. The tableau in the grand manner, the historical painting of studied effects, have disappeared; ... The false is discredited and the truth triumphs. Yes! All historical pictures are false from the roots of the idea to the trappings. Those who think that good composition, correct drawing, brilliant colours, and a lot of trappings, make a good painting, have erred.[28]

Luna's admittance in 1891 to La Société Nationale des Beaux-Arts under Puvis de Chavannes confirmed Luna's social realist leanings as well as allowing him to exhibit ten pictures at the prestigious Champs de Mars without going through the jury.[29]

While Paris fuelled Luna's appetite for experimentation, his representations of women show that he worked within the nineteenth-century discursive construction of femininity, with its commodified representations and oppressive inscriptions of "separate spheres" for the sexes. They are images that move within a specific moment in the history of representation and the social history of women. They lit upon an aspect of modernity that was especially difficult for the propagandistas. It was difficult, as we shall see, because while the propagandistas advocated the most progressive thinking about womanhood, and while their contact with modern femininity in Europe shaped that thinking, the Modern Woman also engendered anxiety and hostility, posing a disturbing challenge to the *ilustrado* male identity.

Suggestive of feminine subversive power and sexual disobedience, Juan Luna's representations of the Modern Woman turn on a dialectic of contradictions — of desire and repugnance, sophistication and innocence, moral corruption and vulnerability. In attempting to illuminate the highly problematic, ambiguous nature of this imagery, it is opportune at this point to consider the works in the light of the political and artistic significance of Luna's move to Paris.

Journeying to Modern Life

For young, ambitious artists, a visit or a move to Paris signified a vastly important step for two reasons. Firstly, triumph at the Paris Salons, the very heart of the Western art world, virtually assured a place for the artist in public and critical esteem, and consequently in the artistic marketplace. Secondly, the increasing influence of the grand dealers who had made the city the international center of their commercial networks allowed for greater marketing opportunities for the artist's work. Seen from this aspect, Juan Luna's career after he had left Manila in 1876 followed a route that was common for Spanish artists of the period. He studied for a year at the Academia de Bellas Artes de San Fernando in Madrid, and then moved to Rome, where he trained for a further five years. In 1882 he returned to Madrid and gained his first measures of recognition and commercial success in its Salons. Paris, with the greater marketing possibilities and artistic prestige it offered, was the logical next step.[30] But of course Paris signified much more than the chance for artistic specialization and success: it provided a novel, irresistible environment for artistic exposure, experimentation and emancipation. And the 1880s was a particularly interesting decade for artists: Renoir, already a figure painter of some renown, was trying his hand at landscape painting with his friend Monet; Vincent van Gogh had made friends with Toulouse-Lautrec and was being introduced to both Monet and Renoir, Pissaro, Degas, Gauguin and others by his brother Theo; Henri Rousseau was preoccupied with his dreamy and sensually humid Jungle paintings and was showing them for the first time at the Salon des Indépendants, the jury-free salon for independent artists. Representing more than a capital city, Paris by the late nineteenth century had become the focus of new modes of learning, thinking and living. It was, to paraphrase Victor Hugo's vivid description in his epigraph to Zola's *Paris*, "the ship of human Progress."[31]

For the Filipino community of students in Spain, Juan Luna's move to Paris carried a weighty significance. At 27, Juan Luna had clinched the first of the three gold medals awarded at the 1884 Exposición General de Bellas Artes in Madrid for his monumental painting *Spoliarium*. This prize aroused great patriotic enthusiasm amongst the ilustrado Filipino community of students and expatriates in Madrid and Barcelona. Juan Luna was not only the first Filipino artist to gain renown in Spain, he was the first Filipino in any field to win recognition in the mother country. This personal achievement had an important political resonance, as his ilustrado compatriots José Rizal and Graciano López Jaena quickly realized.[32]

In his short biography of the painter's life, Rizal grasped the opportunity to criticize the feeble, grudging recognition given to indigenous Filipino talent in the Philippines: "We saw his first canvases, painted in that country so hostile to art, ... and painted under a master who had virtually taught himself."[33] A look at Luna's biographical details, as Rizal rightly recognized, served the dual purpose of appreciating Luna's personal achievement and emphasizing the need for reforms in the Philippines. Neither a mestizo, nor possessing an especially wealthy background, Juan Luna was born in 1857 in the small, Northern Luzon garlic and tobacco town of Badoc to parents who were of the Ilocano ethnolinguistic group. Though the family had achieved some status in their home province of Ilocos Norte, they had not amassed great wealth from sugar, hemp and coffee as other elite families of the region had. After abandoning an apprenticeship as a naval pilot, Juan Luna took up art seriously at the Academia de Dibujo y Pintura in Manila under the direction of the Spanish academician Don Agustín Sáez and the creole Don Lorenzo Rocha. The curriculum at the Academia was patterned after the standard academic program in Europe, and the students were required to spend hours studying imported copies of works by great Spanish masters like Velasquez and Murillo. Their competence was judged by the skill with which they in turn could reproduce the reproductions.[34] The narrow-minded, heavy-handed tuition of Sáez, which the young Rizal also experienced at the Ateneo,[35] curtailed the imaginative spirit and suppressed the artistic ambition of his pupils by demanding that they adhere strictly to the methods and styles of Spanish seventeenth-century painting. Spurning the oppressive doctrines laid down at the Academia, Luna prematurely left his course to continue, under private tutoring, with the self-taught *indio* (native Filipino) maestro Lorenzo Guerrero. Not long afterwards, however, Guerrero advised Luna to leave for Madrid. It seemed that Manila, with its stifling limitations and intellectually oppressive atmosphere, had little to offer the young, ambitious painter.[36]

Luna's resounding gold medal success at the 1884 Madrid Exposición, coupled with that of his compatriot Felix Resurrección Hidalgo, who was awarded a silver medal for his painting *Las Vírgenes Cristianas expuestas al populacho*, was a landmark triumph. The achievement proved the ability of Filipinos to match Spaniards and laid claim, for the first time, to Filipino participation in European culture. The ilustrado

Filipino community in Madrid therefore had high expectations that Luna would succeed in Paris, and as Rizal's diary attests they gave him a rousing farewell:

> 1 (Saturday) All Saints Day
>
> At 10'o clock at night many friends and compatriots gathered at Luna's studio on Gorguera Street, No.14: Paternos, Govantes, Esquiveles, Ventura, Aguirre, Llorente, López, Ceferino, Camillo, Esteban, 3 Benlliures, Mas, Silvela, Paulos and Valle, Arau, Moy and Correa, Conmmaye, Malagamigay, Arnedo, llodijar, Maurin, Maximia, Aramburo, Baera, Aurora, Florinda and others. There was much laughter, much manzanilla and champagne, there was singing, bull dancing (*toros bailo*), guitar, fandango, toasts, comedies. Maximino had an attack. Valentin was very lively. We left at 4'o clock; went on to another place.[37]

In this exuberant *todos los santos* diary entry, Rizal records Juan Luna's *despedida*, a party to celebrate the young painter's departure from the artistic backwater of Madrid to Paris. The comprehensive and hectic quality of this brief entry tries to capture the flavor of a joyous, momentous occasion. Some were long-standing and intimate friends of Rizal from the Philippines and would, like Ventura, Aguirre, Llorente and López, later become propagandistas or otherwise remain closely associated with the reform movement. But it was the context of an expatriate existence that renewed and strengthened such friendships.

Rizal's close and abiding friendship with Luna, four years his senior, had found its basis primarily in the seriousness with which Luna treated his vocation. In a short autobiography written for the Manila newspapers following his Madrid triumph, Luna only hints at the struggle for recognition faced by an indio competing against Spaniards in the metropole: "Truly, I wasted no time whilst studying, aiming to scale in just a small way the heights that Spanish artists have conquered."[38] It was this determined purposefulness that, from the beginning, distinguished Luna from his more slothful, and distracted, ilustrado compatriots studying in Madrid. Impressed by Luna's dedication, as well as sharing a common interest in art, Rizal immediately recognized that Luna's talent "could be signalled as an example to the rest."[39]

Rizal perhaps sensed that Luna's departure for Paris presaged even greater glory and achievement. The party held in Luna's honor seemed to signify a moment of present and future Filipino triumph — in the colonial heartland — by bringing together "friends and compatriots" who dreamed of what they might someday become and achieve. Thus, following the night of celebration, Rizal again records in his diary how the next morning, 2 November 1884, he and the Paterno brothers Maximino and Antonio, accompanied Luna in a mood of great camaraderie to see him take the train to Paris, and to modern life.[40]

Ilustrados and the Allure of Paris

To understand how Luna's departure for Paris could be seen as a journey into modern life, we should first examine the way in which Filipinos experienced the city. The attractions of nineteenth-century Paris, of course, were not unknown to Filipinos passing through Europe. The indio priest Faustino Villafranca who toured the city for a week in 1869, penned a long description of Paris and the city's new *grands boulevards* as a place particularly pleasing to the eye.[41] But whilst it comes as no surprise that a priest would be selective in his descriptions and strip the city of its social texture, Rizal too chose to present a pristine physiognomy of Paris. Writing long letters to his family in the Philippines, Rizal's copiously detailed impressions skip along with the spirited exhilaration of a young traveler eagerly sharing a new urban experience: "shops and department stores everywhere; passers-by animate and throng the streets, the restaurants, cafés, *bouillons*, beer halls, parks and monuments."[42] Piling detail upon detail to encompass the city's myriad features — cleanliness (including urinals on every street that even provide soap), the exhibits at museums (unique, ancient, easily accessible and free), the zoos and botanical gardens teeming with animals, flowers, plants and birds (variegated, exotic, and rare), the spectacle of promenading people (polite and refined) — Rizal's wide-eyed, eager enthusiasm pictures in guidebook style a city overflowing with culture.[43]

The stream of sights that comprise Rizal's *kwento*, or narration of experiences, is however burdened by an anxiousness to picture Paris and its inhabitants from the perspective of an inexhaustible, immeasurable and essentially respectable modernity. The city is constructed both as a site of sumptuous display and as a theatre for the performance of urban idylls. Rehearsing the tasteful recommendations of a tactful guidebook, Rizal summons up an impressive spectacle of modernity, his admiration focused on the physical order of an urban landscape, its excitements, and the visual opportunities it offered — the museums, cafés, wide pavements, architecture and the circulating ease of promenading people. The myth-making aspect of these tourist perambulations is remarkable for what they manage tactfully to evade. Absent from these accounts is the less respectable, the beggarly *foule* (crowd) and the squalid practices of *racolage*, or solicitation, that tarnished Haussmann's gleaming visions.

In many respects, the omission of these aspects of Paris is curious. Rizal for a time lived in the Latin Quarter, an area where cheap lodgings could be found as Rizal told his parents and brother. But it was also known for its "dark alleys," a district where the "dissection of cadavers, the flaying and dismembering of animals and clandestine prostitution coalesce."[44] Upon his arrival in Paris, Rizal naturally headed directly for the area in which Filipinos lived, staying at a certain hotel frequented by Filipinos located in the Rue de Maubeuge, a street in which many of his and Juan Luna's friends had apartments.[45] Moreover, it is likely that Juan Luna, courting Paz Pardo de Tavera at the time, paid frequent visits to her family home at 47 Rue de Maubeuge, a short tram journey from his studio at Boulevard Arago, on the left bank. Many of the addresses of the Filipino ilustrados living in Paris were situated in and around the most lively and fashionable districts of the city. Rue de Maubeuge led to the glamorous *grands boulevards*, branching off towards the Boulevards des Capucines, des Italiens, and Montmartre (see map, Fig. 9).[46] Here, the respectable mingled with the *foule* on the fashionable streets and sidewalks, which in the evenings were illuminated by the modern *éclairage*.

The Boulevard des Capucines and its neighbors, in the phraseology of contemporary commentators, were constantly "invaded" by "swarms" of street-walking prostitutes whose ambulatory *racolage* was seen as a "contamination" of these chic sections of the city.[47] There was a new demand for prostitution, Alain Corbin writes, because the "increased mobility of bourgeois men ... offered ample opportunities for sexual adventure" and "the romantic idealization of the wife made prostitution even more necessary." Wives were supposed to be angelic, to dedicate themselves to motherhood and the home, and within marriage sexual desire and pleasure was to be associated with procreation and the notion of duty.[48]

Unlicensed street prostitutes, claimed moralists, journalists and the police, were threatening a takeover of the city, even and especially its

Fig. 9 Map of Paris, c.1890 (Provided by author)

most prosperous parts. Such was the scale of the "social evil," prurient Paris guides advised their readers, that as many "as 35,000 women were walking the streets of the capital," of whom "not more than five thousand [were] inscribed in the books of the police as carrying on the vocation."[49] Such reports tended to be overblown and sensational rather than accurate, but it remained the case that rampant prostitution, uncontrolled and clandestine, existing at the heart of the city's *beau quartier* fuelled an existing fear that prostitution and Paris could almost be equated. Encounters seemed to be unavoidable and inevitable. Whilst specialized sex guides to Paris explicitly pointed out to the tourist the ample opportunities in which a liaison could occur,[50] the intensity of public anxieties also prompted nineteenth-century medical doctors like Charles Lecour to write extensively, and with some urgency, about the dangers of unregulated prostitution spreading disease, threatening the healthy bodies of male Parisians and infecting the social body of respectable Paris society as a whole:

> Uncontrolled prostitutes, that is to say unregistered, form the majority of the personnel of prostitution in Paris. They are everywhere, in the cafés-concerts, the theatres, and the balls. One meets them in public establishments, railway stations, and even railway carriages. They are there on all the promenades, in front of most of the cafés. Late into the night they circulate in great numbers on all the finest boulevards, to the great scandal of the public....[51]

What all this talk of an invasion of vice amounted to, was an acute anxiety about the visibility of prostitutes on the streets. "The Haussmannization of Paris had multiplied the places where prostitutes could find clients, the venues where men dined, drank, danced, were entertained, all were places that had become more profuse, more conspicuous."[52] That such encounters held a certain personal significance for the young Filipino men is suggested by the inclusion of the intimate trio of male friends found within Juan Luna's painting entitled *Parisian Life* ca. 1892 (also known as *Interior of a Café*) (Figs. 10 and 11). The group of men in the picture bear a resemblance to the artist and his close friends José Rizal and Ariston Bautista, and Luna presented the painting to Bautista to as a remembrance of their time in Paris.[53]

Juan Luna's *Parisian Life* depicts the sort of woman that provoked a mingled state of sexual curiosity and moral opprobrium for the Filipino

Fig. 10 Juan Luna, *Parisian Life*, 1892
[From Santiago Albano Pilar, *Juan Luna: the Filipino as Painter* (Pasig City: Lopez Memorial Museum, 1980)]

Fig. 11 Juan Luna, *Parisian Life*, 1892 (detail) [From Santiago Albano Pilar, *Juan Luna: the Filipino as Painter* (Pasig City: Lopez Memorial Museum, 1980)]

ilustrados residing in Paris. It focuses on an unattended woman inside a café, whose morality is pictorially suggested by various factors. Seated alone, she invites the ogling of the three gentlemen in top hats tightly huddled together in the far corner, one of whom, the gentleman on the right whose view is partially obscured by the urn of spring flowers, is clearly inclining his head in order to get a better look. It is her sociability and the nature of the social situation in which she is placed, rather than any investigation of female solitude, is the subject to which Luna draws the viewer's attention — the other glass of beer on the table, scarcely drunk, the suggestion of a partially smoked cigar, the drawn out chair that directly faces her, mimicking the bodily presence of a male drinking companion who must be the owner of the top hat and coat tossed carelessly inside out and thrown in a discarded, flaccid heap close beside her just at the right of the picture.[54] All these details describe a context in which she is socializing with a man who has briefly left her (perhaps to use the *pissotière*) and whose return she awaits. It is the inclusion of these sartorial accessories that goads the viewer towards a conclusion of impropriety that frames the scene within one of a typically illicit assignation, a recognizably modern Parisian context. It is the final, spicy touch of modernity that fixes her as an absolutely contemporary, sexualized woman, and the moment as the prelude to a calculated process of seduction that would move from café conversation to the coital.

A woman seen sitting alone in a café automatically became the subject of sexual speculation. The format of *Parisian Life* concurred with the dominant ideology of the indecent café woman and Luna's depiction was by no means unusual. Representing the new and modern forms of sexual commerce that had expanded and continued to prosper considerably throughout the 1880s, café women competed in notoriety with women of the brasseries and both — the café woman and the brasserie woman — were two specific and popular representatives of modern Parisian womanhood whose images had become by the late nineteenth century, a familiar expression of moral disapprobation.[55]

The café woman, according to the abundant and eager depictions of journalistic copy and drawings, was a woman who sat about in cafés for no other reason but solicitation and the calculating, mercenary sexual entrapment of men. Judged to be carnal, predatory and sexually illicit, lone café women presented a particularly visible manifestation of the burgeoning urban sex trade and its open forms. Indeed, it was to the extent that the supremely tasteful Karl Baedeker tourist guide of 1888 was concerned enough to protect the sensibilities of its respectable tourist-readers, reminding them to exercise discrimination in their café choices:

> Cafés form one of the specialties of Paris, and some of them should be visited by the stranger who desires to see Parisian life in all its phases.... The best cafés may with propriety be visited by ladies, but those on the N. side of the Boulevard Montmartre and des Italiens should be avoided as the society there is far from select.[56]

The café stood as the perfect venue for the sexually aggressive boulevard prostitutes blatantly putting themselves on sexual display.[57]

The resemblance of the men in *Parisian Life* to the painter and his friends invites the painting to be read as an act of self-representation that places erotic adventure into the familiar, daily orbit of ilustrado activities in the city. The painting epitomizes the ways in which various pictorial resources were used to master and contain the social and sexual force of sexualized women, and Luna's wrestling with the attraction and anxiety the subject engendered.

Parisian Chic

Feminine sophistication and worldliness in European women was compellingly erotic for the ilustrados, but it also provoked great fear. Again, we should recall that many of the young Filipinos were in Europe as students and that most found the exclusive parts of Paris society closed to them. Parisian sophistication, as the following account by Felix Roxas relates, had to be learnt. Acquainting himself with a woman who styled herself as a baroness, a woman "inclined to follow the fashion of the times" and who "stood out as one among the most elegant of women," Roxas recalls his indebtedness and initiation:

> It was she who presented me to Parisian society ... it was she who brought me to well known families; and it was she who initiated me into frequenting the most luxurious and elegant places. She had a finger on everything that concerned me, even how I looked. She quarrelled with the tailor who made my clothes; she was present

when the tailor fitted my clothes, seeing to it that her instructions were closely followed.[58]

Taken firmly in hand by an indulgent, fashionable, worldly woman, Roxas submits himself to an exclusively female form of power and undergoes a Galatea-like transformation: "I had to follow the colour of the necktie she liked, the right patent leather shoes to wear and how to act in places — all these things were controlled by her. Was it possible for a man to be so tied to the apron strings of a lady?"[59]

At a time when a woman's sexual attractiveness was closely linked with modernity and consumption, the Parisian woman obsessed with clothing and her appearance, as the historian Theodore Zeldin observed, was perceived by men to be less vulnerable and more powerful, if only in the field of fashion.[60] It was a power that women wielded which the ilustrados, too, found problematic. There was, for instance, always an underlying fear of committing a fashion faux pas that could make even the most well-dressed of egos look foolish, as the note the baroness discreetly passed to Felix Roxas, standing next to Juan Luna, would surely have achieved: "It would be convenient for you to hint to the swarthy man [Luna] beside you," the note read, "that wearing a blue necktie is always displeasing."[61]

For young Filipino ilustrados like Roxas, the Parisian woman demanded a new style of etiquette, especially in dealing with unexpected situations of intimacy. Recalling an episode where he escorts the baroness home, Roxas explains the new lesson he has learnt:

> Experience had taught the young Filipino that excessive timidity when one found himself alone with a lady, irritated French women because they considered it an insult, a complete indifference to their charms which were usually evident during [such] intimate occasions.[62]

The connection between female self-adornment and sexual allure was thought to be inextricable. Woman and her clothing combined to define femininity: "Where is the man who ... has not enjoyed in the most disinterested manner, a toilette knowledgeably put together, making thus out of the two, the woman and the dress, an indivisible totality?" asked a convinced Baudelaire.[63] Intrigued by female fashion in the modern metropolis, Luna observed the ways in which the structure of a woman's body was altered and held by clothing, how the constraints of clothing dictated deportment, and the influence of a hat on the rectitude of her carriage. The numerous preparatory sketches that appear in his sketchbook of women wearing the latest period fashion illustrate the notice Luna paid to the ways costume created womanliness.[64] Femininity, as many nineteenth-century male commentators like Baudelaire believed, was packaged, and Luna's images of fashionable Parisian women captured the durability of such beliefs.

The rise of the Parisian department store, the appearance of the mass produced garment and the emergence of haute couture were innovations that had drawn women's activities into the realms of fashion. Clothing style underlined a woman's erotic qualities. Yet, a respectable woman who habitually followed the dictates of fashion found herself condemned as fatuous and provoked worries of all kinds. Her interest in shopping and self-adornment was seen as a mania, believed to lead to a peculiarly female form of psychological illness known as "the delirium of consumption."[65] Far worse than this neurosis, in an era when the moral signification of outward personal appearance had itself become a fixation, was the vulgar exhibition of vanity. In polite society, a woman who dressed extravagantly in the latest fashions was seen as immoral, especially if it were known her husband was of limited means. Indeed, a respectable woman's overly energetic interest in personal toilette and dress, it was thought, betrayed a woman's tendency to licentious behavior, even adultery. She could quite easily, it was imagined, dangerously cross over into the sphere of sexual vice — succumb to prostitution, or the world of the fashionable courtesan where success hinged upon the careful display of her looks.

These prevailing social attitudes, we shall now see, offer a context in which the deterioration of Luna's marriage to Paz Pardo de Tavera (Fig. 12), during the last years of his residency in Paris, can be understood. Tension or hostility towards the power of upper class women is an underlying issue in the two images of fashionable women we now consider. Both pictures legibly thematize the intersections between sartorial display, morality and female power, whose force Luna attempted to capture. Luna's picture entitled *Una Dama Francesa* (A French Woman) painted ca. 1890 (Fig. 13) and an early portrait of his wife, Paz Pardo de Tavera, ca.1886 (Fig. 14), makes explicit the power of fashionable women and their ungovernableness by men. Apparent in the two pictures, however, is Luna's moralizing intent. Luna has clearly given an arrogant, disdainful

Fig. 12 *Matrimonio Luna*, 8 December 1886 (Pardo de Tavera Collection, Rizal Library, Ateneo de Manila University)

Fig. 13 Juan Luna, *Una Dama Francesa*, c.1890 (From Lopez Memorial Museum Collection, Philippines)

Fig. 14 Juan Luna, Portrait of Paz Pardo de Tavera in hat, 1886 (Pardo de Tavera Collection, Rizal Library, Ateneo de Manila University)

air to his arresting portrait of the Frenchwoman. Distinguishing her angular, poised profile is an understated elegance: her clothes are clearly well-tailored though lacking in luxurious trimmings; her hat is a masterpiece of millinery, with its highly-structured, sweeping, up-tilted brim and its decoration of two plumes of blue and white feathers. Indeed, her hat provides the dramatic high point to the picture, its shape enhancing the contours of her face, setting off the sharpness of her chin and high-bridged nose. Her haughtily arched darkened eyebrow is a meticulously plucked and pencilled line, her lips closed together. Her expression is one of proud indifference — as she offers up her handsome profile for scrutiny, she merely glances at her viewer from the corner of her eye.

Luna's portrait of his wife Paz is equally striking in the drama her costume enacts. Again, the hat in this picture is a focal point and was possibly one of Paz Pardo de Tavera's own creations.[66] Tall and decorated with what appears to be thin feathers held in place by a band, the sideward tilt of the brim casts a dark low shadow over the eyes, a masked effect that gives her face an aura of mysteriousness. Though it is difficult to see the details of her clothing from this photograph (of the painting, which is no longer extant), she seems to be wearing a dark coat whose stiff, high collar gives her an erect, rather proud and formal bearing. The visible portion of her face is itself a mask of composure, the features betraying no emotion but an overall sense of seriousness and secrecy.

Seen together, the two portraits are more than a document of Parisian women displaying up-to-the-minute costumes of the period. The sense of animosity woven within the fabric of these two representations of women-about-town reveals Luna's awareness of the power that was at stake. In pictorial terms, the artist's accusatory tone is shown in the over-erect pose of the female figures. The women give the impression of independence, and thus seem untrustworthy. Dressed without fussy ornamentation, they are neither flirty nor flouncy. Instead, emanating from Luna's depiction of their stylishness is a cool, silent superciliousness. Emphasized by their staid demeanor and the strong shapes of their hats, their dignified and lofty beauty seems not quite feminine and is therefore to be regarded with suspicion. Their closed lips indicate self-containment, a reserved exterior that appears to limit the artist's intrusiveness and to deny male possession. These are images of proud, confident, powerful women whose elusive, mysterious aura inspires fear

Fig. 15 Photograph of Paz Pardo de Tavera, Juliana Gorricho and Juan Luna (with face scribbled out) (Pardo de Tavera Collection, Rizal Library, Ateneo de Manila University)

Fig. 16 Photograph portrait of Paz Pardo de Tavera (Pardo de Tavera Collection, Rizal Library, Ateneo de Manila University)

and hostility rather than invites male libidinal attention. Photographs of Paz Pardo de Tavera, the first showing her wearing the same hat, standing in front of her mother (see Fig. 15) and the second wearing a hat that was possibly one of her own creations (see Fig. 16) is illustrative of the young woman's poise and confidence.

But there is another set of facts about the woman represented in *Portrait of Paz* that demands another kind of reading of this image. Paz Pardo de Tavera was 24 years old and newly married when her husband painted this portrait of her. Refined and elegant as a number of photograph portraits show, Paz Pardo de Tavera was a young woman who came from a close-knit, cultured family with a long tradition of male intellectuals and female entrepreneurs. Her family was also extremely wealthy, maintaining their comfortable lifestyle in Paris from the revenue generated by their extensive Manila properties.[67] Juan Luna, then 29, had achieved fame and accolade for his art but little money. Impecunious throughout his career, he had recourse to selling "copies" and small studies painted quickly to raise money.[68] Their marriage merged fortune with fame.

If in subsequent years the subject of money came to be increasingly responsible for the strains in the Luna-Pardo de Tavera marriage, the air of haughtiness evoked in Luna's picture may be seen as evidence of a tense situation existing between the couple even prior to the marriage. In a letter written during their courtship, almost a year before their marriage, Luna accused Paz of mocking him in public and reprimanded her for her unseemly behavior:

> I noticed you were doing it seriously.... You please me the least; you offend me. This is not appropriate to your conduct.... In the near future you will be my wife. Be the first to acknowledge my virtues. Do not ridicule me in front of your family by imagining vices that will greatly hurt my honour and the education my parents have given me.[69]

Doña Juliana Gorricho, the mother of Paz, opposed the marriage. She had feared for the future of her daughter whom she had brought up in the ambience of the modern metropolis since the girl was 13 years old. She feared that Luna, as a native Filipino man, did not accord the Spanish lineage of the family the respect she felt it merited. As described by Felix Decori, the appeals lawyer representing Trinidad and Felix Pardo de Tavera (the brothers of Paz), Luna was heard to remark upon his arrest that the Pardo de Tavera family "belonged to that dirty race — the Spanish."[70] Luna had "special ideas about women," Decori stated when the Luna case went to the Court of Appeal. Like all native Filipino men, Decori declared, Luna believed that women were "servile," and saw in the female sex "a kind of slave" ("*una especie de esclava*") who depended for their pride on the name ("*titulo*") and masculinity ("*calidad de hombres*") of their husbands.

Doña Juliana Gorricho had taken her children to Europe alone to escape the threat of persecution from vengeful, anti-reformist *peninsulares* (Spaniards born in Spain) in the Philippines.[71] A dauntless matriarch and a protective parent who enjoyed a close and influential relationship with all of her children, she was, according to Decori, afraid that her daughter and Luna were ill-matched. Nevertheless, the union was endorsed by her eldest son, Trinidad, who assured his mother that Luna was not a "vulgar native; [he is a] civilized man, a great artist; he has talents, he has education, we have nothing to fear in him." Despite her misgivings, Doña Juliana finally acquiesced to the union.[72]

Trinidad Pardo de Tavera's blessing on his sister's choice of husband in fact confirmed the warm reaction the match met in propagandista circles. Although of Spanish noble ancestry, the Pardo de Tavera family were Philippine-born. Their emotional and political ties lay firmly with the Philippines, as their outstanding history of intellectual and political achievement in the country abundantly testified. Indeed, writing home to his parents, Rizal emphasized the Filipino character of the Pardo de Tavera family, especially its female members, commenting more than once on their "Filipino-ness" and the sincerity of the women's patriotism, which he observed each time he visited the Pardo de Tavera home:

> On such days we do nothing else but talk about our country — its likes, food, customs, etc. ... Doña Juliana is a genuine Filipina through and through .... Her daughter Paz speaks French and English and is very amiable, and also very Filipino. She dresses with much elegance....[73]

Situated within the context of the propaganda movement's political strategy of assimilation, the Luna-Pardo de Tavera marriage could be read as affirming a bourgeois sexuality that cut through boundaries of racial privilege and difference. It could be seen as a sexual union that brought two racial categories, Luna's "brown complexion, thick lipped, black eyes, Malayan type,"[74] with the Spanish mestizo blood of Paz.

By the late nineteenth century fear and antagonism towards fashionable women and their show of female power and self-determination were widespread amongst the European bourgeoisie. It was an attitude that the Filipino ilustrados shared. The consequences this attitude had in the field of art production, explains Linda Nochlin, can be seen in the visual structures and thematic choices of pictures that reproduce men's power over, superiority to, difference from, and necessary control of women.[75] In our reading of Luna's representations of fashionable women we can see something of this ideological influence, and the particular critique it gave rise to.

"Monsieur Wants to Kill Madame"

In painting his *Portrait of Paz*, Luna was careful to avoid both flattery and sentiment. He avoided the vapidity and chauvinistic adulation found in much conventional, formal portraiture of the time, choosing instead to show the elegance of his wife as being sharply intelligent and almost menacing. By doing so, Luna compounded the disconcerting quality of the work and retained the disturbing edge that consistently characterized his representations of modern women.

Contrastingly, Luna's more private representations of sexualized women like *En Sueños de Amor*, ca. 1886 (Fig. 17) foregrounded the sexual rapport that had been established between Luna and his wife.[76] In this small, evidently unfinished, canvas the female figure is presented reclining with one arm raised and tucked behind her head. Her hair lies in charming sleep-tousled disarray against the capacious pillow, her eyes and mouth are only half closed, and predictably, an invitational and sensuous expression plays on her sleepy face. Roughly painted brush strokes of yellowish-orange evoke warmth and softness. Lying voluptuously in tender repose, this seemingly "personal" image of his sleeping wife, which was the subject of numerous studies in his notebook, follows certain conventions of nineteenth-century erotic imagery, so embedded in pictorial practice that Luna did not even question it.[77]

In an untitled portrait painted ca. 1890 (Fig. 18), Luna shows a semi-naked female figure languidly resting up against an indiscriminate canopy of softness, staring dreamily at nothing in particular, seemingly oblivious to the fact that her negligee has slipped off, displaying her fleshly shoulders and chest. Just at the crook of her left forearm, a single

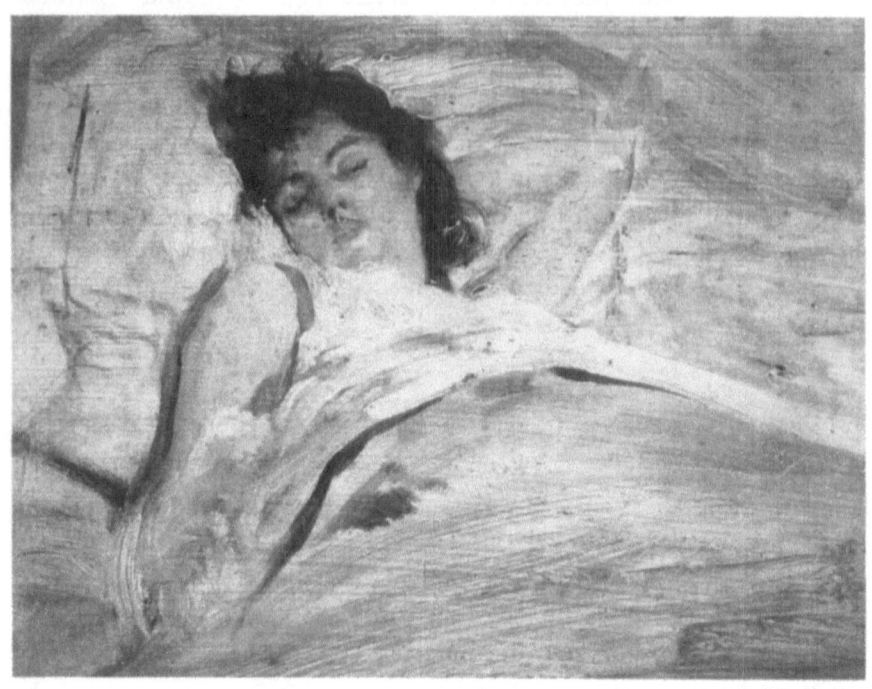

Fig. 17 Juan Luna, *En sueños de amor*, c.1886
(From Lopez Memorial Museum Collection, Philippines)

Fig. 18 Juan Luna, Portrait of woman holding rosary, c.1890
(National Museum, Philippines)

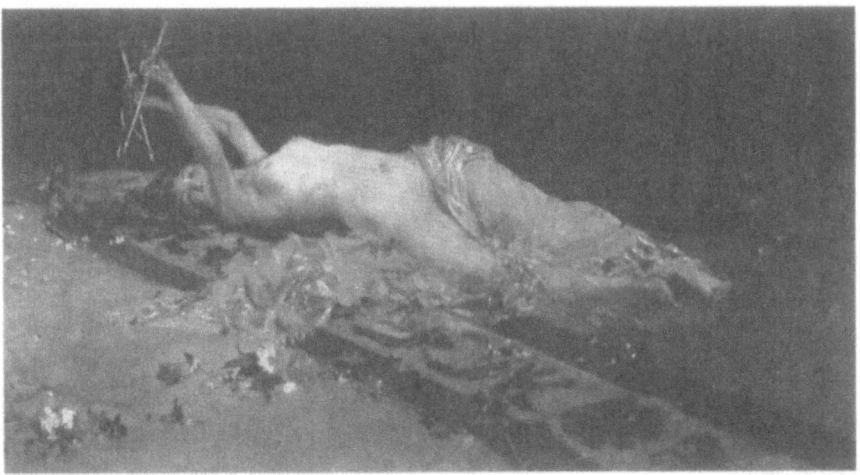

Fig. 19 Juan Luna, *Odalisque*, c.1886
[From Santiago Albano Pilar, *Juan Luna: the Filipino as Painter* (Pasig City: Lopez Memorial Museum, 1980)]

exposed breast surfaces from the froth of lace. She holds in her hands a rosary, its beads dripping through her fingers, the dangling cross at rest upon her body and the delicate material of her lingerie. Beside her lies a closed prayer book and on the little bedside table sits a small lamp.

Presenting a striking analogue to *En Sueños de Amor*, this portrait vividly exemplifies the codes defining nineteenth century female decorum with regard to physical pleasure. Luna's palpably tender handling of paint appears to describe a female body in the aftermath of sexual ecstasy. Her flushed rose-pink flesh, and the sensual roundedness of her shoulders, evoked by a play of pink shades and pearly highlights, seems to signify a skin surface still scandalously moist from slowly subsiding ardour. White lingerie may have been a typical signifier of erotic availability in nineteenth-century sexual fantasy;[78] in pictorial discourse it also served both as a sign of purity and as an exemplary symbolic site for acts of desecration. The fantasy of idealization and degradation is confirmed by the potent concatenations of a rosary cross resting prominently against her indecently displayed negligee, her joined praying hands, and her breast exposed by a lowered, lacy lingerie strap. The twin taboos of feminine desire and carnal pleasure are thus subtly combined. "Having experienced 'ecstasy'," Michelle Perrot writes, the nineteenth-century

Fig. 20 Juan Luna, Study for *Odalisque*, c.1886
[From Santiago Albano Pilar, *Juan Luna: the Filipino as Painter* (Pasig City: Lopez Memorial Museum, 1980)]

bourgeois woman was "obliged to assume the redemptive postures of purity"[79] or, in Sartre's vivid words, "a woman of bourgeois society who had just behaved like an animal was required to play the angel."[80]

Sexual pleasure and propriety came together within a conventional pictorial practice that placed the female nude within the thinnest of narrative pretexts, a practice Luna follows in his painting entitled the *Odalisque*, ca. 1886 (Fig. 19). Possibly inspired by Jacolliot's erotic descriptions of *la bayadère* or temple dancer, the woman is here shown lying on a flower strewn Oriental rug, with jars and jugs just visible at the right of the picture.[81] She is gracefully holding aloft two slender, decorative pipes; her sumptuous orange robe unravelling from her, the last portion remaining entangled around her right thigh. Despite its prone position, this is a body in motion. It is not too hard to imagine this scene as being part of an exotic, erotic dance where Luna has chosen to paint the last bodily movement, the denouement of her dance — a raised torso, a twist of the hip, arms held high and a look at her audience.

Odalisque is a picture fulfilling the formulaic operations of the nude,[82] the candour of her outward gaze works to address her spectator, giving him access to her body.[83] Filipino art historian Santiago Pilar labelled it as a "typical salon piece,"[84] Luna dedicated the preliminary ink and wash sketch to the playboy propagandista Valentin Ventura (Fig. 20), while the finished painting was lavishly framed, and prominently hung like a sexual stimulus, a constantly reassuring reminder of male virility near the couple's marital bed, in Paz Pardo de Tavera's boudoir.[85]

One might also see the physical presence of the *Odalisque* painting in the bedroom, along with that of *En Sueños de Amor*, as evidence of an eroticized married life based on shared pleasure. The Luna-Pardo de Tavera marriage, it seemed, enjoyed some happiness. They addressed each other in affectionate terms using nicknames, "My dear Chiching" (*Mi querida Chiching*), as Luna would write in his letters to his wife, signing himself as "Lulu." Luna was, according to Danet, his defence lawyer, "more than a good husband, [he] had been a lover to his wife, a man deeply in love."[86] For Danet, speaking before a Paris jury in 1893, the portrayal of his client as a man passionately in love with his wife was in perfect keeping with a new type of couple that emerged at the *fin-de-siècle*. During the last quarter of the nineteenth century, men were encouraged to pay more concern to their partner's pleasure. Moralists, educators and doctors enthusiastically supported the eroticization of marriage and favored female orgasm as the best prevention against adultery.[87]

It was therefore entirely understandable, as Danet argued, for a man like Luna who was passionately in love with his wife, to be "devoured by jealousy" when he began to suspect his wife of infidelity. "We are plain, inflexible people with regards to adultery," stated the prosecuting lawyer, Decori, echoing the case of the defence.[88] Indeed, in the context of nineteenth-century sexual mores, both lawyers voiced the prevailing bourgeois adherence to the notion of a double standard of morality. Because the purity of the family had to be preserved at all cost, a wife's adultery was treated with the utmost gravity. It was an act that profaned the sanctity of that domestic temple, the family home — the most serious transgression in the canon of bourgeois morality. As was often the case, a woman found guilty of adultery was banished from hearth and home. This was applied to all women and sanctioned not only within bourgeois mores but also, importantly, in law. While a husband's adultery was punishable only by a light fine and only if the act was discovered to have taken place within the marital home,

Fig. 21 Juan Luna, *Luling castigado por su Mama*, 1892 (National Museum, Philippines)

for adulterous women the Penal Code prescribed harsher punishment, entailing not just a fine but imprisonment. Moreover, if the husband discovered his wife and her lover *in flagrante delicto*, he had the right to kill them both on the spot.[89] But in this case the subversion of the family began not with Paz Pardo de Tavera's three-week vacation at the Mont Doré spa and her alleged flirtation with an older man. Rather, it began with Luna's unease with a wife who was "too modern."

The picture Luna entitled *Luling Castigado por su Mama* ca. 1892 (Fig. 21) was painted only a few months before Luna shot Paz Pardo de Tavera and his mother-in-law Doña Juliana Gorricho. It captures a concrete moment considered to have contributed to the deteriorating marriage — that of Paz Pardo de Tavera in the act of punishing their young son, Luling. An unfinished canvas done in rapid, vigorous brushstrokes, this picture was painted with evident haste, which gives the image a sense of immediacy and urgency adding to its power, a moment whose spontaneity is lent a greater force of truth. It is also a manifestation of the chilling animosity Luna by this time felt towards Paz Pardo de Tavera.

The family was living at the Villa Dupont, on Rue Pergolèse. Luna had consented to move to this house in an expensive residential area near the Avenue du Bois de Boulogne a year before, in the summer of 1891, as it had fewer stairs to aggravate the asthma Paz Pardo de Tavera suffered. It was also a house large enough to accommodate the growing family, with a studio attached that Luna could use. But coinciding with Luna's period of social realism, it was a time of financial hardship for the family when Luna found he was unable to support the household from painting and had become dependent on his wife's money and the financial support of his in-laws. Seeing them struggling, Doña Juliana Gorricho had agreed to live at Villa Dupont paying half of all expenses. However, in reality she shouldered their rent, paid for Luna's studio and most of the household expenses. In addition, Doña Juliana extended some financial support to Juan Luna's younger brother, Antonio, who had also come to live at the house while he studied pharmacy in Paris. As the husband of Paz, Juan Luna had the legal right to control her money and he maintained himself, and at times sent money to his own parents in the Philippines, through the pension his wife received from her share of the Pardo de Tavera real estate investments in Manila. The money, though, was always insufficient and Luna often turned to his brother-in-law, Trinidad, for loans, pawned his wife's jewelry without her knowledge and insisted she ask her mother for extra money.[90]

Luling Castigado was painted not long after the couple's second child, a girl, had succumbed to an illness and died while still in infancy. Luna accused Paz Pardo de Tavera of maternal neglect. In his letters to his wife at Mont Doré, Luna repeatedly reminds her to "take care that Luling," their son, "does not catch cold, for you know very well what the consequences can be."[91] Paz Pardo de Tavera did not only neglect her children, so Luna's accusation ran, she and her equally domineering mother seriously undermined his own paternal authority. As the Court heard, Luna bitterly resented the instances his wife would intervene when he reprimanded their son. Manly pride or *amor propio* steered his anger. One morning, Luna threw everything on the breakfast table at his wife when she dared to intercede, shaking her so violently by the wrists the maids present were terrified.[92] From 1891, the physical beatings Juan Luna had been inflicting on his wife had escalated in frequency and brutality. He had beaten her with a cane so hard it had broken in two and he had attempted to throw her out of the top floor window of the house. The month before the shooting, Luna vented his rage on the body of his wife and her possessions. He destroyed his wife's clothes and forbade her to wear anything but black mourning dresses so that she would not forget the death of her daughter. He prohibited her from wearing make-up, and punched her eyes black and blue when he discovered she had shopped and bought eyebrow pencils, and he had instructed his brother Antonio to follow her whenever she went out to town. Fearing for their lives, Doña Juliana, in a desperate letter to her son Trinidad, recounted Luna's violence and Paz Pardo de Tavera's continuous pleas to her mother: "Mama, I cannot love this man any more in my life. I hate him with my whole body and soul. Nothing, nothing. I love him no more. I will never again love him, and I put up with him only for the sake of my son."[93]

Luling Castigado, then, must be read not merely as a document of domestic conflict involving Paz Pardo de Tavera and her son Luling, but also as a representation of an inimical feminine figure who threatened to overturn the very center of the bourgeois conception of the social order — the institution of the family. The wealth and independence of this Modern Mother mocked the family's representative of patriarchal authority, the husband and father, the *paterfamilias* upon whom wife and children alike ought to depend. The animosity, or outright hostility Luna felt towards his wife, the feeling of inferiority, of being overpowered by dominant women; these, and the inclusion of the signs of instability and fragmentation of a bourgeois patriarchal order are what make the *Luling Castigado* painting disturbing to the modern viewer.

Luna's painting engages directly with the domain of domestic femininity but offers an antipathetic look at "bad" motherhood. The figure of the mother in Luna's painting is shown crossing into the picture, looming large and prominent in the foreground. She casts a sinister figure in her dark clothes and facelessness; tall and bending slightly forwards, she advances with menace towards the little boy, shown cowering by the fireplace across the room. Standing just off-center in the picture, the viewer's eye is led to the figure of the boy, his small frame established by the height of the mantelpiece over the fireplace, which he has not quite managed to reach. His height and slight size, and the nursery knickerbockers he wears, depict his vulnerability and extreme youthfulness. Moreover, contributing to the overall impression of weakness is the color of the boy's clothes. Painted in the same wash of brown as the wall behind him, the human figure lacks definition and clarity and seems to melt into the wall. The boy covers his eyes with his right forearm and hand, in evident terror, is too fearful to look at his mother directly. Her arms crossed behind her, she clutches a long cane that only the viewer sees. With his eyes covered, the little boy can only imagine the punishment that threatens him, and the viewer, in possession of this knowledge, is in the position of the privileged onlooker, powerless but complicit. Emphatically, the scene does not speak of a caring mother administering just punishment to a naughty boy. Rather, it focuses on the fear of an intimidated child.

Holding the cane behind her back, a symbol of masculine authority and discipline, she represents a powerful, aggressive female usurper of male, patriarchal authority. Pictured as an intentional contrast to the domestic delights of a parlor-paradise, the home scene over which she appears to preside lacks warmth. The fireplace is a cold, empty grate, the room bereft of comfortable furnishings, its starkness specified by the single detail of a disordered pile of clothes on a wooden folding chair. She opposes the ideal form of maternal love and emotional intimacy thought natural to women. Her transgressive power stems precisely from the memory of "good" maternal relationships she violates.[94]

But Luna's judgement falls harshly on this mother figure in another way. Luna doted on his little son. Luling had been the subject of a number of studies and paintings by his adoring father and an "inseparable companion" to the artist while out painting landscapes, hiking, and engaging in idyllic country pastimes of catching shrimp and *talangka* (small crabs), as Luna reported in a letter to Rizal.[95] The figure of the little boy, as Luna's pupil son, powerfully signifies the artist's alter ego. Representative of the next generation, the next linking chain of male creative genius, the little boy symbolizes the origins of great art itself. It is here that the "Mama" of this painting commits her greatest crime. She abuses maternal authority and stands as a threatening challenge to masculinity depicted as small, weak and feminized. The inclusion of the mirror, at the far wall over the fireplace insinuates this anarchic reversal in its reflective surface, a witness to a world being turned upside down.

With the distinctive rhetorical flourish of an experienced lawyer, Decori closed his remarks to the jury by declaring: "I know what passion is. It torments jealous souls.... I have come to defend ... those who have killed someone in a fit of jealousy, especially if they surprised the adulterer. You, however, [at first] forgave your wife; instead you snared her ... [and then] you killed her later on."[96] Just as the defense had argued, Decori had described Luna's rages as characteristic of the semi-barbaric peoples of the Tropics, his volatile temper attributed to "Malayan madness." His rages were "like hurricanes ... when they disappear leave so much ruin, grief, tears and death."[97] But Decori considered the murder of the women cold and premeditated. Indeed, having forced his wife at gunpoint to confess to adultery, Luna decided to take the family to Vigo, a small Spanish coastal town where they would all live simply. Luna desperately wanted to take his wife out of Paris. Sensing the danger this presented for her safety, Paz Pardo de Tavera's family immediately decided on the modern solution of divorce, and would have, in all likelihood, called upon the recently passed, and controversial Loi Naquet (1884), a divorce law that provided better conditions of separation for a woman. It was not to be. Upon hearing the screams of her mistress in the house, a panicked maid runs to a nearby café where the brothers Trinidad and Felix Pardo de Tavera are sitting with their lawyer, Antonio Regidor, and bids them to quickly return to the house, afraid that "Monsieur wants to kill Madame."[98] It is the morning of 22 September 1892. Seeing her sons approaching, Doña Juliana shouts from a window of the house warning them not to enter for Luna is armed. Luna appears at another window brandishing a gun, shouting he will kill the first to enter and fires, hitting Felix in the chest.[99] Then, returning to the women, Luna put the barrel of the revolver he bought a few days earlier with his wife's money, to the temples of his wife and mother-in-law and at point blank range "made their skulls fly" (*hacia volar cráneos*).[100]

"Adultery," wrote Zola, "is the plague of the bourgeoisie, just as prostitution is the plague of the people."[101] As voiced here by Zola, the notion that an honest woman, particularly a bourgeois woman, might at any moment lapse into immorality, was a widely held belief that may in part have accounted for Juan Luna's eventual acquittal.[102] Indeed, the impression of rampant, clandestine prostitution in nineteenth-century Paris, compounded the concern over the potential sexual recklessness of respectable women. Bourgeois women, Paris regulationists reckoned, might envy the prostitute's powerful sexuality and emulate it, just as honest women strove to imitate the trend setting style of the hyper-fashionable courtesan. A fear of female sexuality lay at the core of modern femininity articulated by the figure of the "Parisienne." And it was above all the prostitute who was recognized in nineteenth-century mythologies as the supreme allegory of the modern. Luna's painting of *La Parisienne*, as we saw at the beginning of this chapter, captured the monstrous face of modern femininity and sought to directly address its dark side, the dangers it posed to the masculine order. An image emanating whoredom, Luna's representation of the absolutely contemporary Woman invoked disease, with death itself imprinted on her skin.

The Filipino propagandistas were in Europe during a time when the lines of demarcation between adultery, debauchery, moral libertinism and prostitution seemed to be melting. The sordidness of the modern sexual marketplace they discovered in Europe was for many of them contemptible yet alluring, their condemnation was matched by equally strong libidinal desires. The tension found in Luna's pictures of Parisian women bespeaks of a clash between attraction and repulsion, an anxiety towards the modern sexualized woman and the artist's regard for her unmanageability. While Luna held an idea of himself as a passionate artist dedicated to high artistic achievement, identifying with an image of a modern manly man, he considered passion and modernity in women, most especially in his wife, to be base corruptions.

His paintings analyzed the role of make-up, artifice and style and cynically saw them as the stigmata of modernity, part of the commodified spectacle the feminine body presented in the new public spaces and pleasure palaces of Paris. His feminine representations attempted to show that modern urban life corroded Woman's poetic aura, and corrupted her "natural" femininity. Luna mourned this loss with misogynistic violence, his anger guided by *amor propio*, the particular masculine quality that, as we shall see in the following chapter, was central to the ilustrados' concept of male patriotic identity.

Notes

1. Juan Luna (Paris) to José Rizal, 13 May 1891, in *Cartas entre Rizal y sus colegas de la propaganda, 1889–1896* (Manila: Comisión Nacional del Centenario de José Rizal, 1961), p. 659.
2. Walter Benjamin, *Illuminations: Essays and reflections*, edited with an introduction by Hannah Avendt, trans. Harry Zohn (London: Fontana, 1973), p. 166.

3   Alain Corbin, "Commercial Sexuality in Nineteenth Century France: a system of images and regulations," in *The Making of the Modern Body: sexuality and society in the nineteenth century*, ed. Catherine Gallagher and Thomas Laquer (Berkeley: University of California Press, 1987), p. 211.

4   The activities of the *Zorillistas* or *republicanos progresistas* in Madrid and Paris, who agitated for the restoration of the Spanish Republic by means of revolution, were well-known to the Filipino *propagandistas*. Fiercely anti-clerical in his views, Ferrer was Zorilla's principal assistant in Paris at this time and would naturally have been sympathetic to the Filipino patriotic aspirations. See John N. Schumacher SJ, *The Propaganda Movement, 1880–1895: the creation of a Filipino consciousness, the making of the Revolution* (Quezon City: Ateneo de Manila University Press, 1997), p. 21; and James Joll, *The Anarchists* (London: Eyre & Spottiswoode, 1964), p. 233.

5   José Rizal, "[Impressions of Madrid]," written in French in his notebook: Clinica Medica, 1881–87 (Ayer Manuscript Collection, Newberry Library).

6   Ibid.

7   José Rizal (Madrid) to Paciano Rizal, 13 February 1883, in *Letters between Rizal and Family Members* (Manila: National Heroes Commission, 1964), p. 89.

8   Graciano López Jaena, "Biografía de Juan Luna y Novicio," in his collected *Discursos y artículos varios* [1891], Nueva edición revisada y adicionada con escritos no incluido en la primera (Manila: Bureau of Printing, 1951), pp. 186–7.

9   Ibid., p. 187.

10 Felix Roxas, *The World of Felix Roxas: anecdotes and reminiscences of a Manila newspaper columnist 1926–1936*, trans. Angel Estrada and Vicente del Carmen (Manila: Filipiniana Book Guild, 1970), p. 45.

11 Ibid., p. 46.

12 Michelle Perrot, "The New Eve and the Old Adam: Changes in French Women's condition at the turn of the century," in *Behind the Lines: gender and the two World Wars*, ed. Margaret R. Higonnet et al. (New Haven: Yale University Press, 1989), p. 51.

13 Elaine Showalter, *Sexual Anarchy: gender and culture at the fin de siècle* (London: Virago, 1995), p. 38.

14 Tamar Garb, *Bodies of Modernity: figure and flesh in fin-de-siècle France* (New York: Thames and Hudson, 1998), p. 84.

15 For an instructive description of the new Parisian *grand magasins*, see *Paris and Environs with routes from London to Paris: handbook for travellers* (London: Karl Baedeker, 1888), p. 37.

16 As Michelle Perrot has shown, grooming was an activity that was no longer confined to the elite but spread rapidly amongst all classes between 1880 and 1910 serving to heighten, at the same time, the differentiation of sex roles. See Michelle Perrot, ed., *A History of Private Life: from the fires of revolution to the Great War*, trans. Arthur Goldhammer (Cambridge, Mass.: The Belknap Press of Harvard University Press, 1990), p. 488.

17 For a discussion of how transvestitism marked a space of anxiety and crisis about gender identity from the Renaissance to high Modernism see Marjorie Garber, *Vested Interests: cross-dressing and cultural anxiety* (London: Routledge, 1997).
18 For a discussion of these categories and "female types," see Alain Corbin, *Les Filles de Noce: misère sexuelle et prostitution aux XIXe–XXe siècles* (Paris: Aubier, 1978).
19 Indispensable texts that discuss representations of Woman and modernity include T.J. Clark, *The Painting of Modern Life: Paris in the art of Manet and his followers*, revised edition (Princeton, NJ: Princeton University Press, 1999); and Hollis Clayson, *Painted Love: prostitution in French art of the Impressionist era* (New Haven: Yale University Press, 1991).
20 See for example, Jean Beraud's *Avenue des Champs Elysees*, showing an independent boulevard woman, or James Tissot's *The Political Lady*.
21 Tamar Garb, "James Tissot's 'Parisienne' and the Making of the Modern Woman," in her *Bodies of Modernity*, pp. 81–113.
22 Jun Terra, *Juan Luna Drawings: Paris period; from the collection of Dr. Eleuterio M. Pascual* (Makati City: Dr. Eleuterio M. Pascual Publishing House, 1998).
23 Garb, *Bodies of Modernity*, p. 224.
24 Juan Luna, Paris sketchbooks, reproduced in Terra, *Juan Luna Drawings*, p. 46.
25 For a discussion of the term "culture-capital" in relation to European cities at the *fin-de-siècle* see Malcolm Bradbury and James McFarlane eds., *Modernism: a guide to European literature, 1890–1930* (Harmondsworth: Penguin, 1991), p. 42.
26 Although Luna never identified himself with the Impressionist school which was by the time of his arrival in Paris in 1884 already on the wane, the paintings in this study reveal a clear shift away from the teachings of the Spanish Academy. For discussions of Luna, Impressionism and his "impressionistic" style, see E. Aguilar Cruz, *Luna* (Manila: Bureau of National and Foreign Information, 1975); Santiago Albano Pilar, *Juan Luna: the Filipino as painter* (Manila: Eugenio López Foundation, 1980); and Alfredo R. Roces, "Philippine Art: Spanish Period," in *Brown Heritage: essays on Philippine culture, tradition and literature*, ed. Antonio G. Manuud (Quezon City: Ateneo de Manila University Press, 1967).
27 Juan Luna (Paris) to José Rizal, 13 May 1891, in *Cartas*, p. 659.
28 Juan Luna (Paris) to Javier Gómez de la Serna, 26 May 1889, in *Epistolario del Pintor Juan Luna*, ed. José P. Bantug (Madrid: Circulo Filipino, 1955), p. 34.
29 Juan Luna (Paris) to José Rizal, 8 August 1891, in *Cartas*, p. 673.
30 For a discussion of the Spanish School of Art, with which the Filipino painters in Europe have been closely identified, see Carlos Gonzalez and Montse Marti, *Spanish Painters in Paris (1850–1900)* (London: Sammer, 1989).
31 Victor Hugo, "Epigraph to Zola's *Paris*" quoted in Charles Harrison and Paul Wood with Jason Gaiger, eds. *Art in Theory, 1815–1900: an anthology of changing ideas* (Oxford: Blackwell, 1998), p. 883.
32 See the famous, oft-cited tribute *brindis* speeches delivered by Rizal and López Jaena in June 1884 at the Madrid banquet honoring the two painters Juan Luna and Felix Resurrección Hidalgo, in José Rizal, *Political and Historical Writings*

(Manila: National Historical Commission, 1964), p. 20; and Graciano López Jaena, *Discursos*, pp. 30–5.

[33] José Rizal, "Juan Luna," in *La Ilustración-Revista Hispano-Americana* 7: 278 (28 February 1886).

[34] See Carlos Quirino, "Manila's School of Painting," *Philippine Studies* 15 (1967): 348–53.

[35] See Raul J. Bonoan, SJ, "Rizal's Record at the Ateneo," *Philippine Studies* 27 (1979): 53–79.

[36] Pilar, *Juan Luna*, p. 62.

[37] José Rizal, Madrid Diary, 1884: Agenda Bufete (Ayer Manuscript Collection, Newberry Library).

[38] Juan Luna, "Nota autobiografica," in Bantug, *Epistolario*, p. 25.

[39] Austin Coates, *Rizal – Filipino Nationalist and Martyr* (Manila: Solidaridad Publishing House, 1992), p. 74.

[40] This diary entry that establishes exactly when, where and who accompanied Luna on his last day in Spain is only found in the original manuscript of Rizal's 1884 Madrid diary, Agenda Bufete, as cited.

[41] Perfecto Terra Jr, "Villafranca's 'Desde Filipinas a Europa'," *Philippine Studies* 32 (1984): 218.

[42] José Rizal (Paris) to his Parents and Brother, 21 June 1883, in José Rizal, *Diarios y Memorias por José Rizal* (Manila: José Rizal National Centennial Commission, 1961), p. 91.

[43] See especially José Rizal (Paris) to his Parents and Brother, 5 July 1883 and 2 August 1883, in Rizal, *Reminiscences and Travels of José Rizal (1878–1896)* (Manila: José Rizal Centennial Commission, 1961), pp. 239–56.

[44] Corbin, *The Making of the Modern Body*, p. 211; José Rizal (Paris) to his Parents and Brother, 21 June 1883, in *Reminiscences and Travels*, p. 238.

[45] See Francisco Villanueva, Jr, *Reminiscences of Rizal's stay in Europe* (Manila: Loyal Press, 1936), p. 7; José Rizal (Paris) to his Parents and Brother, 21 June 1883, in *Reminiscences and Travels*, p. 234. Though in some parts found to be inaccurately dated, Villanueva's account does, however, provide a useful list of addresses of most of the notable *ilustrado* Filipinos living in Paris at the time. For instance, Don Ramón Ramirez and Don Valentin Ventura, mutual friends of Luna and Rizal, resided at No. 43 and No. 45 respectively throughout the 1880s. During his later visits to Paris, Rizal would stay at the home of Don Valentin Ventura. The close proximity of the Filipino homes in this street suggests that the *ilustrado* community, as in Madrid and Barcelona, tended to cluster together.

[46] Map of the Right Bank of Paris from *Nouveau Plan de Paris: nomenclature des rues du nouveau plan itineraire des omnibus et tramways* (Paris: Lanee, Editeur-Geograph, 1887).

[47] For discussions of the verbal imagery used in contemporary descriptions of this area, see Clayson, *Painted Love*, p. 94; and Clark, *The Painting of Modern Life*, p. 106.

[48] Alain Corbin, *Women for Hire: prostitution and sexuality in France after 1850* (Cambridge, Mass: Harvard University Press, 1990), pp. 193–5.

49 See *Nocturnal Paris and "Paris After Dark" (incorporated) An Indispensable Companion for the Stranger The Only Genuine Night Guide for Gentlemen. Paris after dark containing a description of the fast women, their haunts, habits etc., to which is added a faithful description of the Night Amusements and Other Resorts. Also all particulars relative to the working of the Social Evil in the French Metropolis* (London: n.pub, 1877), p. 39.

50 The following description found in *Nocturnal Paris* illustrates, for example, how dining in public restaurants could even pose as an incentive to vice: "You meet with nymphs who are on the look out for a supper. Say you order a supper for two. You are no sooner seated than a *bouquetiere* comes up and offers you flowers, which your fair one persuades you to purchase. Then a cab driver comes up and presents you with a bill of, say, some twenty francs for her day's drive. And so on through a whole category of little impositions, should the fair one deem you sufficiently good-natured to bear a good fleecing...." Ibid., p. 21.

51 Charles Lecour, *La Prostitution á Paris et a Londres*, quoted in Clark, *The Painting of Modern Life*, p. 105.

52 Ibid., p. 110.

53 Personal communication with Santiago Pilar, January 2003.

54 The detail of the cigar was noticed by Edward Sullivan, "Juan Luna and Transnational Art in the late Nineteenth Century," in *The Pioneers of Philippine Art: Luna, Amorsolo and Zobel* Exhibition Catalogue, Hambrecht Gallery of the Asian Art Museum of San Francisco, 20 October 2006 to 7 January 2007.

55 Reuss, writing in 1889 had noticed an apparent change from the relative decorum found in the brasseries of the 1870s to the indecent and raucous less than a decade later. Quoted in Clayson, *Painted Love*, p. 139.

56 Baedeker, *Paris and Environs*, p. 17

57 Clayson, *Painted Love*, p. 96.

58 Roxas, *The World of Felix Roxas*, p. 174.

59 Ibid.

60 Theodore Zeldin, *Ambition, Love and Politics* [France, 1848–1945, Vol. I] (Oxford, 1973), p. 234, cited in Clayson, *Painted Love*, p. 165.

61 Roxas, *The World of Felix Roxas*, p. 161.

62 Ibid., pp. 160–1.

63 Charles Baudelaire, "Le peintre de la vie moderne" [1863], reprinted in *Curiosités esthetiques, l'art romantique, et autres oeuvres critiques* (Paris: Editions Garnier Frères, 1962), p. 489.

64 Terra, *Juan Luna Drawings*, p. 36.

65 See Octave Uzanne, *Parisiennes de ce temps en leurs divers milieux, états et conditions: études pour servir* (Paris, 1910), especially pp. 345–6; and Ignotus, "Les Grands Bazars," *Le Figaro*, 23 March 1881, p. 1, cited in Clayson, *Painted Love*, pp. 65, 166.

66 Personal interview with Mita Pardo de Tavera, surviving granddaughter of T.H. Pardo de Tavera, 8 December 1999, Manila; also her daughter, Mara Pardo de Tavera, 23 December 1999, Manila.

[67] For a discussion of the lives of the prominent members of the Pardo de Tavera family, see the perceptive account by Ruby Paredes, "The Pardo de Taveras of Manila," in *An Anarchy of Families: state and family in the Philippines*, ed. Alfred W. McCoy (Quezon City: Ateneo de Manila University Press, 1994), pp. 347–417.

[68] See for example Juan Luna (Paris) to Javier Gomez de la Serna, 18 August 1886, in Bantug, *Epistolario*, p. 29. Luna instructs De la Serna to receive small copies of his major canvases and other sketches — a sketch of Margate beach, studies of heads — for quick sale in Manila: "*Por este correo sale para Manila El Pacto de Sangre, el retrato de Legazpi, la copia del Spoliarium, una playa de Margate y otro estudios de cabezas...*"

[69] Juan Luna (Paris) to Paz Pardo de Tavera, 2 October 1885, cited in *Proceso: seguido contra el parricida Juan Luna San Pedro y Novicio, Natural de Badoc (Filipinas) Discurso Pronunciado en la audiencia del 18 Febrero de 1893 Par Maître Felix Decori — Abogado de la Corte de Apelation de Paris*.

[70] The full quote in Spanish reads: "*Al fin era gente que pertenecía a esta sucia raza española.*" Ibid., p. 8.

[71] Doña Juliana's brother-in-law, Don Joaquin, had been one of most prominent *creoles* to suffer exile in the Marianas (now Guam) for his reformist, liberal ideas, after the 1872 Cavite Mutiny. Escaping, Don Joaquin and his wife, Doña Tula, Doña Juliana's sister, fled to Paris where they immediately sent for Doña Juliana, recently widowed, and her family. See Paredes, "The Pardo de Taveras of Manila," p. 369.

[72] The full quote reads: "*Luna no es un indio vulgar, es un hombre civilizado, es un gran artista, tiene talenta, tiene educación, nada debemos temer de el.*" Proceso, as cited.

[73] José Rizal (Paris) to his Parents and Brother, 1 January 1886, in *Letters between Rizal and Family Members, 1876–1896*, p. 204.

[74] Description taken from the Pardo de Tavera statement to the Court of Appeals in Paris, *Cour d'Appel de Paris Chambre des mises en accusation* no. 1750, November 1892.

[75] See Linda Nochlin's pioneering essay, "Women, Art and Power," in her *Women, Art and Power and Other Essays*, pp. 1–2.

[76] In 1887, Luna nevertheless permitted this painting to be reproduced in the Manila art journal, *La Ilustración Artistica*.

[77] For a discussion of erotic imagery in nineteenth-century art and its conventions, see Linda Nochlin, "Eroticism and Female Imagery in Nineteenth Century Art," in her *Woman, Art and Power*, p. 136.

[78] Michelle Perrot, *A History of Private Life*, p. 487.

[79] Ibid., p. 580.

[80] Ibid.

[81] Louis Jacolliot, *Les Moeurs et les Femmes de l'Extrême Orient: voyage au pays des bayadères* (Paris: E. Dentu, 1873), illustrations on pp. 45, 80 and 278.

[82] As T.J. Clark describes, the nineteenth-century nude characteristically achieved the following: "... The woman's body had to be arranged in precise and definite relation

to the viewer's eye. It had to be placed at a distance, near enough for seeing, far enough for propriety. It had to be put at a determinate height, neither so high that the woman became inaccessible and merely grand, nor so low that she turned into matter for scrutiny of a clinical or prurient kind." Clark, *The Painting of Modern Life*, p. 133.

83 Ibid., p. 131.
84 Pilar, *The Filipino as Painter*, p. 126.
85 I thank Ambeth Ocampo for sharing with me a photograph which, coincidentally, showed this painting.
86 "Justice Criminelle: Cour d'Assises de la Seine, Audience du 7 février," *Gazette des Tribunaux*, 9 February 1893, p. 140.
87 Dartigues, *De l'amour expérimental ou des causes de l'adultère chez la femme au XIXe siècle* (1878), cited in Perrot, *A History of Private Life*, p. 599.
88 *Proceso*, p. 6.
89 James McMillan, *Housewife or Harlot: the place of women in French society, 1870–1940* (New York: Palgrave Macmillan, 1981), esp. pp. 16–9; Patricia Mainardi, *Husbands, Wives and Lovers: marriage and its discontents in 19th century France* (New Haven, Conn.: Yale University Press, 2003).
90 Ibid.
91 Juan Luna (Paris) to Paz Pardo de Tavera, 21 July 1892, reproduced in *La Solidaridad* 5 (15 April 1893): 175.
92 *Proceso*, p. 15.
93 Doña Juliana Gorricho (Paris) to Trinidad Pardo de Tavera, 21 September 1892, reproduced in ibid., p. 24.
94 For a critical discussion of nineteenth-century models of bourgeois family structures and its representations in artistic discourse, see Linda Nochlin, *Representing Women* (London: Thames and Hudson, 1999), esp. pp. 163–5. See also Susan Casteras, "The Cult of the Male Genius," in *Rewriting the Victorians*, ed. Linda M. Shires, pp. 117–45.
95 Juan Luna (Benzeval-Houlgate, Normandy,) to José Rizal, 24 July 1890, in *Cartas*, Vol. II, p. 572.
96 *Proceso*, p. 31.
97 Ibid., p. 14.
98 "The Affair of the Villa Dupont, Mr. Trinidad Pardo, His Account of the Murder," *Echo de Paris*, 26 September 1892, quoted in Paredes, "The Pardos de Tavera of Manila," p. 375.
99 *Proceso*, pp. 28–9.
100 Ibid., p. 14.
101 Emile Zola, "L'Adultère dans la bourgeoisie," *Le Figaro*, 28 February 1881, p. 1. Cited in Clayson, *Painted Love*, p. 14.
102 The judgement was upheld in spite of the fact the court had accepted the charge of "voluntary homicide committed with premeditation." See *Cour d'Appel de Paris Chambre des Mises en Accusation* (no. 1750, 6 December 1892), p. 3.

3

Antonio Luna's *Impresiones*: The Anatomy of *Amor Propio*

Disenchantment

Between 1889 and 1891 Juan Luna's younger brother Antonio wrote a series of vignettes of Madrid life that chronicled the disenchantment he felt, and which many of his compatriots shared, when they contrasted the realities of Spanish life with the idealized image propagated by Spaniards in the Philippines. The essays first appeared in *La Solidaridad*, the main organ of the reform campaign, and most were later published in a compilation volume under the title *Impresiones*.[1] Writing under the *nom-de-plume* Taga-Ilog (literally meaning "from the river"), Luna keenly observed life in the Spanish capital in a manner akin to the eighteenth-century satirists, whose works appealed to a shared sense of normal conduct from which vice and folly were seen to stray. Luna's pieces employed "formal" Juvenalian satire, in which the reader was directly addressed.[2]

The essays enabled Luna to articulate a key aspect of the propagandistas' notion of patriotic manhood, *amor propio*. Their second function was to project this particular patriotic identity to a specific audience — the "Filipinos in the Philippines" as a means of countering the power of racist colonial discourse. Imagining a different audience — the Filipino reader — became the guiding spirit for Luna's *Impresiones*. In his prefatory message, Luna attempted to explain his motivations, appealing to the reader to remember that the author had not only spent seven years living in the Spanish capital but was a "Spanish citizen with the freedom to criticize scenes of his own soil."[3] Such words masked his true intentions. Writing to Rizal immediately after its publication, Luna was more explicit: "I believe that, though my book attacks no institution nor any official, it has the wicked presumption of hurling down the idol, smashing the pedestal into smithereens."⁴

Striving to speak from the twin position of the insider, as a Spaniard, and outsider, as a native Filipino, Antonio Luna claimed a special sensitivity to cultural difference. However, as we shall see, the disillusionment Antonio Luna experienced would return him irreconcilably to the category of the foreign, and therefore to being the object of Spanish racism — compelling him to enact various strategies that affirmed his identity both as a Filipino patriot and as a man. In this chapter, Luna's writings will be examined as a form of dialogic engagement with western modes of representation and, as a profoundly important strategy of self-invention. Luna was an observant writer, a romantic and an ilustrado of refined sensibilities. The depth and fervor of his patriotic feeling, as this chapter shows, was intensified by colonial racism and guided by amor propio.

Antonio Luna was 20 years old when he first arrived in Europe in 1886.⁵ The year before, he had spent some time in Manila's Bilibid prison, possibly in connection with an armed rebellion against the Spaniards his uncle had led in the provinces of Pangasinan and Nueva Ecija.⁶ Although quickly suppressed, the episode had serious repercussions on Antonio Luna's family and may have led to his parents' decision to send their youngest son abroad to study and join his elder brother Juan in Paris.

Whilst most ilustrados reacted with disappointment when they saw the dirt and shabbiness of Barcelona and Madrid, it was colonial racism that galvanized their disenchantment into satire and protest. Apologists for Spanish imperialism such as Pablo Feced and Francisco Cañamaque repeatedly provoked the ilustrados in Spain with racist articles. Typically, they employed an orientalist understanding of the Islands, that all-knowing apprehension of the East which had become by the nineteenth century a hallmark of European thinking more usually applied to the Oriental Arab world.⁷ In 1888, Feced published a book entitled *Esbozos y pinceladas* (Sketches and Paintings)⁸ based on a series of light travel sketches and vignettes he had written under the name Quioquiap for the papers *El Liberal* and *Diario de Manila*. His style was comical and his verdicts on Manila and its native inhabitants invariably disparaging. Cañamaque similarly portrayed Philippine scenes with a mixture of shock, disgust and pity.⁹ Writing on Filipino family life, for example, he described the wretchedness of a peasant environment and the overcrowded conditions he believed encouraged a lack of concern over personal decency, hygiene and morality:

> In a miserable hut where six people can hardly stand, the native men and women eat, sleep and live together with their children, young or already mature.... Naturally, morality and hygiene are markedly absent, honesty is a myth, modesty is an illusion: blood affinities get close, become confused, and may God forgive me for thinking evil thoughts but I fear, and the friars are with me in thinking, that it is better not to imagine them...like packed sardines which are sold in Madrid at two *cuartos* a piece.[10]

The moral anxiety Feced and Cáñamaque affected conveyed Spanish racial superiority, the Filipino subjects of their eyewitness accounts being humiliatingly portrayed as dirty, mindless primitives.

> Without the remotest idea of honor (here I wish to say it clearly), ignorant of everything except to the blind satisfaction of their appetites, without remorse or the secret voice of conscience in the heart, alien to the laws of honor and of honesty, awake only to the brutal sentiments of oriental sensuousness, it is logical that the majority of the natives receive from the friars and civilians the appellation of *monkeys*.[11]

Regarded as physically and intellectually immature, uncivilized and effeminate, the native Filipinos, the *indios*, were thought of as no more than "big children," with undeveloped facial and bodily characteristics, unfit to govern themselves and unable to comprehend civilized society. Feced, for example, asked: "What does the poor indio, weak in body and weak in mind ... understand of all this chatter of motherhood and brotherhood, of civilization and of culture?"[12] Intensifying during the 1887 Spanish Exposition on the Philippines that showcased live tribal people of the Islands in Madrid's Retiro Park,[13] such attacks served to strengthen the solidarity of the Filipino community in Spain. Negative press reports aroused the propagandistas who responded to the satirical, scurrilous swipes by Spanish racists with equally energetic rejoinders.[14] Rizal, Graciano López Jaena and the Filipinos' staunch Austrian ally, the Orientalist scholar Ferdinand Blumentritt, returned every criticism back to the core issues in the Philippines — the need for reforms and the expulsion of the friars: "We do not deny that the Philippines is behind times," wrote López Jaena in *El Liberal*:

> ... and this backwardness, far from having as its cause a lack of receptivity to culture, or the incapacity of our race for progress, is due (let us say it in a loud voice), to the friar, who ... has found in the indio an inexhaustible mine of exploitation, burying him in ignorance and fanaticism.[15]

Rarely allowing an assault to slip by without comment, the propagandistas responded with both erudition and satire to the relentless denigration of Filipinos by the arch-racists Feced, the Spanish academician Vicente Barrantes, the colonial bureaucrat and Philippine historian Retana[16] and other detractors. But whilst most rejoinders in *La Solidaridad* treated the flagrant insults as the peddling of convenient theories by the *Castila* (Peninsular Spaniard) to justify colonial conquest, and to perpetuate the exploitation of the native Filipinos,[17] Antonio Luna's short essay "Impresiones Madrileñas de un Filipino" was cleverly different.[18] It overturned the critical tactics employed by the Spanish journalists by converting their field of reference — the proud culture and cities of Spain — into scenes of uncivilized backwardness. In this sense, it is instructive to think of Luna's travel impressions as examples of what literary historian Mary Louise Pratt has insightfully termed "autoethnographic expressions." Referring to instances or modes of impression by which colonized subjects attempt to represent themselves in ways that engage with the colonizers' own terms, "autoethnographic texts" are constructed in response to, or in dialogue with, those metropolitan representations that conventionally constitute ethnographic texts. In Pratt's words, autoethnography invokes "partial collaboration with, and appropriation of, the idioms of the conqueror."[19] Characteristically bilingual and dialogic, "autoethnographic texts" are directed both to the metropolitan reader and to the author's own social group, and therefore elicit a typically heterogeneous reception.

Luna begins his "Impresiones Madrileñas" by recalling the admiration he felt for the Spanish capital before he had ever left the Philippines: "I thought of that nation of valor and gentlemanly nobility (*hidalguía*), [in which] the beautiful city sung by the poets to me occupied first place."[20] Standing on the deck of the ship on which he embarked for Spain, he contemplated Madrid "like a fantastic dreamy illusion." "What would the Puerta del Sol be like?" Luna believes he has the answer:

> Centre of flurry and of life, where the omnibuses, the coaches, the crowded throng meet as if impelled by a secret mechanism; the trams

glide over the net of iron rails, and the humdrum noise of passers-by confuses and deafens. And it is then the words of our Spanish residents in the Philippines resounded in my ears: *Nothing quite like Madrid ... from the Puerta del Sol to heaven.* [Italics in original]

One of the deepest fears harbored by the friars in the Philippines was that the young Filipino men who went to Europe would be contaminated by the liberalism and heterodoxy that were threatening Spanish rule. What the friars had not foreseen, however, was that the Filipino youths would feel a deep sense of disenchantment upon reaching the shores of the Motherland, a reaction that would have the profound consequence of undermining Spanish colonial authority.[21]

Luna imagines Madrid as a relentless fever, a city of excitement, movement, noise and life. In the dazzle of his desire, Luna signifies what Barthes has described as the "amorous subject" for whom Madrid is a "loved being," an aesthetic vision. Yet, as Barthes found, it is a situation of dilemma. Since all that is loved in the Other cannot be fully expressed, the amorous subject resorts to a host of perceptions that come together to form a dazzling impression (the plazas, the rustle of a *chula*'s skirt, the wheels of a tram rolling over iron rails, the throng of passers-by) that blinds and mutes. As Barthes writes, "to dazzle is ultimately to prevent sight, to prevent speech."[22] Madrid becomes the "object of an aesthetically restrained desire," a site to which his, and as he imagines it, every Filipino's desire clings:

> Poor Filipino! Who, living amidst the narrow streets of the walled city, or used to breathe the pure air of our woods and forests where neither rays of the sun nor rain penetrate, or used to watching the tranquil seas that disappear in the blue of the horizon, thought he would be dazzled (*deslumbrado*) by the magnificence of a European city.[23]

Within his own ilustrado culture, a glorified Spain and a glorified Hispanic culture had already existed as ideological constructs, indeed, were sources of Filipino identification and pride, fuelling calls for assimilation with Spain. Here, one can glimpse what it is like to imagine Spain and Europe from the inside out, using materials donated, absorbed and appropriated. Luna thinks of Madrid by experiencing another's memories and employs another's sentiments to speak of his desire.

Having revealed both the source and texture of his Madrid imaginings, Luna proceeds with luscious irony and mocking humor to expose the woeful and indeed unmodern reality of the Spanish capital. Unlike Paris in the nineteenth century, the city of Madrid had been slow to modernize. It did not have a clean water supply until the 1850s, the first public urinal, in the Puerta del Sol, was not installed until 1863, public transport in the form of a mule drawn tram came to the city in 1871 and electric street lights in 1875.[24] The buildings lacked architectural flair, and the dusty plazas were still traversed by antiquated bullock carts and teams of gaunt mules quaintly harnessed with bells.[25] "Illusions and hopes vanished before reality," Luna exclaims. The streets of Madrid were paved with layers of sharp stones, a feature which he facetiously suggests might account for the signs he noticed posted all around the streets advertising the services of a "corn-remover (*callista*)." The crowded, multi-storey slum tenements were in Luna's eyes more like "pigeon huts" than human habitations; far more squalid, indeed, than the native huts in the Philippines derided by Cañamaque. The famed Puerta del Sol, he discovers, is just an ordinary street populated by café idlers who bother and molest other pedestrians, a place which even Madrileños refer to as a "coach terminus with a central fountain for the mules."[26]

More astonishing, however, is the general ignorance of the Spanish towards the Philippines. "And where is that [the Philippines], in China or in America?" a Spaniard asks him. Realising that his interlocutor has not the slightest idea where the Islands are located, Luna gleefully subjects him to scornful dissembling, relishing his mockery of the coloniser: "...[The Philippines is] near China, a province of Japan, north of Siberia," he sardonically supplies. "We were greatly surprised to see that man believing what we said."[27]

Perhaps Luna felt some small sweet revenge in these exchanges. As a native Filipino, Luna was seen as inexorably foreign and inferior. Only Filipinos in whom Spanish blood predominated could expect to find recognition and acceptance in Madrid society. The flamboyant Spanish mestizo and propagandista Dominador Gomez,[28] for example, later boasted how he moved easily through the many social levels of Spanish society: "We reached every place: high class, middle class, low class — now in the *frac* (coat and tails) of the aristocrat, now in the jacket of the bourgeoisie, now in the blouse of the worker.... Never in our long association with the Spanish in Madrid did we see a shade of disdain or a hint of coldness."[29]

For the darker-skinned, more Malay-looking Antonio Luna, however, mixing with the Spanish was not so easily done. The target of racist insults and taunts, Luna's physical difference was the object of derision; his appearance was a visible provocation in public places. Madrid displayed little of the thronging cosmopolitanism seen in Paris, and Luna's native Filipino body, its difference, became itself a source of discomfort:

> My very pronounced Malay figure which had rarely attracted attention in Barcelona, excited in a flagrant way the curiosity of the children of Madrid. There is the *chula*, the young woman, or the seamstresses who turn their heads twice or three times to look at me and say, in a voice loud enough to be heard: Jesus! How frightening (*que horroroso*)! He is Chinese (*Es un chino*). He is an Igorot. (To these people Chinese, Igorots and Filipinos are one and the same.) Small boys and big boys, working class and not working class (*chulos y no los chulos*), not content with this, started to shout like savages: Chinese (*Chino*)! Chi-iine-se (*Chiiniitooo*)! Igorot! In the theatres, in the parks, in gatherings, everywhere there was the same second look at me, the mocking smile ... the half-stupid stare. Often in thinking about these spontaneous manifestations, I ask myself if I were in Morocco, in the dangerous borders of the Riffs, and I come to doubt that I live in the capital of a European nation.[30]

Assaulted by racial insults Luna, appropriating orientalist discourse, views Spain as barbaric. He begins to wonder where he really is, that is, if he is in civilized society or actually elsewhere, in Morocco or the "dangerous borders," places where ignorance and savagery could be expected. Such "scenes of rampant misrecognition" as Vicente Rafael describes,[31] had the effect of estrangement, of alienation. The hostility of a Madrid crowd enables a crucial shift to take place. From the experience, Antonio Luna finds the position in which to situate himself with respect to the multiple, and essentially denigrating, cultural referents that impinge upon him. Responding not to Spaniards, but to "Filipinos in the Philippines," Luna severs his affections like a disillusioned lover and rejects the object of his desire. His "talking back" is achieved through "circumventing the mediation of colonial authority" and directing the transmission of his messages for the benefit of a different audience:

> Filipinos who are in the Philippines: Do not be carried away by the song of the siren to the immense flights of the imagination, because the disenchantment is terrible. We are told so much about her, we think

so much of her beauty ... she is placed so high, so very high ... that, when the illusion fades before the heat of realism, the disappointment is fatal.³²

A Question of Honor

Complaints and negative observations from a colonial subject would always sound to some Spanish ears to have the dangerous ring of filibusterism.³³ If colonial asymmetries tend to play themselves out in texts, the representation of the metropolis by a colonial subject sets into motion a particular process of dislodgement, as Mary Louise Pratt puts it: "For colonies to lay claim to their mother countries ... even a purely verbal claim, implies a reciprocity not in keeping with colonial hierarchies."³⁴

Significantly, Luna wrote his *"Impresiones Madrileñas"* when the Filipinos' propaganda campaign in Europe was at an accelerated pace. Taking over the editorship of *La Solidaridad* from Graciano López Jaena, Marcelo H. del Pilar had moved the newspaper from Barcelona to Madrid, believing the periodical would find more supporters and reach a wider audience in the capital. In addition, contributions from Rizal, Blumentritt, Antonio Luna and Mariano Ponce granted the paper a cutting-edge erudition, and the campaign vigor and ferocity. When Luna's essay appeared on the pages of the propagandistas' paper, for some Spanish critics, it was a show of insolence or worse, a shameless exhibition of ingratitude and disloyalty by a colonial subject of Spain. The editor of *El Pueblo Soberano*, Celso Mir Deas, was outraged at what he saw as the depiction of Spaniards as backward and barbarous.³⁵ Erroneously attributing the article to Antonio Luna's brother, the painter Juan, Mir Deas responded to it by personal insult and accusation: "You [Juan Luna] who have received benefits from Spain, you who have been received by those in the Peninsula better than your own people did ... have the nerve to insult those to whom you owe everything and given you much more than you are worth as an artist and as a man."³⁶ Although Juan Luna wrote to the newspapers coolly disclaiming authorship,³⁷ Mir Deas swept on, taking wider swipes at the Filipino people in general, quoting as his authority the pseudo-scientific travel descriptions of Cáñamaque:

> The native of the Philippines is ... a motley mixture of different and contradictory conditions and qualities.... It is useless to study him....

> His features, always inscrutable, his eyes always sad, his mouth open to a meaningless smile, his step always slow and his ways, always the same, defy reason and distort the most logical of conclusions.[38]

Mir Deas' catalogue of insults was a predictable hyperbolic harangue against the impertinence of the Filipino ilustrado colony in Spain and an invective-filled racist meditation on the natives of the Philippines. The propagandistas were enraged at the challenge to their collective honor, and the Spanish liberal press willingly furnished the site for the ensuing journalistic joust.

Antonio Luna was sent from Madrid as the representative of the Filipino community to Barcelona to demand a public retraction from Mir Deas, whom Luna took to calling Mier Das (punning the name with the Spanish for excreta); if an apology were not forthcoming, Luna would challenge Deas to a duel. Writing to Rizal in Paris, the unmistakable tone of bravado in Antonio Luna's letter reflects the consensus amongst his male contemporaries, reconfirming the rightfulness of Luna's display of manliness:

> Today at three o'clock, I am leaving on the express for Barcelona to ask for reparation by means of arms from the author of the article "To Taga-Ilog" in *Pueblo Soberano*. This gentleman thinks that *Taga-Ilog* is Juan Luna and he accuses him of being an ingrate, *filibustero*, indecent, dirty.... In short, the Filipino colony told me unanimously that I have no other remedy but to go and fight. Those here ... approve of my determination. I do not know if I am doing right but I do not feel in my conscience the remorse of the offender. Goodbye *chico*; I am the author of "Impresiones Madrileñas" and I am the only one responsible for it. Goodbye; if I should come to some misfortune, I ask you a favour to tell Nelly how much I have loved her.[39]

Antonio Luna's claim to heterosexual, virile masculinity is unequivocal. He duels for the sake of honor, not his own but of the Filipino ilustrado community in Europe, thus orienting death in terms of the high, purposeful duties of fraternal comradeship, its very fulfilment a manly pleasure. His farewells have an exaggerated fatalism; in an extravagant declaration of male bonding, he informs his rival, Rizal, to convey his love to Nelly Boustead, a young woman for whom, as we shall later see, both men had a special fondness. The point was clear: it must be shown that Filipinos were not an inherently indolent, undifferentiated, unclean mass lacking courage, passion and taste. By following the Hispanic ideals of masculinity and putting on public display their manliness, the Filipino ilustrados found a dramatic means of refuting the insulting civilization/barbarism dichotomy.

In the flurry of letters they excitedly exchanged over the impending confrontation, the propagandistas in Paris, Madrid and Barcelona scripted themselves into a wholly male, heroic world. Writing to Rizal from Barcelona, Mariano Ponce stresses the importance of Luna's mission, considering contemptible those who are failing to lend their support. "We need your help," Ponce writes urgently.[40] Rizal's response from Paris is swift and determined: "Tell our compatriots there that all of us here shall help with our inner will (*loob*), strength, money and anything else that may be needed over the Luna question and whatever its outcome. We will be sending money there."[41] With the air of a military strategist, Rizal continues, "We have many enemies and other hostile forces, let us use cunning in our struggle so that we may not be scattered."[42]

Writing to Rizal, Luna recounts the dramatic events: "The incident took place at the Café de la Pajarera (Siglo XIX).... I asked him who he was (for I did not know him)...." Luna's actions are dramatic:

> I told him he was infamous, a coward, and a cur, I spat on his face and threw my card to his face. The result: A great disturbance, much disorder, and now I wait tranquilly. The series of insults he has directed to us, without answering our assertions and conclusions, demands no other cause. Be it to death, to luck, as he would like, I will accept the duel. In this way I believe I will show that we Filipinos have more dignity, more courage, more honor than this cringing insulter and coward who has come out in our way.
>
> I believe that I have avenged in this manner our outraged dignity.

Luna's public challenge to duel not only put on display his courage and mettle but also vindicated the collective male honor of the Filipino community in Madrid, and thereby strengthened the bonds of emotional solidarity amongst the ilustrado propagandists.[43] His article "Impresiones Madrileñas" flashed back to his compatriots a highly significant message from the metropolis: Spaniards and Spain were not the ideal of civilized, modern life. This was a bold, arrogant statement from a colonial subject. Antonio Luna strove to project himself and his ilustrado compatriots as more authentically embodying gentlemanly honor than the supposed colonial masters themselves.

Sport and Sartorial Subversion

Drawn from some of the wealthiest and most influential Filipino families, the ilustrados studying in Europe displayed a concern for their clothing and appearance in keeping with their social class. The serious attention that these young men gave to their appearance is wonderfully illustrated by Felix Roxas, who along with fellow ilustrado Tomas Cabangis disembarked at Barcelona in May 1881, after a 42-day sea voyage from Manila. Grooming and sartorial style were their very first priorities:

> Cabangis and I immediately donned our best Manila wardrobe and went out. We went at once to a barbershop ... [to] cut our hair according to the current fashion.... The smoking curling tongs ... taming our straight hair. Cabangis, seeing his curled moustache in the mirror smiled with satisfaction.... We went into the big haberdashery store and provided ourselves with hats, walking sticks, and other essentials. We were about to leave when a lady invited us to see the gloves section. So there we went, discovering two young and pretty attendants, blonde and brunette.... Each counter had a pillow where the client rested his elbow while the sales clerk adjusted the glove. My sales clerk was the blonde one.... She had blue eyes, sweeping eyelashes; a constant heaving of her well-developed bosom punctuated the process of her fitting the glove on my hand, finger by finger, by means of a soft gentle massage....[44]

It is difficult to ignore Roxas' breathless anticipation in this sexually charged description of a glove fitting, in which the physical assets of the female glove seller and the merchandise on offer is juxtaposed. Roxas has appeared to confuse the act of trying on gloves with the fantasy of a blonde glove seller's sexual advances. But it is striking that the young men's first worry after their long sea voyage was the adequacy of their "well-ironed Baxter shirts, patent leather shoes bought from Chinaman Acun, and Manila tailoring".[45]

Frivolity, it seemed, characterized the overall attitude of many young, ilustrado Filipinos and the worry that Filipino males in Europe were showing themselves to be a dandified, precious, pitiful lot, was privately felt by Rizal and Juan Luna. To Rizal especially, his compatriots in

Madrid and Barcelona seemed to be embarrassingly timid, morally weak, indulged, and narcissistic.[46] Observing their dissipation, he remarked with disgust at the endless hours the students wasted in oversleeping, gambling, cafés, women, and discussing little else except "the number of buttons on a coat."[47] Sharing Rizal's sentiments, Juan Luna reported to Rizal what he too saw as a general slackness in focus and intellectual application: "I spent the month of June in Madrid; I saw almost the entire Filipino colony; all as before, some are studious and others, gamblers and layabouts."[48]

Rizal implored his fellow ilustrado compatriots to put an end to their vices, particularly laziness and gambling, and to be diligent in their studies. He exhorted them to remember that they were in a position to bring about national change. In a letter to Marcelo H. del Pilar, he wrote:

> ... If we, who are called to do something, if we, in whom the poor people place their modest hopes, pass our time in these things [gambling], precisely when the years of our youth ought to be used in something more noble and grand by the very fact that youth is noble and generous, I have great fears that we may be struggling for a useless illusion.... I appeal to the patriotism of all the Filipinos to give to the Spanish people a proof that we are superior to our misfortune, and that we cannot be degraded nor our noble sentiments be lulled to slumber by the corruption of morals.[49]

The best defence against the charges of infantilism, effeminacy and effeteness was to demonstrate how mistaken the Spaniards were in their ideas of the Filipino *indio*. The obvious display of a manly physical appearance had an immediate visual impact. Vicente Rafael has shown that a mode of nationalist self-fashioning seemed to operate in the way the Filipino ilustrados wanted to be seen in photographs. As they posed in European clothes, their photographed selves would consciously adopt an expression of extreme gravitas and sobriety "that makes one think of collected interiors in command of their exterior representations, of rational minds holding together bodies in studied repose."[50] Thus pictured, the pose of the ilustrado in European clothes could be understood as an articulation of a nationalist identity by its projection of an image which undercut Spanish racial stereotypes, while simultaneously asserting a construction of masculinity.

Love, Passion and Patriotism

Fig. 22 Ilustrados in Madrid, c.1890
(Filipiniana Section, Philippine National Library)

Wearing the dark costume of the fashionable, European urban male, the Filipino ilustrados photographed gathered on the steps of an imperious Madrid building (Fig. 22) aptly illustrate the way Filipinos mobilized their defence against European racism through bourgeois sartorial style. The men pose confident and dignified. Many sport moustaches, Marcelo H. del Pilar's being the most magnificently curled and stiffened. Next to Del Pilar, José Rizal stands rigidly, his hair carefully combed and brilliantined, his demeanor one of resoluteness. Whether standing or sitting, the men appear in comfortable closeness with one another — arms are linked, are placed on or around shoulders, on knees — in conspicuous gestures of fraternal unity and solidarity. The two leaders Rizal and Del Pilar are careful not to overlap each other, posing with level, shoulder to shoulder equality, Rizal's arm fraternally around Del Pilar.

Indeed, Rizal's attitude towards a manly physical appearance was at times rigidly prescriptive. He was insistent on a manly look that, in his view, ought to be distinctively Filipino and had considered Del Pilar's flamboyant and carefully tended moustache un-Filipino, therefore false (though perhaps not necessarily un-manly). In a letter interspersed with Tagalog words, Rizal (who was himself largely clean shaven, except for a sparse and timid-looking moustache), wrote to Del Pilar to commend him on an essay that had recently been published. Rizal also took the opportunity to advise his compatriot to rid himself of his pretentious facial hair:

> I have finished reading your very interesting pamphlet, written with much common sense (*sentido commun*), much *esprit*, salt, joy and incisive satire that surprises and strikes the reader without leaving time for him to defend himself. The work is written with a concise and robust style that characterizes and should characterize the Filipino style. When a Filipino wants something he first demands it to be strong (*matibay*): the Filipino style before other things is strong (*matibay*) ... the first thing that occurred to me after reading, is that the author must shave himself so that all the world and the Spaniards (*castilas*) will see that he is completely and utterly Tagalog (*tagalog y tagalong na lubos*). Some could take him for a Spaniard by the beard and attribute the merits of the book to Spanish blood (*dugong castila*)....

While Rizal considered his friend's bold writing style impressive, Del Pilar's extravagant moustache irked him and he went on to draw a rather strange comparison. In Rizal's view it seems, one's appearance must conform to the way one writes. The beautiful handle-bar moustache that Del Pilar so lovingly cultivated was not Filipino and lent an aspect to Del Pilar's appearance that was at odds with a writing style that evidently exuded power and strength, a style Rizal deemed to be Filipino. As Rizal cautioned, there was a danger that credit for the book could be given to a Spaniard since Del Pilar's moustache made him look like one.[51]

The detail of the cut of a suit and the quality of its cloth, the starched stiffness of an immaculate white shirt, the utilitarian and restrained use of jewelry and decoration, the essential accessories of hats, gloves, canes that signified the gentleman, all amounted to a weighty sartorial discourse articulating distinctions of class, high education and sober, bourgeois respectability. But as translated by the male, Filipino body, these social codes of clothing and comportment combined to form a uniform image of Filipino men looking out at their viewer with composed, proud, intelligent purposefulness.

Fencing and other sporting activities — pistol-shooting, weightlifting and gymnastics — mirrored the ethics and aesthetics of *la culture physique*, the popular modern body-building movement that served the bourgeois republican aim to re-invigorate the degenerate *fin de siècle* Frenchman.[52]

Fig. 23 Juan Luna, José Rizal and Valentin Ventura, c. 1886
(Pardo de Tavera Collection, Rizal Library, Ateneo de Manila University)

For the Filipinos, fencing captured the essence of aristocratic gentlemanly values — of civilized sportsmanship and chivalry. It became an activity associated with the cultivation of patriotic honor. Rizal and the Luna brothers had taken up fencing during their school and college days in Manila.[53] In Paris the sport was practised much more seriously, either in Luna's *atelier* or at the gymnasium. On Filipino fencing matches in Madrid, Juan Luna remarked to Rizal: "It seems they are behaving with dignity. A contest of 'chino' marksmen in Madrid in the course of the year would not be bad ... we would be respected and the *kastilas de entremes* (farcical Spaniards) would know us better."[54] Impressed by his brother's efforts at encouraging fencing amongst the compatriots, Juan Luna praised the manliness the activity inspired: "It is good they are all dedicating time to the foil, the Filipino is now renowned for being brave and strong (*fama de valientes y de fuertes*) in the use of weaponry."[55] The fencing jousts and pistol-shooting competitions had become battle exercises that prepared young men to fight.

The photograph of Rizal (center), Juan Luna (at left) and fellow ilustrado Valentin Ventura (right) pictured posing during a fencing

Fig. 24 Juan Luna, self-portrait, 1886 (From Lopez Memorial Museum Collection)

exercise (Fig. 23) amplifies this display of manly vigor. The seated figure of the woman in the background, usually cropped out in reproductions of this famous picture, is Juan Luna's wife Paz, a marginal female figure at the periphery who signals, as Rafael observes, "the sexual hierarchy that patriotism reinstitutes."[56] Standing in the courtyard of Juan Luna's Paris home, their fencing foils held momentarily at rest between their legs, the pose of the men is a self-conscious promotion of health, vigor and moral virtue that the activity of physical sport supposed. Indeed, this photograph was evidently one of Juan Luna's favorite pictures, an image of bourgeois masculinity through which an identity was created and described. He would reproduce his photographed pose in a painting (Fig. 24) depicting himself slightly slimmer, his stance slightly more erect with feet set firmly on the ground, the lowered blade of his foil held suitably angled to highlight its length and gleam. He turns to gaze out at the viewer with an expression of conceited arrogance, a look that drew together intensity and virile egotism.

The pleasures of masculine identity and fraternal solidarity found forceful expression in the formation of Los Indios Bravos. Attending the Paris Exposition in May 1889, the group that included Juan Luna and Rizal were impressed by Buffalo Bill's Wild West Show, which featured Native American Indians performing their skills on horseback to the excited applause of the audience. This inspired them to form the all male club Los Indios Bravos whose name subverted the derogatory use of the term *indio* by the Spaniards and fostered instead a sense of patriotic pride.[57] Rather than accepting the term as a humiliating identity, the club's members would wear it as a "badge of honor" representing virile values of bravery and courage.

Even when young, Rizal had an attachment to clandestine all-male societies in which he would assume a leadership role. First he had created the "Compañeros de Jehu," named after a Dumas novel in which the eponymous band of young French aristocrats become highwaymen to steal from Napoleon's Directoire and fund the restoration of the monarchy.[58] Then there were "Three Musketeers," again obviously inspired by Dumas, a gallant trio whom Rizal fancied himself commanding as the dashing captain Treville.[59] The same swashbuckling "all for one and one for all" ethos of male honor and loyalty characterized yet another of Rizal's clubs, the "Babylonians." Exactly what these societies did remains vague, but the core principle was plain: fraternal solidarity and support.

Binding its members to a secret, masonic-like network of mutual trust and aid, Los Indios Bravos perfectly encapsulated the gentlemanly codes of honor promoted by the propagandistas. Despite the spontaneity of its inception, Los Indios Bravos was a serious attempt to broaden the propagandistas' hitherto largely textual counter-discourse. While the underlying purpose seemed to be the "diffusion in the Philippines of all useful knowledge be it scientific, artistic, literary, etc." as Rizal vaguely explained to the Filipino exile José Maria Basa,[60] the interest in developing the physique of the male body; the encouragement of manly skills as shooting and fencing and the emphasis placed on the defence of male honor, were principles Los Indios Bravos upheld. Within this society, the all-male members could collectively posit an image of Filipino manhood that crucially described an alternative idea of identity defined by patriotic ideals, moral virtue and manly vigor. A hint of the club's moral expectations and sexual codes can be glimpsed in one of

Rizal's letters to Los Indios Bravos. Switching from writing in Spanish to Tagalog, Rizal advises one member to mend his ways:

> I should like to remind Lauro that a lot of bad reports (*maraming marami masasamang balita*) about him are being spread or have been spread in Madrid, it is necessary for him to change his behavior (*magbago siya at magbangong puri*) and defend his honor in order the name Indio Bravo may not be tarnished (*huag mabahiran*) and also to ensure that ... [ellipsis in original] should not feel grieved (*sumama ang loob*) should the bad news reach her ears.[61]

Vulgarity

The sense of moral superiority the propagandistas felt over their colonial rulers is apparent in their delight in recounting to their families in the Philippines the scandals, gossip, and decadent culture of Madrid society. Rizal, for example, took pleasure in relating the scandalous affair surrounding the Duque de la Torre's "hermaphrodite" son, whose wife sued for divorce in Paris. "I shall refer to scandals in this Capital [Madrid]," he confided to his brother Paciano, "... which the Manila press ... will certainly not tell you."[62] Marcelo H. del Pilar, in a letter to Pedro Icasiano, similarly comments on the general immorality of the Spaniards, and matches colonial insult with his own observations:

> [The Spaniards] are frivolous, without ideals, with no other conviction than their own personal and momentary convenience. Believe me, *chico*, I came here with flattering dispositions, but each day I go on acquiring the very sad conviction of the incompatibility of this race with sentiments of honour. It is sad to acknowledge it, but we will learn nothing from this accursed race....[63]

What triggers this reaction, we learn, are Del Pilar's forays into Spanish cafés. He is shocked by the informally attired men and women, whom he sees wearing simple shirts, sandals and caps; the entertainment of the *café cantante* is ribald, and he notes that the bawdier it is the better it is appreciated: "I entered these cafés in order to learn for myself the culture that is so bragged about here, and was only disgusted (*masuklam*) by such loathsome (*karumal-dumal*) conduct."[64]

Drawing attention to aspects of Spanish culture the Filipinos found offensive and indecent was the basis of a number of Luna's essays. As his article "Se Divierten" shows, Luna assumed that his readers shared his own high moral values and refined sensibilities.[65] This allowed him to establish a reader-text relationship that reaffirmed those values and sensibilities. In "Se Divierten," Luna recalls a day excursion out of the city. He goes in search for a "rustic atmosphere" like that of a lush, natural Philippine landscape to refresh his soul only to discover arid fields and desert hills.[66] Yet it is not the bleak and dry environment that offends his senses but the activities inside a *merendero*, a provincial drinking house, whose vulgar clientele of "artisans, lady bullfighters, vagabonds" and other "undesirables" become the focus of Luna's attack. In action-filled narrative prose, Luna roams through the scene selecting moments for their dramatic vulgarity:

> There was a fellow attacking the plate with the veritable fury of a savage; others spoke with mouths full, elbows on the table. The women laughed loudly, shouted oaths, terrible blasphemies; screams were heard every moment; this one was chasing a girl around the table; that one was pulling her by the arms.... The men and women were drinking atrociously and between drinks, the smack of a kiss was heard.[67]

Luna assumes the stance of a detached observer; yet, virtuoso-like, he orchestrates the appropriate responses from his readers by punctuating his account with side comments that assumes what is described is being understood as offensive and meriting moral disapprobation. As he recounts, the dancing that takes place is raucous and vulgar, in which "charm in manners, the basic element of decency" is lacking. Luna's concern to press home his point, however, leads his narrative into betraying a prurient fascination for the very act he decries:

> That manner of dancing was the height of indecency: the curves of the woman disappeared completely smothered in the arms of the man; he gazed fixedly on her face, mingling his breath with hers; and the woman, with arms around the man at the back was drawing him close to her, to form together one body. If expert hands were to pass a thread between those two bodies, what a useless task....[68]

Abruptly, Luna's transfixed gaze breaks into astonishment and embarrassment, awakening him not to a state of clarity and illumination but rather, towards further incomprehension: "That was immorality of the highest order; civilization and culture, where?" So great is Luna's disbelief that he can only stutter out his questions, as if stranded in a place of unreality: "I believed that I was dreaming. But no ... confused and ashamed (*avergonzado*), I left that unholy place."⁶⁹ Here Luna's shame and incredulity transforms the lower class provincial Spaniards whose vulgarity he has just witnessed into the exact analogue of the native Filipinos portrayed in Spanish colonial discourse.

The licentiousness and grossness Luna judged to be redolent in lower class Spanish society was offensive to the shared bourgeois sensibilities of the Filipino ilustrados. Refinement, gentlemanliness and honor were to them critically important expressions of equality, if not superiority to the Spaniards and it was imperative to show that their adherence to these qualities was more authentic and true. An attitude of revulsion toward vulgarity indicated as much. However, as we shall see in Luna's works that dealt with Spanish women, revulsion was often marked by sexual desire.

Entering the Contact Zone

Spanish women of both the lower and upper classes pointedly figured, for the ilustrados, as eroticised contact zones.⁷⁰ From the end of 1889 until the summer of 1890, Luna's contributions to the *Artes y Letras* section of *La Solidaridad* dwelt on the theme of Desire. In these accounts, Luna endeavored to describe why the ilustrados found Spanish women sexually fascinating. "The students among us did more or less well in our studies," recalled Dominador Gómez, "interrupted a thousand times by the irresistible delights of the sweet, sweet temptations of Madrid."⁷¹ Europe was construed as a site where Filipino bourgeois manhood should be affirmed, a place that crystallized high activity, male comradeship and adventure, a place where ideas of heterosexual manliness could be constructed, continuously proved and reinforced.

In Luna's stories, the figure of the male Filipino ilustrado was often positioned centrally as the main protagonist either caught or pursuing his love object. Luna describes the beginnings of a love affair between himself and a young Madrileña:

> ... I confess innocently that I could not resist the effects of a strange emotion for one of those precious women. I fell hopelessly in love (*me enamoré perdidamente*) and I thought the feeling was mutual. I became suddenly a fiancé (*el novio oficial*) of that Madrid rosebud.⁷²

The beauty and charm of the eroticized figure of the Spanish woman was enhanced by the city and the ilustrado excitement of urban explorations. As Luna invites the reader:

> Come with me to those narrow crooked streets flanked by ill-kept walls and from the narrow sidewalks contemplate the thin, graceful type of the capital of Spain, or when the sun bids goodbye and darkness falls, when there is a brazen struggle between light and darkness, the struggle of love (*lucha de inamorado*), of caresses, of tenderness which sounds the melancholy note of day — twilight; come with me to Alcala street, wide boulevard with two rows of trees, and there watch not the street girls — Manuelas, Lolas or Carmens — who, according to the French hide a knife under their garters, but the Spanish beauties with sweet kisses on their lips and in their eyes, a treasury of their charms.[73]

For Luna, the "original type that walks around Madrid" could take on a myriad of physical characteristics: "blondes, brunettes and auburn-haired, tall, short, fat, and thin, all breathe the same air. Round faces, brows of delicate porcelain ... ivory complexion ... dark or blue eyes appealing to the senses more than the soul." The intentional, undistinguished generality that the profusion of adjectives portrayed, suggests that intimate contact between the ilustrados and the Spanish woman was treated as an activity of erotic adventurousness, whose nature was mainly looked upon as erotically-driven and sensually-charged experimental liaisons. Spanish women were beautiful but were a "mixture of angel and devil."[74]

But the ilustrados found the flagrant sexuality of Spanish women appealing and exciting only when it was directed toward the satisfaction of male desire. Women who defied their eroticizing fantasies provoked their anger and disgust. Doña Antonia Rodriguez de Ureta, for example, was the only Spanish woman known to have attacked the Filipinos in the Madrid press. For this trangression, she could only be thought of as a whore. Writing to Blumentritt (in German with a sprinkle of Spanish and French words), Rizal vented his contempt for this particular modern woman:

> Concerning Doña Antonia I will tell you the following. She does not deserve your writings. She is a despicable whore (*Sie ist eine unwurdige Dirne*). In the Philippines, she was with a warehouseman

(*almacenero*).... After some time she separated from her husband. She began her life in Manila as a courtesan (*courtisane*) with great scandal.... Afterward she returned to Barcelona and continued her life as a prostitute (*Dirnenleben*) being well known by all. Here in Paris she had also love affairs (*Liebschaften*) with Alsatian Jews, among others, who had been in the Philippines. I received all this information from the family of P.de T. (Pardo de Tavera).... V. Ventura, a Filipino who lived in Barcelona for seven years.... No, she is not worthy of our writings.[75]

Here, Rizal has no qualms in unleashing a patently vicious character assassination of a woman he does not know. He passes on gossip about Doña Antonia that is being circulated by his ilustrado friends and, significantly, sprinkles his diatribe with anti-Semitic sneers.[76] Rizal furnishes Blumentritt with a horde of intimate details concerning her personal life, but he neglects to mention that Doña Antonia was a prolific, well-known Spanish writer, and the author of a respected novel entitled *Pacita* that told the story of the life of a young Filipina.[77]

Choosing to focus not on Rodriguez de Ureta's ignorance or prejudices — which can hardly have been worse than those of her male counterparts — but on her character, Rizal's *ad feminam* attack targeted at what he derisively judged to be her scandalous sexuality and brazen promiscuity. Each line is a scathing condemnation of Doña Antonia's morality: she is a vile whore, a courtesan of great scandal, a prostitute. That Rizal should be so venomous is remarkable in two related ways. If the immorality of a woman's unregulated and illegitimate sexual activity formed the target of the attack, the offence more precisely lay in the fact that a woman — and one of such apparent low morals and merit — should have the temerity to publicly insult the illustrious ilustrado sons of the Philippines.

The imagined merits of Madrid women lay in their sexuality and the novel pleasures and gratifications it offered to the Filipino men. As Dominador Gómez tells it, recalling once again the milieu of the ilustrados in Spain during the late 1880s, the sexual appeal Spanish women held for the Filipinos meant that their presence always remained in demand, and a number of the propagandistas seemed to be remarkably adept at attracting them: "If there was a need to assemble the divinest cluster of enchanting girls," Gómez amusingly reminisced, "the order was given to the prime experts in the feminine line — to a Tomas Arejola ... a

Baldomero Roxas, ... a Kanoy (Galicano) Apacible — who carried out the commission so marvellously that ... graceful, supremely beautiful ladies regularly gathered to enhance the uproarious fiestas of the Philippine colony in Madrid!"[78]

But Spanish women as eroticized objects of desire represented a treacherous terrain of cultural and racial differences to be traversed, testing ilustrado self-affirmation at the level of the quotidian. As Luna's essay "Sangre Torera" details, cultural harmony arising from romance was not to be expected. Contact with a Spanish European love object would sooner or later reveal the great fissures of difference; intimacy was a fragile state of affairs, always in danger of breaking down. Luna describes the lovers' fatal quarrel: "I noticed in her a vice, a very disagreeable one for me, for bulls, the madness for those horny appendages."[79] Luna's masculinist and eroticized narrative questions the viability of this *amorio*, where the disagreement lies in the way courage, *valor*, is being defined, a fundamental and irreconcilable point. The following dialogue between the lovers illustrates not only Luna's patriotic understanding of courage, but also his ideas of womanly behavior:

> My sincere love could not persuade her at all that the spectacle, although a national sport, was not for a young woman. "Don't you see that bloody, horrifying spectacle is not for a young woman?"
>
> "Go on, little boy, how you show that you have no bullfighter's blood in your veins. In your country you do not have courage for such things."
>
> "That is true, because we use it in other ways."

The woman's masculine lust for blood wreaks havoc on the boundaries of sexual difference recognized by Luna and he struggles to restore order. The effort, signalled by his disgust, casts his Spanish love object outside the bounds of desirability. This end of the romance scenario tests Luna's manly sensibilities, which become specified as Filipino. As he watches his sweetheart take pleasure in the bloody, violent culmination of the bullfight, Luna can scarcely conceal his horrified astonishment and offence:

> I covered my face with my hands when I saw my pretty companion taking part fiercely in that noisy protest. She was shouting, insulting the wounded rider. And that girl, all feeling, all tenderness, all sweetness

who fainted at the prick of a needle, was shouting frantically before that bloody picture.[80]

Instead of feminizing him, Luna's display of sensitivity articulates ideas of correctness in relation to sexual difference. Being at odds with certain Spanish social customs served only to highlight these attitudes rather than compromise them. Yet Luna's desire for himself and his country to be viewed in a positive, modern light returned over and over again to haunt his social interactions.

In his essay entitled "Amorios I," Luna describes a scene at a dance, where he surprises his dancing partner, a beautiful Spanish woman named Angela, with his ability to waltz. "Do the people dance in your country like we do?" She asks Luna in amazement.

> "Yes, senorita, we are very fond of dancing."
> "But I thought you did not, because I have seen the dances of those of your people in the Philippine Exposition."
> She was referring to the war dances of the Igorots, the fantasy of some joker. Angela believed those were our dances. Something was really taught by that Exposition.[81]

The Philippine Exposition held in Madrid in 1887, which featured a cultural display of Filipinos from the Cordillera, is here raised as a source of embarrassment and discomfort for Luna, where the binary of civilization/primitiveness was rehearsed in comparisons between the European waltz and the war dances of the Igorot people of the Philippines. Replayed over again in scenes that involved the public display of interracial relations, Luna struggled to sustain the integrity of his bourgeois sexuality in the midst of assaults against his racial distinctiveness. Walking with his Spanish sweetheart in the streets of Madrid, "where everybody's glance was directed at us," he presented an easy target for ready-made cultural disparagements, suffering from overheard comments made by passers-by: "What a beautiful woman, but he...." Although agitated and aroused to anger, his effort to maintain self-control marks out the "truth" of his bourgeois identity, shown here to be lodged in his display of self-restraint and self-discipline.[82]

Sexual desire, as represented in Luna's autoethnographic writings, was structured by the claims of other desires, by amor propio, by the desire to "grasp white civilization and dignity and make them mine," a sentiment Frantz Fanon attributed to the desiring man of color.[83]

Framed by the romance of intimate contact, Luna attempted to account for the colonial dislocations of race and gender. As we have seen, his discursive exploration of sexual desire pointed to the tangled complexity of strategies that turned imitation into mockery and ambivalence into aggressively assertive patriotism whose reference point, the Philippines, was an idealized memory never far from their minds. Cultural nostalgia exerted its own energy and it is to the propagandistas' transformation of this energy into libidinal longing that we shall now turn.

"Does she love me?"

Gatherings in the homes of wealthy, liberal supporters in Spain and in the salons of Doña Juliana Gorricho in Paris were opportunities in which intimate contact between European women and the ilustrados could occur in an atmosphere of relative propriety and decorum. Doña Consuelo Ortiga y Rey, the daughter of a high-ranking, liberal-minded Spanish colonial official who often entertained Rizal and other propagandistas in his Madrid home, recorded in her diary the intense flirtatiousness of these occasions, where European women often found themselves the object of amorous advances, which they entertained or fended off. "I find myself," Doña Consuelo wrote, "in a position of not knowing which side to take: Lete on one side, Rizal on the other, on another the two brothers [Antonio and Maximino Paterno], all attack and I have nothing with which to defend myself except for my head."[84] Rivalry amongst the young ilustrados for the affections of the women they met at these gatherings could be extreme. For Antonio Luna, the rule governing the conduct of erotic triangles was invariably the exhibition of amor propio.

Antonio Luna's courtship of Nelly Boustead occurred at about the same time he had began writing his Madrid impressions for *La Solidaridad*. Along with her younger sister, Adelina, Nelly Boustead, Antonio Luna and Rizal composed an amiable quartet of friends until Luna had begun to sense Rizal's own interest in Nelly Boustead and confronted the growing chill between them:

> We have no reason to be cold to each other for many times I asked you if you felt love for Nelly and you told me no. Consequently I was already sure of you, certain you are my friend ... therefore *chico*, we ought to continue as friends as I thought we never ceased to be.[85]

A familiar presence in the ilustrado milieu of Paris and Madrid, Nelly Boustead had been the subject of much amorous attention and speculation. Tomas Arejola pointed to her impressive attributes: "since last year I have heard a number of times here about this young lady ... who is also a Filipina. I am told she is to be recommended because of her excellent upbringing, her most attractive moral and physical qualities and, in addition, because she is a Filipina."[86] Educated and cultured in the west, yet professedly patriotic, mestiza women raised in Europe presented a mysterious anomaly for the Filipino ilustrados and a sexual challenge.

Returning from Barcelona and the Mir Deas confrontation, Luna despairingly wrote to Rizal: "Your friend and compatriot is asking you this. Does she still love me? I should like to know if I am making myself ridiculous by believing candidly in a love (*cariño*) that no longer exists."[87] Plunged into what Barthes describes as a lover's anxiety, Luna appeals to the fraternity between men. However, wounded pride soon got the better of Luna and he went on to challenge Rizal to a duel after uttering some remarks about Nelly Boustead. Rizal accepted the duel.[88]

As a lover who had lost in a contest of love, Luna's defence of his amor propio is enacted as a ritualistic performance. The seconds appear immaculately dressed in frock coats, gloves and silk hats, and as etiquette dictates, the rules of the duel are spoken with grave formality. The tragedy the situation foretold ended however in comedy: the man who stood as Luna's second was quite deaf, and perhaps to prevent the scene from slipping further into farcical depths, a resolution was prepared "so worded as to save the honor and pride of both gentlemen."[89] Apologizing to Rizal on his brother's behalf, Juan Luna tried to explain his brother's behavior: "It is true that Antonio has a strong character and he is very sensitive. This is good if the cause is just."[90]

Compared to the Mir Deas confrontation, the intended duel between Rizal and Luna has the sense of a performance, in which bourgeois formality and the demands of amor propio are ritualized. Nelly Boustead was the cause that drove a wedge between the two friends. But in the graver question of male honor, her role becomes peripheral or symbolic. She was simply the woman whom the ilustrados deemed worthy enough to squabble over.

Desire led Luna to make comparisons between Spanish and Filipino women, a conceit that revealed what lay at issue — the affirmation and reproduction of male ilustrado bourgeois authority. In "Amorios II" Luna counsels a compatriot who is considering marriage to a European woman with the following judgment:

> [Angela] is more cultured than the greater number of our Filipino women, educated in the colleges of the Sisters of Charity; they who can decorate your house with flowers, embroideries and beads, but who cannot fry an egg for your table; who would interpret fantasies, waltzes, and polkas at the piano, but who do not know how to speak and write grammatical Spanish.... I made him see that our women are darker, with flatter noses, less talkative and therefore not prattlers; but they possess exquisite sensitivity, a faithful character, the demureness of the sex who takes pride in the majestic weakness of women, a soul which says what it means and feels what it says. The Filipino woman whom we could call a song rather than a poem is in a high social position. She is perhaps less educated but in time, she will improve herself and will cultivate her talent.[91]

Luna's comparisons of women turned on the assessment of their relative virtues, beauty and bourgeois skills. The Filipina possessed none of the physical features ilustrados found so alluring in western women and was ignorant of practical skills. This last characteristic of Filipino bourgeois women was a particular point of contention for Antonio Luna. Such "useless" preoccupations as embroidery and beadwork, in Luna's opinion, should be replaced by activities that had a more direct application — cooking food, mending *camisas*, knowing how to write letters and speaking Spanish.[92] Women more than men, Luna reasoned, were responsible for the education of children, the future citizens of the country. It was a common refrain amongst the ilustrados. Luna's evidently limited thinking on the education of women — swapping the fripperies of female handiwork for frying eggs — was however more frank than most.

It is no surprise that the qualities of "sensitivity," fidelity, demureness and feminine weakness that Luna highlighted readily bolstered male patriotic amor propio. These were all positive aspects of a woman's nature the propagandistas thought particularly characterized Filipino women. The next chapter discusses Filipino women's religiosity, the female trait the propagandistas believed gravely threatened family and country and urgently needed to be eradicated.

Notes

1. Taga-Ilog (Antonio Luna), *Impresiones* (Madrid: Imprenta de 'El Progreso de Tipográfico, 1891). Antonio Luna was a scientist by training and published a highly regarded study on malaria. In 1892 he was appointed by the Spanish colonial government to lead a scientific commission investigating illnesses originating from bacteria. Antonio Luna y Novicio, *El Hematozoario del Paludismo su estudio experimental* (Madrid: Est. Tipográfico de G. Pedraza, 1893). For documents pertaining to his commission, see Ultramar, Leg. 5282, Expediente 27, AHN, Madrid.
2. In contrast to the satirical tone adopted by the Roman poet Horace, which was more one of tolerant amusement, Juvenal's satires are fierce denunciations of his fellow Romans in general and of women in particular "who were ruined by wealth and ease hence their follies, vices and crimes." For a discussion of Juvenal's satires see Gilbert Highet, *Juvenal the Satirist* (Oxford: Clarendon Press, 1954), esp. pp. 47 and 99–101; also Niall Rudd, *The Satires of Horace: A Study* (Cambridge: Cambridge University Press, 1966).
3. Luna, *Impresiones*, p. 2.
4. Antonio Luna (Madrid) to José Rizal, 11 April 1891, in *Cartas entre Rizal y sus colegas de la propaganda, 1889–1896* (Manila: Comisión Nacional del Centenario de José Rizal, 1961), p. 645.
5. The most detailed biography of Antonio Luna is Vivencio José, *The Rise and Fall of Antonio Luna* (Metro Manila: Solar, 1986; Renato Constantino Filipiniana Reprint Series). First published in *Philippine Social Sciences and Humanities Review*, 1972. See also Manuel Artigas y Cuerva, *Glorias nacionales: Antonio Luna y Novicio, reseña bio-bibliografía* (Manila: Imp. de La Vanguardia, 1910); Juan Villamor, *General D. Antonio Luna y Novicio: vida hechos y tragica muerte* (Manila: Tipografia "Dia Filipino," 1932); Teodoro Agoncillo, "General Antonio Luna reconsidered", *Solidarity* 10: 2 (March–April 1976): 58–80; Nick Joaquin, *A Question of Heroes* (Manila: National Bookstore, 1981), pp. 176–201; and Ambeth Ocampo, *Luna's Moustache* (Pasig City: Anvil, 1998), pp. 22–35.
6. A short record of Antonio Luna's brief imprisonment, which states that he entered prison on 24 November 1885, is found in a document named *Carcel de Bilibid, Letras* (Ayer Manuscript Collection, No.1393, Newberry Library). For a discussion of the uprising led by Adriano Novicio in the Northern Luzon provinces, see José, *The Rise and Fall of Antonio Luna*, pp. 54–5; also John Foreman, *The Philippine Islands* (Shanghai: Kelly and Walsh Ltd, 1899), p. 398.
7. For an elucidation on western orientalist thinking, see Edward Said, *Orientalism: western conceptions of the Orient* (London: Penguin, 1978).
8. Pablo Feced, *Esbozos y pinceladas por Quioquiap* (Manila: Ramirez y Cia, 1888).
9. Francisco Cañamaque, *Recuerdos de Filipinas: Cosas, casos y usos de aquellos islas: vistos, ordos, tocados, y contados* (Madrid: Anllo y Rodriguez, 1877–79).
10. Francisco Cañamaque, *Recuerdos de Filipinas*, extract reprinted in *La Solidaridad* 1: 21 (15 December 1889): 537. This and subsequent citations from *La Solidaridad* are taken from the Spanish-English parallel text version with translations by Guadalupe

Fores-Ganzon (Quezon City: University of Philippines Press, 1967; republished Pasig City: Fundación Santiago, 1995–96).
11. Ibid., pp. 535–6.
12. Pablo Feced y Temprano, "Ellos y Nosotros," *El Liberal*, 13 February 1887, quoted in Schumacher, *The Propaganda Movement*, p. 63. Feced was the best known and most vicious of the racist polemicists of the time. His column "Ellos y Nosotros" appeared regularly in the Madrid newspaper *El Liberal*.
13. D.J. O'Connor, "Racial Stereotyping of Filipinos in the Spanish Press and Popular Fiction, 1887–1898," Paper presented at "1848/1898–1998: Transhistoric Thresholds" Conference, Arizona State University, 8–12 December 1998.
14. For a broad discussion of the Filipino propagandistas' reaction and response as a counter discourse to Spanish racism experienced in Europe, see Norman Owen, "Masculinity and National Identity in the 19th Century Philippines," *Illes et Imperis* 2 (1999): 23–7.
15. Graciano Lopez Jaena, "Los Indios de Filipinas," *El Liberal*, 16 February 1887, cited in John N. Schumacher SJ, *The Propaganda Movement, 1880–1895: the creation of a Filipino consciousness, the making of the Revolution* (Quezon City: Ateneo de Manila University Press, 1997), p. 63.
16. For a critical evaluation of Retana's role in Philippine history and contribution to Philippine historiography, see John N. Schumacher S.J., "Wenceslao E. Retana in Philippine History" in his *The Making of a Nation: essays on nineteenth century Filipino nationalism* (Quezon City: Ateneo de Manila University Press, 1991), p. 135.
17. See for example the long review by Ramiro Franco (Dominador Gómez), "El libro del Sr. D. Pablo Feced (a) Quioquiap" ("The book of Mr Pablo Feced (a) Quioquiap"), *La Solidaridad* 1: 20 (30 November 1889): 494.
18. Taga-Ilog (Antonio Luna), "Impresiones Madrileñas de un Filipino," *La Solidaridad* 1: 18 (31 October 1889): 682–7.
19. Mary Louise Pratt, *Imperial Eyes: travel writing and transculturation* (London: Routledge, 1992), p. 7.
20. Taga-Ilog (Antonio Luna), "Impresiones Madrileñas de un Filipino," p. 682.
21. Schumacher, *The Propaganda Movement*, p. 216.
22. Roland Barthes, *The Lover's Discourse: fragments*, trans. Richard Howard (London: Penguin, 1978), p. 18.
23. Taga-Ilog, "Impresiones Madrileñas de un Filipino," p. 683.
24. Michael Jacobs, *Madrid Observed* (London: Pallas Athene, 1992), p. 39.
25. Albert F. Calvert, *Madrid: an historical description and handbook of the Spanish capital* (London: John Lane, The Bodley Head, 1909), p. 8.
26. Taga-Ilog, "Impresiones Madrileñas de un Filipino," p. 687.
27. Ibid., p. 685.
28. For details of Gómez's background, see William Henry Scott, "The Union Obrera Democratica, First Filipino Labor Union," *Philippine Social Sciences and Humanities Review* 47, 1–4 (January–December 1983): 170–1.
29. Quoted in José, *The Rise and Fall of Antonio Luna*, p. 105.
30. Ibid., p. 684.

31 Vicente Rafael, "Translation and Revenge: Castilian and the origins of Nationalism in the Philippines," in *The Places of History: regionalism revisited in Latin America*, ed. Doris Sommer (Durham, North Carolina; and London: Duke University Press, 1999), p. 235.
32 Taga-Ilog, "Impresiones Madrileñas de un Filipino," p. 687.
33 In late nineteenth-century Philippines, the term *filibusterismo* was used by the civil or religious authorities to denote any kind of actions or thoughts they deemed to be subversive or seditious. Rizal took the word as the title for his second novel.
34 Pratt, *Imperial Eyes*, p. 190.
35 Rizal, writing in Tagalog to Marcelo H. del Pilar to congratulate him on the excellent quality (*"mabuti sa dilang mabuti"*) of the issue of *La Solidaridad*, immediately recognized the kind of explosive effect Luna's article might have, and complimented it as a work truly well done (*"totoong magaling"*). José Rizal (Paris) to Marcelo H. del Pilar, 4 November 1889, in *Cartas*, vol. II, p. 447.
36 Mir Deas, "To Taga-Ilog," in *El Pueblo Soberano*, 9 November 1889 quoted in *La Solidaridad*, 1: 21 (15 December 1889): 530.
37 "Letters of the distinguished artist Juan Luna to the editor of *La Solidaridad* and *El Pueblo Soberano*," reprinted in *La Solidaridad* 1: 20 (30 November 1889): 489.
38 Cañamaque quoted in Mir Deas, "To Taga-Ilog," as cited, p. 529.
39 Antonio Luna (Madrid) to José Rizal, 16 November 1889, in *Cartas*, vol. II, p. 451.
40 Mariano Ponce (Barcelona) to José Rizal, 26 November 1889, in ibid., p. 457.
41 José Rizal (Paris) to Mariano Ponce, 29 November 1889, in ibid., p. 461.
42 José Rizal (Paris) to Mariano Ponce, 18 November 1889, in *Cartas*, vol. 2, p. 453.
43 For his revenge Mir Deas later denounced Filipino propagandista Mariano Ponce to the police, who arrested him for possessing clandestinely printed pamphlets that allegedly were part of a Filipino conspiracy to "loosen the bonds of union with the mother country." *El Imparcial*, as quoted in *La Patria*, 11 December 1889. Cited in Schumacher, *The Propaganda Movement*, p. 194.
44 Felix Roxas, "First Night in Barcelona," in *The World of Felix Roxas: anecdotes and reminiscences of a Manila newspaper columnist, 1926–36*, trans. Angel Estrada and Vicente del Carmen (Manila: Filipiniana Book Guild, 1970), p. 42.
45 Ibid.
46 For a brief, descriptive overview of the Filipino ilustrado community in Madrid and Barcelona, see Roxas, *The World of Felix Roxas*, pp. 49–54.
47 Austin Coates, *Rizal: Filipino nationalist and martyr* (Manila: Solidaridad Publishing House, 1992), p. 73.
48 Juan Luna (Bouzval-Houlgate, Normandy) to José Rizal, 24 July 1890, in *Cartas*, p. 571.
49 José Rizal to Marcelo del Pilar, in *Epistolario Pilar*, 1: 220–1. Cited in Schumacher, *The Propaganda Movement*, p. 236.
50 Vicente Rafael, "Nationalism, Imagery, and the Filipino Intelligentsia in the 19th Century," in *Discrepant Histories: translocal essays on Filipino cultures*, ed. Vicente Rafael (Pasig City: Anvil, 1995), p. 148.

51. Rizal to Plaridel, London, 3 March 1889, in *Cartas entre Rizal y sus colegas de la propaganda* (Manila: Comisión Nacional del Centenario de José Rizal, 1961), p. 321.
52. This preoccupation with French masculinity was also reflected in the mainstream press. See, for example, L. Hugonnet, *Bulletin de la Ligue nationale de l'education physique* 1 (1888), cited in Tamar Garb, *Bodies of Modernity: figure and flesh in fin-de-siècle France* (New York: Thames and Hudson, 1998), p. 222.
53. See for instance Rizal's entertaining description of the student's dormitory in his second novel *El Filibusterismo*, which mentions the various activities of the college boys including fencing practice: "Concerts of piano and violin of guitar and accordion, alternated with the repeated impact of canes from the fencing lessons. Gathered around a long wide table the Ateneo students write their compositions, solve their problems beside others who write to their sweethearts on rose-coloured embossed paper...." José Rizal, *El Filibusterismo*, trans. Ma. Soledad Lacson-Locsin, ed. Raul L. Locsin (Manila: Bookmark Publishing, 1997), p. 144.
54. Juan Luna (Paris) to José Rizal, 26 May 1890, in *Cartas*.
55. Juan Luna (Bouzval-Houlgate, Normandy) to José Rizal, 24 July 1890, in *Cartas*, p. 571.
56. Rafael, ed., *Discrepant Histories: translocal essays on Filipino cultures* (Pasig City: Anvil, 1995), p. 150.
57. See Schumacher, *The Propaganda Movement*, p.237; Rafael, "Nationalism," p. 149; and Norman Owen, "Masculinity and National Identity in the 19th Century Philippines," Paper delivered at the 6th International Philippine Studies Conference, University of the Philippines, Diliman, 10–14 July 2000.
58. Varios a Primer Consul (José Rizal), circa 1880, in T.M. Kalaw, ed., *Epistolario Rizalino*, vol. I (Manila: Bureau of Printing, 1930), p. 15.
59. Feliciano Cabrera (Manila) to José Rizal, 25 May 1881, in *Cartas entre Rizal y otras personas, 1877–1896* (Manila: Comisión Nacional del Centenario de José Rizal, 1961), p. 20.
60. José Rizal (Paris) to José María Basa, 21 September 1889, in *Cartas entre Rizal y sus colegas*.
61. José Rizal to Los Indios Bravos, 5 October 1889, in *Cartas entre Rizal y sus colegas*, p. 435.
62. José Rizal, (Madrid) to Paciano Mercado, 13 February 1883, in *One Hundred Letters*, p. 85.
63. Marcelo H.del Pilar, (Barcelona) to Ikazama (Pedro Icasiano), 13 March 1889, in *Epistolario de Marcelo H. del Pilar*, vol. 1 (Manila: Imprenta del Gobierno, 1955), p. 63.
64. Marcelo H. del Pilar (Barcelona) to Chanay, 20 March 1889, in *Epistolario de Marcelo H. del Pilar*, vol. 2 (Manila: Imprenta del Gobierno, 1955), p. 7.
65. Taga-Ilog (Antonio Luna), "Se Divierten," *La Solidaridad* 1: 19 (15 November 1889): 713–5.
66. Ibid., p. 713.
67. Ibid., p. 715.

68   Ibid., p. 715.
69   Ibid., p. 717.
70   I have here in mind Mary Louise Pratt's use of the term "contact zone" which invokes, in her words, "the social spaces where disparate cultures meet, clash and grapple with each other, often in highly asymmetrical relations of domination and subordination." Equally pertinent for the purposes of my argument is Pratt's use of the "contact perspective," which places an emphasis on how subjects are constituted in and by their relations to each other, treating the relations not in terms of separateness but of "co-presence, interaction and interlocking understandings." Pratt, *Imperial Eyes*, pp. 4–7.
71   Dominador Gómez quoted in José, *The Rise and Fall of Antonio Luna*, p. 104.
72   Taga-Ilog, "Sangre Torera," *La Solidaridad* 1: 21 (15 December 1889): 797.
73   Ibid., p. 795.
74   Taga-Ilog, "Se Divierten," p. 715.
75   José Rizal (Paris) to Ferdinand Blumentritt, 23 June 1889, in *Rizal-Blumentritt Correspondence* (Manila: José Rizal National Centennial Commission, 1961).
76   The article that caused so much ire amongst the Filipinos had appeared in the Barcelona newspaper *La Nación* (24 May 1889) and directly disparaged the Filipinos in Barcelona. It seems to have come to the attention of Rizal, then in Paris, through fellow *propagandista* Mariano Ponce (Barcelona) to José Rizal, 24 May 1889, in *Rizal's Correspondence with Fellow Reformists, 1882–1896* (Manila: National Heroes Commission, 1963), p. 338. On the anti-Semitism of the time, see for example Linda Nochlin, "Degas on the Dreyfus affair: a portrait of the artist as an anti-Semite," in *The Dreyfus Affair: art, truth, and justice*, ed. Norman L. Kleeblatt (Berkeley: University of California Press, 1998), pp. 103–11.
77   First published in 1885 (Barcelona; Imprenta de Jepus), this novel was subsequently reprinted as *Pacita, o la virtuosa Filipina: novella recreativa de costumbres orientales*, segunda edición (Barcelona: Herederos del V. Pla, 1892). She later wrote another novel, entitled *El Difamador, novella originale* (Barcelona: Tip. de F Altes, 1894).
78   Dominador Gómez quoted in Quijano de Manila (Nick Joaquin), "What signified the expatriates?" *Philippines Free Press* 62: 35 (30 August 1969): 42.
79   Taga-Ilog (Antonio Luna), "Sangre Torera," p. 798.
80   Ibid., p. 799.
81   Taga-Ilog, "Amorios I," *La Solidaridad* 2: 33 (15 June 1890): 398.
82   Ibid., p. 397.
83   Frantz Fanon, *Black Skin, White Masks* (New York: Grove, 1967), p. 63.
84   Diary of Consuelo Ortiga y Rey, September 1882–May 1884, in *Reminiscences and Travels of José Rizal* (Manila: National Historical Institute, 1977), p. 338.
85   Antonio Luna (Madrid), to José Rizal, 9 October 1889, in *Cartas entre Rizal sus colegas de la propaganda, 1882–1889* (Manila: Comisión Nacional del Centenario de José Rizal, 1961), p. 437.
86   Tomas Arejola to José Rizal, 9 February 1891, in *Cartas*, vol. 2, p. 631.
87   Antonio Luna (Madrid), to José Rizal, 27 December 1889, in *Cartas*, vol. II, p. 476.

88 Accounts of this duel are found in José, *The Rise and Fall of Antonio Luna;* Rafael Palma, *Biografía de Rizal* (Manila: Bureau of Printing, 1949); and Encarnación Alzona, *Galicano Apacible: Profile of a Filipino Patriot* (Manila: Heirs of Galicano Apacible, 1971).

89 Rafael Palma, *Biografía de Rizal*, cited in José, *The Rise and Fall of Antonio Luna*, p. 105.

90 Juna Luna (Bouzval-Houlgate, France), to José Rizal, 26 August 1890 in *Cartas*, vol. 2, p. 579.

91 Taga-Ilog, "Amorios II," *La Solidaridad* 2: 34 (30 June 1890): 439.

92 Taga-Ilog, "La maestra de mi pueblo," *La Solidaridad* (30 April 1890).

4

Friar Immorality and Female Religiosity in the Ilustrado Imagination

Eradicating the Human Poison

The Spanish friars in the Philippines tended towards a certain moral laxity. The merchant Robert MacMicking commented that in his native Scotland a minister found to be keeping a mistress would be instantly dismissed and expelled from the Kirk. Yet in the distant colony of Spain it was commonplace to find a priest "openly living in the *convento* with his mistress and natural children" or, just as frequently, to meet numerous half-caste young children being passed off as belonging to a family of some relative although there was "little doubt as to the priest himself being their father."[1] But what shocked MacMicking more than the bare facts of clerical concubinage and concupiscence was the degree to which such breaches of holy vows were tolerated and indulged by society at large. A priest's mistress, he observed, was accepted readily even in the most illustrious and respectable social circles; everyone "perfectly understood the relation in which the spiritual adviser of so large a population … stood to her," and she was viewed as a sort of "privileged housekeeper."[2]

In their youth the ilustrados also came to know that the unchaste friar was a regular fixture of colonial life. In a brief memoir of his student days, for example, Rizal casually recounted that he had shared his boarding house with several Spanish mestizo boys who were the "fruits of friar love affairs."[3] Felipe Calderón, a college student in the 1880s, later recalled fondly that many of his sweethearts had been the daughters of friars. Himself the grandson of a friar, he believed that a chaste friar was as rare as a "snowbird in summer."[4] Rizal's close friend Maximo Viola had the same perception, asserting that in his home province of Bulacan he did not know a single member of the religious orders who had not violated the vow of celibacy.[5]

But the ilustrados' direct first-hand experience of the friar presence in the colony had a much darker side. They belonged to the generation that came to maturity in the aftermath of the 1872 Cavite Mutiny, a period when suspected liberals and *filibusteros* were under the constant threat of persecution, arrest and deportation. Each of the principal propagandistas had some youthful bitter experience of such injustices, perpetrated either directly by the friars or, it was believed, at their instigation and behest. Marcelo del Pilar's elder brother, Toribio, had been one of the Filipino priests arrested and banished to the Marianas in 1872. Marcelo himself had been severely punished whilst still a young law student for questioning the high fee charged by a friar parish priest for a baptism at which he was a godfather. Such insolence cost Del Pilar 30 days inside a prison cell and may have delayed the completion of his law studies at the University of Santo Tomas.[6] In 1885, as mentioned in the previous chapter, the family of Juan and Antonio Luna fell under suspicion after their maternal uncle had led a short-lived uprising against Spanish rule in the provinces of Pangasinan and Nueva Ecija, and the 19-year-old Antonio had been briefly incarcerated in Manila's Bilibid prison.[7] Graciano López Jaena is reputed to have fallen foul of the friars whilst still a teenager in his native Iloilo.[8] When Rizal was but a boy of ten, his mother Doña Teodora was accused of assisting her cousin in poisoning his wife. Although the charge was unfounded, she was arrested upon the orders of the provincial governor, the *alcalde*, and forced to walk a distance of twenty miles to Santa Cruz, the provincial capital, where she was then imprisoned for over two years. The alcalde was regarded locally as "an ally and servitor of the friars."[9] The arrest of his mother, her long absence and her sufferings deeply disturbed the young Rizal, who later recalled his mother's humiliating march in his novel *Noli me tangere*, through the character of Sisa.[10]

These personal collisions with friar authority hardened the ilustrados in their belief that the friars were the chief obstacles to liberal ideas, to progress and modernity. Dispersed far wider than Spanish civil officials, and far less transient, the members of the four friar orders — Augustinians, Dominicans, Recollects and Franciscans — were the mainstay and rigging of colonial rule, hugely influential in Manila (except during a few brief interludes when liberal Governors-General were less accommodating to their entreaties) and veritable petty despots in the pueblos of the provinces. The religious orders and the Jesuits, the Archbishop of Manila proudly informed the Overseas Minister in Madrid in 1887, were "the great auxiliaries of the Administration (and) the main defenders of Spain in every corner of the archipelago ... thanks to them, the Nation, with scant military force, keeps these provinces in utmost peace and submission."[11]

This assessment, the propagandistas would have agreed, was no idle boast; it was the plain truth. Marcelo H. del Pilar classified the system of government in the Islands as a *"frailocracía."*[12] As the Archbishop's remarks suggests, the religious orders took attacks upon them to be attacks upon Spanish rule itself, and as separatist sentiments gathered strength this conviction became progressively more valid. Whether the propagandistas were writing from a reformist or separatist stance, however, the main thrust of their critique was consistent: the "monastic supremacy" was keeping the colony mired in backwardness, poverty and ignorance.[13] "The conflict between friars and Filipinos," wrote Graciano López Jaena, was not fundamentally about religion or nationalism. It was "a struggle for life, for survival; one side defending exploitation, the other fighting for their right to lead a modern life (*la vida de los modernos tiempos*), to lead a free life, to lead a democratic life."[14] "It is said that in certain towns in India," he wrote elsewhere:

> ... are found trees called *manzanillos* whose shade brings death to those who unfortunately seek shelter under their leafy but poisonous bowers.... The friars are the human *manzanillos*, more noxious than those trees, under whose "protective" shade Philippine towns are languishing and agonizing. Having pointed out the evil, the "tree" being known, it only remains for us all jointly to pull it up by the roots and thereby render an immense service to our Motherland the Philippines and to all humanity.[15]

Whilst the country stagnated, the propagandistas alleged, the friars got richer, flagrantly and spectacularly violating their vows of poverty. The religious Orders had acquired extensive landed estates, including several in the most fertile parts of central and southern Luzon, and were resented for land grabbing and for charging their lessees exorbitant rents. Individual parish priests, meanwhile, stood accused of enriching themselves through innumerable opportunistic rackets and ruses: the imposition of exorbitant fees from baptisms, weddings and burials; the constant extraction of donations from the faithful, with special generosity expected on feast days; the sale of candles at mass, prayers and the recitation of novenas; and the insistent peddling of a vast money-spinning assortment of religious paraphernalia — relics, icons, medallions, indulgences, rosaries, reliquaries, phials of holy water, scapulars, cords, shreds of blessed habits and other objects of dubious divine provenance and miraculous effect.

Another source of anti-friar resentment was their Spanish hauteur, their pride in "*la raza.*" Most friars had been born in the Peninsula, and many openly looked down upon the Filipinos as inferior. The Filipinos were a "very pusillanimous race," the Dominican Archbishop of Manila opined, a race whose spirits and "physical organisms" had been sapped by their paltry diet of "a little bit of rice and a small piece of fish."[16] It was true, Rizal countered acidly, that his compatriots were prone to back away from the least strife, but the blame for this pusillanimity rested not with what they ate but with the friars themselves, who from their pulpits and in their classrooms constantly insinuated attitudes of inferiority and subservience into the minds of the Filipinos. Every youth who was educated by the friars had to endure from five to ten years of daily preaching that lowered their dignity and self-respect, an "eternal, stubborn constant labor to bend the native's neck, to make him accept the yoke, to reduce him to the level of a beast."[17] In their school and college classrooms, the propagandistas knew at first hand, the friars excluded scientific, technical and practical subjects from the curriculum or at best taught them archaically and shambolically. They banned the works of countless European thinkers and novelists; scandalously resisted governmental decrees that required the Spanish language to be taught; and consistently suppressed awkward questions and free debate.

The principal charges against the friars, in sum, were that they impeded the nation's progress; sequestered its choicest lands; acted as small-town dictators; exploited for their own profit the gullibility of the faithful; and arrogantly belittled the Filipinos as lesser beings. Frequently perceived by the ilustrados as both "figures of denial but also of excess," as Rafael writes, the Spanish friars appeared to be "retrograde versions" of the young patriots, and easily figured as the "negative moment in the production of ilustrado consciousness."[18]

Friar immorality had only a secondary importance to the ilustrados' litany of complaints, and so too did issues of Catholic theology, as we shall see later.[19] But the scandalous lives of promiscuous priests, real and imagined, were nevertheless a recurrent and relished theme in the anti-friar campaign. Partly this was because allegations of friar degeneracy served as a useful, readily understood, means of highlighting the gulf between priestly profession and practice, of undermining the authority of the friars by exposing them as hypocrites. Partly, too, the friars could be portrayed a threat to young maidens, wives and the moral decency of society at large.[20] And not least importantly, of course, tales of friar concubinage, lechery and decadence provided excellent scope for satire, ribaldry and ridicule.

Sex and the Sacerdotes

In attacking friar immorality, as in other aspects of their campaign against the "monastic supremacy," the propagandistas signalled their affinity with the long tradition of liberal anti-clericalism in Europe. Tracing back any direct intellectual lineages, even were it possible, would be invidious here because it might mistakenly imply that clerical obscurantism and injustice in the Philippines were somehow less grievously real than in Europe, or that Filipino anti-clericalism was a convenient, imitative importation rather than an expression of genuine, deeply felt outrage. Some of the propagandistas, notably Rizal and López Jaena, read and were inspired by great Enlightenment thinkers like Voltaire and Diderot and by nineteenth century humanists like Renan, Sue, Hugo and Zola, but the extent of their acquaintance with the less cerebral, more salacious anti-clerical polemics of the time is simply not known.[21]

All that can be said is that the Filipinos could have readily found such materials in the European cities where they lived, and that their writings about immoral priests and compliant women devotees did sometimes echo European antecedents in content, form and tone. There was intense speculation and suspicion, for example, about what transpired between a priest and a woman when they were alone together in the quiet, dark privacy of the confessional. There was in some depictions of friar lasciviousness a deliberate eroticism, shading into pornography that spiced the anti-clerical message with titillation. And, not least, there was a strong vein of misogyny that followed European writers such as the

French historian Jules Michelet in attributing female religiosity to women's inherent "volatility," "credulity" and "excessive sensibility."[22]

Michelet's work *Du Prêtre, de la Femme, de la Famille* (1845) was particularly influential in setting the tone for attacks on what the historian Stephen Haliczer has termed the "moral solicitation" of women by their confessors.[23] Through the confessional, Michelet contended, priests exerted an inordinate sway over the minds of women and thereby undermined and diminished the influence of their husbands, in whom authority within the household and society at large should properly rest. The Church had used its hold on women to further its conservative political ends and to frustrate plans for liberal and social reforms. Michelet's denunciation was echoed in subsequent decades in works such as George Sand's *Mademoiselle de la Quintinie* (1863), Edmond de Goncourt's *Madame Gervaisais* (1869), Émile Zola's *La Conquête de Plassans* (1875) and the homoeopathist Adrien Péladan's *Le Vice Suprême* (1884).

Other anti-clerical works charged Catholic priests not just of "moral solicitation" but also of habitually using the confessional to solicit sexual favours. Earnest tracts, the popular press and ribald satires alike blasted priestly immorality, and tales of lascivious popes, cardinals, bishops, monks, friars and priests became a staple of nineteenth-century erotica and pornography. Even in England, where the local taste in pornography was mainly for fantasies of sadomasochistic flagellation, there was a ready audience for stories from continental Europe like *The Seducing Cardinal*, a highly lewd and irreverent fiction about the sexual exploits of Cardinal Carrafa, later Pope Paul III, as aided and abetted by Father Ignatius Loyola.[24] By the latter decades of the century, anti-clerical literature, some of it pornographic, was circulating briskly even in Madrid and Barcelona.[25] The pages of *El Motín*, a satirical anarchist weekly, were liberally sprinkled with cartoons picturing lascivious priests, their pliant female lovers and illegitimate progeny. The writer Eduardo López Bago denounced clerical celibacy as an unnatural, soul-destroying human impossibility in his novels *El cura, caso de incesto* (1889) and *El confesionario (satriasis)* (1890).[26]

Respectable husbands should be on guard, some anti-clerical writers warned, and should if possible dissuade their wives from attending confession because of the sexual dangers to which they might fall prey. The manuals used to assist the confessor's relentlessly probing interrogations and to train seminarians in taking confession, they argued, were so lurid and detailed in their descriptions of sexual transgressions as to be veritable "pornographic codes."[27] The seminarians who read them, the anti-clericals worried, were liable to become morally corrupted before they were ordained, and even trained confessors might well be encouraged to engage with their female penitents in all manner of lewdness and sexual perversity.[28] In England, the vigorously anti-clerical Protestant Association circulated pamphlets exposing the "errors of Romanism" to a laity considered ignorant of the revolting contents of confession manuals. One anonymous mid-century work assembled selected extracts, from the manuals then in use, sometimes twisting their context, and annotated the salacious passages with a commentary bursting with scorn and disgust. "Often happens??" the compiler splutters in response to a paragraph about the frequency of seminal spills during "unnatural" sexual acts. "How did he know? There is nothing done, it appears, that can escape the knowledge of a priest."[29]

Anti-clericals in the Philippines made the same dark conjectures and aspersions about what transpired between priest and female penitent in the confessional. The Augustinian friar in the town of Lipa, Batangas, it was alleged, summoned all the young and unmarried women to church every Lent in order to solicit them obscenely in the confessional "through words and manipulations." It was convenient for this "corrupter of youth," it was noted, that the confessional booth was "cornered and buried in the darkest part of the Church," providing perfect privacy for his lewd words and lascivious touches.[30] Other friars, it was gossiped, went so far as to admit the unfair advantage they had over laymen "in the conquest of good looking women, as they relied on the confessional and through it became apprised of facts which made easy the attack, assault, and taking of the stronghold."[31] Marcelo H. del Pilar thought that moral decency was threatened not just by the confessional but also by the ritual of communion. "In our society," he wrote with regret, "there are hundreds of women who approach the sacred communion table every Sunday." "This affects your honour," he cautioned the "virgins of Bulacan," because "the men in charge of the popular conscience" regard a woman's honor "with deplorable indifference."[32]

Rizal's writings, especially his two iconoclastic novels *Noli me tangere* and *El Filibusterismo*, scathingly attacked virtually every aspect of Catholicism as taught and practised by the friars in the Philippines, from catechism classes to convents, from sermon styles to the veneration of images and relics, from the rituals of worship, communion and confession to education in the religious schools and colleges. Banned, and in some towns publicly burned, the *Noli* was famously declared by the Augustinian chairman of the Comisión Permanente de Censura as a "libellous and defamatory" work that deserved the most "acrimonious and severe censure and reprobation, official as well as private, by every honourable person."³³ *El Filibusterismo* suffered similar censure.

In the *Noli*, the degeneracy and venality of Catholicism in the Philippines is personified in the characters of sexually opportunistic and depraved friars. Clerical sexuality, Rizal makes it clear, threatened all that a respectable, civilized bourgeois life held dear — the authority of husband and father, marital life, the family and country. Thus, within the melodrama of the *Noli* lies the damning message that the consequences of entrusting the moral and spiritual guidance of women to priests are treachery, corruption, vice and death. Rizal relates, for example, the story of Doña Pia Alba, a wealthy married woman who is desperate to bear a child. After fruitlessly invoking numerous saints and the Virgin in order to conceive, Doña Pia turns for comfort or advice to her confessor, the Franciscan parish priest Padre Damaso. She finds him obliging, and soon becomes pregnant.³⁴ But she is then filled with remorse, as she later admits in a letter, at carrying a priest's child. She curses it, and desires its death. Together, she and the friar attempt to abort the foetus using drugs, but fail.³⁵

Doña Pia Alba pays for her transgressions by dying of puerperal fever after giving birth to the child she had longed for. The product of the illicit union, María Clara, naturally bears no physical resemblance to her proud and doting putative father, Capitan Tiago, who remains none the wiser.³⁶ Like her mother, María Clara has a tragic destiny and is denied the pleasures of marriage to her childhood sweetheart due to the meddling of another Franciscan friar, Padre Salvi. Sexual entanglements with priests and their consequences brought lasting sorrow in families with the past transgressions of mothers — like Gustave Flaubert's wilful Madame Bovary and her own ill-fated child — being inherited by daughters whose futures became accursed by suffering and tragedy. Bent on preventing her marriage to Ibarra, her childhood sweetheart, the sadistically cruel and politically scheming Padre Salvi seizes the opportunity presented by a private bedside confession to reveal to María Clara her true paternity. Resorting to blackmail, Salvi forbids María

Clara's love for the patriot Ibarra by threatening to make public her paternity and thus cause a great scandal if she does not break off her engagement.[37]

Padre Salvi's obsessive pursuit of Padre Damaso's illegitimate daughter, the chaste and inaccessible María Clara, is fired by base lust. Stalking her throughout the novel, Salvi is a disturbing, lecherous, spying presence. Hinting at the horror in store for women who become the target of a friar's sexual fantasies, Rizal describes Padre Salvi's sexual voyeurism in the salacious tone of anti-clerical erotica: "His sunken eyes glistening at the sight of her beautifully moulded white arms, the graceful neck ending in a suggestion of bosom ... aroused strange sensations and feelings in his impoverished, starved being and made him dream of new visions in his fevered mind."[38] Salvi's lewd imaginings foretell María Clara's tragic fate: she enters the Santa Clara convent as a nun but finds neither sanctity nor peace. Knowing where she is, Padre Salvi insinuates himself into an important position at the nunnery and, Rizal hints, sexually abuses her.[39] Although María Clara remains sexually unobtainable to the priest until the novel's denouement, Padre Salvi seemingly has a reputation for venting his sexual frustration on other female bodies. When blessing attractive young girls, it is noticed, he habitually lets his hand "accidentally" slip down from nose to breast.[40] During a religious procession in the town, a baby with a striking physical resemblance to the Padre spots him in the crowd and happily cries out "Pa ... pa!, papa!, papa!" as if in recognition. Padre Salvi blushes deeply and the amused onlookers exchange a flurry of malicious winks and nudges.[41]

The mestizo offspring and descendants who sprang from sexual liaisons between friars and native women provoked a deep ambivalence in the anti-clerical propagandist imagination. Graciano López Jaena acerbically remarked that the mestizos were a "contraband caste superabundant in the Philippines."[42] Nevertheless, the mestizos were also admired. Prominent in such charged representations as Rizal's María Clara, or the abandoned lovers populating Antonio Luna's *Impresiónes*, or Pepay, the female character in López Jaena's didactic vignette "Entre Kastila y Filipina," the mixed-blood mestiza represented a cocktail of inherited traits and physical attributes that the propagandistas clearly found highly attractive and alluring. "They are always favoured by nature, lovely and graceful," wrote López Jaena, "with the alabaster skin of the father (and the) fascinating dreamy eyes of the mother ... a haughty and vain temperament inherited from the father; sweet, gentle and pleasant speech, a legacy of the mother."[43] The idealization of the racially ambiguous mestiza thus signified a deep-seated contradiction in propagandist rhetoric. The mestiza was desirable, but her beauty had its source partially in the supposed moral, intellectual, and physical attributes of the propagandistas' main target of attack, the Spanish colonial male religious.[44]

In his oft-cited but rarely examined satirical sketch "Fray Botod" — literally "Friar Big Belly" — López Jaena vividly portrays a Spanish cleric so utterly dissipated and depraved that he exists solely to satisfy his carnal appetites. His comical likeness to a "seal without a moustache" belies a noxious and brutal personality: he is physically violent to Filipinos, a glutton, a liar, a cheat and a "worse usurer than a Jewish money-lender."[45] Although a foundling in his native Aragon, and raised by a rustic muleteer, he now enjoys the respect and authority of a king, such is the deference that Filipinos accord to priests. In Fray Botod's room inside the priests' convento the walls are hung with massive, "more or less obscene" paintings of Biblical and religious scenes that all feature nude or semi-nude young women — among them a Susannah being seduced by the Elders, David's concubines being raped by Absalom, and the stripped, captive and forlorn Christian virgins of the Filipino artist Felix Hidalgo.[46] Naked angels and Igorot fertility idols also decorate the room, and amongst the devotional books lying on his bedside table are scattered pornographic *libritos*.[47]

In this room, where the air hangs heavy with the sensuous fragrance of spices, the fat friar enjoys his regular afternoon siesta. Sated by a huge lunch and sprayed with perfume, he wallows amidst tasselled silk covers and luxurious pillows spread on a beautiful bed of carved *kamagong* wood, his every whim indulged by a bevy of nubile native girls whom López Jaena calls "*canding-canding*." Fray Botod's pretence is that he is educating the girls and teaching them the catechism, writes López Jaena, but his true intent is just sensual pleasure. As he reclines in drowsy comfort the *canding-canding* massage, caress, and groom him, tickle his blubbery stomach and whisper in his ear fantastic tales of the underworld, enchantments, witches and fairies. They also please him in other ways "that I know, but will not say" the narrator archly confides.[48]

López Jaena's choice of the term *canding-canding* was itself deliberately salacious. In Spanish, the narrator explains, the term means "young she goats." Left unexplained is the meaning that López Jaena intends to bring instantly to the minds of his Filipino readers via the direct Tagalog homophone *kandeng-kandeng*, which evokes not frolicking young goats but the far more sexually explicit image of dog bitches or other female animals on heat. The humor of López Jaena's word play hinges upon the depiction of female lasciviousness as highly derogatory. In an even bawdier double entendre, López Jaena describes the bell over the convento door as ringing with the sound *"Tilin! Tilin! Tilin!"* Tagalog speakers, again, would immediately recognize that the Spanish word for the tinkle of a bell — *tilin* — is precisely the same as the Tagalog word for the clitoris.[49]

Associating the convento doorway with female genitalia or representing excitable young women as bitches on heat are narrative devices obviously intended to titillate and amuse. But López Jaena's pejorative depiction of women in "Fray Botod," his most vicious attack on clerical dissipation, illustrates how he regarded women's sexuality as being inextricably linked with the perpetuation of friar power. Referring extensively to *Viaje al pais de las bayaderas*, a bestselling Orientalist traveller's tale by the French writer Louis Jacolliot,[50] López Jaena compares Fray Botod's canding-canding to the *bayaderas*, erotic dancers in Hindu temples who sexually gratified their priestly masters, the Brahmins. Both sets of young women, in López Jaena's view, were no better than prostitutes; their "miserable role ... among priests of different religions" was identical.[51] López Jaena's long and indulgent digressions on the bayaderas recount, in lavish detail, the sexually provocative performance of the dancers and the drug-enhanced dream atmosphere of a fictive eastern sensuality that made Jacolliot's book a sensation. Conjuring a seductive *mise en scène* of exoticism and dusky erotic mystery, López Jaena leads his readers into a mythical, sexually transgressive world of strange peoples dedicated to uninhibited sensual pleasures and of lustful, submissive women — motifs that lie at the very heart of traditional Orientalist sexual fantasies represented in any number of Victorian literary accounts of erotic experience.[52] López Jaena has in mind as his readers voyeuristic men who, like Jacolliot's western male travelers, will relish the erotic dances of the bayaderas, vicariously penetrating a culture of prohibited sexual pleasures and mysteries. Attended by discreet servants, the travelers lounge on cushions in a languorous fug of smoke, their privileged eyes feasting on a delirious spectacle of gyrating female bodies that will later satisfy the excitements they arouse.[53]

López Jaena's sexual insinuations and his long, distracting excursion into the erotic world of the *bayaderas* cast doubt on the sincerity of his outraged protestations at the plight of young native women pressed into sexual service by immoral priests. His salaciousness throws into question the genuineness of his professed indignation at the unwholesome life led by the *canding-canding*, an iniquitous fate that he acknowledges could drive women to insanity. His sympathy seems feigned, his protest a thin veil for his more prurient preoccupations and his lingering fascination with the eroticized corporeality of Jacolliot's temple dancers. More revealingly, his titillation shows López Jaena's inclination to think of priest's concubines less as victims and more as sexually lubricious women who are willing, complicit and culpable.

The Ignorance of the Masses

The handmaiden to clerical oppression, Rizal believed, was ignorance. Endeavoring to explain Filipino religiosity in an essay written in 1884,[54] he set his tone with a quotation from César Cantú's *Historia Universal*: "The common man ... saw mystery in everything; and because of his ignorance, he deceived either himself or encouraged the impostures of others."[55] The fervent piety of the Filipino masses, Rizal elaborated, was rooted not in deep understanding, reflection and knowledge but in ignorance and paganism. The essence of Filipino religiosity could be distilled as superstition, indoctrination and blind acceptance, rooted in a desperate desire to atone for guilt and to placate a deity whom the priests portrayed as vengeful and merciless.[56] The only reading matter approved for the faithful was devotional literature and the metrical romances known as *awit*, which Rizal saw as opiates that dulled the people's minds and perpetuated their enslavement.[57]

Rizal's argument was driven by his own ideal of Christian religiosity as a reasoned and reflective faithfulness and by his elitist, severely unforgiving opinion of the Filipino lower classes.[58] Catholicism, he wrote, professed many beliefs and aspirations that were "sublime," but in the Philippines the friars had debased its "holy doctrine." The ignorant and unthinking masses, meanwhile, to his patrician eyes, also merited a share of the blame for the degeneration of the faith into dogmatism, ritual and superstition because they never directly questioned friar teachings.[59] It never occurred to anyone, he regretted, "to inquire about the origin of God or His purpose."[60] Ordinary Filipinos were simple and gullible in their religiosity, unable to distinguish between truth and deception. Novenas and prayers were parroted in Latin or Spanish, obsessively recited by sleepy or distracted minds that understood little of their meaning.

Rizal conceded that the blame for the mental indolence of the masses rested largely with friars and the dire education system. But the masses themselves, he evidently believed, were also culpable, for they suffered from an acute inability to think independently and rationally. Quite often, he lamented, "their intelligence cannot grasp the true meaning of Christian doctrines" and so "they kneel down instead of inquiring and examining their beliefs."[61] It was no wonder, he reflected, that in civilized countries the common man was "an object of anxiety."[62]

Rizal later interwove his critique of Filipino religiosity into the melodramatic plot of his great patriotic novel, *Noli me tangere*. But the *Noli* would have been inaccessible to most Filipinos even had it been permitted to circulate freely, because it was written in Spanish, a language that most Filipinos had difficulty in reading, and published as a book whose cost would have been prohibitive. Taking the anti-clerical message directly to the *pobres y ignorantes* was left to other propagandistas who had a keener grasp of the vernacular idiom, the most notable of whom was Marcelo H. del Pilar, a lawyer from Bulacan. Del Pilar was one of the very few leading propagandistas who became well-known as an anti-clerical and reformist campaigner in the Philippines, before departing for Spain. Throughout the 1880s, until he pre-empted arrest by embarking for Barcelona in late 1888, he worked indefatigably to advance the liberal cause in Manila and his home province.[63] Writing under various pseudonyms, he undermined the vitriolic pamphleteering of priests with his own broadsides satirizing and parodying their messages[64] and vigorously defended Rizal's *Noli* against the fulminations of the Comité Permanente de Censura.[65]

Under the protection and patronage of a carefully nurtured network of liberal Spanish officials, Del Pilar worked for the election of *gobernadorcillos*, town mayors, in Bulacan who were sympathetic to the anti-friar cause. He organized public protests and demonstrations that directly confronted the authority of the friars or humiliated them.[66] One such event was the great anti-friar manifestation held in Manila in early March 1888, which presented a petition to the Governor General calling for the expulsion of the friars from the Philippines. The petition, inevitably, was disregarded, but the protest naturally made the friars and their allies even more anxious about the spreading liberal contagion. Receiving word a few months later that he was about to be arrested and deported, Del Pilar slipped quickly out of the Philippines to join the campaign in Spain.[67]

Surprisingly, Rizal's reaction to the arrival of his fellow nationalist in Europe was distinctly frosty. "To serve our country," he wrote:

> there is nothing like staying in it. It is there that we have to educate the people.... It is all right for young men to come here to study, but those who have already finished their studies ought to return and live there. Marcelo H. del Pilar has already finished his studies and he did not need to come to Europe.[68]

Rizal's antipathy is puzzling. He himself had felt obliged to curtail a visit back home for fear of arrest less than a year previously, and he too, aged 27 when he wrote this letter, had at last finished his studies. Already, perhaps, Rizal could foresee the tensions that would develop between them in Europe, springing in part from a straightforward clash of two forceful personalities but also from their differing approaches to the nationalist campaign. Del Pilar was much more a pragmatist and natural politician than the scholarly, idealist Rizal. He was an organizer, network builder and plotter, and was much more at ease than Rizal with the Tagalog language, vernacular idioms and the everyday lives of ordinary folk. His abilities and sensibilities enabled him to bridge the gulf between the ilustrado propagandistas and the common *tao* (people). Mariano Ponce later recalled that as an orator, Del Pilar was able to adjust his words and the cadences of his voice "according to the intelligence, culture and psychological susceptibility of his audience."[69] It was this ability to speak with people from diverse backgrounds that made Del Pilar a popular figure not only among students and professionals in the city but at gatherings in the rural towns of Bulacan — baptisms, weddings, town fiestas and fight days at the cockpits. He played the violin, piano and flute charmingly, and was renowned too as a troubadour with a special talent for *harana*, the romantic serenades sung by young men when courting eligible *dalagas*.

Del Pilar was able to draw on his deep acquaintance with traditional poetry and song, on native idioms and on the Christian tropes found in devotional texts such as the *Pasyon* to make the anti-clerical and patriotic message readily accessible to the Tagalog masses. "He only needed to take over and renovate what was already available," Bienvenido Lumbera notes in a commentary on the six poems by Del Pilar to have survived:

> This was what the missionaries did when they came in the sixteenth century and were in need of a bridge by which to reach the natives. Del Pilar's insight was to turn the missionary tactics against the friars — to use old forms to propagate new attitudes.[70]

At the center of Del Pilar's didactic style were common familial and gendered motifs. The image of a mother's lament about her daughter, for example, was powerfully employed by Del Pilar in his poem "*Sagot nang España sa hibik nang Filipinas*" to evoke the soured colonial relationship between Filipinas and Spain.[71]

Far more shocking were Del Pilar's parodies of Catholic prayers, reworkings that in the context of nineteenth-century Filipino religious life would have been seen as irreverent in the extreme. Del Pilar's versions of church catechism are burlesque performances in sacrilegious parody — anarchic, comic and profane.

In "*Dasalan at Toksohan*" ("Prayers and Provocations"), Del Pilar attacked clerical hypocrisy and greed firstly by scandalously mimicking such holy orisons as the Lord's Prayer, the Sign of the Cross, the Hail Mary and the Act of Contrition and then by mimicking the catechism with a series of questions and answers on the character of the friar.[72] The catechism, in Del Pilar's view, not only dulled the mind and instilled deference, but also inculcated in the native mind, through insidious mistranslations, the notion that the friars possessed an innate holiness, even a semi-divinity.[73] Del Pilar's subversive Tagalog rendition conveyed a more modest evaluation of their qualities.

The friar's purported obsession with money and sex, so common in the Filipino and European liberal anti-clerical imagination, also appeared prominently in Del Pilar's irreverent renderings. In "*Ang Tanda*," Del Pilar wittily substitutes profanities for key phrases in the prayer uttered by Catholic penitents while making the sign of the cross. Praying for the deliverance of "our carcasses" from "our Lord the Friar," the penitent concludes not in the name of the holy triumvirate — Father, Son and Holy Spirit — but in the name of *salapi* (money); *maputing binte* (a woman's white thighs); and *espiritong bughaw* (the spirit of evil).[74]

Women and riches are the twin idols of the friars, who believe they should be offered both as a matter of divine right. In a corruption of the Ave María, the word *"baria"* (cash) is substituted for the holy name of the Virgin: "Hail Baria, the coffers of the friar overflow with thee ... blessed art thou among things, and blessed is the coffer he fills with thee."[75] In *"Ang mga utos ng fraile"* ("The Commandments of the Friar"), Del Pilar somewhat predictably parodies the Ten Commandments in order to lampoon the sexual relationships of friars and their jealous possessiveness of women. "Do not covet [the friar's] wife," his earthy Commandments stipulate, "nor should she be secretly shared or stolen." The friar must, on the other hand, be permitted to fornicate at will with any other man's wife.[76] If one was stupid enough to disobey the friar's commands, Del Pilar continued ironically, one could expect the "blessings" of enforced servitude to the Church, and the sexual seduction and abuse of one's child.[77] It is significant that in his liturgically styled attacks, Del Pilar tightly linked women and their bodies to money — both were commodities, objects of desire to be possessed by priests. To satisfy the corrupt conventions of friar concubinage, women, more specifically a man's wife or daughter, were seen as having to be in circulation, like money, for the disposal and pleasure of priests.

In the face of friar immorality and abuse, where jail or deportation awaited those who dared to resist the friar's will, Del Pilar uses his profane prayers to incite anger. In his version of *"Pagsisisi"* ("Repentance"), a prayer murmured repetitively by the Catholic faithful in its standard form, Del Pilar addresses not God but the friar, and replaces humble contrition and atonement with indignant outrage: "Thou art my executioner, my most hated Lord and enemy.... I will shun thee ... and I hope some day I will be able to give thee a sound thrashing for the scandalous manner in which you cheat me and in your traffickings of the Cross."[78] His version of the "Lord's Prayer," likewise addressed to the friar, is equally bitter and violent, his sentences quivering with wrath:

> Our stepfather, who art in the convent; cursed be thy name; thy greed depart, thy windpipe be slit on earth as it is in heaven. Return to us this day our daily bread; and make us laugh with thy horse laugh, as you laugh when you fleece us. And lead us not into temptation but deliver us from thy evil tongue. Amen.[79]

Substituting respect and obedience for angry curses, Del Pilar's challenges to the friars were deliberately shocking, and their formulation as bogus prayers would have struck many Filipinos as blasphemous. Yet in a sense they told ordinary folk nothing they did not already know, for they described experiences of friar immorality and racketeering that were an everyday reality. Articulated in an idiom and within a frame of reference readily familiar to the uneducated masses, they carried the messages that friar immorality should no longer be tolerated, and that friar racketeering should no longer be indulged. The friars stood accused not only as corrupt petty tyrants, as racist, lascivious and venal, but also as men who dishonored the God they pretended to serve. Del Pilar's prayers, distorted but not unrecognizable, in some cases the conscious antithesis of God's words, sought to expose to the masses a *frailocracia* that had become the antithesis of God's calling.

Sleeping with the Enemy: The Culpability of Women

Whilst the propagandistas expressed dismay about the misguided religiosity of Catholic Filipinos as a generality, their particular censure was reserved for women. López Jaena was unequivocal:

> You, woman, into what abysses of poverty have you plunged the Filipino people, a rich people, with your superstitions and fanaticism, with your processions and novenas, with your masses and rosaries! ... Through the ministry of your fanaticism, you are the funeral carriage that carries the corpse of the Philippines to the tomb of poverty, the corpse that is devoured voraciously by filthy worms, the Jesuits and the friars, until not a bone remains for them to pick.[80]

López Jaena and Rizal directed a special rebuke at rich Catholic women, whose generous contributions did so much to keep the Church and friars financially buoyant. The money prodigally thrown by devout women into Church coffers, insisted López Jaena, would be far better spent on the establishment of schools, in which could be taught the "true science and useful knowledge" that the Spanish friars were doing their utmost to suppress. The misplaced philanthropy of wealthy women was swindling the country out of a prosperous and civilized present and future. Rizal in his essay on Filipino religiosity and Del Pilar in his *Dasalan at Toksohan* nevertheless also inculpated ordinary non-elite women for pandering to the friars.

But the belief that women were more susceptible to "superstition and fanaticism" than men, and more obsessive in their religious observances, echoed the refrain of European anti-clerical writers like Jules Michelet, and shaded into the same misogyny. Rizal, like López Jaena, could not disguise the sheer distaste he felt at such feminine foolishness. He characterized the daily habits and compulsions of religious women — perpetual praying, kneeling, kissing the hand of the priest, and extravagant almsgiving to the Church — as mere mindless chatter, calloused knees, a badly chafed nose and penury.[81] Just writing down the long litany of women's religious vices exhausted and irritated him so much, he complained, that the effort had given him a pain in his hand.[82] Del Pilar also bemoaned the tendency of Filipino women to believe that piety and virtue could be measured by the time spent in reciting prayers and striking the breast. Such blank-headed religiosity, he wrote bluntly, amounted to a "blot upon the honor" of mothers, sisters and all society.[83]

Countries in which women were not enslaved by religious fanaticism but rather sought knowledge, the propagandistas insisted, enjoyed prosperity and progress. "Fanatical peoples live submerged in deplorable backwardness," wrote López Jaena:

> Morocco, Egypt, Turkey, Russia, China, the interior of India, Zululand, and our own Philippines are incontrovertible proofs of this assertion. Enamored of the past, they lag behind.... [France, England and their colonies, meanwhile, and North America] are ahead of the rest of the world in civilization, because in those countries ... woman is free from prejudices, fanaticism and ardently seeks education and enlightenment. Her cult is work; her priest is her loving husband; her religion is love of family, humanity; and her holy devotion is supervising the education of her children, who are the hope of the country.[84]

Spain, of course, was omitted from López Jaena's list of the countries that were progressing. There too the women, though beautiful, suffered from the same sad defects and vices, and "hence the mother country, Spain, is in decadent state."[85] Rizal drew the same sweeping, simplistic correlation between female religiosity and national advancement in his letter to the young women of Malolos. Asia remained enslaved, he advised, because its women were blinded and chained by religion. In contrast "Europe and America are powerful," because there the women are "learned" ("*marunong*"), possess an "enlightened mind" ("*dilat ang isip*") and "inner strength" ("*malakas ang loob*"). Unlike the enlightened bourgeois women of Europe, Filipinas were intellectually atrophied, their minds dulled by daily religious recitation. "We are aware of all this," Rizal writes with his usual air of superiority: "That is why we are putting our best effort into making sure that the light shining over your fellow women here in Europe reaches you ... though thick clouds envelop our country, we will force the sun's rays to penetrate."[86]

The reasons for women's peculiar piety were a puzzle to the propagandistas. How to explain such a preposterous zealousness and such a close, often emotionally intimate association with the priests? López Jaena speculated only partly in jest that the cause might be a form of psychological bewitchment, the result of hypnotism and suggestion, for otherwise women would recognize that the religion of the friars and Jesuits in fact disparaged them, that there were even "saints who insult women in their homilies and writings."[87] Rizal pondered whether the answer might partly lie in the collective psyche of Filipino women, whose "sweet disposition, lovely personality, gentle manners and modest ways" seemed distressingly to be ineluctably allied to an "absolute deference and obedience to every word, request and order from those who call themselves fathers of the soul."[88] Maybe, he reflected, it was because Filipinas possessed such "immense goodness (and) humility." But more straightforwardly, he thought, the devotion of Filipinas to their priests could be attributed mainly to "ignorance."[89]

Whatever its causes, the blind fanaticism of women was seen as posing a lethal threat to the propagandistas' aspiration that the Philippines should become a modern nation. In an immediate, practical sense, it could even imperil the lives and liberty of the patriots who were laboring to realize that aspiration. Rizal relates in the *Noli* how a woman making her confession to the villainous Padre Salvi divulges the existence of some kind of patriotic conspiracy. The Franciscan friar then breaks the secrecy of the confessional and alerts the Guardia Civil, who then set off to hunt down all the suspected troublemakers and agitators in the locality. The woman's loose tongue and the priest's fear of filibusterism result in the death of the patriotic peasant Elias and the flight into exile of the bourgeois hero Crisostomo Ibarra.[90] The lesson that Rizal wants his readers to draw here, it seems, echoes Jules Michelet's judgment on the French Revolution — that the weakness of unreconstructed, traditionally Catholic women for confessions and priestly counsels made them a dangerous liability to the patriotic and liberal cause.[91]

Female fanaticism was also believed to threaten the institution the propagandistas saw as the bedrock of the modern nation, the patriarchal bourgeois family. Women in countries like England, France and Germany were to be emulated because they had rejected backward religiosity and embraced modern education and individual freedom of thought. They no longer gave their loyalty and devotion to Catholic priests but to where it more properly belonged, to their husbands, families and nation. Repeatedly, the propagandistas stressed how female religious fanaticism abetted and bolstered friar power and concomitantly disrupted and undermined the bourgeois husband, conjugal life, domestic harmony and the moral fabric of society.[92] The rightful authority of the Filipino paterfamilias, López Jaena and Rizal both feared, was liable simply to pass unrecognised by women who were in constant thrall to the men of the Church. Everything that was good and decent was thereby imperilled. Here it is worth quoting at length López Jaena's feelings of dread at a world turned upside down by female religiosity:

> The woman who is devout ... converts the church into a home: morning, afternoon and evening she will be found there kneeling down; in the morning for the Mass, in the afternoon for the novena, in the evening for the prayer for the souls. For her, work is sin; she neglects her duties, her household chores, for prayers; she neglects the education of children for her prayers; she turns away in disgust from the caresses, the love of her affectionate husband for hysterical religious transports; in a word, the church is her dwelling place, the Jesuits and the friars are her family.... From these pernicious habits arise disorder, uneasiness, discord, continuous quarrels in the home; lacking affection the husband becomes depraved, the children ... develop bad habits ... transforming the peace at home into the most frightful confusion, giving rise to great scandals, most unheard of infamy, dishonor.[93]

Marcelo H. del Pilar worried in *Dasalan at Toksohan* that women needed to be protected as objects of desire. Commenting on the motivations of contemporary anti-Catholic polemics in Europe, the French writer Jean Faury discerned a virulent strain of "anti-clerical machismo," a male jealousy and resentfulness that a particular group of other men — priests — should influence and attract women in so powerful a way.[94] In the Philippines the resentment that fuelled this "anti-clerical machismo" would surely be magnified by race, because the men perceived to be abusing their religious office were foreigners.

Anarchy, unhappiness, scandal and dishonor were the bitter fruits society could expect to reap from the religiosity of women.[95] Rizal, in his letter to the Malolos women, echoes López Jaena's concerns in an equally evangelical tone. Foremost in his mind is the damage done to the sons of bourgeois families by the misplaced loyalties of their mothers. Every mother had a duty to bequeath her wisdom to her sons, and yet, Rizal asks:

> what kind of offspring (*supling*) comes from a woman whose only virtue is whispering prayers, whose learning is derived from the *awit*, novena and miracles that stupefy people, who have no other forms of amusements but [religious] petitions or go to the confessional to confess the same sins over again? What kind of sons will she have other than sacristans, errand boys of the curate, or devotees of cockfighting?[96]

Rizal is directing these rhetorical questions to a group of young elite women who had the intelligence, resourcefulness, and the money to establish a school in which they could learn Spanish. Obstructed by the Spanish parish priest, an Augustinian, they appealed to the governor who ruled in their favor.[97] The propagandistas were quick to recognize their courage. Rizal and his fellow nationalists, it is clear, rejoiced at the Malolos women's defiance of the local friar, and cherished the hope that others might follow their example. But for the moment, they recognized, such initiative and determination was remarkable and rare amongst their female compatriots. The generality of Filipino women, they remained convinced, rich and poor alike, were still ignorantly, fanatically and obsequiously attached to a medieval, superstition-ridden Church and its corrupt, hypocritical masters. The Filipina, in Rizal's mind, was already blessed with prudence, a sweet disposition and an "excess of goodness," but lacked "a strong heart," a "dignified character" ("*tibay ng puso, taas ng loob*") and above all a "free mind" — all the qualities denied to her by Spaniards and friars who claimed her to be ignorant, fallen and weak.[98] He and his fellow propagandistas regarded the degradation of Filipinas as a consequence of their meekness and blind obedience to friar authority, their inexplicable devotion to a corrupt and cruel Church.

The propagandistas were likewise united in the belief that the salvation of women, and hence of the country, lay in education and enlightenment. It is important to bear in mind, however, that the propagandistas' wish to impress upon their female compatriots the value of education flows along two tributaries. Firstly, it stemmed from their conviction that they were morally superior to the friars whose authority they were struggling to displace; and secondly from their fear that the feminine nature of Filipinas and their clarity of vision, especially with regard to their true role and duties to their children and society, had become muddied and blurred by their devotion to religion and obedience to the will of the friar parish priest. López Jaena pleaded with his female compatriots to distance themselves from the friars, Jesuits and the Church: "Keep away from fanaticism, winsome compatriots, if you wish the Philippines to advance and progress."[99]

The common thinking of the propagandistas on the importance of educating women may be seen in a letter sent by Del Pilar to his cousin Joséfa Gatmaytan in March 1889, a letter he asked her to share with other women in their hometown of Bulacan. Here he exhorts the women in Bulacan to follow the example of their *coprovincianas* in Malolos, a small town just a few miles away. His letter, he hoped, would encourage them likewise to aspire to learn Spanish and, if necessary, to defy the local Augustinian friar. "I cannot but ask myself," he reflected, "why should a pueblo like Bulacan ... be inferior to the pueblo of Malolos?" It might be true that Bulacan was not as wealthy or fashionable as Malolos, but surely, he reasoned, its women were not inferior "in the aspiration towards knowledge, in the efforts of intellect."[100]

"The young women of today," Del Pilar continued, "single or married, will be the mothers of tomorrow; they must store up knowledge, not only for themselves, but in order to avoid giving their descendants a right to speak ill of the past." López Jaena looked forward more concretely to the establishment of schools run "in accordance with reason and virtue," hospitals that taught the "true science of health," agricultural technology and centers of industry, goals that could be achieved if wealthy women would only redirect their fortunes away from the friars' coffers.[101] The propagandistas felt they had a patriotic duty to inculcate in the Filipina a love for study rather than prayer, reason and intelligence rather than blind devotion. "I exhort you with all the ardor of my soul," Del Pilar said passionately, "learn, instruct, encourage love of study, and you will have fulfilled your mission on earth."[102]

In this discursive effort to sever the bonds between the friars and their female parishioners, the ilustrado portrayal of women revealed a strong strain of misogyny that condemned them as sexually weak willed and intellectually weak minded. Whether women were rich or poor, they were consistently treated as domains in need of male bourgeois instruction and control. Filipino women, they were convinced, had in future to take direction not from the Spanish friars but by the legitimate figures of moral authority and arbiters of moral rectitude, bourgeois patriots such as themselves.

Supplanting the Friars: Bourgeois Men and the Path to Redemption

In seeking to give a new direction to Filipino women, as their messages to Malolos show, the propagandistas felt it natural to start their proselytizing within their own elite circles. And ahead of all others in their minds, of course, were the female members of their own families. Rizal, as we shall see in a later chapter, liked to relay his thoughts from Europe on women's duties and obligations back to his sisters in the province of Laguna. Also revealing is the personal correspondence of Marcelo H. del Pilar, one of the very few propagandistas in Spain who had a wife and children back home.[103] He had married a distant cousin, Marciana, ten years before his hasty departure from the colony, and had two daughters, Sofia and Anita.[104]

A thick volume of letters in Tagalog dated from 1889 to 1895 survives as tangible evidence of Del Pilar's devotion to his wife, whom he affectionately addressed as Chanay, and to his young girls.[105] Only to his wife did he speak frankly and at length about the physical ailments that regularly plagued him, particularly during the Spanish winters, which he found insufferably chilly, and about his constantly parlous finances. When the contributions collected by sympathizers in Manila failed to reach him or were insufficient, he often relied on Chanay to scrape together whatever she could to provide the wherewithal for the bare necessities of existence. His letters did not, as a general rule, share with his wife more than a few fragments of information about his political activities or contacts with his fellow propagandistas, but he did frequently relay his impressions of daily life in Spain. He particularly liked to depreciate Spanish customs and behavior that struck him as vulgar, boorish and offensive. Filipinos, his didactic and patriotic message was clear, were in many respects more civilized and refined than their colonial rulers.

His absence from his home worried Del Pilar incessantly. Although his wife and daughters, in the typical fashion of a bourgeois Filipino family, could rely on an extensive network of relatives, Del Pilar made certain his wife did not feel he had abandoned her in terms of his paternal duties. His letters consequently were filled with advice, particularly in relation to the upbringing of Sofia, his pre-pubescent daughter who had just left the home in Bulacan for the first time to attend a school in Manila. "You must always remind her to do well at school," he counselled his wife:

> ... she should ... avoid those who curse; she ought not to become friendly with them nor turn them into enemies, exercising tact in her avoidance ... she should appear dignified to all, and confide only to her mother. This ought never to be far from her thinking: no one can love her in the way her parents love her. If it happens that the world deceives her no one will be frank and honest with her except her parents ... all her joys, all her sorrows, all her dreadful fears should be confided only to her mother.[106]

The filial loyalty Del Pilar insists upon would not be unusual advice if heard today. However, what is important to highlight here is that in Del Pilar's instructions to Chanay lies the implicit rejection of the friar's traditional role in the counselling and confessing of children. Del Pilar is adamant that no one should be entrusted with the moral upbringing of Sofia other than her parents, and he clearly expects Chanay herself to continue to seek and follow his guidance despite his long absence from the family home.

Sofia and her younger sister Anita inhabited Del Pilar's night time dreams. He constantly reminds his wife to be heedful of the mundane concerns of his little girls; to restore the peace when they squabbled;

to make sure their pet kittens did not scratch them; and to warn them about the dangers of being run over by a *carromata*, a horse drawn cart, as they crossed the road. Often he learnt about such domestic minutiae not from Chanay herself but from Deodato Arellano, his sister Hilaria's husband, whom he relied upon to keep a solicitous watch over his family.[107] Upon hearing from Deodato that his wife had not visited Sofia in Manila for several days, he immediately sent a letter admonishing her:

> It is best if you visited her more often, lived with her for several days. If it were a boy then I would be sending you different advice; but because she is a girl her mother needs to be close by every minute.[108]

In Del Pilar's view, girls away from home clearly required extra vigilance and control. He repeatedly urges Chanay to instruct Sofia in diligence and industry, to make certain the child studies hard, rises "before the rays of sunlight strike her bed" and, imperatively, familiarizes herself with "*gawa ng babae*" — the work of a woman.[109]

Once Sofia could learn how to write, he warmly encouraged her and began to send her letters directly. In these affectionate notes, Del Pilar asks his child to pray — for her father's health, strength and their eventual reunion: "Every night pray one 'Our Father' so that our reunion will be hastened. Depend upon God to listen to you if your conscience is sincere and true when you pray."[110] His stance on religion, like Rizal's, was neither atheistic nor even agnostic. He thanked the Almighty for relief from sickness, success in his campaigns and the well being of his family. "Through God's mercy I have not fallen ill" was a recurrent refrain. There was a way of devotion to God, he plainly believed, that was true, genuine and sincere, a faith and spirituality that needed to be proclaimed and nurtured as a counterpoint to the false, corrupt and hypocritical perversion of Christianity purveyed by the friars. In a letter to a niece, Del Pilar showed he was well aware that the friars and their supporters would misrepresent his anti-friar position as irreligious. The best person to dispel these deliberate falsehoods, he advised his niece, would be her cousin, his own young daughter Sofia:

> No doubt they will slander my religious sentiments in order that you may not believe my words; but you all know me, and if you do not, there is my daughter, at an age when she can not yet dissimulate her real belief; interrogate her, scrutinise her conscience with regard to

religious matters, and the judgement which you will then form will enable you to judge the religious sentiments of the father.[111]

Del Pilar did not, however, place on record any clear statement of his beliefs, and neither, with the partial exception of Rizal, did the other leading propagandistas. The religious aspect of their thinking has not been adequately studied by historians of the nationalist movement, and cannot be given the attention it deserves within the restricted scope of this dissertation. It is nevertheless important here to emphasize the crucial difference between the religious sentiments Del Pilar and the other leading ilustrado anti-clericals espoused and the beliefs and practices of their Catholic compatriots, especially the women. First and foremost, as we have seen in this chapter, what the propagandistas rejected was the version of Catholicism sowed and nurtured by the Spanish friars in the Philippines, a version in their view so full of falsehoods and superstitions that it discredited the very name of religion. What the friars were doing in the Philippines, Rizal told his friend Ferdinand Blumentritt, a Catholic who lived in Bohemia, was "ghastly:"

> They abuse the name of religion for a few pesos. They hawk their religion to enrich their treasuries. Religion to seduce the innocent young woman! Religion to get rid of an enemy! Religion to perturb the peace of marriage and the family, if not to dishonor the wife! Why should I not combat this religion with all my strength when it is the primary cause of all our sufferings and tears?[112]

Often, too, the propagandistas made a point of including the Jesuits — a non-friar order — in their anti-clerical attacks. It was true, some conceded, that the Society of Jesus appeared less obscurantist and more progressive in some ways than the Dominicans, Franciscans, Augustinians and Recollects, but this was a strictly relative measure. By the standards of modern Europe, as Rizal's fictional sage Filósofo Tasio averred, the Jesuits were reactionary (*"retroceso"*). They only gave the semblance of being forward-looking in the Philippines because the colony was "barely beginning to emerge from the Middle Ages;" it was "at least three centuries behind the cart."[113]

In the same conversation Filósofo Tasio also takes a swipe at the Pope of the time, Leo XIII. The old scholasticism of the Dominicans, he argues, the reliance for theological guidance on the Church Fathers, is now dead "in spite of Leo XIII," because "there is no Pope who can resurrect what common sense has executed."[114] Del Pilar also expressed anti-papal sentiments in a letter to Rizal, looking forward to the "weakening of the power of the Pope" in their priest-riddled country.[115] And this irreverence towards the Holy Father, in the context of the 1880s, was tantamount to a personal renunciation of Catholicism itself. Rizal wrote about "the shipwreck of my faith"; and López Jaena about how European philosophers such as Voltaire, Diderot, Renan and Lammenais had "proven palpably and brilliantly" the "absurdities and contradictions contained in Catholicism."[116]

Given the paucity of written testaments of faith, however, the best pointer to any collective standpoint or any broad consensus in religious sentiments among the propagandistas is the fact that after arriving in Europe the majority joined Masonic lodges. The five patriots who figure most prominently in this study — Juan Luna, Antonio Luna, Del Pilar, López Jaena and Rizal — all became Freemasons at one time or another, and so too did countless other Filipinos in Madrid, Barcelona, Paris and London in the 1880s.[117] Masonry in Spain, France and elsewhere in Catholic Europe was at this time intimately linked with anti-clericalism and liberal politics, and was anathematized by the Church. In line with several of his predecessors in the Apostolic See, Pope Leo XIII spelt out the horrors in a special Encyclical, *Humanum Genus*, in which he identified Freemasons as partisans of the kingdom of Satan, hell-bent on heading an evil worldwide uprising against the Church and God.[118] Any propagandista who joined a Masonic lodge had made a conscious, defiant decision to separate himself from the communion of the Church, and knew that he would incur the penalty of excommunication.

Masons profess to be tolerant of all faiths, yet at the same time condemn the intolerance of all faiths. "The blood spilled over different beliefs and creeds, over different divinities," Del Pilar wrote, "has never stained the apron of the working Mason but has enhanced the whiteness of its purity, making it a banner of peace."[119] They believe in the existence of the Creator, the "Great Architect of the Universe," but deliberately avoid, in Del Pilar's words again, determining the "attributes" or "sphere of action in heaven or on earth of divinity."[120] The evidence for God's existence, most late nineteenth century Masons would have argued, comes not as a revelation from the divinity, set down in scripture and interpreted by priests, but from the power of human reason. Man has only to look at the awe-inspiring size, complexity and beauty of the natural universe about him to know its creation cannot have been an accident, to recognise everywhere design, order and the necessity of an ultimate cause. The majority of propagandistas who became Masons, in other words, could be called deists, albeit, as the Dominican historian Fidel Villarroel has aptly remarked in relation to Del Pilar, deists who still heard echoes from their Catholic pasts.[121]

Rizal, for example, felt obliged after three years in Europe to calm his mother's fears that he had strayed too far from the faith of his childhood. He gently reassured his mother that he still believed in the "fundamental principles" that underpinned his duties as a Christian. He made it clear to her, however, that he did not base his beliefs on illusions and falsehoods. His conscience, he insisted, only permitted religiosity if its beliefs and practices were compatible with reason. "I would fail in my duty as a rational being," he wrote, "if I would prostitute my reason and accept the absurd. I do not believe God would punish me if, in trying to approach Him, I should use reason and intelligence his most precious gift."[122] This understanding of religion served as the guiding light for the attack on friar governance. The propagandistas wanted their countrymen to be able to distinguish between religion based on human reason and religiosity founded on ignorance.

Women, especially bourgeois women, were a prime target in this campaign not just because they were seen as being more fervently pious than men, but also because they were supposed to possess a higher sense of moral rectitude, as being society's standard bearers of honor and virtue. A good woman, for Del Pilar, acted not only as a "balm for the rigors of life, but an element which imperceptibly leads man on the road of virtue or on the path of perversity and cowardice." Wherever women were virtuous, he wrote, "there vice is timid and dignity predominates in the customs of the people" but wherever women lacked honor the menfolk too bore "the stamp of immorality" and neglected their duties in family and society.[123] More importantly, women in their role as mothers held in their hands the future of the country. As mothers, women determined whether their sons, and hence the nation, progressed and prospered or whether they continued to tolerate the current condition of poverty and subjugation. In the attack against friar power, women — their hearts, minds and bodies — became the site of fierce ideological struggle. The intimate relationship between women and priests had to be severed because it imperilled the nation. Hence while the way to the country's redemption, indeed of the broad mass of Filipino men, lay through the bourgeois wife, mother and future mother, ultimately, it was a way that would be directed by ilustrado elite men.

But there was another aspect to the propagandistas' emphasis on education for women. Promoting education laid stress on activities of the mind and demotion of the body resulting in a parallel emphasis on female chastity, celibacy, shame and modesty. As we will see in the next two chapters, the propagandistas used the weight of their scientific reasoning to argue the belief that women should expressly avoid sensual pleasure and restrain their sexual nature. Their aim was to reform women's sexual behavior, but in so doing, paradoxically, they like their European anti-clerical counterparts came to echo the age-old teachings on female sexuality of the Catholicism they so bitterly fought.

Notes

1. Robert MacMicking, *Recollections of Manilla and the Philippines during 1848, 1849 and 1850*. Edited and annotated by Morton J. Netzorg (Manila: Filipiniana Book Guild, 1967), p. 67.
2. Ibid., p. 68. The native female propensity to form carnal unions with the friars, as MacMicking's remarks suggest, was obviously linked in part to the mundane attractions of wealth and status. Scholars have speculated that it may also have been rooted, at least in the early decades of Spanish rule, to women's desire to tap into the spiritual power of the alien shamans. See John Leddy Phelan, *The Hispanization of the Philippines: Spanish aims and Filipino responses 1565–1700* (Madison: University of Wisconsin Press, 1959), pp. 36–9; and Filomeno Aguilar, *Clash of Spirits: the history of power and sugar planter hegemony on a Visayan Island* (Quezon City: Ateneo de Manila University Press, 1998), pp. 41–3.
3. P. Jacinto [José Rizal], "Memorias de un estudiante de Manila" [1878], in *Diarios y Memorias por José Rizal* (Manila: Comisión Nacional del Centenario de José Rizal, 1961), p. 12.
4. From the testimony given by Don Felipe Calderon, 17 October 1900 in *Lands Held for Ecclesiastical or Religious Uses in the Philippine Islands, etc.*, United States, 56th Congress, 2nd Session, Senate Document No.190 (Washington: Government Printing Office, 1901), p. 139.
5. From the testimony given by Maximo Viola, of San Miguel de Mayumo, Bulacan, 23 October 1900, in ibid., p. 157. In the mid-1880s there were 24 parishes in Bulacan, all held by Spanish friars — 17 by Augustinians and 7 by Franciscans. Both at the time and subsequently, apologists for the religious orders have dismissed such allegations as hugely exaggerated. A very few friars, they concede, were wayward

and unedifying, but these rare reprobates were weeded out by their superiors as soon as their transgressions became known.

6. Fidel Villarroel OP, *Marcelo H. del Pilar at the University of Santo Tomas* (Manila: University of Santo Tomas, 1997), p. 37.
7. *Carcel de Bilibid, Letras* (Ayer Manuscript Collection, No.1393, Newberry Library).
8. Gregorio F. Zaide, *Great Filipinos in History* (Manila: Verde Book Store, 1970), p. 256.
9. Austin Coates, *Rizal: Filipino nationalist and martyr* (Manila: Solidaridad Publishing House, 1992), pp. 19–20.
10. P. Jacinto [José Rizal], "Memorias," p. 9; José Rizal, *Noli me tangere* [1887], trans. Ma. Soledad Lacson-Locsin, ed. Raul L. Locsin (Honolulu: University of Hawai'i Press, 1997), pp. 127–8.
11. "Exposición del Arzobispo de Manila, Msgr. P. Payo OP, al Ministro del Ultramar, 26 de noviembre de 1887" [Archives of the University of Santo Tomas], cited in Fidel Villarroel OP, *Marcelo H del Pilar: his religious conversions* (Manila: University of Santo Tomas, 1997), p. 8.
12. Mh. Plaridel [Marcelo H. del Pilar], *La frailocracia Filipina* (Barcelona: Imprenta Ibérica de Francisco Fossas, 1889).
13. See, for example, Jonathan Fast and Jim Richardson, *Roots of Dependency: political and economic revolution in 19th century Philippines* (Quezon City: Foundation for Nationalist Studies, 1979), pp. 61–2; Fidel Villarroel OP, *The Dominicans and the Philippine Revolution, 1896–1903* (Manila: University of Santo Tomas, 1999), pp. xxvi–vii; Rolando de la Rosa, *Beginnings of the Filipino Dominicans: history of the Filipinization of the Religious Orders in the Philippines* (Manila: University of Santo Tomas, 1990), pp. 125–6.
14. Graciano López Jaena, "Filipinas en las Exposición Universal de Barcelona," in *Discursos y artículos varios* [1891] Nueva edición revisada y adicionada con escritos no incluido en la primera (Manila: Bureau of Printing, 1951), p. 16. The case that López Jaena's anti-clericalism can be seen more meaningfully as an expression of modernism than of formative nationalism is elaborated in Clement C. Camposano, "Rethinking López Jaena's Struggle against Monastic Supremacy," unpublished MA dissertation, University of the Philippines, Diliman, 1992.
15. Graciano López Jaena, "A los Filipinos" [Barcelona, 1891], Dedication of his volume *Discursos y artículos varios*, p. v.
16. From the testimony given by the Archbishop of Manila [Bernard Nozaleda, OP], 4 August 1900, in *Lands Held for Ecclesiastical or Religious Uses in the Philippine Islands, etc.*, p. 103.
17. José Rizal, "Sobre la indolencia de los Filipinos (IV)" ["On the Indolence of the Filipinos"], *La Solidaridad* 2: 38 (31 August 1890): 574.
18. Vicente Rafael, "Nationalism, Imagery, and the Filipino Intelligentsia in the 19th century," in *Discrepant Histories: translocal essays on Filipino cultures*, ed. Vicente Rafael (Pasig City: Anvil, 1995), p. 138.
19. "Immorality" in the Filipino sense of the word, as Trinidad H. Pardo de Tavera advised a US fact-finding commission in 1900, "simply meant sexual departures

from morality." At the same hearings Pedro Serrano Laktaw intimated that he found the specifics of the subject simply too filthy to discuss: "The details of the immorality of the friars are so base and so indecent that instead of smirching the friars I would smirch myself by relating them." Testimonies given before the Philippine Commission, 22 and 24 October 1900 respectively, in *Lands Held for Ecclesiastical or Religious Uses in the Philippine Islands, etc.*, pp. 160, 164.

[20] Ilustrado depictions of Spanish friars were not confined to images that presented friars as sexual predators but also as impotents and effeminates who wore women's dress, which alluded to the wearing of the soutane. See Leon Ma. Guerrero, *The First Filipino: a biography of José Rizal* (Manila: National Historical Institute, 1963), pp. 82, 115 cited in Vicente Rafael, "Nationalism, Imagery, and the Filipino Intelligentsia in the 19th century," in *Discrepant Histories*, ed. Rafael, p. 138.

[21] Esteban de Ocampo, "Rizal as a Bibliophile," in *The Bibliographical Society of the Philippines*. Occasional Papers No. 2 (Manila: Unesco National Commission of the Philippines, 1960); Graciano López Jaena, "Una frase de amor: persuasiva a las bellas y elegantes damas de Filipinas" ["A Phrase of Love: an appeal to the beautiful and elegant ladies of the Philippines"], in *Discursos y artículos varios*, p. 253. Rizal was particularly inspired by Voltaire. He counselled Del Pilar to take lessons in French so that he could read Voltaire's complete works and taste his "beautiful, simple and correct style" and know his "way of thinking." José Rizal (London) to Marcelo H. del Pilar, January 1889, in *Cartas entre Rizal y sus colegas de la propaganda, 1882–1889* (Manila: Comisión Nacional del Centenario de José Rizal, 1961), p. 274.

[22] Olwen H. Hufton, *Women and the Limits of Citizenship in the French Revolution* (Toronto: University of Toronto, 1992), pp. xviii–xx. For discussions of anti-feminist currents within the French Revolution itself, see Lynn Hunt, *Politics, Culture and Class in the French Revolution* (Berkeley: University of California Press, 1984); and Joan B. Landes, *Women in the Public Sphere in the Age of the French Revolution* (Ithaca, NY: Cornell University Press, 1988).

[23] Stephen Haliczer, *Sexuality in the Confessional: a sacrament profaned* (Oxford: Oxford University Press, 1996), p. 194.

[24] Julie Peakman, *Mighty Lewd Books: the development of pornography in eighteenth-century England* (Basingstoke: Palgrave MacMillan, 2003); Ian Gibson, *The Erotomaniac: the secret life of Henry Spencer Ashbee* (London: Faber and Faber, 2001); *The Seducing Cardinal or Isabella Peto, a tale founded on facts* (London: Published as the Act Directs by Madame Le Duck, Mortimer St., 1830) cited in Pisanus Fraxi, (Henry Spencer Ashbee), *Bibliography of Prohibited Books* (New York: Jack Brussel, 1962), n.p.

[25] Haliczer, *Sexuality in the Confessional*, p. 188. Lou Charnon-Deutsch, "Pornography and the Becquer Brothers' Bourbons in the Raw," in *The Representation of Sexualities in the Hispanic cultures and literatures*, ed. Roberto Reis and David William Foster (Minneapolis: University of Minnesota Press, 1996), pp. 274–94.

[26] Eduardo López Bago, *El cura, caso de incesto* (Madrid: Juan Munoz Sanchez, 1889); also *El Confesionario (satiriasis)* (Madrid: Juan Munoz y Compania, 1890).

[27] Michel Morphy, *Les Mystères de la Pornographie Cléricale* (1884); and Leo Taxil and Karl Milo, *Les Débauches d'un Confesseur* (1885) cited in Haliczer, *Sexuality in the Confessional*, p. 187.

[28] Haliczer, *Sexuality in the Confessional*, p. 187.

[29] *The Confessional Unmasked: showing the depravity of the priesthood, immorality of the confessional, being the questions put to females in confession, etc., etc.*, extracted from the theological works now used by Cardinal Wiseman, his bishops and priest, with notes by C.B. (London: Thomas Johnston, 1851), p. 56.

[30] Testimony given by José Templo, native and resident of Lipa, Batangas, landed proprietor and agriculturist in *Lands Held for Ecclesiastical or Religious Uses in the Philippine Islands, etc.*, p. 202.

[31] José Garcia del Fierro, "The Problem of the Friars," written submission dated Nueva Caceres, 11 September 1900, in *Lands used for Ecclesiastical and Religious Purposes etc.*, p. 215.

[32] Marcelo H. del Pilar (Barcelona) to Joséfa Gatmaytan, 13 March 1889, in *Epistolario de Marcelo H. del Pilar*, Tomo I (Manila: Imprenta del Gobierno, 1955), p. 57.

[33] Father Salvador Font, cited in Plaridel [Marcelo H. del Pilar], "*Noli me tangere*: before monkish hatred in the Philippines" (Plaridel's defense of José Rizal's *Noli me tangere*). Reprinted in *Rizal's Correspondence with Fellow Reformists, 1882–1896* (Manila: National Heroes Commission, 1963), pp. 735–6.

[34] Rizal, *Noli me tangere*, p. 39.

[35] Ibid., p. 401.

[36] Ibid., p. 39.

[37] Ibid., p. 401.

[38] Ibid., p. 149.

[39] Ibid., pp. 422–6.

[40] Ibid., p. 354.

[41] Ibid., p. 200.

[42] Graciano López Jaena, "Entre Kastila y Filipina" [Between the Spaniard and the Filipina], in *Discursos y artículos varios*, p. 167.

[43] Ibid.

[44] For an exploratory study of how capitalism and colonialism is inscribed on the Filipino female body see Jeanne Illo, "Fair Skin and Sexy Body: imprints of colonialism and capitalism on the Filipina," *Australian Feminist Studies* 11: 24 (1996): 219–25.

[45] Graciano López Jaena, "Fray Botod (Estudios al natural)" [Fray Botod: a true-to-life study], in *Discursos y Artículos*, pp. 204–6. Another stereotypical caricature of the friar as an overweight, avaricious and licentious glutton is Rizal's statuette "Orate Fratres" ["Pray Brothers"], now displayed in the Rizal Library of the Ateneo de Manila University. On the friar's bulging belly hangs a reliquary depicting the profile of a woman; in his hand he holds a tray with wine, and by his feet lies a lumpy sack, presumably filled with money.

[46] Historians more commonly cite López Jaena's patriotic celebration of Hidalgo's "*Las Virgenes cristianas expuestas al populacho*," which he praised together with Juan Luna's "*Spoliarium*" for expressing "the lamentations and woes of this race upon

whose head has long weighed the stigma of unjustified prejudices." His inclusion of the famous canvas in Fray Botod's private gallery of "obscene" paintings shows that he also recognized the work as powerfully erotic. "Las virgenes" won Hidalgo a silver medal at the 1884 Madrid fine arts exposition. This (and other internal evidence) casts grave doubt on the claim found in numerous sources that López Jaena first wrote "Fray Botod" in 1874, when he was only eighteen and had not yet left the Philippines. The only version of "Fray Botod" that has survived, in any event, seems to be that published in López Jaena's collected speeches and essays in 1891. Graciano López Jaena, "En honor de los artistas Luna y Resurreccion Hidalgo" [1884], in *Discursos y artículos varios*, p. 33.

47 López Jaena, "Fray Botod," pp. 218–9.
48 Ibid., p. 220.
49 Ibid., p. 211.
50 Louis Jacolliot, *Les Moeurs et les Femmes de l"Extrême Orient: voyage au pays des bayadères* (Paris: E. Dentu, 1873). The first Spanish edition appeared three years later: Luis Jacolliot, *Viaje al pais de las bayaderas* (Madrid: Imprenta de Manuel G. Hernandez, 1876).
51 López Jaena, "Fray Botod," p. 221.
52 Edward Said, *Orientalism* (New York: Vintage, 1979).
53 López Jaena, "Fray Botod," pp. 221–3.
54 José Rizal, "The Religiosity of the Filipino People" [1884], in *Miscellaneous Writings of Dr. José Rizal* (Manila: National Heroes Commission, 1964), pp. 92–106. This essay, which Rizal left unfinished, has apparently never been published in the original Spanish, even though the manuscript — "Estado de religiosidad de los pueblos en Filipinas" — is preserved in the Philippine National Library.
55 Ibid., p. 92.
56 Ibid., pp. 94–5.
57 In an age of strict literary censorship, these were the only reading materials readily available and could safely be enjoyed by the common tao. See Damiana L. Eugenio, *Awit and Corrido: Philippine metrical romances* (Quezon City: University of the Philippines Press, 1987); and Bienvenido L. Lumbera, *Tagalog Poetry 1570–1898: tradition and influences in its development* (Quezon City: Ateneo de Manila University Press, 1986).
58 Rizal's essay has been conspicuously neglected by Catholic scholars who have looked at popular Filipino religiosity. See, for example, Miguel Bernad, *The Christianization of the Philippines: problems and perspectives* (Manila: Filipiniana Book Guild, 1972); Jaime Bulatao, "When Roman Theology meets an Animistic Culture: mysticism in present-day Philippines," *Kinaadman* 6: 1 (1984): 102–11; and John N. Schumacher, "Syncretism in Philippine Catholicism: its historical causes," *Philippine Studies* 32 (1984): 251–72.
59 Rizal, "The Religiosity of the Filipino People," p. 100.
60 Ibid.
61 Ibid., pp. 95–9.
62 Ibid., p. 94.

63 In 1882 Del Pilar was the founding editor of *Diariong Tagalog*, the first Spanish-Tagalog bilingual daily newspaper in the Philippines. It was a shortlived paper that spoke out courageously in support of various reforms and through Del Pilar's eloquent translation, brought one of José Rizal's first major essays, "El amor patrio" ["Love of country"] to the attention of a Tagalog reading audience. Magno S. Gatmaitan, *Marcelo H. del Pilar, 1850–1896* (Quezon City: Munoz Press, 1966), p. 166.

64 Under the pseudonym of "Dolores Manapat" Del Pilar published *"Caiigat cayo"* ("You are eels"), a play on Father Rodriguez's pamphlet *"Caingat cayo"* ("Take care"), a work warning people away from Rizal's *Noli*. John N. Schumacher, SJ, *The Propaganda Movement, 1880–1895: the creation of a Filipino consciousness, the making of the revolution* (Quezon City: Ateneo de Manila University Press, 1997), p. 121.

65 Plaridel [Marcelo H. Del Pilar], *"Noli me tangere*: before monkish hatred in the Philippines," Appendix I to *Rizal's Correspondence with Fellow Reformists, 1882–1896* (Manila: National Heroes Commission, 1963), pp. 735–43.

66 Villarroel, *Marcelo H. del Pilar: his religious conversions*, pp. 9–10.

67 For an account of Del Pilar's campaign and his political methods see John Schumacher, *The Propaganda Movement, 1880–1895: The creation of a Filipino consciousness, the making of the Revolution* (Quezon City: Ateneo de Manila University Press, 1997), pp. 120–7; and Epifanio de los Santos Cristobal, "Marcelo H. del Pilar." Photocopy taken from mimeograph copy in the library of Dr. Domingo Abella, p. 56. This article was published in *Philippine Review* 3 (1918): 775–803, 861–85 and 947–75.

68 José Rizal (London) to José Ma. Basa, January 1889, in *Cartas entre Rizal y sus colegas de la propaganda, 1882–1889*, p. 287.

69 De los Santos, "Marcelo H. del Pilar," p. 11.

70 Lumbera, *Tagalog Poetry 1570–1898*, p. 143. The six poems are: *"sagot nang España sa hibik nang Filipinas"* ("Spain's Reply to Filipinas' Lament"), *"Dupluhan"* ("Verse contest"), *Dalit* ("song"), *"Epigrama"* ("Epigram"), *Ang mga kahatolan nang fraile* ("The counsels of the friars"), and *"Pasiong dapat ipag-alab nang puso nang tauong babasa sa kalupitan nang fraile"* ("The *Pasion* that should inflame the hearts of those who read about the cruelty of the friars").

71 Reynaldo Ileto, *Filipinos and their Revolution: event, discourse and historiography* (Quezon City: Ateneo de Manila University Press, 1998), pp. 11–9. Del Pilar's *"sagot"* was written as a response to a poem by another Tagalog propagandist, Hermenegildo Flores, *Hibik ng Filipinas sa Inang España* ("Filipinas' Lament to Mother Spain") ([Manila]: n.p.: c. 1888) [In the scrapbook on Marcelo H. del Pilar by José P. Santos, Bernardo Collection, Ateneo de Manila archives.] This poem also used familial imagery.

72 Del Pilar wrote *Dasalan at Toksohan* swiftly and secretly together with Pedro Serrano Laktaw and another Bulacan townmate, Rafael Enriquez, on the day of his hasty departure for Europe. Once in Barcelona, Del Pilar had the verses printed and sent back to the Comité de Propaganda in Manila. Schumacher, *The Propaganda Movement*, pp. 124–5.

73 Mh. Plaridel [Marcelo H. del Pilar], *La soberania monacal en Filipinas: apuntes sobre la funesta preponderencia del fraile en las islas, así en lo político como en lo económico y religioso* (Barcelona: F. Fossas, 1888), p. 30.
74 Marcelo H. del Pilar, "Ang tanda" ["The Lesson"] [1888], in De los Santos, "Marcelo H. del Pilar," p. 42.
75 Marcelo H. del Pilar, "Ang aba guinoong baria" ["Our Holy Money"] [1888], in ibid., p. 43.
76 Marcelo H. del Pilar, "Ang mga utos ng fraile" ["The Commandments of the Friar"] [1888], in ibid., p. 44.
77 Marcelo H. del Pilar, "Ang mga biyayang ng fraile" ["The Blessings of the Friar"] [1888], in ibid., p. 45.
78 Marcelo H. del Pilar, "Pagsisisi" ["Repentance"] [1888], in ibid., p. 43.
79 Marcelo H. del Pilar "Ama namin" ["Our Father"] [1888], in ibid., p. 43.
80 López Jaena, "Una frase de amor," pp. 257–8.
81 José Rizal, "Sa mga kababayang dalaga sa Malolos" ["To my compatriots, the young women of Malolos"] [February 1889], in *Cartas entre Rizal y sus colegas de la propaganda, 1882–1889* (Manila: Comisión Nacional del Centenario de José Rizal, 1961), pp. 305–6.
82 José Rizal (London) to Plaridel [Marcelo H. del Pilar], 22 February 1889, in *Cartas*, pp. 301–2.
83 Marcelo H. del Pilar (Barcelona) to Joséfa Gatmaytan, 13 March 1889, in *Epistolario de Marcelo H. del Pilar*, Tomo I, p. 57.
84 López Jaena, "Una frase de amor," p. 259.
85 Ibid.
86 Rizal, "Sa mga kababayang dalaga ng Malolos," pp. 307–8. By suggesting that the generality of European women had become freethinkers, the propagandistas were of course sacrificing objectivity in the interests of polemical effect. Anti-clerical writers in Europe, as they well knew, remained deeply vexed by the sway ecclesiastical power still had over women. In countries like France the gulf between male and female religious observance had been widening since the late eighteenth century, with men steadily withdrawing from active Church attendance and religiosity being increasingly identified with women. Haliczer, *Sexuality in the Confessional*, p. 194; Michelle Perrot, ed., *A History of Private Life: from the fires of the revolution to the Great War*, trans. Arthur Goldhammer (Cambridge, Mass: The Belknap Press of Harvard University Press, 1990), pp. 556–8.
87 López Jaena, "Una frase de amor," pp. 254–7.
88 Rizal, "Sa mga kababayang dalaga sa Malolos," p. 304.
89 Ibid.
90 Rizal, *Noli me tangere*, pp. 355–64.
91 Hufton, *Women and the Limits of Citizenship in the French Revolution*, p. xix.
92 Rizal, "Sa mga kababayang dalaga sa Malolos," pp. 303–6; Graciano López Jaena, "Una frase de amor," pp. 252–3.
93 López Jaena, "Una frase de amor," p. 258.

94 Quoted in Perrot, ed., *A History of Private Life: from the fires of the revolution to the Great War*, pp. 557–8.
95 See also Graciano López Jaena, "Amor a España, o A las jovenes de Malolos" ["Love for Spain, or To the Young Women of Malolos"] [February 1889], in *Discursos y artículos varios*, pp. 241–5.
96 Rizal, "Sa mga kababayang dalaga sa Malolos," p. 305.
97 For a biographical background of these famous women, a detailed account of this episode and its social, political context see Nicanor G. Tiongson, *The Women of Malolos* (Quezon City: Ateneo de Manila University Press, 2004).
98 Rizal, "Sa mga kababayang dalaga sa Malolos," p. 308.
99 López Jaena, "Una frase de amor," p. 251.
100 Marcelo H. del Pilar (Barcelona) to Joséfa Gatmaytan, 13 March 1889, in *Epistolario de Marcelo H. del Pilar*, Tomo I, p. 56.
101 Ibid., pp. 251–2.
102 Marcelo H. del Pilar (Barcelona) to Joséfa Gatmaytan, 13 March 1889, in *Epistolario de Marcelo H. del Pilar*, Tomo I, p. 57.
103 The only other prominent patriot known to have started a family before leaving for Spain is Pedro Serrano Laktaw, and his personal correspondence has not survived.
104 José P. Santos, *Buhay at mga sinulat ni Plaridel* (Manila: Palimbag ng Dalaga, 1931), pp. 1–2.
105 *Epistolario de Marcelo H. del Pilar* Tomo II (Manila: Imprenta del Gobierno, 1958). The letters from Chanay to her husband are unfortunately no longer extant.
106 Marcelo H. del Pilar (Barcelona) to Chanay [Marciana del Pilar], 2 May 1889, in ibid., pp. 19–20.
107 Arellano, who worked as a clerk with the artillery corps, was also Del Pilar's main political confidant back home. Del Pilar's correspondence with Arellano and other propagandistas both in the Philippines and in Europe is collected and published in *Epistolario de Marcelo H. del Pilar*, Tomo I (Manila: Imprenta del Gobierno, 1955).
108 Marcelo H. del Pilar (Madrid) to Chanay [Marciana del Pilar], 29 April 1890, in *Epistolario de Marcelo H. del Pilar*, Tomo II, p. 59.
109 Marcelo H. del Pilar (Madrid) to Chanay [Marciana del Pilar], 8 July 1891, in ibid., p. 103.
110 Marcelo H. del Pilar (Madrid) to Sofia del Pilar, 14 September 1892, in ibid., p. 140. This encouragement of his daughter's prayerfulness prompted Del Pilar's grandson, a Jesuit priest, to claim erroneously that Del Pilar had shifted in his thinking, and repented his earlier anti-clerical stance. See the remarks of Vicente Marasigan SJ, quoted in Ambeth Ocampo, "Plaridel Anecdotes" and "The Pain of the Hero's Family," in Ambeth Ocampo, *Looking Back* (Pasig City: Anvil, 1990), pp. 134–7.
111 Marcelo H. del Pilar (Barcelona) to Joséfa Gatmaytan, 13 March 1889, in *Epistolario de Marcelo H. del Pilar*, Tomo I, p. 56.

112 José Rizal (Paris) to Ferdinand Blumentritt, 20 January 1890, in *The Rizal-Blumentritt Correspondence, 1890–1896* (Manila: National Historical Institute, 1992), pp. 322–3.
113 Rizal, *Noli me tangere*, pp. 351–2.
114 Ibid., p. 352.
115 Marcelo H. del Pilar (Barcelona) to Pedro Icasiano, 25 March 1889, in *Epistolario*, I, pp. 72–3.
116 López Jaena, "Una frase de amor," p. 253.
117 A more detailed indication of the prevalence of Masonic attachments amongst the propagandistas is given in the biographical appendix to this study.
118 Pope Leo XIII, *Humanum Genus* [Encyclical on Freemasonry; promulgated on April 20, 1884].
119 Quoted in Juan Causing, *Freemasonry in the Philippines* (Cebu City: G.T. Printers, 1969) p. xx; see also Reynold S. Fajardo, *The Brethren: Masons in the struggle for Philippine Independence* (Manila: Enrique L. Locsin, 1998), pp. 65–90; 101–2; and T.M. Kalaw, *La Masonería Filipina: su origin, desarollo y vicissitudes, hasta la epoca presente* (Manila: Bureau of Printing, 1920).
120 Quoted in Villarroel, *Religious Conversions*, p. 25.
121 Villarroel, *Marcelo H del Pilar: his religious conversions*, p. 25.
122 José Rizal (Madrid?) to Dona Teodora Alonso, c.1885, in *Letters between Rizal and Family Members, 1876–1896* (Manila: National Historical Institute, 1993), p. 175. This stance is also strongly reflected in Rizal's correspondence in 1892–93 with Pablo Pastells SJ, one of his spiritual mentors in his student days at the Ateneo de Manila. See Raul J. Bonoan SJ, *The Rizal-Pastells correspondence: the hitherto unpublished letters of José Rizal and portions of Fr. Pablo Pastell's fourth letter and translation of the correspondence together with a historical background and theological critique* (Quezon City: Ateneo de Manila University Press, 1994); and Miguel A. Bernad SJ, *Rizal and Spain: an essay in biographical context* (Manila: National Book Store, 1996), pp. 92–105.
123 Marcelo H. del Pilar (Barcelona) to Josefa Gatmaytan, 13 March 1889, in *Epistolario de Marcelo H. del Pilar*, Tomo I, p. 55.

5

Pathological Visions: Rizal, Female Sexuality and the Sickness of Society

Truth in Science

In a letter written in 1892, the Jesuit priest Pablo Pastells suggested to Rizal that he must have been driven to write his controversial, patriotic and anti-clerical novel *Noli me tangere* through raw resentment and bitter, wounded pride. For Rizal, who strove to write with clear-headed reasoning rather than emotion, Pastells' remarks may have been quite galling to read. But his response was reflective, showing that he had become both familiar with and adept at handling such criticism of his work. He claimed that the unjust treatment and assaults to his dignity he had suffered while young were not what had moved his pen. Instead, he kept in mind "a clear vision of the reality of my motherland, the vivid memory of what was happening, and a sufficient dexterity to judge the etiology."[1]

In these few concise words, Rizal delineated for the benefit of his clerical interlocutor not only the approach he had taken in writing his first novel but also the overall method he used in dealing with the problems of his country. To see with clarity, to remember, and to think of origins and causes pointed to a specific scientific style that was fundamental to Rizal's literary process and thinking — the logic of clinical analysis as a "narration of pathological events." Philippine colonial society in Rizal's eyes was analogous to a living organism attacked and slowly consumed by disease whose cure lay in the expertise of the enlightened ilustrado. This chapter and the next will track Rizal's application of this medical perspective to his study of Philippine society and history to give an account, based on a variety of sources that include Rizal's lesser known sculptures and letters as well as the *Noli*, of female sexual desire as it came to be perceived within what was essentially Rizal's overall pathologizing vision. Situated inside a larger matrix of national pathologies, the sexual nature of Filipino women was represented by turns as a passion dangerous or hysterical in need of moral reform and restraint. Yet Rizal's scrutiny of female sexuality, as will be seen, was also influenced by his European milieu, and in this world, conversely, the European woman came to be enjoyed as a particular, private male Filipino bourgeois pleasure.

Aside from law, the most popular field of study for the young Filipino ilustrados who came to study in Europe was medicine. From 28 medical students who enrolled at various universities in the Peninsula and France, almost half attended the Universidad Central de Madrid, including Rizal who entered in the autumn of 1882.[2] In parallel with his studies in the Faculty of Medicine, Rizal took several courses in the Faculty of Philosophy and Letters, including history, Latin, Greek and Hebrew, Spanish literature and Arabic.[3] By 1884 Rizal was joyfully informing his parents he had obtained the licentiate in medicine, a qualification that enabled him to practise medicine even though he had not yet earned the doctorate, which required the submission of a thesis: "At last I am a physician," he wrote to his family.[4] Abandoning the doctorate, Rizal then chose to specialize in ophthalmic surgery, being only the second Filipino to have done so. His graduate studies in ophthalmology led him to train at clinics in Paris and Heidelberg in Germany for a further two years (1885–87).[5] After qualifying, however, he practised ophthalmology only sporadically and when he was in financial need. He received patients at his family home in Calamba, saving the fees for his European travels, and later financially assisted his exiled family by briefly setting up his own eye clinic in Hong Kong. During his exile in Dapitan, he operated on patients who journeyed to the remote town to be treated by him. Accompanying one of his patients was a young woman of supposed Anglo-Irish descent named Josephine Bracken, who later returned to Dapitan and became his lover.[6]

As numerous scholars have pointed out, Rizal's academic background in medicine exerted a strong influence on his literary imagination and he drew freely upon scientific metaphors and the analytical procedures of clinical diagnosis in particular to describe his own writing process and literary approach.⁷ In October 1882, at the beginning of his first year at the Universidad Central de Madrid, Rizal carefully noted his first lesson in clinical diagnosis, whose method and procedure was emphasized as the key to understanding a patient's illness and the application of an appropriate treatment. "Clinical history," wrote Rizal in his exercise book:

> ... is the narration of pathological events with their antecedents and final outcome which have occurred in a patient.... It is divided into three parts: first, the anamnesis, that is, the antecedents, second the present condition with the diagnosis and the prognosis and third, treatment or management prescribed by the physician.

At first sight, it would be easy to dismiss these jottings as run of the mill lecture notes. But the methods of clinical diagnosis and the scientific scrutiny of pathological conditions he was learning offered him a rich source of provocative metaphors to mine. He likened, for instance, the cowardice of his countrymen to a disease whose cure lay in the drastic but life-saving procedure of cauterization, for "if the people are cowardly like a diseased organ suffering from infection and near degeneration, then the remedy is treatment by fire."⁸ As a *"narration* of pathological events," clinical diagnosis formed the basis of an intellectual framework upon which he could harness the production of a patriotic discourse. Certain qualities associated with the nerve and skill of the physician or surgeon also appealed to Rizal in a fundamental way. In neat script, Rizal carefully wrote:

> [For the] prognosis to be accurate [it] should be based on a good diagnosis, (besides) the events should be considered in their chronological order, that is, the whole anamnesis should be recalled. Judgement, calculation, common sense, and a clinical eye, are the necessary qualities. It is perhaps the most delicate part of clinical medicine. Treatment is dictated by the physician's knowledge in relation to the present condition and the prognosis. In the end, the patient is either cured, convalesces, is relieved or continues in the same state, worsens or dies. Then, the clinical history is completed by the autopsy.⁹

The physician had to adopt a certain approach to illness and follow given procedures that required a systematic gathering of knowledge and its objective ordering. Clinical diagnosis depended on a "methodical" and "accurate" construction of a patient's medical and social history;

it assumed a fidelity to "truth" and accuracy; it required the qualities of cool rationality, of "judgement," "calculation," "common sense" and the "clinical eye" of the physician who dictated and controlled a process that moved progressively and logically towards either prognosis and treatment or the ultimate moment of truth — the autopsy.

This scientific perspective appealed to Rizal and can be seen even in his private correspondence. Writing in Tagalog sometime during the autumn of 1891, Rizal urged his fellow ilustrado patriots abroad to return to the Philippines when they had completed their studies. Bringing with them their enlightened ideas, fruits of a European education, ilustrado patriots were figuratively the medicine to cure his ailing country. Writing in Tagalog, Rizal stated his unequivocal position: "... How we can help (*maitutulong*) ... is with our lives in our country (*ang ating buhay sa ating bayan*).... Medicine should be brought to the sick (*Ang gamot ay dapat ilapit sa may sakit*)."[10]

In adopting the language and approach of biomedical science, Rizal's strategy would not have been wholly unfamiliar to the European middle class literate public. From newsprint to novel, the reading matter of the European middle classes had become saturated throughout the nineteenth century with a political discourse that described social conditions in terms of physiological symptoms affecting a nation's health and strength or weakness and illness. Preoccupied with the living conditions of their burgeoning urban populations, the political elites and social planners of the industrializing West readily plundered the language of medicine and science for metaphors to explain the social crisis occurring in their cities. In Britain for example, eugenic notions of degeneration fuelled increasing concerns about the unregenerate poor, the "dangerous classes," whose crowded slums were variously depicted through biological images of disease, pestilence and contagion. Voicing the typical anxieties of the Victorian elite towards the increasing numbers of vagrant poor in the capital, Thomas Carlyle for example, visualized all of London as a malignant ulcer debilitating the national body politic.[11]

The imaginative dimensions of medical science had similarly appealed to French writers and political historians such as Jules Michelet and Emile Zola, whose works Rizal read and admired and circulated amongst his propagandist friends.[12] Inheritors of the late Enlightenment, these authors combined literature, science and medicine in their works, using the scientific vocabulary of medicine and pathology and its systems of representation in their discussions of French society. While Michelet authored numerous popular works epitomizing the blend of science and literature,[13] Zola revealed his own attitude to his art by comparing the work of the realist writer to that of the surgeon. The realistic novelist, thought Zola, ought to approach his craft with the same clinical precision of the surgeon and "put on the white apron of the anatomist and dissect, fibre by fibre, the human beast laid out completely naked on the slab of the amphitheatre." [14]

The effect of introducing these kinds of scientific analogies in the Philippine context by an indio was incendiary. As the friars' vehement condemnation of Rizal's work attested, the *Noli* was seen as an especially dangerous species of social critique, a blend of fiction and truth that was in an important sense scientific. Although only a few hundred copies reached the Philippines (the rest being held up or confiscated at customs), a committee appointed by the rector of the University of Santo Tomas officially condemned the book as subversive to the State and "heretical and impious to religion." Its circulation was banned by the Comisión Permanente de Censura and even its possession was deemed an arrestable offence.[15] Archbishop Payo of Manila was said to have sent word to the parishes that all copies of the *Noli* should be gathered and burned.[16] In August 1887, after five years of absence, Rizal returned to the Philippines and saw for himself the commotion his book had stirred: the friars clamored for Rizal's exile and excommunication, his family were harassed, his friends put under surveillance, and he had become known as a dangerous literary celebrity. He found himself caught in the midst of a maelstrom of rumors that had been circulating about himself and his book even months before his arrival. Undermining the colonial and clerical proscription of the book, the rumors not only transformed the messages the *Noli* carried well beyond Rizal's imagined intentions, they also re-created Rizal into a potent symbol of hope and salvation, especially amongst the folk of Calamba, his own provincial town.[17]

In 1890, a detailed critique of the *Noli* written by Vicente Barrantes, formerly a high-ranking colonial official in the Philippines, appeared in the Madrid literary review *La España Moderna*. Barrantes denounced Rizal as "a spirit twisted by a German education."[18] In a fiery and combative response, Rizal conceded that his spirit had been twisted, but insisted the damage long predated his contact with Germany. "My spirit is twisted," he wrote:

... because I have been reared among injustices and abuses, because since a child I have seen many suffer stupidly and because I too have suffered. My "twisted spirit" is the product of that constant vision of moral ideals succumbing before the powerful reality of abuses, arbitrariness, hypocrisies, farces, violence, and other vile passions.... Yes I have depicted the social sores of "my homeland"; in it are "pessimism and darkness" and it is because I see much infamy in my country; there the wretched equal in number the imbeciles. I confess that I found a keen delight in bringing out so much shame and blushes, but in doing the painting with the blood of my heart, I wanted to correct them and save the others ...[it is because of the existence of this corruption] I have written my *Noli me Tangere*, I ask for reforms so that the little good that there is may be saved and the bad may be redeemed.[19]

Rizal's reaction to Barrantes illustrates the crystallization and maturation of the political thoughts he had carried with him throughout the writing of the *Noli*. First, Rizal felt deeply that exposing the moral backwardness of his own people would make them realize their culpability for their miserable state: "I wanted to awaken my countrymen from their profound lethargy, and whoever wants to awaken does not do so with soft and light sounds but with explosions, blows, etc." as he wrote to his Austrian friend Blumentritt.[20] Secondly, Rizal situates this "backwardness" in the context of the immorality, oppression and brutality of Spanish misrule, a specific condition which could be examined by applying the rigors of scientific method. Thirdly, Rizal wanted to formulate an alternative to colonial ideology, and he believed that to achieve this it was necessary to tell the truth. The corruption of the existing order would be exposed by the truth, and in truth lay the seeds of social transformation.

How Rizal told the truth gives the *Noli* its power. In his reply to Barrantes, he had referred to his portrayal of vice-ridden Philippine society as a "painting done with the blood of my heart," applying the phrase Blumentritt had used three years earlier in a congratulatory letter to him on the *Noli*'s publication.[21] Rizal clearly felt that Blumentritt's emotive phrase had aptly captured his intensely personal and passionate effort, a work that had been inked, as he imagined, with his own blood. As only his closest friends and confidantes were aware, the writing and publishing of the *Noli* had taken Rizal to the brink of physical and financial exhaustion. Personally, Rizal harbored great hopes for his novel and meant to achieve some fame from it: "With this [work] I wish to make myself known," he confided privately to his brother Paciano, "for I suppose that it would not pass unnoticed; on the contrary, it will be the object of much discussion."²² Rizal had begun the book whilst still a medical student in Madrid in 1885 and had completed the manuscript the following year in the peaceful, rustic surroundings of Wilhelmsfeld, a village a few kilometers distant from Heidelberg, where he was studying ophthalmology. With financial help from his close friend Maximo Viola, Rizal published the manuscript himself in Berlin at the cheapest printers he could find. He sent one of the first copies off the Berlin presses to Blumentritt in Leitmeritz on 21 March 1887, with a letter attached in which he described his novel as:

> ... the first impartial and bold book on the life of the Tagalogs. The Filipinos will find in it the history of the last ten years. I hope you will note how different are my descriptions from those of other writers. The government and the friars will probably attack the work ... but I trust in the God of Truth and in the persons who have seen our sufferings at close range. Here I answer all the false concepts which have been formed against us and all the insults which have been intended to belittle us. I hope you will understand it well.²³

Neither aesthetic merit nor artistic recognition, Rizal declared, had been his main concern in the *Noli*. His primary aim was to reveal the truth by countering the defamatory representations of his country by the colonizers and portraying the harsh reality:

> I have unmasked the hypocrisy which, under the cloak of Religion, came among us to impoverish us, to brutalize us; I have distinguished the true Religion from the false, from the superstitious, from that which traffics with the sacred word to extract money, to make us believe in foolishness which Catholicism would blush at if it had knowledge of it. I have unveiled what lay hidden behind the deceptive and brilliant words of our government; I have told our compatriots of our faults, our vices, our culpable and shameful complacence with these miseries.²⁴

Rizal imagined his country and people were suffering from an illness and pain too acute to touch. His chosen title *Noli me tangere* held a clinical rather than a biblical metaphor and was less concerned with Jesus' first words spoken to Mary Magdalene after his resurrection

(John 20:17) than evoking the diseased state of the social body. As he explained: "The book contains, then, things that nobody in our country has spoken of until the present. They are so delicate that they cannot be touched by anyone."[25]

In unpacking the question of truth in the *Noli*, Caroline Hau correctly links Rizal's commentary not simply to his brand of social realism but also to his ethical thinking.[26] The ambivalent interaction between fact and fiction found in the *Noli* functions as a critique of the colonial order, itself made possible by an appeal to higher standards of morality and a belief in a human ability to enact change. Rizal confronts his people stunted in their progress and compares his country with Europe, the site of cultural production, modernity and change. His dual vision enables him to approach the mechanisms of Spanish colonial power with the eyes of the outsider, while simultaneously retaining the intimacy and passion, of the insider. Aptly summed up by Hau as the "enforced rootedness" of the "insider-outsider," this double consciousness gives the *Noli*'s narrative perspective its sharp insight.[27]

Rizal's work was only the second novel to be written by a Filipino. The first, *Ninay*, written by Rizal's friend Pedro Paterno and published in Madrid in 1885, was experimental and mediocre. Cluttered with superficial footnotes on Philippine customs, flora and fauna, Paterno's work deferentially avoided issues that might cause offence to a Spanish readership.[28] In contrast, Rizal drew his readers deeply into the mire of Manila and provincial Tagalog society and brought into exquisite, excruciating focus the hypocrisy, cowardice, stupidity and ignorance that made colonial domination in his country possible. His supporters recognized the realism of his portrayal. He was pleased to share with Blumentritt a letter from the award winning Filipino painter Felix Resurrección Hidalgo, who had sent him this reaction:

> I have read some pages of your book and I have found them full of truth.... I admire your courage in saying plainly what you think and the inspiration reflected in your work which makes one feel the palpitations of the heart of a man who loves his country.[29]

As the initial readers of the *Noli* found, there was something unnervingly familiar in the book's scenes and characters. The Spanish lawyer Antonio Regidor, writing to Rizal from London, complimented him on showing the "defects and virtues of our idolatrous countrymen (*idolatradas paisanas*)" with a "marvellous hand (*manera maravillosa*)." He saw the characters as instantly recognizable, even identifiable, and asked Rizal which of the many female victims of "the concupiscence of the religious colonial" had served as the model for María Clara. With only small variations, he wrote, the misfortunes of this "expiatory martyr" brought to mind those of "Lucia of Imus ... Anita of Binondo ... Isabel of Pangasinan, etc. etc. Which of these women's lives did you use to write your drama?"[30] In the following section we will examine how the answer to Regidor's question became the basis of Rizal's depiction of female mental weakness and hysteria.

Chengoy's Gossip and "The Eastern Question"

One of Rizal's closest friends was José M. Cecilio, nicknamed Chengoy. Boarders together in their schooldays and *compañeros* throughout their adolescence, they kept in close touch as young men, and after Rizal's departure for Europe in 1882 Chengoy became his main informant about the circles of Manila society he had left behind. It was a role that Chengoy positively relished. His letters related in rich detail the everyday lives of Rizal's admirers and amours. He regaled Rizal with lively anecdotes about girls they knew and about his young sweethearts' preoccupations. The thought of a number of well-born *dalagas* waiting and pining for his return, needless to say, served Rizal's vanity and flattered his ego.

Embroidered with his own observations and spiced with personal opinion, Chengoy's *tsismis*, or gossip, had at its core a "primordial understanding" where names, jokes or scenarios required neither explanation nor elaboration since all that was talked about in all its significations and contexts was already intelligible and tacitly understood.[31] Gossip became a private, intimate form of communication that the two men enjoyed exclusively; a mode of speech they employed within the pleasurable context of male homosocial bonding. In another important sense, gossip brought Rizal closer to the life he had left behind. It became a discourse that permitted Rizal to participate, albeit semi-vicariously, with unbroken continuity in Manila's social whirl; allowed him to believe that he could still exert an influence in the lives of his girlfriends despite being abroad. Finally, Chengoy's gossip provided fertile soil in which Rizal cultivated his imagining of female sexual desire that ultimately came to be embodied in the character of María Clara, the putative heroine of his first novel *Noli me tangere*, and his most enduring vision of ideal Filipino female sexuality.

Cecilio and Rizal could speak on the complex subject of women in perfect accord. In their shared code, women were often identified just by an initial, their place of residence or a meaningful phrase; they were "M," "O," the "Santa Cruz girls," "the dear P, of dwarfish love."[32] One young woman, Cecilio reported, found Rizal's sudden absence particularly difficult to accept:

> Poor girl, what tears has she not shed from the first days when she arrived from her hometown and did not find you in the house but instead five thousand leagues from Manila! Your sister María can tell you about it, because she was in tears before her. One day she told me that she was not in the mood for anything, not even for her intimate friends, and that she wanted to dye all her clothes. I replied that she should not despair because the years pass by quickly...and that one of your greatest sorrows, if not the only one, when you left was that you had to be separated from her. We have to console her some way.[33]

It would prove extremely hard, as Chengoy would later discover, to comfort Leonor Rivera. She was 15 when Rizal left and had thought of him as her fiancé. Her family was distantly related to Rizal's and she had attended the same private school as his sisters. Her father, Antonio Rivera, managed the Casa Tomasina, the student boarding house in Intramuros where Rizal and his friends lodged while studying at the University of Santo Tomas. Leonor was 13 when Rizal boarded at Intramuros. Younger than him by six years, she displayed the accomplishments of a young woman typical of her class and upbringing — she could sing, play the harp and piano and was educated enough to read and write in Spanish.

Whilst early letters show they regarded each other with affection, she signing her name as "Taimis," the codename Rizal had given her, their love affair developed when Rizal was abroad, through a six-year correspondence, undoubtedly nourished by the encouragements of Rizal's skilful proxy. The inscription on a photograph Leonor sent to Rizal three years after his departure speaks of her unabated romantic ardor. Writing first with formal decorum "To José from his faithful cousin," Leonor liked to keep up the pretence to secrecy she and Rizal had established, adding below it her true dedication in their coded language: "To my unforgettable and dearest lover, this picture is dedicated by his devoted Leonor."[34] But her efforts and hopes came to nothing. Despite their pledges of love and Leonor's fidelity, Rizal allowed opportunities to marry Leonor Rivera slip away. Leonor, meanwhile, manipulated by her mother who seemed to have grown tired of her daughter's misplaced and futile devotion, was made to finally accept the proposal of an Englishman, Henry Kipping, a railway engineer working on the Manila to Dagupan line. Entering into the union unhappily, Leonor burnt all of Rizal's letters, set the conditions that her mother would share their marital home and vowed never to play the piano nor sing again. She died giving birth to a second child, scarcely two years into her marriage.[35]

As Cecilio recounts in his letters, Rizal's departure had a huge psychological effect on Leonor Rivera. Her gaiety vanished; she lost weight and sleep, became wan and sickly.

> The person who suffers on your account — of this you should not have the least doubt, inasmuch as the sky is cloudless and the stars can be seen clearly — left her retreat for being sick. She is suffering from insomnia and angina, and she is thin. The persons who appreciate her no longer know what to do for her, but our physician friend, who was consulted about her ailments said that insomnia was natural at her age. But anyone who had seen him when he said this would suspect that there was some ambiguity in his words. This unfortunate person must be praying that the *no* in that phrase *Hasta el amor no se olvida* [Even love is not forgotten] be never erased or remain in it forever.[36]

Months pass; Cecilio's letters are cluttered with news of other women.[37] Meanwhile Leonor vacillates, "one day well another day ill," but mostly despairs. Rizal had become remiss in writing to Leonor. It was not the first time he had caused her to doubt the sincerity of his affections, for in the past she had thought him too impulsive "like a newly opened rose, very flushed and fragrant at the beginning, but afterwards it begins to wither."[38] Cecilio tries to comfort the woman he and Rizal refer to as "the little landlady," with good results. He assures her that Rizal remains true and she spurns other suitors; he tells her jokes and relates the way Rizal writes to him about her, and her spirits are lifted: "I do this to her so as to console her somewhat in her distressing situation."³⁹ Despite the passage of time, Cecilio reports, Leonor's longing continues unabated:

> The truth is, dear namesake, this young woman is sick of fever every week and as you can very well understand, this is the effect of the ardent passion she feels for you.⁴⁰

Meanwhile, a second girl, Leonor Valenzuela, nicknamed Orang, is also being led to believe by Cecilio that Rizal remains devoted to her. "Orang," he writes to Rizal, "asked me what it was you told me in your letters and I answered that you continue loving her."⁴¹ The two Leonors had very different personalities, and Rizal would have been wrong to believe Cecilio's reassurances that both women missed and desired him with the same intensity. Unlike Leonor Rivera, Orang does not suffer because of Rizal's absence. She remains sociable, cheerful and healthy. She denies that she is Rivera's rival, allows a string of admirers to court her simultaneously and with an opportunistic attitude that evens the score on both manipulative men, checks with Cecilio every now and again, as he becomes increasingly aware, that her beau abroad continues his interest in her.⁴²

Nevertheless, Rizal still vainly views the two women as choices that merely await a decision. Rizal raises the issue with Cecilio, referring to Leonor Rivera as the "Eastern Question," a jocular allusion to the diplomatic dilemma then preoccupying the European great powers. Considering the contrasting personalities of the two women Cecilio gives his friend crucial advice:

> In reply to your question as to whom I would choose of the two L's, if I were in your place, I am going to tell you that I favour the longstanding Eastern Question, because she is more feminine (*hembra*), more yielding (*ductil*), more docile, sweeter (*dulce*), softer (*suave*), nicer (*dengosa*), more sweetly affectionate (*acaramelada*) and above all more educated. This does not mean that the other one is detestable, for she is industrious, hardworking, and she is not stupid in regard to earning a living.⁴³

The importance of Cecilio's reply to Rizal's question cannot be underestimated. It is worth remembering that Rizal has known Leonor Rivera for seven years and both families approve of the relationship. Although Rizal's letters to Cecilio and to Leonor Rivera have not survived, we know that Rizal was touched by Leonor's letters and enjoyed reading her sentimental disclosures. Rizal was moreover fully aware of her illnesses and accepted that the cause was the intensity of her desire for him.[44] Finally, while it may be that a seed of doubt could have been planted in Rizal's mind by a dream he had in which Leonor was unfaithful, her regular correspondence and Cecilio's reports would surely have put paid to his anxiety.[45] Because Cecilio has been so energetic in his task as Rizal's proxy, both women are led to believe they are Rizal's *novia*, sweetheart, just as the two men have calculated, assuredly then Rizal therefore feels confident he can choose between the two Leonors. In the light of this, Rizal's diary entry of 31 March 1884 in which he feels he has somehow lost out in love is rather self-absorbed aggrandizing:

> The women of my country please me very much. I don't know why, but I find in them I know not what that enchants me and makes me dream.... So many young women who could have illumined my life even for one day and yet nothing. I'm going to become like those travellers who go through a path strewn with flowers: they pass by without touching them with the hope of finding something uncertain, until the road becomes more arid and they find themselves at last in a bare region regretting the past. I have no regret except perhaps having deprived myself of many pleasures. I feel that my heart has not lost its capacity to love, only I don't find anyone to love. I have used this sentiment but little.[46]

Rizal struggles to find words to describe what qualities he finds pleasing in the Filipina, what it is about them that makes him fall into pleasant, dreamy reverie. He imagines himself as a traveler embarked on some uncertain purpose in which love and pleasure is fleeting and ultimately sacrificed. He feels that he cannot find anyone to love and even thinks he is not well-versed in the emotion. But these vain musings mask the convoluted machinations Cecilio has been carrying out on Rizal's behalf. As his correspondence with Cecilio makes evident, Rizal actively encouraged love and desire in the two women by giving, at the very least, the impression he himself was in love.

Cecilio's reply to Rizal's question is considered. He weighs up their contrasting qualities and the feisty, flirtatious, spirited, independent, intractable Orang who is resourceful and clever enough to make her own living comes short of Cecilio's ideal of womanliness. Unlike the devoted, lovesick and easily pitied or patronized Leonor Rivera, Orang was disconcerting; her sexual desires attractive as well as anarchic. And Rizal believed he had a choice. After pondering over Cecilio's judgement for some months, Rizal gives his answer. Cecilio is pleased:

> I congratulate you on your wise selection of the woman who will be your faithful companion. She is not at La Concordia but in Dagupan, Pangasinan, beside her parents and I believe that she will not come to Manila until next December, and I do not know if she will enter again La Concordia and finish her education.[47]

Compensating for Leonor's erratic education, presumably, are the feminine qualities Cecilio has defined. And what of Orang? By this time, it is rumored that she is betrothed. Subsequent letters show Leonor Rivera's continued fidelity to Rizal. She discontinues her formal education, lives with her parents in the provinces and spurns the attentions of numerous prospective suitors and admirers. It is not known whether Rizal formally disclosed his decision to her; within Cecilio's letters she remains known as the "beautiful but frail Eastern Question," pining and waiting for Rizal's return. Rizal on the other hand had begun his first novel and, inspired by Leonor Rivera's devotion, manifested so spectacularly in her psychosomatic illnesses, wrote the first Filipino literary representation of the force of native female sexual desire.

Mad, Bad and Hysterical: Female Sexuality in *Noli me tangere*

Near the beginning of Rizal's *Noli me tangere*[48] is a scene charged with sexual tension. The winsome mestiza María Clara is awaiting the arrival of Crisostomo Ibarra, the man to whom she is betrothed. Childhood sweethearts, Ibarra and María Clara have not seen each other for seven years, and now each passing moment increases her impatience and excitation. But, like any wellborn young woman expecting a gentleman visitor, María Clara cannot appear too eager, and she occupies herself knitting a silk purse in a vain endeavor to distract herself and calm her nerves. Her concentration is focused on the noises outside that might herald the arrival of her sweetheart: "Each sound from the street, each carriage that passes by causes the maiden's bosom to throb, and makes her tremble."[49]

In this scene, Rizal sets out to give narrative shape to María Clara's feelings for Ibarra, the novel's idealistic patriot hero. Rizal traces back María Clara's attraction to the happy times she and Ibarra had shared as children in the provincial town of San Diego. Their intimacy is sentimentally rooted in their childhood games, quarrels and secrets. At puberty their paths had decently diverged, Ibarra departing to pursue his studies in Europe and María Clara being dispatched to a strict, almost penal convent school in Intramuros. The sweethearts would not see each other again for seven years.

Rizal establishes the bond between María Clara and Ibarra as being both pure and propitious — a union of youthful innocence which brought together the son of the richest *capitalista* in the whole province with the daughter of a man who had left San Diego for the city and had become the wealthiest property owner in Binondo. But the ultimate justification for the union, Rizal stresses, is love. Only love can explain María Clara's tremulous excitement and trepidation, and love itself is beyond explanation: "If you who read this have loved, you will understand," Rizal claims, "if not it is useless for me to tell you."[50] Love, rather than lasciviousness, justifies the flesh and blood pressures of María Clara's corporeal sensuality and legitimates the inclusion of libidinal excitement in the text.

Electrified by desire, María Clara's body expresses her love for Ibarra by breaking free from her conscious control. She finds herself unable to speak and allows her aunt to answer her father's questions. At the sound of a carriage stopping and the mention of her sweetheart's name, she is gripped in a state of rigid tension. She "pales" and drops her knitting: "she wanted to move but could not," Rizal relates, "a nervous trembling seized her body."[51] Penetrated, as it were, by sound, María Clara seems to respond only to powerful erotic impulses generated by Ibarra's arrival. Hearing his steps on the stairs and the sound of his "virile" voice abruptly sends her body flying into energetic movement. In order to retain her modesty and hide her urgent, thrilling amativeness, she flees to the oratory, a room her father has filled with his "house-gods" or religious icons.

> Pale and breathing rapidly, the maiden pressed her heaving bosom and sought to listen. She heard the voice, that voice so dear to her, which for a long time she had heard only in her dreams: he was asking for her. Mad with happiness she kissed the nearest image, Saint Anthony.

Fortunate saint! In wood as in life, prey to sweet temptations. Then she found the keyhole to peep through and contemplate him.[52]

Only in private, closeted in a silent chapel, can María Clara relish the voice that has nourished her fantasies and delighted her in her dreams; only by spying on her lover through a keyhole can she savor his physical form.

Being unmarried and chaste and forced to show restraint, María Clara suffers at once from the excess of her sexual desire and the social compulsion to appear moral and respectable. Her experience of sexual excitement is marked by concealment, displacement and speechlessness. Discovered by her elderly aunt in an apparently dishevelled state, María Clara is plunged into embarrassment and is led, docile and subdued, into the private and taboo space of the young woman's boudoir. "'Come! Fix yourself up, come!' prodded the old woman ... the maiden allowed herself to be led like a little child. They closeted themselves in her room."[53] Shame quiets María Clara and tames her ardour. Her lack of sexual self-control is seen as necessitating the intervention of authority and her physical confinement.

"Love" in this scene not only explains María Clara's behavior. It also performs the vital narrative function of uniting the progressive patriot Crisostomo Ibarra with the perfect Filipina maiden. Like the "foundational fictions" of Latin America, the *Noli* employs erotic rhetoric to provide a framework for patriotic dreams, and thereby ascribes a key role to heterosexual desire. The relationship between Ibarra and María Clara marries "national destiny to personal passion."[54] Ibarra's love for María Clara is bound to the very same youthful memories that form the wellspring of the love he has for his country, Filipinas:

> You seemed to me the nymph, the spirit, the poetic incarnation of my country: lovely, simple, amiable, full of candour, daughter of the Philippines, of this beautiful country which unites with the great virtues of Mother Spain the lovely qualities of a young nation — just as all that is lovely and fair and adorns both races is united in your being. Hence my love for you and that which I profess for my Motherland are blended into a single love.[55]

Significantly, the hero of the *Noli* is not only an idealistic patriot but also a healthy, virile and energetic man newly returned from Europe, the fount of enlightenment and modernity. Dressed formally in a European cut black suit, Ibarra's "commanding height, his features, his movements, exuded an aura of wholesome youthfulness in which body and soul had developed and blended equally well."[56] Equally significantly, Rizal couples this active, masculine embodiment of the patriotic, the enlightened and the modern, with an idealized incarnation of passive femininity whose most treasured qualities are simplicity and virtue. Her eyes are habitually cast downwards as a sign of her modesty. She "manifested her love with that virginal grace which knows only pure thoughts."[57] It is ironic that the seven cloistered years María Clara has spent in the care of Catholic nuns, an education that neither Rizal nor his patriot hero Ibarra would applaud, has moulded a young woman whose sweet innocence they idolize.

Besides her moral virtues, needless to say, María Clara is blessed with a radiant beauty. She is a "fantastic vision," otherworldly, perfection incarnate:

> ... a deity, a sylph, advancing without touching the floor, circled and surrounded by a luminous halo. At her presence the flowers bloom, the dance frolics, melodies awaken, and a choir of devils, nymphs, satyrs, genii, maidens, angels, and shepherds, dance, shaking tambourines, gyrate and at the goddess, deposit, each one, a tribute.[58]

María Clara's virtuous chasteness and ethereal loveliness enable her to personify the nation and to inspire male patriots like Ibarra to action. But her feminine charms also distract him from his patriotic tasks, and he shows his irritation. "You have made me forget that I have my duties."[59]

Oscillating between extreme emotions, María Clara embodies an exaggerated notion of femininity in which maidenly proprieties and sexual desire framed her selfhood, a construction that served to define Filipina female sexuality as shameful, sinful and guilt-ridden. Masochism and sexual prudery was María Clara's lamentable legacy to Filipino women. As Carmen Guerrero Nakpil perceptively writes,

> It is the element of guilt and disaster that we must lament most — it is so well rooted in our mores that the average Filipina, though she may not have read through Rizal's novels, has a compulsive sense of sin and doom, of sadness and shame, she feels obliged to see terror in the delights of love and sex and to offset these, as María Clara did, by a kind of frantic piety.[60]

Rizal seems to agree with Tasio, the philosopher of his fictional San Diego, that: "A woman, to be good, must have been, at least at some time, a virgin or a mother."[61]

As the only mother that is sympathetically portrayed in the *Noli*, Sisa, the simple-minded peasant woman provides an emotive appeal to the patriot's noble purpose.[62] She suffers grievously in both body and spirit: maltreated by her abusive husband, in anguish over her missing sons, horse whipped and falsely arrested, Sisa is figured as a helpless mother whom patriots are duty bound to protect and defend. However, her eligibility for patriotic compassion seems to hinge on two conditions. First, Sisa conforms dutifully to the maternal model of doting mother and faithful wife, lavishing affection on her sons and endlessly tolerating her husband's absences, idleness and cruelty. Secondly, Sisa is sexually honorable. Rizal repeatedly contrasts her decency with the immorality of the 'shockingly attired women whom the town called the soldiers' mistresses', women from whom Sisa herself recoils.[63] They walk in the streets without any "overskirt or *tapis*," wearing only an "underskirt or *saya* of yellow and green, and a blouse of blue gauze."[64] Sisa, on the other hand, though her face is lined by hardship, manifests a wholesome and unadorned brown-skinned beauty, *kayumangging-kaligatan*, a natural simplicity.[65]

In a scene that recalls his own mother's unfounded arrest and humiliation, Sisa is marched between armed soldiers to the town jail and stripped of her honor and respectability. She agonizes that she has descended even lower than the mistresses of the soldiery, one of whom taunts her as she is escorted like a criminal through the town plaza. Thrown into the soldiers' barracks, she is plunged into despair and sickened by the sight of wanton women wallowing in their own licentiousness: "a mistress was lying down on a bench, pillowed on a man's thigh, smoking and looking at the ceiling in boredom. Other women helped the men to clean garments, or weapons etc., singing lewd songs in low voices."[66]

Rizal's empathetic treatment of Sisa is premised on the representation of an essentially passive and self-sacrificing female nature that requires protection from the pernicious effects of a corrupt and brutal colonial system. Rizal's pity is accompanied by his criticism of woman's "weakness," a mental and moral weakness that he perceived to be responsible for fuelling the conditions of woman's subjugation. If Sisa is a defenseless victim of social injustice, exploited and oppressed by abusive friars, her husband, and the *guardia civil*, it is because she is "weak of character and with more heart than brain." She "knew only how to love and to weep."[67]

In stark contrast to María Clara and Sisa stand two female characters who are emblematic of the moral and cultural corrosiveness of Spanish colonial rule, the horrific Doña Victorina and Doña Consolación. These women are so distasteful that as the novel draws to its close the narrator laments their continued survival; he wishes they could have been killed off "for the good of the public."[68] Emphatically neither virtuous virgins nor loving paragons of motherhood, the two doñas image the anarchic and degenerate, the "negative opposite to a propagandist project of creating identity."[69]

Doña Victorina and Doña Consolación are caricatures drawn to represent Filipina women who despise their own language, dress and people. Refusing to speak in their native Tagalog tongue, they instead speak in a mixture of "murdered Tagalog" and mangled Spanish in a pretentious attempt to adopt the airs of the Hispanic elite, or the European, succeeding only in outrageous imitation. Victorina, a woman of means, wears badly fitting European clothes and applies copious layers of rice powder to hide her brown complexion.

Both women attempt to distance themselves further from their indigenous identities and status by marrying Spaniards. Doña Victorina spurns every native suitor, including the extremely wealthy Capitan Tiago, and eventually settles for the worthless quack doctor Don Tiburcio Espadaña, a lame, stuttering, bald and toothless colonial: "she would have preferred a Spaniard who ... had more mettle and a superior air — as it was her habit to say. This class of Spaniards, however, had never approached her to ask for her hand."[70] Here Rizal criticizes the tendency of his fellow indios to accord too much deference to Spaniards, even those who in the Peninsula had been criminals, failures or social outcasts. Despite Don Tiburcio's worthlessness, Doña Victorina expends great effort on cultivating her investment. Money allows her to transform her husband physically and mould him closer to the image of her desires: she fits him with good dentures, clothes him using the best tailors and prohibits him from walking in public because of his limp, ordering instead the finest horses and carriages to transport them grandly around the town.[71] Doña Consolación, Rizal informs us, at one time a *lavandera* or washerwoman, had escaped her humble origins by marrying a Spanish corporal who later rose through the ranks to become an *alferez* or lieutenant and was assigned to command the Guardia Civil detachment in San Diego. Within this tiny backwater, Rizal wryly observes, the alferez had the power of a King, just as the parish priest was like the Pope.

In describing the sheer badness of both Victorina and Consolación, Rizal dwells at length on their physical hideousness, discerning an equivalence between their character and appearance. To indicate the decayed state of Doña Victorina's soul, Rizal draws upon the familiar imagery of the crone, and brings to mind Ovid's portrayal of the repellent Invidia in *Metamorphoses*.[72] "Her luxuriant hair," Rizal writes, "had been reduced — according to her maid — to a tiny bun the size of a head of garlic; wrinkles furrowed her face, and her teeth had begun to loosen; her eyes had also suffered quite considerably; she frequently had to squint...."[73] Victorina's prolonged search for a good Spanish husband spoke of an unassailable vanity, because "she was no longer passable; she was passé," Rizal jests.[74] Echoing the traditional misogynistic logic that marks old and aging women as evil and threatening, Rizal's rendering of Victorina's physical decrepitude simultaneously expresses his moral condemnation. Victorina has become "ugly and ridiculous" and "a hag,"[75] and has desperately, uselessly tried to compensate by falsifying her very femininity. She is bedecked in a profusion of artifices: false ringlets and curls, lace, rice powder, ribbons, and during an imagined pregnancy, bright colours and flowers. All this feminine paraphernalia, Rizal seems to say, was a dangerous deception, an attempt to conceal corruption and decay.

While Doña Victorina is ridiculous, Doña Consolación is pure evil. She is likened by Rizal to Medusa. Here is a woman who frightens people simply by gazing upon them with full raging rapacity, a long cigar wedged between thick, grimacing purple lips. Her body is a carapace containing her own violence; her throbbing veins carry not blood but sour "vinegar and gall."[76] She is saturated in her own bile; her hair is sparse and stringy, her thighs thin and collapsed. Wearing grimy rags, sitting alone in dirt and semi-darkness, puffing clouds of cigar smoke, she has the same mythic fearsomeness as the *mangkukulam*, the witch that terrorizes the Filipino psyche. She surpasses even Doña Victorina in her ugliness, and exceeds her likewise in corruption and evil. Rizal mines the glossary of horror to evoke a woman who was no longer human:

... she was seen pacing from one end of the room to another, silent as if meditating on something terrible or malignant. Her eyes glittered like a serpent's, caught and about to be crushed underfoot. They were cold, luminous, piercing, akin to something slimy, filthy and cruel.[77]

Not content with this imagery, Rizal's imagination turns to nature, as violent and unpredictable, for further metaphors. Doña Consolación is likened to the force of a gathering storm, a tempest that leaves terrible destruction in its wake. Her body is no longer composed of flesh, but has become a core of pure electrical energy "threatening to explode into a terrible tempest. Everything around her bent like rice stalks at the first gust of a hurricane."[78]

Besides being reflected in their physical appearance, the moral decadence of Doña Victorina and Doña Consolación is manifest in their aberrant sexuality and their deviant marriages. They both violate the boundaries of sexual difference: Doña Victorina is "imposing and masculine;"[79] Consolación also had "masculine features."[80] Victorina subjugates her husband Don Tiburcio to the point of complete capitulation. With sadistic cruelty, Doña Victorina targets her husband's Achilles' heel, his lack of teeth, and to humiliate and punish him she periodically rips out his dentures:

> Whatever she said had to be followed. She had come to the point of completely dominating her husband, who for his part, did not put up any resistance. He had become like a kind of lap dog to her. If she was annoyed she did not allow him to go out; and when she was really angry she pulled out his dentures, leaving him unsightly for one or two more days, depending.[81]

Doña Consolación is no less a sadist than Doña Victorina. Although regularly beaten by her violent and cruel husband, Consolación matches if not surpasses his brutality. Indeed, Rizal explicitly highlights the sexual charge found in Consolación's sadism and her violent marital relationship. If the alferez's lessons in Spanish were reinforced by beatings, she for her part, responded to her husband's painful tutorials with equally vicious gusto, scratching, gouging and pulling at the "tufts of hair on his chin and at another portion of his anatomy" until her husband, all bloody, cried out and "asked for forgiveness ... a shirt torn to shreds, many hidden parts of the body laid bare...."[82] Yet the servants know that the ferocious escalation of anger and violence was infused with sexual energy and was a prelude to the couple's sexual intimacy. As Rizal writes, the heavy sound of boots being removed caused the servants to "wink at each other," and the discordant sounds within the "darkness of the bedroom," are too terrible and pornographic for him to relate: "A scream, the sound of a falling body, imprecations, moans, curses, blows, hoarse voices.... Who can describe what took place in the darkness of that room?"[83]

Rizal writes the character of Doña Victorina as if he were unmasking woman's terrible falsehood, warning against the illusions of femininity. Her physical charms, so he reveals, are counterfeit; her sexual fickleness merely concealed a lustful sexual appetite, in Doña Victorina's case, an illicit appetite for men who were not Filipinos. Saved by indigestion on their first wedding night, Don Tiburcio conducts himself "honorably" by the second night and consummates the union. If the experience traumatizes him, "he had aged at least ten years more" as Rizal imagines for his readers, it is not because the unfortunate man has been confronted by a sexually inexperienced maiden. Doña Victorina was no virgin. Inclined to "lay her nets to fish in the sea of worldly waters for the object of her sleepless nights," Rizal delicately writes, Doña Victorina was wont to bestow her sexual favors on her foreign lovers having "not a few times" or so Rizal hints, delivered "jewels of inestimable value into the hands of foreign adventurers and nationals."[84]

Rizal's representations of women who did not fulfil their self-abnegating role of wife and mother, who resisted domestication, took on an even more monstrous incarnation in the figure of Doña Consolación. She believed herself to be beautiful, and neither Rizal nor her own husband can beat her into submission, or make her understand that she could not be exposed to human society let alone be allowed to take her place in it.

In tracing the path of Consolación's descent into hell, Rizal tracks the iniquitous route in prostitution. She is outrightly considered a prostitute, "a mistress of the soldiery" with a bodily odour betraying her lustful immorality.[85] The sexualized cruelty of Doña Consolación and Doña Victorina might be viewed in the light of Krafft-Ebing's famous elucidation of sadism, who defined the behaviour as "the experience of sexual pleasurable sensations produced by acts of cruelty, bodily punishment ... or when witnessed in others, be they animals or human beings. It may also consist of an innate desire to humiliate, hurt, wound or even destroy others in order thereby to create sexual pleasure in one's self."[86] If Rizal found it difficult, or unseemly, to describe the events that followed between the alferez and his wife, his confinement of the action inside the "darkness of the bedroom" pointedly emphasizes the intensely sexual nature of what occurs and the interpretations we must make.

Whether they were depictions of female domesticity and selfless maternalism, or images of spiteful cruelty and evil, essential to Rizal's contradictory and intrinsically ambivalent representations of female subjectivity, is a surprisingly unvarying notion of female sexuality chiefly characterized as being highly unstable and volatile. In Rizal's eyes, sexual desire festered in women from all classes. In the impoverished Sisa, desire was fatally self-immolating and psychically destructive, a product of a weak generosity all too easily exploited; while María Clara may not have been conscious of her bodily sexual impulses, she is shown to have suffered from such promptings of the flesh and the effort to repress them. Driven by selfishness, sinfulness and spite, Doña Consolación and Doña Victorina lose their humanity and become little more than bizarre, visual entities. Half-blind and sporting a wig of ringlets, the latter is a figure of curiosity and comedy, and the former, abandoned by her husband, wholly gives herself up to vice and is simply a nightmarish vision, an epiphany of horror, instilling fear in all who behold her. Whether woman's downfall comes as a consequence of yielding to the desires of a womanish heart or sensuality, lustfulness and sheer excess are the cause, a lexicon of doom and condemnation articulates Rizal's conceptions of female nature — illness and madness, immorality and evil.

Within this frame of biopolitics, the gender crises and sexual anarchy wrought by the characters of Doña Consolación and Doña Victorina in the *Noli* told of a society in moral disarray. As either nightmarish figures of gender disorder and pathological sexuality, or vulnerable targets of sexual and emotional abuse, Rizal's major female characters in the *Noli* enact moral fables, personify ethical lessons with underlying messages that critique the colonial social order. The characters of Doña Consolación and Doña Victorina are posited as examples of moral and sexual degeneracy and symbolize chaos incarnate, existing outside the boundaries of ilustrado patriarchal culture as well as being its disrupters. Even the legitimate love between María Clara and Ibarra is considered a serious distraction from the higher purposes of patriotism and service to one's country.

Rizal's frightening picture of female sexuality and dominance could find its justification in a view on the relationship between gender and intelligence espoused by the contemporary social analyst Raimundo Geler. In his controversial book *Islas Filipinas: Reseña de su organización social y administrativa*, Geler maintained the doctrine of separate spheres through a logic which argued that "in those people who advanced with civilization, man excels the woman, while in civilizations that have declined, the contrary happens and the woman excels the man." Bolstered by the scientific proof found in the cranial data accumulated by numerous European scientists, Geler's logic identified the larger cranial capacity of males as the defining mark of progressive civilizations and the "more perfect races." In such societies, Geler thought, it was the natural right of men to exercise their superiority. Only in decaying societies did the opposite occur.[87] A writer respected by the propagandistas for his anti-friar polemics, Raimundo Geler was the pseudonym of Manuel Regidor, the brother of the London-based lawyer Antonio Regidor. Rizal implored Blumentritt to attend closely to Geler's book: "I beg you to read it," he wrote emphatically from London, "it is written by a Spaniard and tells many truths. If only there were fifty Spaniards like Geler, I would give and shed the last drop of my blood for Spain."[88] Influenced heavily by contemporary European scientific research, Geler's ideas were perfectly in accord with the image of sexual crises Rizal presented in the *Noli*, where the anarchy caused by female sexual desire and women who dominated was meant to be understood as symptoms of a society in decline.

Rizal's Patria

Rizal imagined he could approach the social conditions of his country in the manner of a physician obtaining an accurate diagnosis in order to propose a cure. If truth had the ability to "unmask" hypocrisies, or to show the inner nature of things, telling the truth was akin to the methods of clinical diagnosis. The intertwining of literary conventions and scientific metaphor is apparent from the beginning in the *Noli*, even from the title. As mentioned earlier, Rizal claimed that the title was inspired by Jesus' first words spoken to Mary Magdalene immediately after his resurrection, an episode described in the Gospel according to St. John. Certainly, this "Noli me tangere" scene had long been a source of inspiration for artists since the Renaissance and Rizal may have even viewed Corregio's evocative interpretation in the Prado.[89] It is more likely, however, that Rizal had its most popular usage in mind, "Noli me tangere" being common parlance for a cancerous type of ulcer that particularly afflicted the face. Indeed, the vulgate Latin phrase and a malignant ulcer were held synonymous according to Corlieu's *Memorandum de Medicina, Cirujía y Partos* (1876) and Cuesta's *Vocabulario de Medicina* (1878), just two of the books widely used by medical students like Rizal at the time.[90]

Rizal's prefatory dedication of the *Noli* to "Mi Patria" delineates at the outset the clinical metaphor that would permeate the entire novel. Rizal meant to treat his country as a physician would a diseased body whose cure lay in the accuracy and veracity of clinical diagnosis. At its essence, the dedication presents an emotionally-charged image of a diseased mother attended by her patriot-physician son:

> In the annals of human adversity, there is etched a cancer, of a breed so malignant that the least contact exacerbates it and stirs in it the sharpest of pains. And thus, so many times amidst modern cultures I have wanted to evoke you, sometimes for memories of you to keep me company, other times, to compare you with other nations — many times your beloved image appears to me afflicted with a social cancer of similar malignancy.
>
> Desiring your well-being, which is our own, and searching for the best cure, I will do with you as the ancients of old did with their afflicted: expose them on the steps of the temple so that each one who would come to invoke the Divine, would propose a cure for them.
>
> And to this end, I will attempt to faithfully reproduce your condition without much ado. I will lift part of the veil that conceals your illness, sacrificing to truth everything, even my own self-respect, for as your son, I also suffer in your defects and failings.[91]

This gendered symbol of the homeland constitutes several distinctive features particularly associated with science and female sexuality. First, the maternal potency of this image lies in its capacity to stimulate familial and sympathetic connection. She is comforting, familiar and ever-near. She is the immutable point of reference in the patriot's innumerable comparisons with other nations, with other "modern cultures." Yet, the dedication is clearly not an anthem of adoration to an ideal maternal femininity. And this is the second point: Rizal's Patria is an object of helplessness and pity. She is described as undergoing horrors of suffering, a cancer of particular malignancy corroding from the inside out. While she elicits sympathetic concern, she is simultaneously an interesting medical case to be solved. Thirdly, her face is so disfigured by disease that it must be concealed behind a veil. The patriot says he will lift the veil that hides her illness and confront the full horror of what lies beneath, even though this would mean "sacrificing everything." Here the binds of filial duty and love do not solely dictate his actions for the patriot understands how he too is implicated in her illness. Thus, fourthly, being her son, he feels contaminated by her affliction, and this realization adds urgency to his search for a cure.

Rizal's allegorizing partly borrows from classical antiquity and refers specifically to the allegorical image of a corrupted, diseased female body that is deeply rooted in the Christian tradition. As the paintings and sculptures examined by Marina Warner show, a woman's body was perceived as both entrapping and contaminating, corruption occurring equally within the soul and body, one mirroring the other.[92] Certainly, Rizal's education at the hands of the Jesuits and Dominicans would have made these depictions of sinfulness and this Christian mode of thought with its inherent misogyny all too familiar. The physical disintegration and mortality of Rizal's Patria harnesses this moral outlook and once again articulates the age-old cipher of the fallen woman upon whose wasted and diseased flesh is imprinted vice and sin.

Given the negative value Rizal places on his personified Patria, the veil she wears thus carries the implication of shame and guilt, rather than female sexual modesty, just as it simultaneously works to conceal the grotesque truth of her affliction. Yet, while religious and classical influences dovetail in the single key image of a veiled woman, its deployment was also tightly bound to the secular, masculinist authority of modern scientific discourse. As Ludmilla Jordanova has shown, the veiled/unveiling woman was one of the most powerful and pervasive sexual metaphors found in western scientific culture, presenting a rich metaphorical field that science and medicine has traditionally exploited. Rizal's use of this image tellingly reveals, in Jordanova's phrase, a general "physiognomic mentality." A way of thinking characteristic of the western scientific and medical tradition, the physiognomic approach was premised on the idea that the decoding of visual signs could reveal the true inner nature of things. It encouraged an intellectual enquiry behind surface appearances, of moving beyond visible signifiers towards a deeper, inner level — a method that the metaphor of unveiling vividly articulated.[93] By invoking the principle of physiognomy, Rizal tapped into a western intellectual tradition whose authority was not only firmly entrenched in science and medicine but also had for centuries set the intellectual terms for the acquisition of natural knowledge.

Placed on the steps of the temple, Rizal's weak, wasted and veiled female Patria is to be examined by each passing learned man. It is however the male patriot son endowed with reason, control and intellect who is ultimately able to comprehend her by unveiling. Within the discursive frame of Rizal's dedication, the metaphor of unveiling braids together scientific endeavor with the issues of truth and knowledge. Simultaneously, the strain of moral condemnation implicit in the diseased and disfigured female figure of Patria makes it also an image that perpetuates ancient Christian themes by integrating these associations within a discourse that was both secular and modern. In writing his dedication, Rizal made clear the triumph of male medical power and knowledge over a female afflicted with a deadly disease.

Sculpting the Sensual

Despite Rizal's exceptional empathy towards his Patria, at no point does he overturn the symbolic code that equates wasting, diseased and disfigured flesh with sin, lust and death, or, to reverse the symbolic imagery, equates a healthy, young female body with virtue. Rizal simply does not challenge these aesthetic constructions and symbolic equations.

To represent allegorical images of virtue, interestingly, Rizal chose not prose or poetry but sculpture, favoring allegorical statuary and the soft medium of clay to depict the beautiful female nude. It seems Rizal liked the way in which the erotic and sexual appeal of the youthful female nude could be transfigured in the mould of high-minded ideals. Female sexuality could be contained and masked in allegories of virtue but also enjoyed. It seems the malleability of clay agreeably lent itself to the almost literal rendering of sensual, life-like, naked female skin and flesh. For Rizal, the practice of sculpting clay held an almost physical, visceral engagement, a process in which libidinal enjoyment, even in furtive and fugitive thought, could be derived from handling the soft, warm, supple clay and shaping it into erotic ideal. Moreover, it is significant

◄ Fig. 25 José Rizal, *The Triumph of Science over Death*, or *Scientia*, 1890 [Austin Craig, *Lineage, Life and Labours of José Rizal* (Manila: Philippine Education Publishing Co., 1913)]

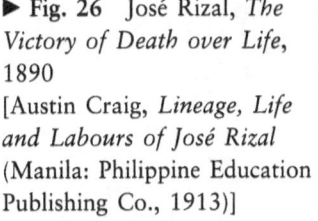

► Fig. 26 José Rizal, *The Victory of Death over Life*, 1890 [Austin Craig, *Lineage, Life and Labours of José Rizal* (Manila: Philippine Education Publishing Co., 1913)]

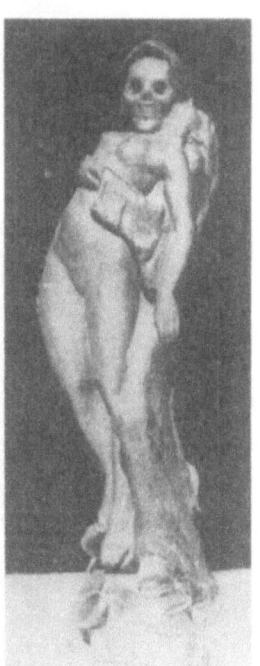

to note that the female images examined here all possess western facial features.

Rizal modeled at least three statuettes in the early summer of 1890. He dispatched two as a gift to Blumentritt and a third to his close friend and compatriot Valentin Ventura. To the pair of sculptures given to Blumentritt, Rizal gave the titles the *Triumph of Science over Death*, or *Scientia* for short (Fig. 25) and the other as the *Victory of Death over Life* (Fig. 26). The title of the figure sent to his close friend and compatriot Valentin Ventura (Fig. 27) is unknown. As erotic objects, the female bodies in these sculptures can be seen to represent the reverse, or counter images to Rizal's Patria.

In the letter accompanying *Scientia* and the *Victory of Death*, Rizal wrote to Blumentritt that they were "originals not copies" and were intended as "little tokens of remembrance." While this gave the impression that they were trifling gifts, Rizal was evidently proud of these sculptures and thought it was still worthwhile sending the *Scientia* despite being already broken.[94] The *Victory of Death over Life* shows Death as a cloaked skeleton who carries in his skeletal arms the limp

Fig. 27 José Rizal, *Reclining Nude*, 1890
[Austin Craig, *Lineage, Life and Labours of José Rizal* (Manila: Philippine Education Publishing Co., 1913)]

body of Life; *Scientia*, and here Rizal had in mind the Latin word for knowledge, is portrayed standing triumphantly upon a skull bearing aloft a flaming torch.

The iconography carries multiple meanings that intertwine themes of Nature, classical conceptions of Truth and Christian ideas about nakedness and virtue. Rizal's *Scientia* and *Life* turn on the central premise that the Otherness of the female body could express an ideal, and nakedness articulated disclosure and truth. Whether *alethia* in Greek, *veritas* in Latin, as Rizal would have been well aware, Truth was feminine in gender, personified in the female form that embodied nature, integrity and wholeness. As Marina Warner writes, "naked truth," *nuditas naturalis*, possesses an "eschatological body, transfigured and innocent; sprung out of the earth, she is also primordial and aboriginal, like nature, the origin of living things."[95]

Rizal's sculptures of *Scientia* and *Life* echo and harness these multiple meanings. Both figures visualize vitality and virtue in the smooth, young, unblemished condition of the female body. Traditional signs of beauty are manifest in the flow of long abundant hair; ardour and bounty find expression in the rounded conical breasts; female genital hairlessness, as opposed to the unruly display of curly pubic hair, conforms to a sense of innocence and aesthetic tastefulness. Yet, while the sensuality of bare flesh is apparent in both sculpted female figures, they are sharply contrasting in their relative hardness and softness.

Strong and erect, Scientia stands poised and proud on the crown of the skull; as prized knowledge, she is reminiscent of La Liberté and holds erect the same sacred flame. Indeed, the Statue of Liberty and the torch she holds may have directly inspired Rizal, who had gazed in awe at the American monument barely two years previously, while sailing out from New York harbor in May 1888 on his way to England.[96] These parallels are not simply coincidental. The creator of Liberty was inspired by the symbols of Freemasons and intended to evoke staid control and light; Rizal, it should be remembered, was also a freemason and his sculpture both identifies with such imagery and alludes to similar meanings.

But, unlike the Statue of Liberty, *Scientia* was meant to be viewed privately and Rizal did not have to worry at all about public codes of respectability. Scientia is naked yet her nakedness appears respectable. This is because she remains trapped by the symbolic conventions that govern depictions of allegorical virtue. These necessitate the precise, petrified pose which must speak unambiguously of the ideal integrity her emblematic character represents. Rizal emphasizes inviolate power and invincibility in Scientia's nakedness. The musculature of her torso and flatness of her belly possess the strength and firmness of youth. There is no mistaking the primal integrity of this personified abstraction. Scientia, illuminating the virtue of learning and Knowledge, is impervious and sound, a body solid and whole, a conqueror of mortality.

In contrast, *Scientia*'s companion piece, the *Victory of Death*, reinforces the yielding vulnerability and eroticism of the naked female body through the emphasis of rounded contours. Death lifts and clutches Life closely against itself, carrying the body as if it were a trophy. However, the impression of lifelessness seems to be somewhat superficial, for the female body arches against Death with erotic abandon. Life falls heavily against Death yet her naked body, with its smoothly sculpted sumptuous curves, is unmistakably posed to provide visual enjoyment. Her torso is oriented towards the front, drawing the gaze directly to her exposed sex; her slender arms drape over Death's shoulder and her head is thrown back to accommodate Death's skull which rests underneath the soft crook of the neck. Her face is difficult to see so we cannot be certain of her expression, but it is her body that is the point of focus. It presses closely against Death; a cloaked arm grasps it firmly below the rounded breasts; bony fingers sink into a fleshly thigh, an upper thigh and buttock is nestled by Death's protruding thigh and knee. Death appears to simultaneously possess and enjoy the naked female body as well as presenting it for exhibition. This visual seductiveness belongs firmly in the sphere of sexuality and invites a tactile and visceral response from its viewer.

Blumentritt liked the two statuettes very much, and particularly admired The *Victory of Death*, complimenting Rizal on its "magnificent conception."[97] But Rizal esteemed Blumentritt as a scholarly father figure and perhaps for this reason, he chose allegory as an appropriate vehicle from which to regard the sexualized female nude. In contrast, the statuette of the reclining woman Rizal sent to Valentin Ventura was explicitly erotic to a degree which he may have thought a sober, bookish friend such as Blumentritt would consider a breach of propriety.

A powerful streak of voyeurism informs Rizal's clay statuette of a reclining woman. Her long hair falling about her face, eyes half closed, mouth slightly open, a hand lightly resting on her belly, the tactility of a rounded, well-defined bosom constitute a familiar repertoire that make her autoerotic pose sexually thrilling. She is aware and yet unaware of her viewer hence increasing the element of sexual excitement. Far from passive, her supine frame is charged with erotic energy: her hand is in the midst of peeling away the last fragment of cloth concealing her sex. It is a movement signifying that what Rizal chose to mold into clay was a vivid moment of delicious sexual anticipation on the part of a sexualized female object and the eager male viewing subject that is imagined. Even to Ventura, his confidante, Rizal was unable to articulate in words the candid sexuality of this particular clay figurine. Indeed, in this case, Rizal seems to have committed a deliberate and telling act of self-censorship.

Sometime in May 1890, Valentin Ventura received an unexpected parcel from Rizal containing a clay figure of a semi-naked woman reclining on a chaise longue. Strangely, the gift was not accompanied by any letter. After five days with still no word, Ventura decided to claim the statuette and finally sent Rizal his thanks. Ventura found the figure so alluring that he asked his friend about the model: "Tell me frankly if the model you used lives in Brussels, because truly, if she lives there, it will be worthwhile to make a trip to that city to admire her and make her acquaintance."[98] Ventura's question remained unanswered; Rizal did not reply to this letter or to Ventura's subsequent messages. As Ventura sensed, this was odd behavior for Rizal, who normally responded dutifully to all his correspondence. "I have not received a letter from you for a century. What is happening to you? Are you sick? Let me know."[99] There is no record of Rizal ever responding to Ventura's queries, and the statuette has remained surrounded in mystery. Austin Craig, Rizal's American biographer, has speculated the figure to be a composite creation where the woman's head may have been copied from a painting and the body from an engraving.[100] Whether this speculation has any basis or not, it is perhaps more fruitful to view Ventura's gift in the context of Rizal's short stay in Brussels in 1890.

Representing one of the least explored periods of Rizal's life, Rizal's eight-month Brussels sojourn is left, in most biographies, stupendously vague. This is surprising given that it was in Brussels that Rizal revised, edited and published *El filibusterismo*, his second novel. Practical reasons, Leon Guerrero suggests, may have been behind Rizal's move to Brussels, a city cheaper than Madrid or Paris and with printers in nearby Ghent that charged far less than either. With his family dispossessed and the Calamba hacienda despoiled, Rizal was living on very little money and José Alejandrino had invited him to visit.[101]

At the end of January 1890, Rizal arrived in the Belgian capital and lodged with José Alejandrino on the Rue Philippe de Champagne, paying rent to two sisters, Marie and Suzanne Jacoby. Also living in the household was a niece, Petite Suzanne, with whom Rizal developed a certain intimacy during his stay. The extent of their familiarity can be glimpsed from letters Petite Suzanne wrote after his departure.

> Where are you now? Do you think of me once in a while? I am reminded of our tender conversations reading your letter.... How pleased I would be to follow you, to travel with you.... You wish

me all kinds of luck, but forget that in the absence of a beloved one a tender heart cannot feel happy.

A thousand things serve to distract your mind, my friend; but in my case, I am sad, lonely, always alone with my thoughts — nothing, absolutely nothing, relieves my sorrow. Are you coming back? That's what I want and desire most ardently — you cannot refuse me. I feel very unhappy thinking that perhaps I might never see you again... You know with one word you can make me very happy. Aren't you going to write to me? She who wishes to protect you from all harm.[102]

Petite Suzanne's gentle pleas and melancholic yearning attests to the closeness that she and Rizal had enjoyed. Rizal evidently had encouraged their intimacy only to leave her in a state of uncertainty — she remains unclear whether he intends to return or if in fact she has been abandoned. In any case, she deeply laments their separation and, under the illusion that she still retains some emotional hold upon her lover, speaks of her wish to join him, to travel with him believing she would not be denied.

Rizal, it would seem, had led Petite Suzanne to think that travelling together might be a possibility giving her, at the very least, the feeling that he considered the idea desirable. It is significant to note here that this was not the first time Rizal had left his foreign *amours* with this impression and in this position of uncertainty. In London, he had begun a flirtatious relationship with a daughter of the English family with whom he lodged, a relationship that ended just as abruptly. Gertrude Beckett brought Rizal his breakfast tray in the mornings and had assisted him in sculpting a bust. Like Petite Suzanne, Gertrude Beckett became intimate with the family's Filipino lodger. She pined for him when he left, "Oh I was so miserable then," she confessed, and reflected on the fantasy of accompanying him on his travels as she later wrote: "Now suppose if I had come with you, we should have had a dear little room and not apt (sic) fidgeting about so."[103]

Rizal sent Beckett brooches and fashion magazines that for a time kept their relationship alive through correspondence. For Petite Suzanne, bereftness gave way to joyous hope when she was brought encouraging news of her lover's possible return by an unnamed friend of Rizal's who visited the Jacoby house: "One of your compatriots is already here. Come quickly and bring with you some twenty more.... I hope your heart is open and I shall not have to wait a long time for your decision.... There will never be any home in which you are so loved as that in Brussels, so, you little bad boy, hurry up and come back."[104]

Tantalizing as they are, Petite Suzanne's teasing, sexually playful letters are not the only reason behind the discomfort felt on the part of Rizal's biographers when dealing with his Brussels sojourn. His companion José Alejandrino fondly remembered how he and Rizal sometimes visited two sisters who he described as *palomas de bajo vuelo*, literally "low flying doves" but more prosaically prostitutes.[105] In his memoirs Alejandrino recalls how Rizal followed a routine where he carefully managed his time. He filled his leisure hours usefully "making clay statuettes ... binding a book, making a wooden box for his pistols."[106] Rizal himself reported to Antonio Luna that he spent his time on other innocuous activities — studying, writing, going to the clinic, the gymnasium, the fencing hall and shooting practice. Together with his letter he sent Luna bullet-ridden cardboard targets that showed his excellent marksmanship.[107]

When relating his doings to his compatriots, Rizal meant to set a laudable example, especially to the younger ones like Antonio Luna. About his private life, however, he had become extremely guarded, and it was only to very select friends like Valentin Ventura that he felt he could confide anything at all salacious. Responding to some such confidence, Ventura ribbed his friend in February 1890 that:

> I was afraid that after having lived eight months in Paris and with our great manliness (*las grandes hombradas*) you would be bored there. But I see that you really have the qualities of a traveler, on which I congratulate you, for these are very useful, so that you would not be married or be chased, which is the same thing (*para que no se case O que le cazen que es lo mismo*).[108]

Clearly, Rizal had found a way to add spice to his time in Brussels. Ventura's subtle play on the Spanish verbs *casar* and *cazar*, to be wed and to be chased, intimates an amorous indulgence which Rizal appeared to have been enjoying rather soon after his arrival and which he was careful to keep under discreet control. Perhaps this alluded to the visits he and his fellow lodger Alejandrino periodically paid to two sisters somewhere in the city. Choosing his words with delicacy, but still making his meaning plain, Alejandrino recalled that:

> Rizal was a puritan, but his puritanism was reasonable and without hypocrisy. Recently arriving in Brussels and not being able to speak French I hardly went out of the house. One day he invited me to amuse ourselves (*divertirnos*), telling me we could pass the time in the house of two sisters whom he knew. We went there and I came to like the amusement very much, because a few days later I asked him when we could return for more fun, but then he grew serious, saying that he considered such entertainment was necessary once a month, but more than once was already a vice, and he was not willing to encourage vices.[109]

Written after Rizal's martyrdom, Alejandrino's words intended to distance the Philippines' national hero and himself from explicit commercial sexual relations. In seeking to appear curious and innocent of the "amusement," a man acting only on Rizal's initiative and following the advice of the knowing physician, Alejandrino gives an innocuous impression of their "amusement" with two sisters, entertainment justified by Rizal as medically approved practice and by Alejandrino as novel adventure.

Alejandrino was not alone in his desire to sanitize Rizal's more clandestine activities. In the summer of 1886, Rizal stayed with his friend Maximo Viola in Barcelona; some months later, they met again and set off together to travel around Europe. Reminiscing about their adventures, Viola too records Rizal's interest in "centres of amusement," which in Barcelona just as in Brussels, included houses where male visitors were entertained by *"palomas de bajo vuelo,"* or "low flying doves." Viola, writing in 1913, expurgates his memories in the same manner as Alejandrino. The nature of Rizal's forays to brothels, he claimed, were more "investigative than voluptuary," deriving not mainly from lust but from a keen academic interest in brothel "customs, luxury or poverty" and "ways in the refinement of vice:"

> He was eager to know everything, because the day when, as a writer, he would have to combat such a vice in its diverse manifestations for being unnatural and anti-physiological, according to him, he would be informed of its cause the better to correct it. It must be noted that in these excursions ... he always hinted to me that he had never been in favour of obeying blindly the whims of nature when their call was not duly justified by a natural and spontaneous impulse.[110]

Four years later, in his travels with Alejandrino, Rizal seems to have changed his mind, believing that strictly regulated frequency was better than responding to a "natural and spontaneous impulse."

Unlike Alejandrino however, Viola relates a specific incident though told with the same guarded, constrained formality and reverence. This is Viola's recollection of Rizal's encounter with a prostitute in Vienna whose physical charms are so extraordinary it appears she was sent to him and Rizal is unable to resist:

> ... The image of a temptress (*tentadora*) in the form of a Viennese woman, of the family of Camelias or Margaritas, of extraordinary beauty and irresistible attraction, who seemingly had been expressly invited to offer for a moment the cup of mundane pleasure to the apostle of Philippine freedom.[111]

It is significant to note that Viola compares this nameless Viennese woman to the beautiful and honourable courtesan Marguerite of Alexandre Dumas fils' *La Dame aux Camelias* (1852), rather than to some common street-walking trollop. Viola's explanation consciously panders to the refined sexual tastes and sensibilities expected of the Filipino ilustrado bourgeois male. The Viennese woman was both sexually irresistible and honorable, therefore the encounter, or Rizal's "only slip" as Viola insists, is understandable and reasonable.[112]

Reading Viola's recollections in conjunction with Alejandrino's, reveals a pattern of evasion of any explicit account of Rizal's sexual adventuring on the part of those who were his key companions or confidantes. Yet, however elusive Rizal's erotic experiences are to track, commercial or non-commercial, what is clear is that the voluptuous, venal or romantic foreign woman seemed to hold for Rizal a special allure. Exiled in Dapitan from 1892 until 1896, Rizal, it should be recalled, was apparently not attracted to the Filipino women around him and preferred to live in loneliness and solitude until the arrival of Josephine Bracken, a woman of considerably low intellect, uncertain origins and whom biographers have described as "flighty and unreliable, undomesticated and superficial." Possessing "distinctly European" features, Josephine Bracken quickly became Rizal's lover. Defying his family and sisters who were suspicious and hostile towards the stranger, Rizal fell as Austin Coates writes, "within hours, within minutes perhaps" deeply in love.[113]

Whether Rizal paid for his monthly entertainment in Brussels is open to speculation. Correspondence shows that Rizal had borrowed money from Ventura and sent him an account of his expenses. Brussels, Ventura could only conclude after scrutinizing Rizal's financial admissions, was turning out to be as expensive as Paris after all.[114]

We are not given any more details about what Rizal had been spending his money on, but a few months later Rizal decided to make a few cuts in his expenses. Applauding the step, Ventura wrote Rizal: "I congratulate you on jilting (*planton*) your *chiquita*, because it saves on various things: money, time and ... Providence."[115] By his reference to Providence, one presumes, Ventura meant to congratulate Rizal on having avoided the fateful dangers of an amorous entanglement, be they marriage, illegitimate offspring or disease.

But the financial cost of his indulgences was not the only aspect preying on Rizal's mind. A series of disturbing vivid dreams that ominously foretold of his death had begun to upset Rizal during the spring of 1890. He was, as he described, assailed by nightmarish images of dead loved ones; of following a path that led deep into the bowels of the earth. He became gripped with a need to finish his work and felt he didn't want to be caught off-guard by the uncertainty of life, of tragedy and death. "*Laong laan* is my true name," he wrote, believing more firmly in the pseudonym he used for his *La Solidaridad* articles that meant "ever ready."[116] Whether it was because of these dreams, or the troubling events taking place in Calamba or intrigues amongst the propagandistas and within *La Solidaridad*, the life Rizal was enjoying in Brussels abruptly ended. The true cost of these sexually illicit "amusements" seemed to lie in suffering inner conflict, not borne out by guilt for enjoying sensual gratification, rather, for allowing himself to be overly distracted by pleasure. Rizal's mood of sobriety and seriousness is reflected in a letter sent to Marcelo del Pilar. Writing partly in Spanish and Tagalog, Rizal resorts to the abstract, language of the dedicated patriot; a vocabulary in which Rizal easily slipped when he needed to remind himself of his (and what he believed to be every young Filipino man's) duty:

> We do not have the luck of other young men to dispose of our time as we please ... our mother needs to be rescued from captivity: our mother is pawned, we need to redeem her first, before we can have pleasure (*ang ina nati'y nasasanla, kailangang ating tubusin muna, bago tayo makapagaliw*).[117]

Brussels had briefly provided Rizal an interlude of sexual freedom where he could indulge, in relative anonymity, his taste for foreign women, the Caucasian European woman whose seemingly insatiable sexuality he found dangerously attractive and erotically appealing. Rizal's clay gift to Ventura is a voluble admission of this, a rare confessional gesture in the face of a morality that advocated sexual discretion, propriety if not abstemiousness. Memoirs and recollections by Rizal's friends give little more than fleeting glimpses of Rizal's erotic experiences; brief accounts buried amidst thick layers of sanitized, reverential rememberings.

Proposing a correlation between biographical context and Rizal's sculptural representations of the female nude enters slippery terrain. However, in the absence of any aesthetic or historical account of the clay statuettes Rizal made during this period, these experiences as they report upon Rizal's conceptualization of the foreign woman's sexuality crucially situates the statuettes in a context of ambivalence. What he enjoyed privately Rizal could only articulate in the formal language of his sculptural female forms, in his conventionally aestheticized and eroticised renderings of the unclad female body.

Rizal's clay female figures are a rare representation of the insatiable female sexuality he had attributed to the non-Filipino woman. But this was a libidinal attraction that was selective and plainly excluded the "New Woman" types or the masculine looking women who wore their hair "short like men" and went about without "holes in their ears" as the decidedly un-feminine German and English women he had seen on his travels.[118] These were features of the more stridently independent European woman Rizal recoiled away from, neither wishing his countrywomen to imitate or to emulate and which he himself found physically repulsive. Rizal idealized the tenderness, the softness, the submissiveness of a pliant and yielding femininity; qualities he imagined characterized Filipino women and which he sought in European women. In his diagnosis, sexual desire in Filipino women and their experience of sexuality were part of a sick society suffering from a range of pathological symptoms.

Notes

1   José Rizal (Dapitan) to Fr. Pablo Pastells, 11 November 1892, in *Miscellaneous Correspondence* (Manila: National Heroes Commission, 1963), p. 204.
2   Luciano P.R. Santiago, M.D., "The First Filipino Doctors of Medicine and Surgery (1878–97)," *Philippine Quarterly of Culture and Society* 22 (1994): 103–40.

3   Miguel María Varela, "Rizal's Studies in the University of Madrid," *Philippine Studies* 9: 2 (April 1961): 294–300.
4   José Rizal (Madrid) to his parents, 28 June 1884, in *One Hundred Letters of José Rizal to his Parents, Brother, Sisters, Relatives* (Manila: Philippine National Historical Society, 1959), p. 185.
5   Geminiano de Ocampo, "Our Foremost Ophthalmologist," *Historical Bulletin, Philippine Historical Association* 5: 1–4 (December 1961): 298; also José P. Bantug, "Rizal, the Physician," *Journal of History* 5: 1–2 (1957): 41–4.
6   Biographers have given much attention to this period of Rizal's life. See for example Austin Coates, *Rizal: Filipino nationalist and martyr* (Manila: Solidaridad Publishing House, 1992); and Leon Ma. Guerrero, *The First Filipino* (Manila: Guerrero Publishing, 1998). Guerrero's biography was first published in 1961.
7   See for example Raul J. Bonoan, S.J., "José Rizal: revolution of the mind," in *The World of 1896*, ed. Lorna Kalaw-Tirol (Manila: Ateneo de Manila University Press, 1998), pp. 213–35; and Miguel A. Bernad, S.J., *Rizal and Spain: an essay in biographical context* (Manila: Navotas Press, 1986).
8   José Rizal (Paris) to Mariano Ponce, 18 April 1889, in *Epistolario Rizalino*, ed. T.M. Kalaw, vol. 2 (Manila: Bureau of Printing, 1933), p. 167.
9   José Rizal, "Clinica Medica," notebook 1881–87 (Ayer Manuscript Collection, Newberry Library).
10 José Rizal [Europe] Fragmentos de una carta en Tagalo, c. October 1891, in *Epistolario Rizalino*, ed. T.M. Kalaw, vol. 3 (Manila: Bureau of Printing, 1933), p. 250.
11 Anne McClintock, *Imperial Leather: race, gender and sexuality in the colonial contest* (London: Routledge, 1995), p. 46.
12 Esteban de Ocampo, "Rizal as a Bibliophile," in *The Bibliographical Society of the Philippines*, Occasional Papers No. 2 (Manila: Unesco National Commission of the Philippines, 1960), pp. 27–52; see also the letter of Ceferino de Leon (Madrid) to José Rizal, 19 December 1885 requesting Rizal to send him a novel by Zola, in *Miscellaneous Correspondence*, p. 77.
13 Ludmilla Jordanova, *Sexual Visions: images of gender in Science and medicine between the eighteenth and twentieth centuries* (Madison: University of Wisconsin Press, 1989), pp. 85–6.
14 Elaine Showalter, *Sexual Anarchy: gender and culture at the fin de siècle* (London: Virago Press, 1992), p. 134.
15 Wenceslao Retana, *Vida y escritos de Dr. José Rizal* (Madrid: Libreria de Victoriana Suarez, 1907), pp. 128–9. Clerical attacks on his novel gave Rizal the opportunity to display his talent for satirical humor. In response to Father Font's attack on the *Noli*, Rizal published "*Por Teléfono*," an imagined telephone conversation between Madrid and the Philippines that served to poke fun at the stupidity of a character closely resembling Font. In 1888, the Augustinian friar Father Rodriguez published his attack on Rizal's *Noli* in the form of a treatise on the moral dangers of reading books forbidden by the Church. It elicited a pamphlet from Rizal, entitled "*La visión de Fray Rodriguez*" in which God punished the friar for his literary foolishness by condemning him to continue writing to eternal public ridicule. Written using Rizal's

Masonic name, "Dimas Alang" ("Touch me not"), the pamphlet was published secretly in Barcelona in 1889 by Maríano Ponce, sent to the Philippines via José Basa in Hong Kong and circulated in churches in Manila by the Comité de Propaganda. W.E. Retana, *Aparato bibliográfico de la Historia General de Filipinas* (Madrid: Imp. de la Sucesora de M. Minuesa de los Rios, 1906), vol. 3, p. 1129, entry no. 2711.

16 Alex Schadenberg (Vigan) to José Rizal, 9 April 1889, in *Miscellaneous Correspondence*, p. 106.
17 For an insightful reading of the folk reception of Rizal, see Reynaldo Ileto, "Rizal and the Underside of Philippine History," in *Moral Order and the Question of Change: essays on Southeast Asian thought*, ed. David K. Wyatt and Alexander Woodside (New Haven: Yale University Southeast Asia Studies, 1982), pp. 278–337.
18 José Rizal, "To His Excellency Don Vicente Barrantes," *La Solidaridad* 2: 25 (15 February 1890): 67.
19 Ibid.
20 José Rizal (Brussels) to Ferdinand Blumentritt, 2 February 1890, in *The Rizal-Blumentritt Correspondence, 1890–1896* (Manila: National Historical Institute, 1992), p. 328.
21 Ferdinand Blumentritt (Leitmeritz) to José Rizal, 27 March 1887, in *The Rizal-Blumentritt correspondence, 1886–1889* (Manila: National Historical Institute, 1992), p. 63.
22 José Rizal (Leipzig) to Paciano Rizal, 12 October 1886, in *Letters between Rizal and Family Members* (Manila: National Heroes Commission, 1964), p. 245.
23 José Rizal (Berlin) to Ferdinand Blumentritt, 21 March 1887, in *The Rizal-Blumentritt Correspondence, 1886–1889*, p. 62.
24 José Rizal (Berlin) draft letter to an anonymous friend, 5 March 1887, in *Rizal's Correspondence with Fellow Reformists, 1882–1896* (Manila: National Heroes Commission, 1963), pp. 83–4. The full quote originally written in French is in *Clinica Medica*, unpaginated MSS.
25 José Rizal (Berlin) draft letter to an anonymous friend, 5 March 1887, in *Rizal's Correspondence with Fellow Reformists, 1882–1896*, p. 83.
26 Caroline Hau, *Necessary Fictions: Philippine literature and the nation, 1946–1980* (Manila: Ateneo de Manila University Press, 2000), p. 77.
27 Ibid., p. 81.
28 Scholars have recently reassessed the life and achievements of Pedro Paterno in terms of his incipient nationalism. See Resil B. Mojares, *Brains of the Nation: Pedro Paterno, T.H. Pardo de Tavera, Isabelo de los Reyes and the production of modern knowledge* (Quezon City: Ateneo de Manila University Press, 2006); Portia L. Reyes, "A 'treasonous' history of Filipino historiography: the life and times of Pedro Paterno, 1858–1911," *South East Asia Research* 14: 1 (March 2006): 87–121.
29 Cited in José Rizal (Berlin) to Ferdinand Blumentritt, 29 March 1887, in *Rizal-Blumentritt Correspondence, 1886–1889*, p. 67.
30 Antonio Regidor (London) to José Rizal, 3 May 1887, in *Cartas entre Rizal y sus colegas de la propaganda, 1882–1889* (Manila: Comisión Nacional del Centenario de José Rizal, 1961), p. 119.

31. The phrase "primordial understanding" and my interpretation of gossip here is drawn from Martin Heidegger's insightful discussion on gossip as a form of "idle talk" and its importance in the interpretation of everyday life. Martin Heidegger, *Being and Time*, trans. John Macquarrie and Edward Robinson (New York: Harper and Row, 1962), pp. 211–5.
32. José Cecilio (Manila) to José Rizal, 9 January 1885, in *Miscellaneous Correspondence*, p. 60.
33. José Cecilio (Manila) to José Rizal, 16 September 1882, in *Epistolario Rizalino*, vol. 1, p. 49.
34. Coates, *Rizal*, p. 54.
35. Ibid., pp. 186–7.
36. José Cecilio (Manila) to José Rizal, 15 December 1882, in *Miscellaneous Correspondence*, p. 28.
37. Ibid.
38. Taimis (Leonor Rivera) (Manila) to José Rizal, 28 December 1881, in ibid., p. 21.
39. José Cecilio (Manila) to José Rizal, 15 September 1883, in ibid., p. 47.
40. José Cecilio (Manila) to José Rizal, 9 March 1884, in ibid., p. 50.
41. José Cecilio (Manila) to José Rizal, 9 January 1885, in ibid., p. 60.
42. José Cecilio (Manila) to José Rizal, 9 January 1885, in *Miscellaneous Correspondence*, p. 60.
43. José Cecilio (Manila) to José Rizal, 18 April 1885, in *Cartas entre Rizal y otras personas, 1877–1896* (Manila: Comisión Nacional del Centenario de José Rizal, 1961), p. 68.
44. Rizal's entries in his diary kept from 1 January 1883 up to 1 November 1885, written in Madrid, briefly record his receipt of Leonor's letters and his thoughts on them. See for instance the entry for 10 January 1884, in which Rizal writes (in code): "Leonor's letter is loving with a most pleasant ending;" 13 April 1885: "Today I received letters from Leonor, Uncle Antonio [Leonor's father], and Chengoy. I'm fairly contented with what they tell me, though not with the condition of Leonor." José Rizal, "Madrid Diary," in *Reminiscences and Travels of José Rizal* (Manila: National Historical Institute, 1977), pp. 81–101.
45. José Rizal, Madrid Diary entry dated 25 January 1884: "Tonight I had a very sad dream. I imagined I returned to the Philippines, but what a sad reception! My parents didn't show up and Leonor had been unfaithful; but her infidelity was so great that it had no remedy." Ibid., p. 89.
46. José Rizal, Madrid Diary entry dated 31 March 1884, in ibid., pp. 96–7.
47. José Cecilio (Manila) to José Rizal, 30 September 1885, in *Miscellaneous Correspondence*, p. 70.
48. Rizal wrote *Noli me tangere* (in Spanish) in 1884–86 and the novel was first published in Berlin in 1887 by the Berliner Buchdruckerei-Actien-Gesellschaft. A facsimile of this first edition was published in Manila in 1978 by the Instituto Nacional de Historia. The best English translation is that by Soledad Lacson-Locsin (edited by Raul L. Locsin) and the citations in this dissertation refer to the edition published

in Honolulu by the University of Hawai'i Press in 1997. In some instances, however, the translations have been slightly modified.

49 Rizal, *Noli me tangere*, p. 41.
50 Ibid., p. 42.
51 Ibid.
52 Ibid., pp. 42-3.
53 Ibid., p. 43.
54 Doris Sommer, *Foundational Fictions: the national romances of Latin America* (Berkeley: University of California Press, 1991), p. 27.
55 Rizal, *Noli me tangere*, p. 45.
56 Ibid., p. 13.
57 Ibid., p. 183.
58 Ibid., p. 28.
59 Ibid., p. 48.
60 Carmen Guerrero Nakpil, "María Clara" [1956], in *Woman Enough and Other Essays* (Manila: Ateneo de Manila University Press, 1999), p. 36.
61 Ibid., p. 167. See also Vicente L. Rafael, "Language, Identity, and Gender in Rizal's *Noli*," *Review of Indonesian and Malaysian Affairs* 18 (Winter 1984): 128-9.
62 See for example Violeta López-Gonzaga, "Images of women and their role in society in José Rizal's writings," in *José Rizal and the Asian Renaissance*, ed. M. Rajaretnam (Kuala Lumpur: Institut Kajian Dasar; Manila: Solidaridad Publishing House, 1996), p. 175; Caroline S. Hau, "Philippine literary nationalism and the engendering of the revolutionary body," in *Body Politics: cultural representations of women's bodies*, ed. Odine de Guzman (Quezon City: UP Center for Women's Studies and The Ford Foundation, 2002), pp. 58-9.
63 Rizal, *Noli me tangere*, p. 126.
64 Ibid., p. 127.
65 Ibid., p. 90.
66 Ibid., p. 128.
67 Ibid., p. 89.
68 Ibid., p. 422.
69 Alma Jill Dizon, "Felipinas Caliban: colonialism as marriage of Spaniard and Filipina," *Philippine Studies* 46 (First Quarter, 1998): 42. See also Alma Jill Dizon, "Beyond the Melodramatic Vision: national identity and the novels of José Rizal," PhD dissertation, Yale University, 1996.
70 Rizal, *Noli me tangere*, p. 284.
71 Ibid., p. 286.
72 "... Her whole body lean and wasted, and she squinted horribly; her teeth were discoloured and decayed, her poisonous breast of a greenish hue, and her tongue dripped venom," in Ovid, *Metamorphoses*, II (London: Penguin Classics, 1955), lines 775ff., pp. 70-1.
73 Rizal, *Noli me tangere*, p. 284.
74 Ibid.
75 Ibid., pp. 285, 287.

76 Ibid., p. 259.
77 Ibid., p. 260.
78 Ibid., p. 261.
79 Ibid., p. 285.
80 Ibid., p. 59.
81 Ibid., p. 286.
82 Ibid., p. 263.
83 Ibid., pp. 267–8.
84 Ibid., p. 282.
85 Ibid., p. 260.
86 Richard von Krafft-Ebing, *Psychopathia Sexualis: a medico-forensic study, with especial reference to the antipathic sexual instinct* [1887] Trans. from the twelfth German edition and with an introduction by Franklin S. Klaf (New York: Arcade Publishing, 1998).
87 Raimundo Geler, *Islas Filipinas: Reseña de su organización social y administrativa y breves indicación es de las principales reformas que reclaman* (Madrid: Cargo de J.E. Morete, 1869), extract in *Documentary Sources of Philippine History*, compiled, edited and annotated by Gregorio F. Zaide, additional notes by Sonia M. Zaide, vol. 7 (Manila: National Book Store, 1990), pp. 228–9.
88 José Rizal (London) to Ferdinand Blumentritt, 13 October 1888, in *Rizal-Blumentritt Correspondence, 1886–1889* (Manila: National Historical Institute, 1999), pp. 205–6.
89 Antonio Allegri, known as Corregio (1489–1534), *Noli me tangere*, c. 1534. Oil on canvas entered the Prado in 1839. See *The Prado* (London: Scala Publishers, 2000), p. 141.
90 J.M. Simon, S.I. Simon and G. Simon, "San Juan y La '*Noli me tangere*'," in *Archivos de la sociedad Española de oftalmología* 6 (Junio 2002).
91 Rizal, *Noli me tangere*, n.p.
92 Marina Warner, *Monuments and Maidens: the allegory of the female form* (London: Wiedenfeld and Nicholson, c.1985), p. 296.
93 Ibid, p. 92.
94 José Rizal (Brussels) to Ferdinand Blumentritt, 5 July 1890, in *The Rizal-Blumentritt Correspondence, 1890–1896*, p. 369.
95 Warner, *Monuments and Maidens*, p. 315.
96 Entry dated New York, 13–16 May 1888, in Rizal's travel diaries, published in *Reminiscences and Travels of José Rizal*, pp. 149–51.
97 Ferdinand Blumentritt (Leitmeritz) to José Rizal, 9 July 1890, in *Rizal-Blumentritt Correspondence 1890–1896*, p. 371.
98 Valentin Ventura (Paris) to José Rizal, 15 May 1890, in *Rizal's Correspondence with Fellow Reformists, 1882–1896*, p. 455.
99 Valentin Ventura (Paris) to José Rizal, 19 May 1890, in ibid., p. 457.
100 Austin Craig, *Lineage, Life and Labours of José Rizal* (Manila: Philippine Education Company, 1913), p. 102.
101 Guerrero, *The First Filipino*, p. 249.

102 Undated letter (now destroyed) attributed to (Petite) Suzanne Jacoby, in English from the original French in Carlos Quirino, *The Great Malayan: the biography of Rizal* (Manila: Philippine Education Company, 1949), p. 192.
103 Gertrude Beckett to José Rizal, undated letter in ibid., pp. 154–5.
104 (Petite) Suzanne Jacoby (Brussels) to José Rizal, 1 October 1890, translated from the original French and in *Miscellaneous Correspondence*, p. 141.
105 Ambeth Ocampo, "Rizal and the two Suzannes," in *Rizal Without the Overcoat* (Manila: Anvil Publishing, 2000) pp. 143–4. Ocampo does not however provide a citation for Alejandrino's other remarks.
106 José Alejandrino, *The Price of Freedom*. Translated from the original Spanish by Atty. José M. Alejandrino, Filipiniana Reprint Series (Manila: Solar Publishing, 1986), p. 2.
107 José Rizal (Brussels) to Antonio Luna, 3 July 1890, in *Rizal's Correspondence with Fellow Reformists*, p. 477.
108 Valentin Ventura (Paris) to José Rizal, 5 February 1890, in *Cartas entre Rizal y sus colegas de la propaganda, 1890–1896*, p. 493.
109 José Alejandrino, *La senda del sacrificio: episodios y anecdotas de nuestras luchas por la libertad* (Manila: Loyal Press, 1933), p. 5.
110 Maximo Viola, "Mis viajes con el Dr. Rizal," *The Journal of History Special Rizal Edition 5*: 1–2 (Manila: Philippine National Historical Society, 1957), pp. 53–79.
111 Ibid., p. 71.
112 Ibid.
113 Coates, *Rizal: Philippine Nationalist and Martyr*, p. 264.
114 Valentin Ventura (Paris) to José Rizal, 24 February 1890, in *Rizal's Correspondence with Fellow Reformists*, p. 436.
115 Valentin Ventura (Paris) to José Rizal, 16 April 1890, in *Cartas entre Rizal y sus colegas de la propaganda*, p. 521. (Ellipsis in original.)
116 José Rizal (Brussels) to Marcelo del Pilar, 11 June 1890, in ibid., p. 549.
117 Ibid., p. 550.
118 José Rizal, Journal entry, August 1886 on the Rhine between Heidelberg and Leipzig, in *Reminiscences and Travels of José Rizal*, p. 114.

6

Silencing the Flesh: Rizal's Erasure of Female Sexual Pleasure

Sex and Civilization

In the introduction to his famous work *Psychopathia sexualis* the German psychiatrist Richard von Krafft-Ebing affirmed that sexual life was the finest measure for determining the degree to which a culture could be called civilized. Primitive societies, he observed, were characterized by "gratification of the sexual instinct" being "the primary motive in man as well as in beast;" by men and women having sexual intercourse openly and unashamed of their nakedness; and by a relatively low value being placed on women's "virginity, chastity, modesty, and sexual fidelity."[1] Woman in uncivilized societies was the "common property of man, the spoil of the strongest and mightiest ... a 'chattel,' an article of commerce, exchange or gift, a vessel for sensual gratification, an implement for toil." Certain "savage races" illustrated this uncivilized condition most strikingly, and the very best examples, in Krafft-Ebing's opinion, were the "Australasians, Polynesians, (and the) Malays of the Philippines."[2]

Critics of Krafft-Ebing attacked his assertion that civilization was the critical factor in the aetiology of sexual psychopathology, insisting that sexual perversions were not culturally acquired but innate, and were evident amongst primitive and civilized peoples alike. Iwan Bloch, for instance, drawing upon the work of the German anthropologist Heinrich Ploss, cited the sexual "epicureanism" of the primitive men from the island of Pohnpei in Micronesia who liked to put fish inside a woman's vulva to savour by cunnilingus. But this gustatory practice,

Bloch observed, differed little from the "sexual gourmandism that occurs in Parisian brothels in the form of *pollution labiale*" and was neither more nor less pathological than the *divertissement* of the English "earl who inserted strawberries into his mistress's genitalia and later ate the fruits thus marinated."³ Few however, would disagree with the general polar distinctions drawn by the Spanish physician Felipe Monlau. "The Orient," he summarizes, is characterized by "polygamy and sensuality." Misery and despotism naturally resulted from harems, seraglios, venereal excesses, barbaric mutilations, sodomy, indolence and ignorance that were features of the oriental way of life. The Occident, with its observation of monogamy and Christian austerity however, enjoyed domestic harmony, equality and liberty, its citizens active and productive.⁴

Rizal lived in Germany in 1886–87 and was well attuned to European scientific and intellectual currents. Possibly he was aware of Krafft-Ebing's work, and certainly he was keenly interested in the wider debate over whether the sexual behavior of a culture reflected its level of civilization. Spanish apologists for colonial rule, as we have seen, persistently argued that the Filipinos remained in many ways a backward, primitive people, and delighted in alleging in support of their case, that lasciviousness and promiscuity were widespread in the Philippines. These allegations caused deep offence to Rizal and his fellow propagandists, who wanted as a matter of patriotic honor to repudiate such colonialist slurs. But countering the same argument when it appeared to carry the weighty authority of European science was less straightforward. Physicians and ethnographers, Rizal saw, were prone to categorize mankind into different physical types and to draw sweeping generalizations about how these types differed in their intellectual capacity, cultural attainment and refinement, personal morality and sexual behavior. Rizal did not object in principle to generalizations of this nature, but he did object forcefully to their lack of discrimination. Emphatically, he did not accept any generalizations that attached imputations of primitiveness to Hispanized lowlanders like himself.

Krafft-Ebing's reference to the Philippines gave added currency to the notion that Filipinos could be classified as primitive on the basis of their reputedly unbridled sexual life. In the context of contemporary ethnographic thinking, though, it is surprising that he specifically mentioned the "Malays of the Philippines" as opposed to the Negritos, whom the academic literature then deemed to be both "non-Malay" and significantly more primitive. According to the "migration waves" theory propounded by the Austrian scholar Ferdinand Blumentritt, the original Negrito settlers in the archipelago had been displaced by two subsequent "Malay" waves. The first of these had been the ancestors of the Igorots and other "mountain tribes" who had resisted subjugation and conversion to Catholicism; the second had been the ancestors of *"los Filipinos civilizados,"* the Tagalogs and other lowland peoples who to varying degrees had endured or embraced Hispanization. Blumentritt, therefore, would have taken grave exception to Krafft-Ebing's blanket inclusion of the "Malays of the Philippines" among a roll call of the "savage races." He too drew a correlation between civilization and sexual behavior, but in direct contrast to Krafft-Ebing credited the second-wave "Malay" migrants — whom ilustrados like Rizal would have regarded as their own ancestors — as having "a higher civilisation and milder morals" than the earlier inhabitants.[5]

To understand Krafft-Ebing's assertion that the "Malays of the Philippines" possessed a primitive sexual life, it is instructive to trace its intellectual genealogy. Ultimately, we shall see, it rested on Spanish sources that the propagandistas saw as tainted by racial prejudice and imperial self-interest. Krafft-Ebing's footnote reveals his indebtedness to Heinrich Ploss, whose ambitiously titled magnum opus *Das Weib in der Natur-und Volkerkunde* first appeared in 1884.[6] To establish the primitiveness of Philippine sexual life, Ploss in turn relied primarily on the works of three authors, all of whom Rizal later met: Ferdinand Blumentritt;[7] Alex Schadenberg[8] (who had studied the Negritos); and Fedor Jagor[9] (who had travelled widely in the archipelago).

Blumentritt in particular was a key source, especially his *Versuch einer Ethnographie der Philippinen*, which was published in 1882 — four years before the Austrian orientalist became acquainted with Rizal and the Filipino propaganda campaign. From this volume, Ploss extracted the information that in pre-Hispanic times women in the Visayan region of the Philippines fashioned artificial penises so as to be able to appease their insatiable appetites. Evidence of the same lasciviousness had been remarked upon by travellers to the Visayas down to the present day. Ploss also repeated Blumentritt's observations that even the Tagalogs of Luzon, notwithstanding their "higher civilization and milder morals" in relation to the Negritos and "mountain tribes" manifested a pronounced lack of sexual modesty. Blumentritt commented that the civilization of the Tagalogs had been further advanced by a long history of inter-marriage with foreigners: "Let it be remarked that the Tagalogs have plenty of foreign blood flowing in their veins, not only Chinese and Spanish but also Japanese (16th and 17th centuries), which mixtures have bettered the race as a whole."[10] Yet, despite this history of miscegenation, not even the so-called primitive Igorots of the Cordillera, who were known to guard the virginity of their young girls, could surpass the loose sexual morals of the Tagalogs and the Visayans.[11] Moreover, Blumentritt went so far as to imply, the Tagalogs displayed a number of animal-like faculties. They were remarkably adept at manipulating their toes to pick up small objects, and they retained an acute sense of smell, especially the women who "are able to find out whether the men nearby them are sexually excited or not."[12] The excessive immorality of the Visayans and the sensuality of the Tagalogs, Blumentritt affirmed, were part of the "pagan legacy" that endured despite the evangelizing efforts of the Spanish friars.

In making these assertions, Blumentritt drew upon, and thereby gave added credence to, the travel observations of Francisco Cáñamaque, a Spanish journalist and traveler whom the propagandistas would later energetically attack.[13] Immorality, Blumentritt gleaned from Cáñamaque, was widespread both in Manila and in the countryside of the Tagalog region:

> Immorality is widespread not only in Manila but also in the rural areas. Virginity is not a virtue for the girls easily give themselves up to any of their lovers, and only a small number of them are still virgin when they are brought before the altar for marriage. This may still be blamed on the time when they were still pagans and when virginity was not prized. Sexual intercourse, according to Cáñamaque, is performed without any ceremony even in the streets. The same writer claims that fornication is also a children's vice. Cáñamaque says that they are a people without any feeling of shame. Women and men especially in the provinces, allow themselves to be seen completely naked. Prostitution is present.[14]

Surely, then, there is some irony in the fact that the work of German scholars whom Rizal esteemed for their scientific rigor and objectivity — men like Blumentritt, Jagor, Meyer whose work on the primitiveness of Filipino sexual life proceeded to influence other German scientists like Ploss and Krafft-Ebing — was founded on Spanish writings.

Despite his close correspondence with the ilustrado Filipinos and the enthusiastic support he gave to the propagandist campaign shown by his contributions to *La Solidaridad*, Blumentritt had not thought to revise nor retract the assertions of primitiveness he made concerning Tagalog sexual life in his *Versuch einer Ethnographie der Philippinen*. But stirred perhaps by Rizal's work on the Morga, revisions of a sort did occur to a limited extent in the form of an article entitled "The morality of the pagan peoples" which he published in *La Solidaridad* in December 1890. Questioning accusations of savagery made by a Spanish author writing on several indigenous tribal peoples, Blumentritt asked whether "this immorality is inherent in the natives" by which he meant the un-Christianized examples of natives, the Samals, Bagobos, Mandayas, Subanon, Kalingas and more. As he insisted, "no-one can dispute with me the fact that sexual immorality is incompatible with intellectual superiority."[15]

Blumentritt's later allusions to the sexual life of the Filipinos were decidedly coy. Within the forum of the propaganda campaign, he intentionally understated the level of German scholarship on native sexuality and was reticent in revealing German scientific interest in native sexual practices. In his bibliographical review of foreign scholarship on the Philippines, Blumentritt chose not to cite a brief note on sex in the Visayas by Fedor Jagor — "sexuelle Abnormitäten bei den Bisayern Philippinen." He also conspicuously omitted a work by his close friend Professor A.B. Meyer on the "penis perforations of the Malays,"[16] whereas he did cite an essay by the same author on the safer subject of Malayan teeth filing customs.[17]

The profound influence exerted on him by the German historical and ethnographic tradition undoubtedly contributed to Rizal's veritable blindness towards the racism, errors and inconsistencies in Blumentritt's 1882 account on Filipino sexual behavior. Traveling around Germany with Maximo Viola in 1886 and 1887, Rizal had the opportunity of meeting several important German scholars through letters of recommendation furnished by Blumentritt. He made the acquaintance of Hendrik Kern, a Dutch professor of Sanskrit who taught in the Netherlands at the University of Leiden; and Wilhelm Joest who had written on the Philippines and was a professor at the University of Berlin. In Dresden Rizal called upon Professor A.B. Meyer, director of the Ethnographic Museum, who enthusiastically showed him his collection of "instruments of ravishment and priapism."[18] Immediately afterwards, it must be said, Rizal went off to the Catholic Church to hear High Mass.[19] In Berlin, Fedor Jagor had invited him to attend the meetings of the Geographical Society (where Rizal became a member) and introduced him to the most eminent German scientist of the time, the pioneering pathologist Rudolf Virchow, president of the Berlin Society for Anthropology, Ethnology and Prehistory (who admitted Rizal as a fellow).

Disdainful of Spanish scholarship which seemed fatally flawed by colonial interests, to Rizal Germany in contrast presented the "great laboratory of oriental studies," where studies in anthropology, linguistics, botany and zoology were guided by scientific rigor and pursued without direct political intentions. "Thanks to the German scholars we get accurate information about our country," Rizal wrote to Blumentritt. "When ... we wish to verify the historical accuracy of certain facts we shall have to come to Germany to search for these facts in German museums and books! It is sad to arrive at this conclusion, but it is the truth."[20]

Rizal maintained a lively correspondence with German intellectuals until his death. Yet he neither challenged German scholarship on the sexual life of Filipinos nor engaged in that aspect of German research. Spanish chronicles, especially those written by the friar missionaries, remained firmly Rizal's target. "Who among Filipinos and Spaniards wrote the first insulting books?" Rizal asks passionately and accusingly. "Who started slandering? Who was the first to compare people to animals? Who tried first to humiliate an obedient people?"[21] Rizal had resolutely trained his sights on countering Spanish colonial representations by appealing to the scientific authority claimed by German scholarship. It was a strategy energetically attacked by Spanish reactionaries, most especially by Retana who launched vicious salvos aimed to discredit the scholarship of Blumentritt, calling it belittlingly (amongst a myriad of other epithets) German *gansaditas* (little nonsenses).[22]

Scholars have long acknowledged Rizal's close intellectual relationship with Blumentritt, particularly in the writing of Philippine history. The role Blumentritt played in Rizal's decision to annotate Antonio de Morga's *Sucesos de las islas Filipinas* was pivotal. It was Blumentritt who first brought the book to Rizal's attention and whom Rizal thought of as being the most able to write his country's history.[23] But though he had a modest reputation in oriental studies, Blumentritt was a rather marginal figure in German intellectual circles. A man who disliked travel, Blumentritt did not ever visit the Philippines and rarely disrupted his home life and teaching routines by undertaking speaking engagements or trips to meet with the Filipino propagandistas outside his Bohemian home town. His voluminous correspondence instead shows that his involvement with the ilustrado Filipinos provided him with a ready reservoir of native informants with specialized knowledge on the Philippines, while the exchange of data through letters allowed him to conduct his research and writing from his study at home in Leitmeritz which he preferred. Yet, it seemed perfectly reasonable to Rizal to favor this reclusive and peripheral Bohemian scholar as an appropriate person to write his country's history. As a citizen of a country without political interests in the Philippines, Blumentritt appeared to Rizal as an objective, scientifically motivated scholar whose "disinterested" opinion, Rizal described, appeared as it were politically uncontaminated and founded on scientific integrity and therefore trustworthy.

> The Philippines should be grateful to you if you would write a complete history of our country from an impartial point of view.... You profess the Catholic religion, but you don't have an iota of fanaticism. And you don't have to see the country personally; the historian contemplates the past. I believe that you are the best qualified for the task.[24]

That Rizal preferred, at least initially, a foreigner's construction of a Philippine past over indigenous attempts are details that have been glossed over if not left unexplained in Philippine historiography.[25] Rizal was profoundly impressed by the extent of Blumentritt's depth of knowledge about the Philippines. He closely read and even translated Blumentritt's own works, and allowed his own reading to be guided by the Bohemian's suggestions, references that he meticulously sought out and consulted.[26] Through Blumentritt, Rizal deepened his own knowledge on current anthropological theories of race and civilization reading the classic work of Waitz and Gerland, *Anthropologie der Naturvölker* (Anthropology of Primitive Peoples),[27] which propounded the idea of the unity of the races.[28]

But as Rizal was well aware at the time of his proposition, other Filipinos were engaging in the writing of Philippine history, most notably the flamboyant ilustrado Pedro Paterno who published the first of his historical works, *La antigua civilización tagalog*, in 1887. Moreover,

Blumentritt was in close correspondence with a young and prolific Filipino journalist, the Ilocano-born patriot Isabelo de los Reyes. Rizal's hunger to know the pre-colonial past and present it as a source of identity was matched by the insatiability of Isabelo, who would publish in Manila between 1887–90, at least eight pioneering works on Filipino folklore and pre-colonial history.[29] Blumentritt admired de los Reyes' work and wrote to Rizal with high praise: "Your Ilocano countryman, my dear and esteemed friend I. de los Reyes is working incessantly. I'm pleased with his valuable ethnographic works. It is a pity that he has not studied ethnography which would make his studies even more brilliant."[30] Unlike the history writing of Pedro Paterno, whose work was riddled with bizarre conclusions and exaggerations, de los Reyes held no desire to show a golden age and could be considered as the more reliable historian.[31] If, predictably, the Spanish reactionary Wenceslao Retana was insulting in his criticism of Isabelo's work *"Don Isabelo no es un historiador,"*[32] the hubristic Pedro Paterno was moved enough to call him the "Father of Philippine folklore" in 1886, and T.H. Pardo de Tavera commended his culturally insightful research. While Rizal and other ilustrado propagandistas were easily persuaded by Blumentritt's "migration wave" theory, and were expending considerable effort in proving their ancestors equal to Europeans, Isabelo took a radically different view. He found Blumentritt's theory unconvincing, and held instead an unshakeable belief in the Filipinos as one people, calling himself what other ilustrados felt insulting, if not inconceivable — "brother (*hermano*) of the wild Aetas, Igorots and Tinguians."[33] Neither did Isabelo feel the need to prove the Filipinos were not racially inferior to Europeans. To him, this was plainly evident. Whilst ilustrado Filipinos like Rizal had become enamored by Europe and German intellectuals, Isabelo, a scholar and a journalist working in the Philippines, preferred to orient his efforts towards highlighting customs that distinguished Filipinos from Europeans.[34] However, there is little evidence that Rizal gave any direct encouragement or advice (which was his habit) to Isabelo, who had been working on his groundbreaking historical and ethnographic works around the same time as Rizal's own efforts.[35] Indeed, the two later came into conflict regarding the issue of impartiality. Rizal's reserve towards Isabelo's historical scholarship, in contrast to his warm and repeated endorsement of Blumentritt, tellingly made his position clear.

Failing to persuade Blumentritt to undertake the task of writing his country's history, Rizal decided to do it himself. That Rizal did not trust his compatriots to write this history was an attitude he later underlined to Blumentritt:

> I have first to give an example to my compatriots, combat their bad qualities, and afterwards, when they are already reformed, then will emerge many writers who can represent my native land before proud Europe, like a young lady who is presented to society after having finished her schooling.[36]

Arriving back in Europe from the Philippines, Rizal chose to proceed to London rather than Madrid or even Berlin, though he knew a copy of the Morga and other early Spanish chronicles could be consulted in libraries of the latter cities. Upon his arrival in the afternoon of 25 May 1888, he stopped briefly at the Midland Grand hotel, the gorgeous Gothic pile at the front of St. Pancras railway terminus, where he could not have failed to notice the elegant smoking room exclusively for ladies.[37] Then, 16 August, having been granted a reader's pass to the British Museum, Rizal formally signed in for the first time at the Reading Room, attaching the professional title of "doctor" to his confident signature. While the good number of female readers surely could not have escaped Rizal's observant eyes, the young Filipino unknowingly worked in the Reading Room with H.G. Wells, and in and out during the period of his visit were Rudyard Kipling, Eleanor Marx and Peter Kropotkin.[38]

Like Paris and the cities of Germany he had visited, London made civilized Europe evident, where women were often seen busy reading in libraries, were respected, serious-minded and learned. But there lay a terrifying underside to the civilized city. The women of London were gripped by fear, as Rizal was later to note in *La Solidaridad*. At the time of his stay a sexual psychopath who identified himself as Jack the Ripper roamed the streets disembowelling women in the shadows of the East End.[39]

Footnoting Fornication: Rizal's Annotations of Antonio de Morga's *Sucesos de las islas Filipinas*

Written in 1609, Antonio de Morga's *Sucesos de las islas Filipinas* was one of the more objective accounts by an early Spanish chronicler.[40] Rizal regarded the author as "a learned explorer" who possessed "nothing of the superficiality and exaggeration so peculiar to the Spaniards."[41] Equally important, he had been a high-ranking colonial official, and not a friar; indeed, he regarded the religious orders as a source of lamentation and trial.[42] Rizal published his edition of the Morga in Paris in 1890.[43] His annotations distilled, in several crucial ways, the ilustrado effort to build what cultural historian Resil Mojares has called "a nationalist counter-narrative." To paraphrase Mojares, Rizal's aims were part of an ilustrado determination to counter colonialist denial of a Filipino history outside Spanish rule; to resist colonialist denigration of native culture and to claim a pre-existent identity (*antigua nacionalidad*) violated, interrupted and erased by colonialism. Given these purposes, Mojares concedes, Rizal was not above "misreading his sources (whether innocent or intentional) by selectively highlighting details, leaving out others, or displacing contexts."[44] These faults in Rizal's work did not escape the scrutiny of his contemporaries. Even his friend Blumentritt, writing in the preface that otherwise heaped glowing praise on the work for presenting the perspective of the colonized, gently chided Rizal for indulging his anti-friar prejudices and for censuring the "occurrences of centuries past in accordance with the concepts that correspond to contemporary ideas."[45] Isabelo de los Reyes, meanwhile, commented that Rizal's patriotism, though "laudable," had undermined his objectivity and led him to exaggerate the level of civilization attained by the natives of the Islands before the Spanish conquest.[46]

The biases and historical flaws in Rizal's annotations provide an insight into how Rizal responded to the early chroniclers' accounts of a sexually permissive native culture. Confronting this aspect of the historical record had been difficult for Rizal, because reports of permissiveness obviously did not support his overall thesis about the high level civilization attained by the pre-Hispanic indios. In a rejoinder to Isabelo de los Reyes, Rizal asserted that his arguments were grounded in, and drew upon, a range of sources. Patriotism, he insisted, had not undermined his partiality to the extent that he would attempt to challenge what appeared to be incontrovertible:

> Whether or not patriotism has blinded me, somebody can always criticise me for not disproving the claims of Morga about Filipino women. I did not wish to deny what I had found in the testimonies of all the authors, just as I do not wish to accept what is said contrary to reason.[47]

Rizal saw, in other words, that Morga's account concerning Filipino women was offensive and ought to be disproved. If he had been acting in the interests of patriotism alone he would have refuted Morga. But he had concluded it would be wrong to do so because Morga's allegations appeared to be supported by similar descriptions given independently by other authors.

When working on his annotations, Rizal mined an array of sources that included the Spanish missionary accounts of Martin de Rada (1575), Juan de Plascencia (1589) Pedro Chirino (1605), Francisco Colin (1663) and Gaspar San Agustin (1698) as well as travel narratives by Antonio Pigafetta (1521), Miguel de Loarca (1582), Thomas Cavendish (1588) and others. He found these early narratives and chronicles were replete with detailed descriptions of a variety of sexual behavior, relationships, and practices socially sanctioned in native society. Inclined to view native sexual life as mortal sins and perversions, and certainly aberrant, the chroniclers reported witnessing practices they pejoratively called fornication, adultery or concubinage, incest, forms of polygyny and polyandry and sodomy, the "sin against nature" that encompassed homosexual, heterosexual and bestial anal penetration. Sex to the pre-colonial natives clearly entailed much more than the propagation of the species; it was also enjoyed purely in the pursuit of carnal pleasure.

Predictably, the Spanish chroniclers principally blamed indio women for the keen sexual proclivities of the natives. They repeatedly remarked upon the lascivious and unchaste *mujer indigena*, and what they perceived to be her shockingly unmanaged sexual desires. Miguel de Loarca's observation in 1582 was typical:

> The women are beautiful, but unchaste. They do not hesitate to commit adultery, because they receive no punishment for it.... [They are] extremely lewd, and they even encourage their own daughters to a life of unchastity; so that there is nothing so vile for the latter that they cannot do it before their mothers, since they incur no punishment.[48]

Morga described the pre-colonial culture of the Islands in the eighth and final chapter of the *Sucesos*, and it was this chapter that provided Rizal with the best opportunity to amplify his case for the pre-Hispanic inhabitants having a superior "ancient morality" that contact with the Spaniards subsequently corrupted and destroyed.

Rizal fussed over the detail of Morga's descriptions of the native's noble comportment, luxurious dress, elaborate jewellery, tattoos, filed teeth, bodily cleanliness and perfumed corporeality,[49] but was especially quick to censure any mention of parading naked flesh. He wanted to excise the sensuality inherent in the image of the pre-colonial native woman portrayed by Morga, clearly intending to replace it with an undebauched, moral, if not prudish representation. He cited liberally from the 1605 account of the Jesuit missionary Pedro Chirino, whose picture of restrained, modest and fully clothed natives was much better suited to his purposes.[50] Quoting Chirino, Rizal relates that even when bathing women kept their bodies "bent and almost seated for modesty, immersed in the water until the throat, with the greatest care not to be seen, though there may not be anybody who can see them."[51] They were characteristically "circumspect and careful in covering their bodies with extreme modesty and bashfulness."[52]

The Spanish chroniclers had also disparaged the marriage and divorce customs they encountered, claiming they illustrated the amorality, sexual primitiveness and lack of respect for women in native culture. Paying "bride wealth" rather than the giving of a bridal dowry, they concluded, meant in effect that wives were bought. Divorce and the dissolution of marital ties, they remarked, could occur for the most "trivial causes".[53] Responding to these arguments, Rizal contended that the marital arrangements enjoyed by the ancient Filipina were in fact more egalitarian than both the traditional European dowry system and more contemporary European inheritance and marriage customs. Pre-colonial marriage appeared to him as a union of equals:

> Naturally the woman did not and does not carry a dowry. The character of the Filipino woman, to be a help rather than a burden to the husband, reject this custom necessary to the European woman because if she is not a burden, in general she increases the husband's budget. In the Philippines the woman does not fish for a husband, but she chooses a husband; the husband does not take a heavy burden or the matrimonial yoke, but a companion to help him and introduce economy in the irregular life of a bachelor.... The sad spectacle that many European families present who seem to be in a hurry to get rid of their marriageable daughters is almost never seen in the Philippines.... The Tagalog wife is free and respected, she manages and contracts, almost always with the approval of her husband, who consults her

about all his acts. She is the keeper of the money, she educates the children... She is not the European woman who marries, purchases the husband's liberty with her dowry, and loses her name, rights, liberty ... her true dominion being limited to reign over the salon, to entertain guests, and to sit at the right of her husband.[54]

Filipino women, Rizal asserted, brought to the domestic domain far more than a dowry. Valued in her own family who customarily are reluctant to let daughters go, the Filipina enjoys sexual autonomy, insofar as she is at liberty to marry the husband of her choice. The Filipina, he claimed, was able to restrain her passions and therefore to inject "economy" in the "irregular" life of a single man. This greater self-control, Rizal assumes, extends to the management of family finances and material possessions. A "help" rather than an economic burden to her "husband's budget" she brought to the marriage her own inheritance from her parents. Yet the household budget was not the only important aspect of family life entrusted to her. She was responsible for the education of her children, independently conducted financial business as she saw fit, while her husband sought out her counsel and respected the decisions she made. This image of high moral rectitude underscored the key roles Rizal considered a woman played within the marital and domestic spheres of his own times. The allusion to her careful business sense outside the home is presented as an ability firmly oriented towards nourishing the well-being of her family.

Isabelo de los Reyes, like Rizal, detailed customs relating to inheritance, marriage and divorce and concluded that these practices were "generous" and "very much favoured" the woman. Unlike Rizal, however, Isabelo was not afraid to highlight the pagan culture of the Filipinos. Writing in *El Folklore Filipino*, Isabelo discussed pre-Hispanic women in relation to the power and influence they wielded in their communities. He spoke of their role as shamans, the powerful intercessors between the divine and the human known as *babaylanes* in the Visayas, or *katalonans* by the Tagalogs.[55] He talked of epics that sang of cunning and clever women; referred to ancient Philippine mythology which revered a host of *diwata*, heavenly female deities, or spirits, and correctly identified the most feared demons as being the female *asuang*, and *mangkukulam*.[56] Where Rizal liked to relate the elegant attire of indio women with various civilized sartorial counterparts — the long flowing Moorish styles, the sculpted coiffure and kimonos of the Japanese for instance,

Isabelo de los Reyes saw no need to make such comparisons.[57] Preferring to judge them by their own merits and uniqueness, he was admiring of pre-conquest indios who walked resplendently wreathed in gold and jewels, their legs strung with garters of semi-precious stones.[58] Again in contrast to Rizal, Isabelo de los Reyes did not feel the urge to idealize pre-conquest sexuality in the interests of patriotism and propaganda. He noted that polygamy had been practised in the Visayas and that abortion and infanticide had been common everywhere, practised either to preserve family honor or because another child would be an economic burden to the family.[59] Nor did Isabelo deny the claim that virginity was little valued, noting that in the Visayas an artificial penis was ceremonially used to break the hymen of unmarried girls.[60]

Morga made frequent mention of native sexual life and peppered the entire chapter with his observations. He found indio women loved money so much they readily yielded themselves up for the promise of pecuniary gain.[61] He was scandalized by the observation that future husbands considered virgin brides to be such an inconvenience and virginity a "disturbance and impediment" that there were men paid to end the virginity of young women before their marriage.[62]

To these observations Rizal responded in page after page of annotations, but his arguments, smooth when affirming gender equality, were less assured with regard to the egalitarian joys of sex. He was inclined to frame sex in terms of biological determinations and considered the sexuality of the pre-conquest inhabitants, indio women especially, as a manifestation of a "sincere obedience to nature and instincts" or their *"facilidad"* to obey their instincts to reproduce. But there was a limit to how far he could stress this "sincere" and "natural" desire without falling into the same exaggerations he was accusing the friar chroniclers of committing. On the one hand, Rizal was acutely aware that political motivations were often the reasoning behind the exaggerations. In a letter to Blumentritt, Rizal criticized the distortions found in the sixteenth century account of Father Martin Rada. "I should like to believe that he cherished good intentions," comments Rizal on Rada:

> ... but perhaps on account of religion, he did not want the Spaniards to abandon the Philippines, so he described the natives differently from the other writers, as if they were worse than wild animals. He says that almost all mothers kill their children before birth when they already have more than one or two.... And the unfortunate young women who conceive children follow the same procedure.[63]

In answer to this depiction of infanticide, Rizal cited the Jesuit Chirino, who gave a rather more flattering account of the civilization of the indios. But his more confident rhetoric in defence of pre-conquest indio women was based simply on his own convictions, without reference to any source. They were not the only women in history, he insisted, who prostituted their bodies for money. Europe too had a long history of sexual licentiousness, of worshipping the "cult of Venus, Priapus, Bacchus ... of orgies and Bacchanalia ... of prostitution in Christian Europe, and above all in the Rome of the popes." In this matter, he rightly said, "no nation can cast the first stone." He felt, nevertheless, that whatever the excesses of the past, "the Filipinas of today have no reason to blush before the women of the most chaste nations of the world."[64]

The prevalence of sexual promiscuity among young people that Morga remarked upon gave Rizal the opportunity to refine his argument. There was little sexual modesty:

> Because they saw nothing sinful in the act of reproducing the species. The ancients, as in many other places, did not see in it more than a natural instinct to be satisfied. The same Mosaic Religion did not prohibit it except adultery. Only Christianity made the act a mortal sin because, it saw every thing carnal as corrupt, bad, like something from the devil.... Between prostitution and gloomy and barren Cenobite anti-naturalism there is a middle ground: obedience to natural laws without corruption or frustrating the purposes that all things have.[65]

But then Rizal suffers a failure of nerve, abruptly drops this "natural instincts" line of argument and returns to his defence of the honor of pre-conquest Filipino women. Failing to find solid evidence in support of his case in the primary sources, he turns instead to a secondary source which he knows to be not only dubious but far-stretched to the point of fantasy — Pedro Paterno's *La antigua civilización Tagalog*. Completely suspending his critical faculties and professed allegiance to scientific method, he even applauds the imaginative ethnography of Paterno as an "erudite" tome which in his view refuted "magnificently" the imputations about Filipino women that Morga perpetrated and later writers echoed.[66]

Equally troubling to Rizal was the recurrent mention of incest and sodomy in historical sources. Rizal sensibly called Morga's claim of incest as an "ordinary" practice an exaggeration. While conceding incest may not have been totally absent, he felt it reasonable to argue that in other places "even worse are recorded ... in the annals of the great peoples and families of Christian and devout Europe." Furthermore, Morga's comments reminded him of the slanderous scribblings of certain Spanish hacks whose own sense of morality was questionable. Rizal parried: "In order to assert such dirty stupidities it is necessary to have witnessed them, or believe himself capable of doing the same if placed in the same circumstances."[67]

Rizal's response to Filipino promiscuity was immediately followed by a footnote vociferously condemning sodomy. Here, the offence he takes against this particular sexual act is grievous. Rizal saw sodomy as an abominable crime. He believed it occurred when men either became "disgusted by prostitution," and here he offered the examples of Europe or China, or through "excessive privation," a state that often led to wandering down "mistaken paths" which happened "in certain single sex convents and schools."[68]

Morga had claimed that sodomy had become more widespread after the arrival of the Chinese. Much inclined to this vice, they had succeeded in contaminating indio men and women. Writing not long after one of the first and bloodiest massacres of the Chinese by the Spaniards in 1603, killings enthusiastically aided and abetted by the Tagalogs in Manila, Morga evidently continued to harbor a common, deep-seated Spanish prejudice against the Chinese.[69] Rizal also makes plain his own antipathy towards the Chinese:

> Despite what Morga says and despite the fact that almost three centuries have already elapsed since then, the Filipinos continue abhorring this crime and they have been so little contaminated that in order to commit it the Chinese and other foreigners make use of their compatriots, of indio women and those who are their wives or of some miserable vagabond children.[70]

There are two critical features to note in this diatribe against sodomy. Firstly, Rizal vehemently refutes Morga's claims of pervasive sodomitical practices amongst the Filipinos and asserts that the relative "uncontamination" of the Filipino is a result of an historical hatred towards sodomy which continues even after three hundred years. Secondly, the "Filipinos" Rizal speaks of here refers not to indio men and women in general but exclusively concerns men. Rizal's stance against sodomy was all too plain. Ancient Filipino men vigorously resisted and were, so to speak, impenetrable. Thus, Chinese men and other sodomising foreigners had little choice but to use their fellow countrymen, native women and wretched stray children. Morga had thought sodomy was an abomination and Rizal had been inclined to agree. Rizal's long footnote declared his disgust and refuted its incidence among indio men by stating that the practice was abhorred by them and hence contained, restricted to foreigners and their hapless weak partners.

Yet the criminality of this sin against nature paled in comparison to another sexual practice that Morga regarded as far more shocking, not least because of its unfamiliarity to European eyes. The brief remarks on sodomy were immediately followed by a description of a practice which in Morga's opinion exceeded sodomy in its depravity and wickedness. This was the custom of men in the Philippines, especially the tattooed people (*Pintados*) of the Visayas to pierce their penises. Credit for the invention and demand for this bloody and devilish practice was unequivocally attributed by Morga to the unrelentingly lustful indio women:

> The natives of the Islands of the *Pintados*, especially the women, are very vicious and sensual, and their malevolence has led them to invent lewd (*torpe*) ways of intercourse between women and men. The men have a custom that they practice from their youth onwards. They make a hole in their *miembro viril*, close to its head, and pass through it a device that resembles a serpent's head made of metal or ivory, which is then secured in place by material of the same substance. With this device they have intercourse with a woman, and are unable to withdraw long after coitus, for women are so addicted and find delight in it despite shedding much blood and receiving other injuries. These devices are called *sagras*....[71]

Morga had not been alone in documenting these painful penile piercings. Indeed, his was one of the later observations. To European chroniclers the practice was so spectacularly savage that it figures in numerous narratives of Southeast Asian travels, and a perusal of just a handful of historical sources would have made Rizal familiar with male genital mutilation. Miguel de Loarca had made a note of penis pins in 1582,[72] and the Englishman Thomas Cavendish while visiting Capul Island off Samar in 1588 saw a "nayle of Tynne thrust quite through" the heads of men's "privities."[73] The Italian merchant Francesco Carletti ruminated over pleasure and pain upon seeing the devices between the legs of Visayan men in 1596.[74] According to the Boxer Codex of 1590, women especially found the wheels or rings so immensely satisfying that their use could not be prevented, even though the Spaniards punished the makers, the wearers and the pleasured with beatings.[75] Pigafetta, however, was the first European to record his fascinated, horrified reaction to the penile implants and incisions so common in Southeast Asia. In Java, he had heard the delicate sound of tinkling bells emanating from the penises of men who had come, on the pretense of urinating, to serenade their sweethearts with the melodious music they made by shaking their penises.[76] But subtle music-making in Java was a far cry from the assortment of flesh-tearing wheels, stars, spurs and gold bolts as large as a "goose quill" in use in the Philippines that Pigafetta scrupulously went on to detail.[77]

Rizal had made good use of Pigafetta's enthralling, richly detailed account and would have found it impossible to miss the Italian's startling descriptions of penile erotic surgery. But surely what was striking about the numerous accounts given by the historical sources was not the variety of penis devices being used and their dispersion throughout Southeast Asia; nor was it the difficult technique that needed to be employed which the astonished chroniclers were only too happy to relate to their readers in graphic detail. The striking characteristic feature of all the accounts was the common reason that prevailed to explain the punctures and insertions. Men endured the agony of penile operations and wore the devices, Pigafetta related, principally for the enhancement of female sexual pleasure: "They say that their women wish it so, and that if they did otherwise they would not have communication with them."[78] This essential explanation reached by fifteenth and sixteenth century European writers like Pigafetta has proved to be a resilient one. Today's ethnographers of the region do not attribute the use of the penis perforations and inserts to the native woman's wicked sexual nature, but some do still conclude that the purpose of penis pins is to heighten a woman's erotic pleasure and genital arousal.[79]

Morga's description of the Filipino penis perforations appears within a sequence of paragraphs that deal with the pre-conquest sexuality in general — about the promiscuity of young people, sodomy, "*herbolarios y hechiceros*" (herbalists and witch doctors), and men whose task was to deflower young women.⁸⁰ All these topics provoked lengthy annotations from Rizal in which he plainly relished the opportunity to modify, correct and refute. How then did Rizal respond to Morga's account of penile mutilation? One would expect a footnote. But here Rizal's prolixity came to a conspicuous halt, his silence made more deafening by the long annotations on its flanks.

Rizal's silences in the Morga are rare occasions but important ones. They indicate an opinion. For example, noticing Rizal's silence in relation to Morga's characterizations of the Negritos as savages, the historian Filomeno Aguilar correctly interprets the silence as an expression of Rizal's view of Negritos. Aguilar takes the silence to mean that since Rizal did not consider the Negritos as part of his imagined Filipino national community, they were therefore undeserving of his defence.⁸¹ Rizal's silence on the subject of penile mutilation is equally telling. The bulk of his historical sources had carried similar descriptions and more importantly, had similarly attributed the practice to female lasciviousness. Given the weight of the historical evidence that confronted him, we can only surmise that on this point he felt unable to refute Morga. Inwardly, he must have accepted that the pain and trauma of male genital mutilation could only be explained by a compulsion to satisfy the wicked, insatiable sexual appetite of women. As we noted, Rizal had in mind female sexuality when he tried to rebut the accusations of bias leveled at him by Isabelo de los Reyes: "I did not wish to deny what I had found in the testimonies of all the authors."

But Rizal's silence was an uncomfortable one. Throughout his combative annotations, Rizal had manfully tried to defend the pre-conquest indias from the calumnies of the Spanish chroniclers. But he also attempted something more ambitious. Highlighting customs of bilateral inheritance and divorce, Rizal pointed to a historical legacy of gender equality and constructed a historical image of enlightened, civilized femininity. The pre-conquest indio woman became a positive signifier, possessing qualities the contemporary Filipina should inherit or emulate. Wives in pre-Hispanic times were wise, prudent, nurturing, industrious, entrepreneurial, and conducted themselves with modesty in her attire and comportment.⁸²

The issue of the ancient indio woman's sexuality was a recurrent one in the main text and its frequency was reflected in Rizal's dialogic annotations. Allegations of women's inordinate sexual appetite were persistent, and Rizal found it difficult to maintain a coherent and plausible argument. He admitted the existence of female sexual desire and explained women's fondness for sex in terms of a "sincere obedience to natural laws and instincts." He attributed the pre-conquest indio's habitual infidelity to an old superstitious belief recorded by Chirino, which held that when a woman died she needed her former lovers to lead her safely by the hand across the dangerous river that separated this world from the next.[83] In a later footnote, in a predictable attempt at making female sexuality more palatable, Rizal narrowed his concept of female sexual instincts by explicitly linking them to the desire to reproduce. Clearly, he found dealing with the historical evidence of the indios' strong libido a painful struggle. It is difficult to ignore, for instance, the uneasy squirming and sense of desperation in his appeal to Paterno's questionable work, or in a tortuous analogy he drew between loss of virginity and inexperience in ballroom dancing.[84] Rizal's laborious efforts to rationalize, order and at times suppress the indio's independent sexuality resulted in uneven and often tenuous responses. When the issue flared up most startlingly on Morga's pages, as in the passage on male genital mutilation, Rizal pondered the weight of evidence and lapsed into silence.

A Lexical Detour: Defining Desire in Serrano Laktaw's *Diccionario*

The image of the unchaste, sexually immodest Filipina and the perception of native female desire as anarchic and indecorous haunted the ilustrado valorization of scientific order, rationality and bodily discipline. In the realm of language, this unease about disorderly female sexual activity is well illustrated in the *Diccionario* produced by Pedro Serrano Laktaw, the foremost Tagalog grammarian and lexicographer of the day. Serrano Laktaw was an important figure in the propaganda movement who had collaborated with Marcelo H. del Pilar in writing anti-friar tracts and was later a pivotal figure in the foundation of Masonic lodges in and around Manila. Here we shall examine how Serrano Laktaw, by inscribing terms for female genitalia and sexual desire with connotations of immorality and decadence, ironically followed in the very same path as the Church he disdained as obscurantist.

In the process of compiling dictionaries, confession manuals and codes of etiquette, Spanish missionaries had perforce to mention the aspects of female corporeality they found distasteful and the actions they wanted to suppress. Their works, as Resil Mojares has remarked, point to the existence of a rich, highly developed native vocabulary relating to the body, its motions and sensuality, a "body dialect" that the "missionaries found disquieting and threatening, suspicious of what libidinal devilish impulses may lie within." The natives, they believed, had a "surplus of physical expressiveness."[85] By attaching condemnation to the meanings of words to do with sex, the religious translators asserted both their own superiority as moral arbiters and the broader civilizing claims of Hispanic colonial authority.[86]

The missionary ascription of sinfulness to Tagalog terms relating to the sensual body and the erotic can be traced back to the early decades of Spanish contact. In a *Vocabulario Tagalo* published in 1624, for example, the Franciscan friar San Antonio rendered *hindot*, a word for intercourse, as "a lewd act performed by a man upon the arched body of a woman bent forward." Rather than ascribe the word *libog* its correct meaning of sexual desire, San Antonio traduced it as "excessive lustfulness." Taking this moralizing to its logical conclusion, he did not even attempt to offer a Spanish equivalent for *tilin*, a Tagalog term for the clitoris. All that the users of his *Vocabulario* needed to know, he decided, was that this was a "most lewd word."[87] The words themselves, like the bodily acts and parts they signified, were consciously stigmatized in the service of Catholic morality.

Over a century later, in the Tagalog-Spanish dictionary produced by Frs. Juan de Noceda and Pedro de Sanlucar in 1754, the word referring to the sexual desire of the Filipinos, *libog*, is again ascribed the qualities of lustfulness, carnality and shame. Readers are also warned again that *tilin* is a "lewd" word, although Noceda and Sanlucar, unlike San Antonio, do at least disclose its actual meaning, the *"clica de mujer."*[88] Compiled expressly for a "religious, learned and distinguished" readership, their *Vocabulario* did in fact record a profusion of words relating to the sexualized body and its erotic gestures; words that did not simply refer to male and female genitalia but were terms designated to states of excitement and flaccid rest, fecundity and manliness. Inevitably, such nuances were sometimes lost in translation. The post-coital peace of a penis that the word *quinsol* evoked, for example, was rendered flatly as the "shrinking miembro viril" or a man's "repentance."[89] The fluidity of gender recognized by the Tagalogs in words such as *bayoguin*, an effeminate male, was given a pejorative slant by the imputation of cowardliness to any man "who dresses in women's clothing."[90] Entries in the *Vocabulario* that referred to women's sexuality had an especially negative tone, the tarnish perhaps rooted in popular slang but enthusiastically echoed by San Antonio rather than ignored. He noted, for instance, that *quiqui*, a word for the female genitalia, was employed as an insult, hurled to humiliate.[91] And he recorded a repertoire of synonyms, like *talandi* and *quiri*, that could be used to stigmatize a woman deemed to be flirtatious or lascivious.[92]

In 1872, a Spanish mestizo named Rosalio Serrano followed the friars' didactic example when compiling a Spanish-Tagalog dictionary specifically intended for use in schools of primary instruction.[93] So keen was Serrano to impart his moral message, in fact, that he included a number of words not normally found in dictionaries designed for children. Two especially surprising inclusions were *copula* and *concupiscencia* as they appeared in his dictionary. In his entry for *copula*, Serrano first offers *tali* and *pagcatali* ("tie together" and "be entwined") as the colloquial vernacular equivalents but then adds the noun *pagaapid* (*pakikiapid*), which refers to adultery or some other expressly illicit sexual union. He thereby invests *copula*, in Spanish the straightforward, value-free word for coitus with connotations of illegitimacy and transgression.[94] *Concupiscencia* he explains with delicate sensibility but rather unspecifically, by tendering the figurative phrase "*pagcahilig na ualang tuto sa manga cagalingan sa lupa*," which might be freely translated into English as a "inordinate desire for earthly pleasure."[95] Concupiscence, or sexual desire, is thus presented by Serrano to his young readers as an inclination for carnality, a base desire contrary to morality and what is civilized and governed by intellect.[96]

The *propagandista* Pedro Serrano Laktaw was the son of Rosalio Serrano. Born in 1853, he became a primary school teacher, married and fathered a large family before departing for Spain in about 1888 to study for the *Normal Superior* teaching qualification in Salamanca. The first part of the work that made his name, the *Diccionario hispano-tagalog*, was published in Manila in 1889.[97] Highly praised by the propagandistas, the dictionary was also endorsed by foreign orientalists,[98] recognition that later secured him the position of tutor to the young Prince of Asturias, the future King Alfonso XIII of Spain.[99] Together with Rizal and Pardo de Tavera, Serrano Laktaw revived the pre-Hispanic syllables "ka" and "wa" and was the first to employ the new Tagalog orthography in a published work.[100] But more significant in the present context are his censoring omissions and censorious definitions. Whilst he included some words referring to the male genitalia like *titi* (penis) and *bayag* (testicles),[101] he systematically excluded from his *Diccionario* certain words in the Tagalog vernacular relating to the female genitalia and those that referred to intercourse. Not included were common words for the vagina such as *pocqui* and *poclo*; for the clitoris as *tilin* and *tinggil*; and for the sexual act, *hindot*. Putting these words into a dictionary, Serrano Laktaw, presumably felt, would have been grossly indecorous.

Serrano Laktaw used his father's work as a basis for his own *Diccionario* and he clearly had the same desire to use the power of translation in order to propagate good morals. This desire was not driven by prudishness alone. In compiling a dictionary for use by an awakening, increasingly self-confident people who aspired at least to greater autonomy if not to independence, Serrano Laktaw wanted to demonstrate that the high morality and civilization of that people entitled them to their place in the modern world. Even more than in his lexical lacunae, Serrano Laktaw's purpose is manifest in his definitions of the sexual terms he does include. To his father's definition of *copula*, for example, Serrano Laktaw added after *pagapid* (*pakikiapid*) or adultery the supplementary meaning "*o pakikialam nang lalaki sa babayi o nang babayi sa lalaki*" ("or a man interfering with a woman or a woman with a man"). This explicitly links the illicit sexuality of *pagapid* (*pakikiapid*) to *pakikialam*, a word whose meaning ranges from an intrusive, unwanted meddling to an extreme act of harassment. The effect of doing so is unequivocal. The term for a consensual, if illicit, sexual relationship, becomes riveted to a description of an interaction far more threatening and even violent, whether done by a man towards a woman or vice-versa.[102] With *concupiscencia*, Serrano Laktaw again appended his own gloss or moral garnish to his father's Tagalog definition, volunteering two derogating synonyms — *nasang mahalay* (lewd desires) and *kalupaan* (carnality) — that serve to underline the baseness of concupiscence.

In lexical terms Serrano Laktaw's elaborations were often superfluous, adding little clarity or accuracy. The negative meanings inherent in these translations from Spanish to Tagalog translations defined sex and sexual desire, concupiscence, as profane, morally degrading and spiritually imperilling. This emphasis plainly accorded with conventional religious restraints, but it also pointed to Serrano Laktaw's wish to assert his own authority as a native translator whose renditions of words were aimed at a native audience and sought both to affirm and to reinforce the indigenous moral sensibility. Filipino claims to equality as Spanish citizens, he believed, would be bolstered by a mastery of the language of the colonizer and a matching of the public morality that Spaniards liked to profess. In writing the prologue to the *Diccionario*, Serrano Laktaw's friend Marcelo H. del Pilar welcomed the work explicitly as part of the wider "civilizing mission."

This motivation is also apparent in the second volume of Serrano Laktaw's *Diccionario*, which gave his Spanish equivalents for Tagalog words.[103] Here too, his renditions go beyond any superficial and impersonal translative frame of rhetoric and meaning. His unusually long entry, for example, to *libog*, the Tagalog word for sexual desire, strikingly illustrates his proselytizing ambition:

> **Libog;** *kalibugan.* Lujuria; concupiscencia; lascivia; liviandad; sensualidad; carnalidad; crápula; torpeza; deshonestidad; impudencia [sic]; impureza; obscenidad.f. malicia; impúdica. *Nakahihikayat sa kalibugan.* Voluptuoso, sa; sensual; lasciva, va. Adj.- *Malibog* Lujurioso, sa. Sensual; carnal; crapuloso, sa. Deshonesto, ta impudente; impudico, ca; impuro, ra; obsceno, na; voluptuoso, sa; liviano, na; lascivo,va; libidinoso, sa; adj. braguetero, m. *Nauukol sa kalibugan.* Carnal; lascivo, va; pornográfico, ca. Adj. Sinon.de *iyag.* [104]

Kalibugan might be translated in English as sexual lustfulness; *malibog* as sensuality, and tacked on at the end is the synonym *iyag*, or lustful desire. Examples of how *kalibugan* might be used in a sentence are provided by the phrase *nakahihikayat sa kalibugan*, which may be loosely translated in English as "seduced by sexual lustfulness," and *nauukol sa kalibugan* as "drawn to sexual lustfulness." With these derivations and usages, Serrano Laktaw points to the fertile possibilities of the Tagalog root and to the rich indigenous vocabulary of physical expressiveness recorded by the early Spanish missionaries and explorers. *Libog*, we learn, is a root word whose vernacular arms sinuously twist to articulate the myriad physical states of sensuous, sexually yielding corporeality. *Libog* is desire, lustful, earthy and physical. *Libog* is seductive and enticing; *libog* is a crisis of engulfment, and an irresistible succumbing.

In the discourse of Tagalog sexual life, *libog* was then and resiliently remains a common word used to describe sexual desire. Recognizing the power of this word, its importance in the erotic vocabulary, its linguistic flexibility and its popularity, Serrano Laktaw immersed *libog* in a sea of Spanish words that described the sins of the flesh, associating the word inextricably with moral filth and decadence. If he had little option given the negative connotations that European words carried, he did not resist their moralizing ascriptions. He submerged *libog* deep in the Spanish lexicon of sinful lust — carnality, shamefulness, lasciviousness, indecency, and dissipation. In the mind of the ilustrado translator, a propagandista who like Rizal was keen to prove the morality and civilization of his countrymen, the most common word in the Tagalog lexicon of physical desire, *libog*, conveyed feelings that were not just impure but obscene, pornographic and downright wicked.

The Elusiveness of Virtue

Serrano Laktaw's febrile denunciation of sexual desire reflected how deeply the male ilustrados were troubled by the dangers of uncontrolled and undisciplined female passions. Sexual desire, it was feared, contaminated the heart of every woman, making distinctions between the virtuous and the "guilty," the chaste and the "fallen" neither certain nor clear. In May 1891 the propagandista Dominador Gómez treated readers of *La Solidaridad* to a long-winded tract on this perplexing subject.[105] Given the sheer perfidy of female nature, he affirmed, even intact virginity or marital fidelity were unreliable criteria for assessing a woman's virtue. Men might know what women were doing, but not what they were thinking, for regrettably the "recesses of conscience are impenetrable and shielded from human investigation."[106]

Addressed to "mothers and daughters," his two-part essay was an attempt, in his words, to define the "feminine characteristics [of] purity, modesty, honour, and integrity." Everyday chatter among the propagandistas about these vexed issues, he felt, displayed an "annoying confusion," which as a physician he considered himself well qualified to dispel. His opinions, he assured his readers, were supported by "extensive study" and the authority of medical science. As a doctor, he possessed an informed understanding of female nature and the biological basis of a woman's sexual appetites. Could virtue exist in women, he asked, in a form that was true, sincere and genuine? No, he answered flatly; perfect virtue was a pristine state of the soul that women could ultimately never attain. Due to their biological make-up, women had an inherent moral weakness. The bodily urges they felt, the sexual longings they hid in their hearts and minds, nourished as they were by a thousand quotidian temptations, meant that women could never transcend the force of their sexual desire.

Impressionable young women were led into error by priests in the confessional, who put impure thoughts into their minds and fostered "licentious impudence." But insidious dangers existed too in the gamut of bourgeois rituals and leisurely pastimes; they lurked in the pleasures of intimacy, conversation and the beguilements of stylish masculine grooming. In enumerating these dangers, Gómez incriminates men like himself in the process of corruption, for the diversions and ruses he discloses are precisely those he knew would arouse the erotic interest of women from his own social class: watching "lascivious and scandalous" spectacles in the theatre; reading "obscene" books such as romantic novels; the flattery of a "young *caballero*;" exchanging whispers on a moonlit balcony; pressing close during the slow rhythm of a gentle waltz; kissing ardently; and the virile appeal, even, of a black and shiny moustache and well-trimmed side burns.[107]

All these myriad enticements led women inexorably to harbor and conceal fleshly longings, whether or not they successfully resisted the pleasures themselves. And resistance, for Gómez, was in a sense a greater evil than submission. "The unfaithfulness of a soul in dreaming, thinking and savouring pleasure with a man, even when not carried into actuality," he stated emphatically, "is infinitely more serious than actual disloyalty and adultery." In other words, the "adulterer in thought" deserved more scalding opprobrium than the "adulterer in fact."[108] Wherever sexual desire was hidden it festered in the soul, and society was denied the opportunity to offer redemption, to forgive the afflicted woman and to direct her instincts and energies into the proper channels of dutiful wedlock and childbearing.

Women who succumbed to temptation but cunningly managed to avoid detection likewise escaped public censure and the chance of subsequent repentance, forgiveness and deliverance. Society condemned the "fallen" woman who persisted openly in her transgression but mistakenly lavished praise on innumerable others who knew how to evade "the inquisitorial eyes of vigilant censors" because their "repeated indiscretions with lovers" had made them wily. [109] Many of the outwardly most respectable women, Gómez observed, harbored dark secrets.

And some women carried an especially deep shame. Driven by depravity, yet fearful of illegitimate pregnancy, they indulged their lustfulness with their own sex, rather than with a man, satisfying their carnal appetites in *amor lesbio*. In a discourse that generally made no mention of same sex desire, this was a rare allusion to lesbianism. Like Rizal's diatribe against sodomy, Gómez's disgust towards lesbianism underscored the clear-cut distinctions the ilustrados drew between healthy normative sexuality and that which they condemned as aberrant, immoral, dissolute, and un-Filipino. Sodomy, Rizal had said, was abhorrent to Filipinos; it had been unknown in pre-Hispanic society and in later centuries had been practised only upon the pernicious insistence of Chinese and other foreigners. Lesbian love, in Gómez's similarly unequivocal view, was among the worst forms of vice and perversion. Women who lay with women were corrupt in their bodies and fatally damaged in their very souls.[110]

Gómez did concede that individual circumstances, such as an abusive or wayward husband, might make a woman's sexual transgressions understandable. But that did not alter the fact that the woman was compromised by her biological desires. Society's fond pretensions about women's virtue, in sum, were false and hypocritical. True virtue — the possession of an "iron will to overcome the tortuous demands of the flesh" — remained a fanciful ideal. As a doctor, Gómez believed his view of female sexuality was informed by reason and medical science; it demonstrated that he was in tune with modern thinking. Like his fellow propagandists, he aimed to supplant the old, traditional authority of Catholic priests and specifically to discredit the influence they held over women. Religious preaching on moral and sexual matters, he affirmed dismissively, was "nonsensical." He explicitly urged women to stop listening to priests and to reject religious ideas that were "opposed to the modern egalitarian spirit of this age of progress."[111]

Paradoxically, though, Gómez's essay was uncannily similar in its prescriptive moralizing to the priestly homilies he professed to despise. His concluding advice to women could have come from the pulpit: "Keep alive the undying fire of a great love for your husbands; look up to them and do not think of anything else but their being the fathers of your children."[112] His vaunted application of reason and modern scientific knowledge to questions of female sexuality claimed objectivity but finally arrived at familiar conclusions. Enlightenment and modernity, for the ilustrado scions of the nascent Filipino elite, entailed in matters of sex a vigorous affirmation of the bourgeois values of moral propriety and self-control; a confinement of female sexual desire firmly within the legitimate channels of marriage and family life. Science had shown female sexual desire to be biologically inherent, and to be such an inexorable and potent force that it could threaten the social order. It was the patriotic and patriarchal duty of modern, enlightened Filipino men to ensure this fearsome force was strictly contained within decent and civilized bounds.

Sex Education

Dominador Gómez imperiously addressed his *La Solidaridad* essay on feminine virtue to "Our Mothers and Daughters," but in reality its readers would mostly have been male ilustrados like himself who cultivated the habits and tastes of bourgeois European gentlemen. To these readers, Gómez's admixture of moral and medical preoccupations would not have been unfamiliar. Similar pontifications filled the pages of the sex manuals that proliferated during the late nineteenth century. Intended for both men and women, these manuals sought to make sexuality safe and hygienic, dispensing advice on genital cleanliness, venereal diseases, the calamitous effects of masturbation, remedies for male impotence and sterility, condoms and other forms of prophylactic contraception, physical indications of female virginity, and the proper etiquette for the conjugal bed. The books promised their readers an accessible yet purportedly scientific basis for understanding female sexuality and sexual pleasure.

In addition to the huge body of literature on sexuality being produced by physicians in France, Germany and England, doctors in Spain were also keenly developing the new specialty of sexology. Physicians such as Felipe Monlau and Amancio Peratoner, for example, were prolific and influential pioneers in the field whose numerous works the Filipino expatriates would have probably encountered whether or nor they were studying medicine. Peratoner's sex manuals aimed to keep Spanish men abreast of the latest thinking on sex and sexuality. In *Fisiología de la noche de bodas* (1875), for instance, the author assured his readers on his title page that his work drew upon an array of acclaimed, mainly French, physicians, moralists and philosophers.[113] He interpreted in a popular style what the dominant contemporary European discourses distinguished as a normative sexual life. His writings reveal the often speculative, androcentric and confusing nature of contemporary scientific understanding of sex, but they merit brief attention here because they show the particular climate of opinion in which the propagandists developed their views about male and female sexuality. Most crucially, following the French savants he so admired, Peratoner placed a high value on marital, reproductive sexuality and disapproved of non-procreative sex. This was a stance with which the propagandists would have professed themselves fully in accord, even when behaving contrarily.

Peratoner defined sex as the "intimate union of the sexes and the consummation of the act of generation." "Normal" women's sexuality, in his estimation, was solely the means to reproduction and maternity, and "normal" female sexual pleasure was realized solely by penile penetration and ejaculation.[114] Women, indeed, only had an incidental role in intercourse, as the passive receptacles of male spermatic energy. It was the man's task, Peratoner pronounced, to introduce his organ and ejaculate the "prolific liquid" and the woman's duty to receive the male organ and its liquid cargo. For men, ejaculation involved "voluptuous sensations," a "considerable loss of fluid" and "violent spasms." For women, the spasms of orgasm were a longer but smaller and more internal process, entailing "convulsive intermittent contractions" that sent out a "channel of fecundating liquid, some of which was absorbed by the neck of the uterus." Female orgasms should neither be felt nor manifest, neither audible nor visible. "Small spasms" were normal, but "ardent venereal voluptuousness" was manifested only by "nervous" women. Orgasm for these women involved "distressing sighs and violent contractions; and in others shouts, almost epileptic howls ... and convulsions similar to attacks of hysteria." These sensations, Peratoner emphasized, were not normal. They were "abuses."[115]

The source of excessive female sexual pleasure, Peratoner discerned, was the clitoris. As with all other parts of the female genitalia, the clitoris found its homologous parallel in the male organ and was simply "a man's penis in miniature," the sole difference being the absence of the urethral canal.[116] At the same time, it was a most dangerous organ, the cause of all the sexual disorders that afflicted the nineteenth-century woman: lesbianism, masturbation, depression, marital dissatisfaction and nymphomania. Monlau blamed the clitoris fot the vice-ridden women of ancient Rome and Greece who practised tribadism, subrigatrice and fricatrice.[117] An enlarged clitoris signified female atavism, the legacy of the primitive past; it identified a promiscuous woman, explained an inclination towards prostitution and encouraged masturbation which, Peratoner agreed with his eminent sources, led to the corruption of the female sensibility and madness. In extreme cases the clitoris had to be removed, and leading physicians practised the "harmless operative procedure" of clitoridectomy as a cure for a multitude of women's illnesses.[118]

Popular books on sex and medicine, which the works of Monlau and Peratoner exemplified in Spain, concerned themselves with the sexual health and marital well-being of both men and women. Men were enjoined to avoid a multitude of practices if they were to avoid sickness from sexual diseases. Amongst the causes of venereal and syphilitic disorders that could afflict a man, Peratoner cited masturbation, excessive copulation, and sex with a woman suffering from any number of defects and illnesses from cancer to ovarian cysts.[119] For both sexes, the manuals warned, copulating excessively held dire consequences. Men were threatened with a host of disorders from impotence, debilitated genitals, atrophied testicles, ruptured blood vessels, loss of hearing and memory, to pulmonary diseases, digestive problems, mania, spasms, convulsions and epilepsy. Likewise, women would suffer from genital irritations, irregular menstruation, cancer of the womb, of the uterus and vagina, sterility, morbidity and hysteria.[120]

Peratoner's *El mal de Venus*, published in 1881, contained several graphic warnings about the dangers of female sexuality.[121] Readers were instructed, for instance, how to discern signs of venereal disease in the female genitals. A gentleman could reassure himself that a woman was healthy and hence safe for sexual intercourse by simply comparing "the mucous parts of the genital organs" with the "lips of the mouth." Intended to disclose what was dangerously hidden, here was advice carrying the implicit message that women were dissembling, their bodies breeding grounds for disease, corporeal hiding places for lethal contaminations which physicians were morally obliged to reveal. This was advice edged with urgency, potentially even life-saving: "If the assembly of the vulva appears red, inflamed, warm, burning ... its colorations greenish yellow," Peratoner sagely counselled, then the gentleman should practise "absolute abstention."[122]

Sex for men was regarded as little more than part of a therapeutic regime whose frequency had to be determined by age, moderation and the "rules of hygiene."[123] Men (supposedly, of course, only married men) in their twenties and thirties, might in Peratoner's estimation find it beneficial to expend their spermatic energy about three times a week. Rizal, in his late twenties, evidently shared Peratoner's belief in libidinal thrift but thought the good doctor's allowance far too generous. Whilst living in Brussels in 1890, we may recall, he had introduced his visiting compatriot José Alejandrino to an unspecified "amusement" at the house of two sisters. Looking forward to being "amused" again, Alejandrino was disappointed to be told sternly by Rizal that a "good time" was necessary only "once a month." Indulgence more often would be yielding to vice.[124] Sexual self-control, Rizal plainly agreed with Peratoner, entailed the observation of a regular, "normal" and moderate regime of bodily expenditures that prevented moral and physiological enfeeblement and ensured the salubrity of a man's *vita sexualis*. Practising spermatic thrift was an important aspect of Rizal's sober management of time, money and energy. Whilst companions like Alejandrino might have misinterpreted this thrift as high-mindedness and resented his preachy admonishments, Rizal's self-rationing in fact reflected an pseudo-scientific idea of sex in terms of excess or deficits of energy, and an apprehension of sexual behaviour as being either normal or pathological. This reasoning was anchored not only to the traditional, Catholic moral discourse on deviant sexuality but also to the new medical discourse on sexual perversion.

The need to guard against an excessive avidity for sexual stimulation or unconventional sexual practices was tightly woven into Rizal's medical training. As a medical student, Rizal was taught how to identify and treat symptoms of perversity and, more fundamentally, how to understand perversions and their moral and physiological ramifications in the reductive terms of nosologies of degeneracy. A brief look at Rizal's medical notes on masturbation illustrates this influence on his thinking.

As we have already seen, Rizal began his medical studies by learning the principles of pathology and clinical analysis. In his "Clinica Medica" notebook he recorded the symptoms, diagnosis and treatment of patients in the Hospital San Carlos, the hospital where he and other medical students at the University of Madrid underwent their practical training. Among the cases he studied on ward rounds with his professor, Dr. Santiago Encinas, were several in which masturbation was held to be significant. Masturbation, Rizal's notes reveal, was viewed as causing a range of mental and physiological illnesses that could be treated by therapeutics, anaphrodisiacs or penile surgery. A patient who complained of abdominal pain accompanied by involuntary night time emissions, for example, was swiftly diagnosed as suffering from spermatorrhea and administered tinctures of iodine, extracts of sage, prescriptions of potassium iodine and several "rainbaths."[125] Viewed as a direct consequence of the "abuse of masturbation," such diagnoses implied the patient's own culpability for their morbid condition.[126] A patient diagnosed with congenital phimosis, or involuntary retraction of the prepuce, was observed to be in a dangerous state of almost perpetual sexual stimulation. "Phimosis causes a stimulation conducive to onanism, which weakens the intellectual faculties," Dr Encinas observed.[127] Referring to a case of hypospadias, a condition in which the meatus, the opening from which urine passes is not located at the tip of the penis, Dr. Encinas reasoned that masturbation had led to the patient's impotency, "since the semen cannot come in contact with the vagina."[128] Finally, in case of epithelioma, in which the penis had become diseased from "friction" and the passing of urine, masturbation was ultimately blamed for the complete loss of the male organ, because the only remedy was amputation.[129]

The ancient Hebrews, opined Dr. Encinas, had introduced the practice of circumcision partly for reasons of cleanliness but also in order to discourage men from gaining over-frequent "gratification" by the rapid and repetitive retraction of the prepuce. Here Rizal was clearly tickled by the wry parallel his professor drew between Jerusalem in Biblical times and the imperial capital in which they now lived. "A city whose food came from Manna," Dr. Encinas told his class, "could not be but a vagrant people; a city of vices; a city of filth; a city of corruption, filled with impurities, a city like Madrid."[130]

In the light of a medical training that attributed horrendous consequences to masturbation and sexual excess, Rizal's calls for restraint, moderation and self-discipline were more than mere rhetoric. Sexual self-discipline signified self-mastery and the ideal disposition of manliness. Male hygiene, virile health and sexual regulation were hallmarks of a respectable, civilized citizenry. To underscore this understanding of sexual behavior, T.H. Pardo de Tavera sought to inculcate the values of personal hygiene and cleanliness in men by writing a booklet designed to educate the "lay person" in sanitation. Published in Manila in 1895 and promptly translated into Tagalog from the original Spanish to reach a wider audience, *Arte de cuidar enfermos* was a direct challenge to certain superstitions in relation to the care of the sick. It offered practical advice which superseded as well as incorporated the earlier teachings of priests often found in books of manners. By filling this manual with instructions on how to properly wash the body, hands and genitals to prevent disease and infection, Pardo de Tavera emphasized cleanliness as a moral imperative, positing personal hygiene as a sign of social improvement and enlightened progress.[131]

Brotherly Advice

Publishing works on medicine, hygiene or even his chosen specialty ophthalmology did not figure in Rizal's scholarship despite his life-long interest in science.[132] Rather, Rizal's personal correspondence with scientists, curators, orientalists and members of his family bring to life the relentless curiosity and excitement of a man who embraced the promises he believed modern science held for human progress. Letters to his family in particular give an impression of Rizal's enthusiasm and intellectual adventurousness, a young student released into a world of scientific learning and freedom that Europe, especially Germany and France represented. And Rizal intended for that light of science and modernity he perceived to shine so brightly over the peoples of Europe to reach his fellow countrymen. Rizal's educational ideals, specifically his belief in the education of women makes Rizal a sympathetic and familiar voice to today's feminist historians. Further, affection, respect and mutual concern are immediately discernible in letters between Rizal and his beloved sisters. He brought them news of his activities and travels and they kept him in tune with the rhythms of family life. More intimately, they related to him their private health and medical concerns, a gesture that indicated their trust in him. Here, Rizal had a striking opportunity to influence and educate the women closest to him on fundamental issues concerning all women — female sexual and reproductive health.

Yet in matters relating to the pragmatic health concerns of his sisters, Rizal's letters reveal a basic unease. Rizal's sisters were acutely aware of the advantages of having a brother studying medicine in Europe and searched his letters for news of innovative medical technologies and methods for the advancement or improvement of women's sexual and reproductive health. They enjoined their brother to study and implement these ameliorating solutions and recounted in detail their needs. Rizal however responded to his sisters' call with relative dispassion. True, he regularly reported on his activities as a medical student but Rizal neither discussed the merits or advances being made in the science of reproductive biology, nor more crucially, did he provide his sisters with the much needed medical advice they sought. Rizal preferred to focus his concerns on women's morality and the moral dangers that a woman's vehement sexual passions presented.

Rizal was not averse to trying remedies currently in vogue, using new treatments on himself and prescribing them to friends and relatives. Over many years, for example, he regularly took Fowler's solution, a liquid form of arsenic, believing that it eased the chest pains he thought were the lingering vestiges of illnesses he suffered as a child.[133]

Rizal believed fervently in the efficacy of the poison and went through periods of arsenic intoxication, suffering the classic side effects of over-excitement, chronic thirst and excessive perspiration.[134] Feeling nevertheless that the benefits of arsenic outweighed these unpleasant consequences, he recommended Fowler's solution to members of his family without a second thought. When he heard that his brother Paciano felt unwell, he advised him always to carry with him "a little bottle of Fowler's arsenical liquor, taking daily two or four drops in a little cup of water."[135] Writing to his sister Saturnina from Dapitan in 1893, Rizal prescribed five drops a day of the "arsenical liquor" to treat herpes.[136] When a brother-in-law thought he suffered from glaucoma, Rizal, unable to examine his eyes at first hand, thought the illness might instead be malaria and wrote advising a strong dose of arsenic "beginning with ten drops daily ... and increasing by two every day until thirty drops."[137]

Rizal's enthusiastic endorsement of arsenic illustrates that he was willing, even eager, to share with those back home the medical knowledge he was acquiring in Europe. He was selective, however, about the information he chose to relay. In particular, he was conspicuously reticent in sharing his knowledge on female sexual and reproductive health, even though his medical notes attest to his familiarity with this area of medicine. He told his family that his first lectures at the Hospital San Carlos were on obstetrics. For a time his sisters might even have thought their brother was developing a special interest in gynaecology and obstetrics. His professor in obstetrics, he told them, was the flamboyant

Andres López Busto, whom Rizal knew by his title "Marquis de Busto."[138] Rizal was impressed by Busto's refined ways and jested that he felt honored to be taught by such a highly cultured gout sufferer.[139] When he was in Paris, Rizal visited the Laennec Hospital with the esteemed Filipino obstetrician Felipe Zamora and noted that its facilities were far superior to those found in Madrid.[140] Again in Paris, he accompanied Felix Pardo de Tavera to examine women's illnesses at the Lariboisiere Hospital.[141] Writing to his sister Saturnina, he later mentioned using water as an effective treatment for women's diseases.[142]

Encouraged by these reports of his activities, Rizal's sisters made it clear to their brother that women's reproductive health was crucially important to them. Writing in Tagalog, his eldest sister Saturnina firmly told her younger brother:

> I am sending you news that I now have two children, the eldest is Alfredo, next is Adela, and now I am eight months pregnant. Study well how you may be of assistance to our situation, certainly with so many of us there will always be someone suffering the hardships of this sickness.[143]

Referring to the physical arduousness of parturition as a "sickness" (*saquit*) that repeatedly plagued each of Rizal's childbearing sisters, Saturnina added more than a note of exasperation in her request. She is ordering her younger brother to work towards alleviating the suffering periodically afflicting his sisters. Giving birth to children, in Saturnina's experience, was always painful and carried the threat of death. She had endured the "rigors of parturition for a period of twenty-four hours" with the birth of her first child in 1882 and anticipated another painful labor. "I hope I shall be able to deliver safely and we will still see each other again," she wrote, clearly regarding the impending birth of her next child with profound and understandable trepidation.[144] The desire to give birth painlessly and safely was a matter of utmost importance to all of Rizal's sisters. Reiterating her sister Saturnina's appeal for advice on methods of painless parturition, Lucia asked Rizal also to tell his sisters about ways to increase and prolong the supply of breast milk. "This is what we need," she emphasized.[145]

Having nine sisters, of whom only two, Joséfa and Trinidad, remained unmarried, Rizal was well aware of his sisters' fecundity. The news Rizal regularly received from home was riddled with announcements of pregnancies, new births, children who were sick or had died, and the health of mothers. At the end of 1883, Rizal's mother Teodora Alonso sent a letter to her son in which she listed the names and arrival dates of her newest "debts to Our Lord," 6 new grandchildren within a period of less than 12 months, born to 4 daughters who, as she noted, were undeterred by the high rates of maternal death, the ravages of a cholera epidemic, beri-beri and the destructive violence of typhoons.[146]

With extraordinary good fortune, the principal members of the Rizal family survived the major cholera outbreaks of 1882 and 1888. But to Rizal's sisters, child bearing posed just as great a danger as epidemic disease. Lucia urged her brother pointedly to offer pragmatic solutions, to proffer not "beautiful words" but "positive deeds." Writing in 1886 to inform him about his sister Narcisa's miscarriage and other miseries, Lucia pointedly told Rizal that "We have no other treatment for our hardships other than the Spanish word for *paciencia* (patience). If you have better medicine than this then don't forget to bring it with you."[147] Later, Narcisa only narrowly survived a serious bout of puerperal fever that struck her down three days after childbirth.[148] In 1887 the family mourned the death of Olimpia, the third eldest sister, who had survived two difficult deliveries and the birth of a stillborn but then died in the course of another labor. "She lost so much blood that she died in less than thirteen hours," Rizal informed Blumentritt sadly.[149]

As members of the elite, Rizal's sisters had better access to doctors, medicines and treatments than most. They could call on the services of physicians trained in Europe and buy medicines imported from Europe as well as turn to indigenous healers, the *arbolarios* and local midwives. The expertise of ilustrado physicians and obstetricians like Felipe Zamora, Ariston Bautista Lin or Galicano Apacible, all of whom were friends and contemporaries of Rizal in Europe, represented the most advanced form of medical care for parturient women and women's illnesses available in the Philippines. As letters from Rizal's family show, these ilustrado physicians were frequently called upon to attend to the illnesses of the female members of the family. After the death of Olimpia, for instance, Soledad, the youngest of the sisters, fell sick and was immediately treated by Galicano Apacible;[150] Saturnina sought out Felipe Zamora in Manila concerning a disorder of the uterus.[151] This increasing willingness of Rizal's sisters to entrust their well-being to western medical practices and the hands of male medical professionals evinces a general reorientation towards a more scientific approach to health and medicine. Even Lucia, already mother to six children, solicited advice from Rizal on how best to care for her latest new born, her seventh child.[152]

But such changes in attitude were neither consistent nor unequivocal. The rising prestige of the ilustrado physicians did not so much supplant as supplement the role of local healers, midwives, and the use of herbal and home remedies. Paciano wrote to Rizal about a sickness in Calamba he called "*la locura,*" insanity, which had affected mainly "the poorer classes" but also their sister Narcisa. As Paciano explained, a treatment of mustard plasters (*sinapismos*) was applied to their sister, failing which she would be sent for a course of hydrotherapy.[153]

Neither was it the case that elite women always heeded the advice of their western trained physicians. In 1890, Rizal received news from Saturnina that she had gone to Manila to be treated by Zamora, whose diagnosis was that her "uterus was swollen, out of place and dirty." "But I do not feel the symptoms he mentions," she remarked, writing to her brother in Tagalog:

> This is my second examination and he won't tell me the charge so I don't know how much I should pay. He has asked me to buy a vaginal syringe and to take three types of medicines, belladonna, estramonio and sauco.[154]

Three months later, Saturnina again told Rizal about her condition:

> I'm now well, by God's mercy. I think Zamora misled me in saying my uterus was swollen. I have still not used the medicines he prescribed and I don't feel anything different from before.[155]

Although she disregarded her physician's advice and preferred to get better without medication, Saturnina was not generally sceptical about western medicine and treatment. Rather, implicit in the doubts she harbored towards Zamora's diagnosis was an underlying belief, one she shared with her sisters, that her brother's opinion might be more illuminating, more trustworthy. It is important to recognize that the receptiveness of Rizal's sisters towards western medicine essentially hinged upon the esteem in which they held Rizal and their personalistic faith in him. Western medicine was deemed only safe, reliable and effective in the hands of someone whom they felt to be utterly dependable. In relating their illnesses to Rizal, his sisters held some anticipation of a response, an expectation that informed advice would be offered. Craving information, Rizal's sisters would surely have benefited from knowing, even in the simplest terms, what medical treatments were being administered to European women.

However, Rizal's attitude towards his sisters' medical concerns was ambivalent. He professed a general interest in obstetrics but did not accede to their request that he specialise in that field and did not offer them the practical advice they urgently sought. On the pressing issue of painless parturition, he would have been aware that physicians in Europe had employed ether and chloroform to anaesthetize parturient women since the mid-nineteenth century. He might either have endorsed this practice or alternatively have cautioned his sisters about chloroform's undesirable effect of producing a prolonged period of inexplicable sexual excitation, a factor that made its use during childbirth questionable.[156]

Rizal, it should also be noted, was in Europe during a period when modern contraception was veritably exploding into the public consciousness amidst debates on Malthusian projections of a population explosion. Tampons or vaginal sponges were a popular and respectable contraceptive in nineteenth-century Europe, as was douching using vaginal syringes. Popular in Germany since the 1870s, the standard device was known as the "irrigator," an apparatus that squirted a douching solution consisting of water, vinegar and carbolic acid into the vagina through a thin nozzle that immobilized and flushed out spermatozoa. A more convenient model, the Ebell irrigator, was fitted with a bulb to collect the solution thus permitting douching to be done in bed.[157] And surely, too, Rizal would have heard of the mechanical contraceptive enthusiastically launched by Dr Wilhelm Mensinga in Leipzig in 1882, called the "diaphragm." Mensinga and the thousands of doctors who advocated the use of the diaphragm viewed therapeutic contraception as being as moral as therapeutic abortion but much safer.[158] The cervical cap had already been promoted since the 1830s, and in the mid-1880s the London pharmacist Rendell began eagerly marketing chemical contraception in the form of tablet suppositories. Finally, by the 1890s, spermicidical powders constituting boric, citric and tannic acids in a gum base had become available throughout Europe, a popular brand being Dr Huter's vaginal powder which sprayed directly into the vagina to coat the surface.[159]

Rizal finally, could also have let his sisters know how high-powered douches and other forms of hydrotherapy were being used to treat women's illnesses in European spa resorts, or he might have mentioned a new instrument known as the electro-mechanical vibrator that physicians employed to relieve a host of hysteroneurasthenic disorders in women.[160] Involving genital massage, the treatment was intended to induce female orgasm, a state defined under clinical conditions as the crisis of an illness, or "hysterical paroxysm." Whether attained by mechanized technology such as the "water-cure," or by the traditional use of fingers (properly dipped in fragrant oils and scented waters) as performed by a doctor, massage of the genitals to orgasm was considered a legitimate medical therapy that only fashionable women could afford.[161]

It is apparent from Saturnina's letters that her brother did not gratify her with a response on either Zamora's diagnosis or his prescriptions. Nor did he make any comment on her condition. Correcting a malposition of the uterus was straightforwardly achieved by physicians in the nineteenth century with the use of intra-uterine devices of various kinds, and Rizal might have asked his sister whether Zamora had attempted this.[162] Perhaps he tactfully refrained because he felt that giving an opinion would have undermined Zamora's expertise and diagnosis. Perhaps too he felt a lack of confidence in this area following a traumatic experience in the San Carlos clinic. There he had operated on a young woman diagnosed with a tumor found in the ovary and uterus. The neck of the uterus was also found to have "deviated" from its correct position. Complications occurred during the operation and the patient in their care slowly bled to death. In his notes Rizal recorded his alarm, dismay, and feelings of inadequacy: "We were sure that was the uterus.... We could not explain what was there, what was happening. It is intolerable.... During the autopsy another uterus with its ovary and a vagina were found.... How can there be two uteri?"[163]

But even if this experience disturbed Rizal enough to discourage him from advising on uterine disorders (especially from a great distance), he might still have explained Zamora's prescribed use of vaginal syringes to his sister. Vaginal syringes in the Philippines were probably expensive items available only in exclusive Escolta pharmacies. Consisting of a rubber balloon filled with water injected into the vagina through a rubber tube, this was an indispensable tool for douching, a legitimate hygienic function that also served as a covert method of contraception. Saturnina may have also wondered what her brother thought of Zamora's prescription of belladonna, estramonio and sauco. Belladonna is sourced from deadly nightshade and estramonio from jimson weed, both of which had powerful hallucinogenic properties. It is unclear why Zamora prescribed these remedies, but like the third preparation, sauco, which is extracted from elderberry, they were probably administered by physicians for all sorts of conditions.

Rizal's persistent reluctance to advise on the health issues his sisters brought to his attention becomes all the more conspicuous when contrasted with his readiness to dispense moral and social guidance to them. In February 1886 he wrote stuffily from Germany to a younger sister, María:

> The object of this letter is to relate to you some particular things that may be of interest to you and besides of use to you, like for example how German and French women keep their houses.[164]

Including sketches in his letter to make clear what he meant, Rizal took great pains to show his sisters how they might imitate the bourgeois interiors of European homes. Dining rooms in the best houses, he advised, were adorned with paintings depicting pleasant landscape scenes, still life of crustacea and fruit but "nothing serious or sad, for some people would get indigestion." It was no longer fashionable to place large dishes of fruit at the centre of dining tables, but was chic to provide guests with a scattering of several tiny dishes of sweets, pickles and fruits, interspersed with tasteful arrangements of fresh flowers. This practice, Rizal thought, could be easily copied in the Philippines. Antique plates with gay designs could be hung on walls as was done in Germany and Holland, or precious Chinese porcelain could be stylishly displayed, as it was in the Pardo de Tavera residence in Paris. Rizal then went on to give detailed instructions as to how these dinner plates should be hung, carefully specifying the required types of hooks and lengths of wire. To complement the plates, Rizal suggested, wine jugs could be suspended from the corners of the ceiling, "the more covered in cobwebs the better," in the then fashionable manner of a Mediterranean cafe.[165]

Rizal clearly wanted to transplant into the family house in Calamba the styles of interior décor then found in haute bourgeois homes in Europe, styles he thought would raise the Rizal residence a modern, modish cut above its neighbors. But one wonders how much his sisters appreciated his tips on interior design when what they really wanted in his letters was a response to their pleas for medical advice. Rizal's virtual silence on the medical issues concerning female physiology essentially barred his sisters from partaking in a dialogue with him on women's physical nature. This is a critical point because it highlights exactly where Rizal's thinking was focused. First, he wanted to affirm bourgeois material culture, embodied and displayed in the family home, as a triumph of civilization and modernity. Secondly, and crucially, Rizal aimed also to secure bourgeois *morality* in the domestic domain, a site where it could be reinforced as easily as it could be undone. It was not accidental that Rizal chose María as the recipient of his advice on setting dining tables and hanging plates. The sixth sister, the unmarried María's undomesticated spirit was well known to Rizal.[166] Brash and opinionated, a fearless rather than elegant horsewoman and unafraid of men, María seemed to Rizal to display unfeminine habits that required reform.

Between Rizal and his sisters lay an abiding and mutual affection, respect and concern, as their correspondence amply attests. But Rizal took his role as a brother to his sisters seriously and his high moral stance is evident in words and tone throughout his letters. Feminist historians have discerned an emancipating trajectory in Rizal's letters. They have especially highlighted Rizal's concern for the well being of his mother, for the education of his sisters, and for the good conduct of his nephews and nieces. Most scholars agree that Rizal's stress on the virtues of reason, a well-cultivated mind, good character and a moral upbringing, combine to present positive evidence of Rizal's desire to develop the potential of Filipino women as participatory citizens in the public sphere. In this respect, Rizal's early letters to his sisters foreshadow the thinking on the role of women in civil society he set out in his oft-cited "Letter to the young women of Malolos," which we shall discuss presently.[167]

Indeed, Rizal encouraged his sisters to write to him regularly; he relentlessly hectored the younger ones to read attentively and to apply themselves to their studies; to combat indolence and to cultivate knowledge as the principal adornment of women rather than the fripperies of clothing. He commended to them the example of German women, whom he lauded as diligent, simple and serious. To his younger sister

Trinidad, for example, he recalled how German women displayed none of the coquettish frivolities and sartorial fripperies of the Filipina:

> ... Their clothes do not have plenty of colour, and generally they have only three or four, they do not pay much attention to their clothes nor to jewels. They dress their hair simply, which is thin.... They go everywhere walking so nimbly or faster than men, carrying their books, their baskets, without minding anyone and only their own business ... they are home-loving and they study cooking with as much diligence as they do music and drawing.[168]

While Rizal evidently approved of a more subdued if not dour and plain show of femininity that was "more concerned with substance than with appearances," his prescriptions favored women's cultivation of the intellect firmly within the frame of submissive sexuality and soft, yielding femininity. On the other hand, that German women seemed unwomanly, "somewhat masculine" and "not afraid of men," was repugnant to Rizal. He unkindly teased his big-boned elder sister, María, by comparing her physically to the masculine-looking German women.[169] The ideal for Rizal lay in combining the Filipina characteristic of "tenderness" with the intellectual qualities of the European woman. "If these qualities [the virtue of industry and tenderness] that nature gives to women [in the Philippines], were exalted by intellectual qualities, as it happens in Europe, the Filipino family has nothing to envy the European."[170]

Rizal's emphasis on education and good character turned on a single fundamental diktat that feminist historians have neglected to scrutinize. What he demanded from his sisters most of all was the vigilant guard of their sexual honor. In a letter that we might see in parallel to his message to the women of Malolos, Rizal severely admonished his youngest sister, Soledad, for bringing dishonor upon the family. Soledad, he had learnt, had eloped with her secret lover, Pantaleon Quintero, and had married without the blessing of her parents. The wilful Soledad was only 19 years old when news of her shameful secret elopement reached Rizal. His aunt, Concha Leyba, wrote to him in April 1890 remarking on the troublesome behavior of Soledad that always seemed to concern her boyfriends, "*noviazgos.*"[171] By early June, both Trinidad and Narcisa had reported Soledad's illicit marriage to Rizal: "Soledad got married on 23rd April," commented Narcisa. "Nobody in our family went to her wedding, nor was anyone invited either."[172] Writing from Brussels, on

6 June 1890, Rizal coldly let Soledad know what he thought about her rebellious behavior. Soledad in his view had disgraced her family, brought unhappiness to her parents and, even more odiously, had set a bad example of sexual dishonor to the younger girls in the family.[173]

In his letter of rebuke to Soledad, he drew a contrast to his own behavior, which he felt had "dignified" the family, and her own, which had brought only the stain of dishonor. He felt his own moral authority was unquestionable: "I'm a man," he wrote, "and when I returned [to Calamba], I was much older, with more experience, more wisdom than you." Pre-empting any imputations that he too might have been guilty of sexual transgressions, he assured Soledad that his enemies could never "accuse me of anything that will make me blush and lower my head.... I can tell you that in my love affairs I have always presented myself with nobleness, because I myself would feel humiliated."[174]

The letter was addressed to Soledad but plainly Rizal intended its message also to reach his other sisters, Trinidad and Josefa, so they too could sit up and take notice of his moral prescriptions. These he elucidated in no uncertain terms:

> Always keep before your eyes the honour and good name of all. Don't do anything that you cannot say and repeat before every one with a raised head and satisfied heart. If you have a *novio* (sweetheart), do not attempt secret meetings and conversations that only serve to lower a woman's worth in the eyes of a man. Conduct yourselves nobly and with dignity. Men should be noble and worthy and behave like men not as thieves or adventurers who hide. A man afraid to come out in the open should be despised. You should value and esteem greatly your honor and you will be more greatly esteemed and valued.[175]

Rizal cited himself and his wilting, long-suffering fiancée Leonor Rivera as models of sexual self-abnegation. He enjoined his sisters to save themselves and the family from "*deshonor*" at all cost. The honor of oneself, one's family, and future generations lay in the upholding of female sexual honor:

> You are no longer a child, all of you are no longer children, nor are you uneducated. Thanks to our parents you are educated and informed. I speak to you as my sisters and I repeat: remember the old age of our parents, your honor and that of ours. You have many nieces; place yourselves as a good example and dignify yourselves.[176]

The mark of a civilized man, as Rizal was at pains to show, was careful self-discipline and sobriety that kept unruly drives and passions in check. Rizal wrote his letter to Soledad during his stay in Brussels. As we have recounted, it was a stay that involved liaisons with women whose frequency he carefully regulated for reasons of physical health. Care, thrift, discipline, moderation and discretion determined the acceptability of his actions. Imposing his exacting moral standards more absolutely upon Filipino women however, Rizal saw sexual honor as determining the worth of the Filipina and defining her civilization.

Just as he had done in his annotations to the Morga, Rizal in his message to the women of Malolos, defended the Filipina and her culture by emphasizing that a country's civilization was apparent by its respect for women. But in his letter to the Malolos women, the desire to defend the Filipina co-existed with his equally strong desire to rebuke her. It was the Filipina's purported moral weakness (*karupukan*) and foolishness (*kamangmangan*), he noted, that made herself, her husband and sons, her family and country perpetually vulnerable to attack. Filipino women, he emphasized, had to change. "If the Filipino woman will not change," wrote Rizal severely, "she should not be entrusted with raising her children, but only be used to conceive and give birth (*kundi gauing pasibulan lamang*); her rights and authority in the home should be removed because unwittingly she will betray her husband, children, country and all."[177]

Women should awake and open their eyes, because their tasks and obligations were of the utmost importance, Rizal exhorted. Motherhood and the education of their children were their special contributions to the future of the nation. It was their patriotic duty to:

> awaken and prepare the inner spirit (*loob*) of the child to every good and desirable idea; love for honor (*puri*), a true and steadfast character, clear thinking, clean conduct, noble actions, love for one's fellow man, respect for God — this is what children should be taught.... The country should not expect honor and prosperity whilst children are raised defectively, as long as women who raise children are degraded and foolish. Nothing can be drunk in a turbid and bitter spring; no sweet fruit can come from a sour seed.[178]

It was also the duty of a woman to instil courage in her chosen man, to demand of him a "noble and honorable name" and a manly heart (*pusung lalake*) that could protect her womanly weakness. She should cultivate in her man activity and industry, noble behavior and worthy sentiments. As a wife she should help and encourage her husband, "share in every hardship, drive away his woes, strengthen her husband's inner reserve, share with him all perils and bring joy when there is sorrow."[179]

In this vision of ideal, unselfish and unsexed womanhood there is no place for female sexual desire. Rizal's discourse instead reproduces and intensifies familiar stereotypes of female sexlessness and purity proliferating throughout the late nineteenth century. Rizal envisioned women as being both chaste and maternal, transcendent of sexuality thus requiring the Filipina to live an oxymoron. This model of civilized womanhood was perfectly in keeping with late nineteenth-century medical scientific thinking. On the one hand physicians had begun to accept the idea of women's capacity for sexual pleasure yet on the other, the notion of women's intrinsic purity and spiritual superiority could never be completely abandoned. Women, especially educated bourgeois women who suffered orgasm, it was reported, felt nothing. As society advanced, women's bodies correspondingly adapted to the demands of culture subordinating sexual feelings to the civilizing processes of mental power and moral discipline.[180] As Thomas Laqueur found in his study on sexual pleasure and its relationship to reproduction, civilization, in all its political, economic and religious manifestations, had branded its effects on female bodies. Civilization drew mankind away from "scenes and habits of disgusting obscenity among those barbarous people whose propensities are unrestrained by mental cultivation" to a state in which "bodily appetites or passions, subject to reason, assume a milder, less selfish, and more elevated character."[181]

If civilized women were purged of base, sensual appetites, what distinguished a civilized and advanced society was a refined sexual life in which relations between the sexes were monogamic and mutual and the exercise of sexual functions was governed by shame and modesty. A developed society, Krafft-Ebing had argued, treated women as individual beings and encouraged their intellectual and moral advancement. A woman's sublime virtues were perceived as her abilities to be a man's companion and comfort in life, a wife in charge of a settled home and a mother who guarantees that offspring progress physically, morally and intellectually. Such distinguishing features of civilized society became active elements in Rizal's own rhetoric on Filipino women and Philippine society in general. In the process, female sexuality became central to the ilustrado drive for social reform; became both battleground and casualty in the war between the propagandist, ilustrado claims to cultural civilization versus colonial discourse on the ungovernable Filipino libido. But while the ways in which female sexual desire was denounced, denied and fettered to maternity by Rizal rested ultimately on the rhetorical exigencies of the moment, the effect of silencing the female body, and the erasure of erotic pleasure has proved to be long lasting.

Notes

[1] Richard von Krafft-Ebing, *Psychopathia sexualis, with especial reference to the antipathic sexual instinct* [1886], trans. Franklin S. Klaf (New York: Arcade Publishing, 1998), p. 2. Upon its publication in Vienna, *Psychopathia sexualis* was instantly heralded as a landmark in the history of psychiatry and acknowledged as the first medical classification of sexual disorders. See Renate Hauser, "Krafft-Ebing's Psychological Understanding of Sexual Behaviour," in *Sexual Knowledge, Sexual Science: the history of attitudes to sexuality*, ed. Roy Porter and Mikulas Teich (Cambridge: Cambridge University Press, 1994), pp. 210–27.

[2] Krafft-Ebing, *Psychopathia sexualis*, p. 1.

[3] Iwan Bloch, *Beitrage zur Aetiologie der Psychopathia Sexualis* (Dresden: H.R. Dorn, 1902), vol. I, p. 2; f.p. 5.

[4] Dr. D. Pedro Felipe Monlau, *Higiene del Matrimonio, ó el libro de los casados en el cual se dan las reglas e instrucciones necesarias para conservar la salud de los esposos, asegurar la paz conyugal y educar bien a la familia*, Cuarto edicion (Paris: Librería de Garnier Hermanos, 1883), p. 157.

[5] Ferdinand Blumentritt, *An attempt at writing a Philippine ethnography [Versuch einer ethnographie der Philippinen]* [1882]. Translated from the original German text by Marcelino N. Maceda (Marawi City: University Research Center, Mindanao State University, 1980), p. 14. See also Filomeno V. Aguilar Jr, "Civilisation and Migration: 'Igorrotes' and 'Negritos' in the ilustrado national imagination." Paper read at the Fourth European Philippine Studies Conference, Alcala, Spain, September 2001; and Reynaldo Ileto, "Rizal and the Underside of Philippine History" [1982], in *Filipinos and their Revolution: event, discourse, and historiography* (Quezon City: Ateneo de Manila University Press, 1998), pp. 29–78.

[6] H. Ploss, *Das Weib in der Natur-und Volkerkunde: Anthropologische Studien* (Leipzig: Th. Grieben, 1884). Undergoing numerous re-publications, the work was continued and revised after the author's death by his collaborators Max Bartels and Paul Bartels. In its final incarnation, published in 1935, Ploss's work expanded into three volumes which with the aid of numerous intimate illustrations "dealt fully," its editor boasted, "with those aspects of a woman's life which are little known even

to gynaecologists." Herman Heinrich Ploss, Max Bartels and Paul Bartels, *Woman: an historical, gynaecological and anthropological compendium*, trans. and ed. Eric John Dingwall (London: William Heinemann Medical Books Ltd, 1935).

7   Besides relying extensively on Blumentritt's *Versuch einer Ethnographie*, Ploss also consulted the same author's "Der Ahnenkultus in. die religiosen Anschauungen der Malayen des Philippinen-Archipel," *Mittheilungen. d.k.k. Geographie Gesellschaft in Wien*, 2–3 (1882): 177ff.

8   A. Schadenberg, "Ueber die Negritos der Philippinen," *Zeitschrift fur Ethnologie* (1880): 133ff.

9   F. Jagor, *Reisen in den Philippinen* (Berlin, 1873); Idem., "Sexuelle abnormitäten bei den Bisayern, Philippinen," *Verhandlungen der Berliner Gesellschaft für Anthropologie, Ethnologie und Urgeschichte* 12 (1880): 90–1.

10 Blumentritt, *Versuch*, p. 57.

11 Ibid., p. 75.

12 Blumentritt, *An Attempt at Writing a Philippine Ethnography*, pp. 34–5.

13 Francisco Cáñamaque, *Recuerdos de Filipinas: cosas, casos y usos de aquellas islas*, 2 vols. (Madrid: Librería de Anllo y Rodriguez: 1877; Librería de Simon y Osler, 1879).

14 Ibid., p. 46. This passage is closely paraphrased by Ploss in *Das Weib*, vol. 1, p. 223.

15 Ferdinand Blumentritt, "La moralidad del indio salvaje," *La Solidaridad* 2: 46 (31 December 1890): 598–604.

16 A.B. Meyer, "Ueber die Perforation des Penis bei den Malayen," *Mittheilungen anthropologischen gesselchaft in Wien* 7: 9 (1877): 242–4. Blumentritt also contributed to this respected journal.

17 Ferdinand Blumentritt, "Lo que escribieron los extranjeros sobre Filipinas: apuntes bibliográficos," *La Solidaridad* 5: 107 (15 July 1893): 328–34.

18 For an idea of the collection Rizal viewed, see A.B. Meyer, *Bilderschriften der ostindischen Archipels und die Südsee* (Leipzig: Verlag von A. Nauman und Schroeder, 1881), esp. p. 2, "Die Palau, Tafel 2."

19 José Rizal, Diary entry for 31 October 1886 (Dresden), in *Reminiscences and Travels of José Rizal* (Manila: National Historical Institute, 1977), p. 123.

20 José Rizal (Berlin) to Ferdinand Blumentritt, 13 April 1887 in *Rizal-Blumentritt Correspondence*, p. 71.

21 José Rizal (London) to Ferdinand Blumentritt, 12 October 1888, *Rizal-Blumentritt Correspondence*, vol. I, p. 203.

22 Wenceslao Retana (Desengaños), *Apuntes para la historia (aniterías y solidaridades)* Folletos Filipinos II (Madrid: Manuel Minuesa de los Rios, 1890), p. 35.

23 Ferdinand Blumentritt (Leitmeritz) to José Rizal, 14 November 1886, in *Rizal-Blumentritt Correspondence*, p. 19; José Rizal (Berlin) to Ferdinand Blumentritt, 22 November 1886; and 28 November 1886 in ibid., pp. 21, 24.

24 José Rizal (Berlin) to Ferdinand Blumentritt, 13 April 1887, ibid., p. 73.

25 See for example John N. Schumacher, S.J., "The Propagandists' Reconstruction of the Philippine Past," in *The Making of a Nation: essays on nineteenth century Filipino*

nationalism (Manila: Ateneo de Manila University Press, 1996), pp. 102–18; and Ambeth Ocampo, "Rotten Beef and Stinking Fish: Rizal and the writing of Philippine history" [First delivered at the International Rizal Conference, Kuala Lumpur, Malaysia, October 1995], in *Meaning and History: the Rizal lectures* (Pasig City: Anvil, 2001), pp. 75–155.

26   José Rizal (Berlin) to Ferdinand Blumentritt, 28 November 1886, ibid., p. 25.
27   Theodor Waitz, Georg Gerland, *Anthropologie der Naturvölker*, 6 vols. (Leipzig: F. Fleischer, 1859–72). Rizal announced his intention to translate the fifth volume, which deals with the Malay peoples.
28   José Rizal (Berlin) to Ferdinand Blumentritt, 28 November 1886, in *Rizal-Blumentritt Correspondence*, p. 25.
29   In chronological sequence, these works were *Filipinas* (Manila: J.A. Ramos, 1887); *Expedición de Li-mahong contra Filipinas en 1574* (Manila: n.pub, 1888); *Triunfos del rosario, o los Holandeses en Filipinas* (Manila: n.p., 1888); *Artículos varios sobre etnografía, historia y costumbres de Filipinas* (Manila: n.p., 1888); *Historia de Filipinas* (Manila: Imp. de D.E. Balbas, 1889); *Las islas Visayas en la época de la conquista* (Manila: Tipo-litografía de Chofre y Cia., 1889); *Historia de Ilocos* (Manila: Establecimiento tipográfico La Opinion, 1890); and *El Folklore Filipino* (Manila: Imprenta Santa Cruz, 1890).
30   Ferdinand Blumentritt (Leitmeritz) to José Rizal, 14 November 1886, in *Rizal-Blumentritt Correspondence*, p. 20.
31   T.H. Pardo de Tavera, *Biblioteca Filipina* (Washington: Government Printing Office, 1903), nos. 2370–78. For a detailed summation and analysis of Isabelo de los Reyes' scholarly contributions to Philippine ethnography and history see William Henry Scott, "Isabelo de los Reyes: father of Philippine folklore," in *Cracks in the Parchment Curtain and Other Essays in Philippine History* (Manila: New Day Publishers, 1996), pp. 245–65; and Benedict Anderson, "The Rooster's Egg: pioneering world folklore in the Philippines," *New Left Review* 2 (March–April 2000): 47–62.
32   Wenceslao Retana, (Desengaños), *Sinapismos, (bromitas y critiquillas)*, Folletos Filipinos III, (Madrid: Librería de Fernando Fe; Manila: Librería Amigos del Pais, 1890), p. 30.
33   Isabelo de los Reyes, *El Folklore Filipino* [1890], published with an English translation by Salud C. Dizon and María Elinora P. Imson (Quezon City: University of the Philippines Press, 1994), pp. 20–1.
34   William Henry Scott, "Isabelo de los Reyes: provinciano and nationalist," in *Cracks in the Parchment Curtain*, esp. pp. 273–6.
35   Rizal was decidedly economical in his acknowledgement of Isabelo de los Reyes' work, and particularly snooty about his special focus on the Ilocos region from which he hailed. "I see that many folklorists and future anthropologists are appearing in Ilocos," he cautioned Blumentritt. "In view of the fact that the majority of Filipino folklorists are Ilocanos and they use the epithet Ilocano, anthropologists will classify authentic Filipino customs and usages as Ilocano. I have Isabelo's works.... He has committed some errors because he does not speak Tagalog well." José

Rizal (San Francisco) to Ferdinand Blumentritt, 30 April 1888, in *Rizal-Blumentritt Correspondence*, vol. 1, p. 167.

36 José Rizal (London) to Ferdinand Blumentritt, 26 August 1888, *Rizal-Blumentritt Correspondence*, vol. 1, p. 196.

37 *Dickens's Dictionary of London, 1888, An Unconventional handbook* [1888] (Old House Books Facsimile edition, 1993), p. 130; Hotel advertisements in Post Office London Conveyance Directory for 1887, *Trades and Professional directory*, 1887, p. 86.

38 British Museum signature of readers, 4 June 1887–11 October 1888, unpublished volume, British Museum Reading Room archive.

39 See *La Solidaridad*, vol. 2, 30 April 1890, p. 195.

40 Antonio de Morga, *Sucesos de las islas Philipinas* (Mexico: n.pub., 1609).

41 José Rizal (London) to Ferdinand Blumentritt, 17 September 1888, *Rizal-Blumentritt Correspondence*, p. 201. Antonio de Morga obtained his doctorate in canon law from the University of Salamanca in 1578. He was appointed to Manila as lieutenant governor in 1593 and five years later became a judge in the Supreme Court of the colony, the *Audiencia*.

42 J. S. Cummins, "Editor's Introduction," in Antonio de Morga, *Sucesos de las islas Filipinas*, trans. and ed. J.S. Cummins (Cambridge: Cambridge University Press, 1972), p. 4.

43 Antonio de Morga, *Sucesos de las islas Filipinas. Obra publicada en Méjico el año de 1609, nuevamente sacada a luz y anotada por José Rizal, y precedida de un prólogo del Prof. Fernando Blumentritt* (Paris: Librería de Garnier Hermanos, 1890).

44 Resil Mojares, "Rizal Reading Pigafetta," in *Waiting for Maríang Makiling: essays in Philippine cultural history* (Quezon City: Ateneo de Manila University Press, 2002), pp. 61–2.

45 Ferdinand Blumentritt, "Prólogo," in Morga, *Sucesos* (1890), p. xii.

46 De los Reyes, *Historia de Ilocos*, p. 103. For Rizal's irritated, angry response to this criticism, see José Rizal, "Una contestación a Don Isabelo de los Reyes," *La Solidaridad* 2: 42 (31 October 1890): 504–7. Juan Luna, a friend of both men, tried without success to end their discord; see Juan Luna (Paris) to José Rizal, 8 November 1890, in *Cartas entre Rizal y sus colegas de la propaganda*, Tomo II, Segunda Parte (Manila: Comisión Nacional del Centenario de José Rizal, 1961), p. 587.

47 Rizal, "Una contestación," p. 507.

48 Miguel de Loarca, *Relación*, in *The Philippine Islands, 1493–1898*, ed. Emma H. Blair and James A. Robertson, vol. 5 (Cleveland, Ohio: A. H. Clark, 1909), p. 1618.

49 Ibid., p. 246.

50 On the distortions of the early missionary reports see William Henry Scott, *Barangay: sixteenth century Philippine culture and society* (Quezon City: Ateneo de Manila University Press, 1995), p. 3.

51 Rizal in Morga, *Sucesos* (1890), p. 262.

52 Ibid., p. 288.

53 Ibid., pp. 301–2.
54 Rizal in Morga, *Sucesos* (1890), p. 53.
55 For an insightful discussion of the Filipino female shaman see Alfred McCoy, "*Baylan:* animist religion and Philippine peasant ideology,"*Philippine Quarterly of Culture and Society* 10: 3(1982): 141–94.
56 See for example the description given by Raul Pertierra, "Viscera-suckers and Female Sociality: the Philippine asuang," *Philippine Studies* 31(1983): 319–37.
57 Rizal in Morga, *Sucesos* (1890), p. 261.
58 Isabelo de los Reyes, "La Filipina en los primitivos tiempos, " in *El Folklore Filipino* [1889], pp. 286–96.
59 De los Reyes, *Historia de Ilocos*, vol. 1, p. 128. For an overview of how these acts were an accepted part of family and social life in the culture of the early Filipinos see Rámon Pedrosa, "Abortion and infanticide in the Philippines during the Spanish contact," *Philippiniana Sacra* 18(1983): 7–37.
60 Isabelo de los Reyes y Florentino, *Las islas Visayas en la época de la conquista* (Manila: Tipo-litografía de Chofre y Cia., 1889), p. 33.
61 Morga, *Sucesos* (1890), p. 263.
62 Ibid., p. 309.
63 José Rizal (London) to Ferdinand Blumentritt, 8 November 1888, in *Rizal-Blumentritt Correspondence*, vol. 1, p. 210.
64 Ibid.
65 Ibid., p. 289.
66 Ibid., p. 308.
67 Rizal in Morga, *Sucesos* (1890), p. 307.
68 Ibid., p. 308.
69 Henry Kamen, *Spain's Road to Empire: the making of a world power, 1492–1763* (London: Allen Lane, Penguin Press, 2002), p. 208. Wenceslao Retana's annotations to the Morga also provide details of the Spanish laws enacted to prohibit sodomy in the colonies. See Antonio de Morga, *Sucesos de las islas Filipinas por el Dr. Antonio de Morga, nueva edición enriquecida con los escritos ineditos del mismo autor ilustrada con numerosas notas que amplien el texto y prologada extensamente por W.E. Retana* (Madrid: Librería General de Victoriana Súarez, 1909), p. 475.
70 Rizal in Morga, *Sucesos* (1890), pp. 308–9.
71 Morga, *Sucesos de las islas Philipinas* (1609), p. 145.
72 Loarca, *Relación*, p. 116.
73 Thomas Cavendish in Francis Pretty, "The admirable and prosperous voyage of the worshipfull Master Thomas Candish [Cavendish]," in *Hakluyt Voyages* (London: Everyman's Library, 1907), vol. 8, p. 242.
74 Francesco Carletti, *Rogionamenti di Francesco Carletti* (Firenzi, 1701), p. 178, cited in Fedor Jagor, "Sexuelle abnormitäten bei den Bisayern, Philippinen," *Verhandlungen der Berliner Gesellschaft fur Anthropologie, Ethnologie und Urgeschichte* 12(1880): 90.
75 The "Boxer Codex," trans. Carlos Quirino and Mauro Garcia, *Philippine Journal of Science* 87: 4(December 1958): 42.

[76] Antonio Pigafetta, *Magellan's Voyage around the World*, the original text of the Ambrosian MS, with English trans. notes, bibliography and index by James Alexander Robertson and Emma H. Blair (Cleveland: The Arthur H. Clark Company, 1906), vol. 2, p. 169.

[77] Ibid., vol. 1, p. 167.

[78] Ibid.

[79] Anthony Reid, *Southeast Asia in the Age of Commerce, 1450–1680*, vol. 1, *The lands below the winds* (New Haven: Yale University Press, 1988), pp. 148–50; Tom Harrisson, "The 'Palang': Its history and proto-history in West Borneo and the Philippines," *Journal of the Malaysian Branch of the Royal Asiatic Society* 37: 2(1964): 162–74; and Donald Brown, James W. Edwards and Ruth Moore, *The Penis Inserts of Southeast Asia: an annotated bibliography with an overview and comparative perspectives* (Berkeley: Center for South and Southeast Asian Studies, University of California Berkeley, 1988). In a later paper, Donald Brown revises his opinion with regard to Borneo, where he is less certain what the "penis pin is all about." Donald Brown, "The Penis Pin: an unsolved problem in the relations between the sexes in Borneo," in *Female and Male in Borneo: contributions and challenges to gender studies*, ed. Vinson H. Sutlive, Jnr. (Borneo Research Council Monograph Series, Ashley Press, n.d.), pp. 435–54.

[80] Morga, *Sucesos* (1890), pp. 308–9.

[81] Aguilar, "Civilization and Migration," p. 42.

[82] Rizal in Morga, *Sucesos* (1890), p. 263.

[83] Ibid., p. 263.

[84] Ibid., pp. 309–10.

[85] Resil Mojares, "Catechisms of the Body," in *Waiting for Maríang Makiling*, p. 177.

[86] Vicente Rafael, *Contracting Colonialism: translation and Christian conversion in Tagalog society under early Spanish rule* (Durham: Duke University Press, 1993), especially pp. 23–54.

[87] Francisco de San Antonio, O.F.M., *Vocabulario Tagalo* [1624], ed. Antoon Postma (Quezon City: Ateneo de Manila University Press, 2000), pp. 211, 149, 118 and 268 respectively.

[88] Juan de Noceda y el P. Pedro de Sanlucar, *Vocabulario de la lengua Tagala compuesto por varios religiosos, doctos y graves* [1754] (Manila: Impr. de Ramirez y Giraudier, 1860), pp. 179 and 338 respectively.

[89] For words relating to the male genitalia, as a whole and its parts, flaccid and erect, see for example ibid., pp. 14,16, 68, 267.

[90] Ibid., pp. 16, 45.

[91] Ibid., p. 406

[92] Ibid., pp. 406, 317.

[93] Rosalio Serrano, *Nuevo diccionario manual Español — Tagalo para el uso de las escuelas de primera instrucción* (Manila: Establecimiento tipográfico "Ciudad Condal" de Plana y ca., 1872). By profession Serrano was a government surveyor in his home province of Bulacan; his lexicography seems to have been a self-taught

94 Serrano, *Nuevo diccionario*, p. 113.
95 Ibid., p. 108.
96 This moralising tone was also evident in Tagalog phrasebooks. The Castilian phrase for an illegitimate child, for example, was rendered in Tagalog by one compiler as "a child of the soil." V.M. De Abella, *Vade-mecum Filipino, o manual de la conversación familiar español-tagalog seguido de un curioso vocabulario de modismos manilenos* (Manila: C. Miralles, 1874), p. 21.
97 Pedro Serrano Laktaw, *Diccionario hispano-tagalog* (Manila: Estab. Tip "La Opinion" a cargo de G. Bautista, 1889). The second part, *Diccionario tagalog-hispano*, was published in Manila by Santos y Bernal in 1914, and a facsimile edition of the complete work was published in 1965 — Pedro Serrano Laktaw, *Diccionario hispano-tagalog* (Madrid: Ediciónes Cultura Hispanica, 1965).
98 See for example the review by Hendrik Kern, "Review of Diccionario Hispano-Tagalog," *La Solidaridad* 3: 68(30 November 1891): 585–7. Marcelo H. del Pilar complimented Serrano on producing a work that would be most welcome "*a este mundo de las penalidades estomacales y monacales.*" Marcelo H. del Pilar (Barcelona) to P. Ikazama [Pedro Icasiano], 30 May 1889, in *Epistolario de Marcelo H. del Pilar*, Tomo I (Manila: Imprenta del Gobierno, 1955), p. 158.
99 E. Arsenio Manuel, *Dictionary of Philippine Biography*, vol. 2 (Quezon City: Filipiniana Publications, 1970), p. 361. Indicative of propagandist support for his work, *La Solidaridad* closely followed and reported on the activities of Serrano Laktaw. See "News in Brief" items in *La Solidaridad* 2: 37(15 August 1890): 381; and 2: 65(15 October 1891): 513.
100 For details of the orthographic revision see José Rizal, "On the New Orthography of the Tagalog Language," *La Solidaridad* 2:29(15 April 1890): 181.
101 Serrano Laktaw, *Diccionario* (1965), pp. 118 and 1304 respectively.
102 Ibid., p. 155.
103 Serrano Laktaw originally conceived his work in two parts and had intended to publish the Tagalog-Spanish volume at the same time as the Spanish-Tagalog. He later recounted that he had started work on the Tagalog-Spanish volume in the 1880s, but for some unknown reason it was a generation in gestation and did not ultimately appear until 1914.
104 Serrano Laktaw, *Diccionario* (1965), p. 402.
105 Ramiro Franco (Filipino) [Dominador Gómez], "Women's Virtue: to mothers and daughters," *La Solidaridad* 3: 55(15 May 1891): 227–31; and 3: 56(31 May 1891): 261–7.
106 Ibid., p. 227.
107 Ibid., p. 261.
108 Ibid., p. 265.
109 Ibid., p. 231.
110 Ibid., p. 263.
111 Ibid., p. 265.

Note: Footnote 94 is preceded by the line "enthusiasm. See E. Arsenio Manuel, *Dictionary of Philippine Biography*, vol. 1 (Quezon City: Filipiniana Publications, 1955), pp. 403–4."

112. Ibid.
113. Amancio Peratoner, *Fisiología de la noche de bodas: misterios del lecho conyugal*. Seguido de un estudio del Dr. A. Tardieu (Barcelona: Establecimiento tipográfico-editorial de José Miret, 1875). The title page of this work promises the reader information on "copula – virginidad – desfloración – anafrodisia – impotencia – esterilidad – adulterio" based on the opinions "de los eminentes moralistas, filosofos, fisiólogos y medico – legistas: Balzac, Bayle, Buffon, Clement, Debay, Fodere, Janet de Ligne, Mahon, Mayer, Michelet, Mentaigne, Orfila, Petigars, Plutarco, Velpeau, Virey, Zacchias, etc.etc. redactado en vista de sus obras, y de varios preciosos manuscritos de las Bibliotecas Nacional y de las Escuela de Medicina de Paris."
114. Ibid., p. 2.
115. Ibid., pp. 24–6.
116. Ibid., pp. 13–4, 19.
117. Monlau, *Higiene del Matrimonio*, p. 140.
118. Elizabeth A. Sheehan, "Victorian Clitoridectomy: Isaac Baker Brown and his harmless operative procedure," in *The Gender/Sexuality Reader: culture, history, political economy*, ed. Roger N. Lancaster and Micaela di Leonardo (London: Routledge, 1997), pp. 325–35.
119. Amancio Peratoner, *El mal de venus estudio medico-popular sobre las enfermedades venereas y sifilíticas tomado de las obras de los eminentes sifiliógrafos Belhomme, Cullerier, Diday, Lancereaux, Martin, Mireur, Ricord, etc., etc.* (Madrid: Simon y Osler, 1881).
120. Monlau, *Higiene del matrimonio*, pp. 169–70.
121. Peratoner, *El mal de venus*, p. 28.
122. Ibid., f.p. 206.
123. Peratoner, *Fisilogia de la noche de bodas*, p. 27.
124. José Alejandrino, *The Price of Freedom: episodes and anecdotes of our struggles for freedom*, trans. José M. Alejandrino (Manila: M. Colcol, 1949), p. 6.
125. Case listed as "Bed No. 4 – Men – First Observation: Spermatorrhea tabes mesenterica," in *Clínica Medica*, in *Miscellaneous Writings of Dr José Rizal* (Manila: National Heroes Commission, 1964), p. 78.
126. A basic diagnosis echoed by medical practitioners in England; see for example Roberts Bartholow, *Spermatorrhea: its causes, symptoms, results and treatment* (New York: William Wood, Co, 1879), pp. 2–14. For a perspicacious overview of the subject, see Thomas Laqueur, *Solitary Sex: the cultural history of masturbation* (New York: Zone Books, 2003).
127. Rizal, *Clínica Medica*, p. 202.
128. Ibid., p. 203.
129. Ibid.
130. Case listed as "Bed No. 21 – Men 28 – Phimosis (congenital)," in ibid., p. 202.
131. T.H. Pardo de Tavera, *Arte de cuidar enfermos* (Manila: Tipografia de Chofre y Comp., 1895), p. 5. The work was translated from Spanish to Tagalog by Inigo Regalado y Corcuera and published as *Paraan sa pag-aalaga sa maysaquit* (Manila: Imprenta de J. Atayde, 1895).

132 Rizal's only medical article was a brief unpublished essay on the treatment of mental illness thought to be caused by supernatural possession. Written in 1895, whilst he was exiled in Dapitan, the article was entitled "La curación de los hechizados. Apuntes hechos para el estudio de la medicina Filipina." See Luciano P.R. Santiago, "Centennial: the first psychiatric article in the Philippines (1895)," *Philippine Quarterly of Culture and Society* 23(1995): 62–75.

133 José Rizal (Berlin) to Ferdinand Blumentritt, 9 December 1886, in *Rizal-Blumentritt Correspondence*, vol. 1, p. 30; José Rizal (Berlin) to Ferdinand Blumentritt, 30 December 1886, in ibid., p. 33. In the nineteenth century arsenic was recommended by physicians for everything from malarial fever to skin diseases, uterine disorders, diabetes and bronchitis. Applied externally it was used to remove warts and "cancers;" drank as a general tonic it was reputedly beneficial to the complexion and was a favorite cosmetic with prostitutes, taken to restore a rosy color to wan, pale cheeks. See J.S. Haller, "Therapeutic Mule: the use of arsenic in the nineteenth century *Materia Medica*," *Pharmacy in History* 17(1975): 87–100; *Merck's 1899 Manual of the Materia Medica*, Facsimile edition (New York: Merck and Co., 1999).

134 José Rizal (Berlin) to Ferdinand Blumentritt, 30 December 1886, in *Rizal-Blumentritt Correspondence*, vol. 1, p. 34; José Rizal (Berlin) to Ferdinand Blumentritt, 26 January 1887, in ibid., p. 43.

135 José Rizal (Dapitan) to Manuel Hidalgo, 1 August 1893, in *Cartas entre Rizal y los miembros de la familia*, Tomo II, Segunda Parte (Manila: Cómision Nacional del Centenario de José Rizal, 1961), p. 434.

136 José Rizal (Dapitan) to Saturnina Hidalgo, 25 October 1893, in ibid., p. 439.

137 José Rizal (Dapitan) to Manuel T. Hidalgo, 13 March 1894, in ibid., p. 453.

138 Born in Madrid 1832, Busto was head of the obstetrics clinic at San Carlos when Rizal enrolled. See José M. López Pinero, Thomas F. Glick, Victor Navarro Brotons and Eugenio Portela Marco, eds., *Diccionario historico de la ciencia moderna en España*, vol. 1 (Barcelona: Nova-Grafik, 1983), p. 141; Andrés del Busto, *Título memorial razonado para la reforma de la enseñanza clínica de la especialidad de ginecología y paidología* (Madrid: Imprenta de Enrique Rubiños, 1881).

139 José Rizal (Madrid) to his family, 10 October 1882, in *Cartas entre Rizal y los miembros de la familia 1876–87*, Primera Parte (Manila: Cómision Nacional del Centenario de José Rizal, 1961), p. 54.

140 José Rizal (Paris) to his family, 21 June 1883, in ibid., p. 117.

141 Ibid., p. 118.

142 José Rizal (Madrid) to Saturnina Hidalgo, 29 January 1883, in ibid., p. 91.

143 Saturnina Hidalgo (Calamba) to José Rizal, 16 July 1885, in ibid., p. 187.

144 Ibid.; Manuel T. Hidalgo (Calamba) to José Rizal, 24 September 1882, in ibid., p. 42.

145 Lucia Herbosa (Calamba) to José Rizal, 2 February 1886, in ibid., p. 216.

146 Teodora Alonso (Calamba) to José Rizal, 27 November 1883, in ibid., p. 147. For a clear assessment of the nineteenth-century Philippine experience of cholera and beri-beri, see Ken de Bevoise, *Agents of Apocalypse: epidemic disease in the colonial Philippines* (Princeton: Princeton University Press, 1995), esp. pp. 165–84.

147 Lucia Herbosa (Calamba) to Rizal, 29 August 1886, in *Cartas entre Rizal y los miembros de la familia*, vol. 1, p. 253. The Tagalog phrase Lucia uses to describe Narcisa's loss is *"nacunan"* or literally "taken away."

148 Antonino López to Rizal, 14 May 1890, in *Letters between Rizal and family members 1876–1896* (Manila: National Historical Institute, 1993), p. 347.

149 José Rizal (Calamba) to Ferdinand Blumentritt, 26 September 1887, in *The Rizal-Blumentritt Correspondence*, vol. 1, p. 137. In his letter Rizal does not confirm whether he was his sister's attending physician nor does he disclose the complications that arose. Filipino physician and medical historian José Bantug acknowledges a personal communication from Rizal's nephew, Dr Leoncio López-Rizal who assumes Rizal's presence at the delivery and speculates that placenta praevia was the cause of Olimpia's death. Placenta praevia is a condition where the placenta becomes implanted at the bottom of the uterus and above the cervix or near it thus preventing a normal vaginal delivery. See José Bantug, "Rizal the Physician," *The Journal of History* 5: 1–2(1957): 42.

150 Concha Leyba (Manila) to Rizal, 23 September1887, in *Cartas entre Rizal y los miembros de la familia*, vol. 1, p. 285.

151 Saturnina Hidalgo (Manila) to José Rizal, 2 June 1890, in ibid., vol. 2, p. 340.

152 Lucia Herbosa (Calamba) to José Rizal, 27 March 1887, in ibid., vol. 1, p. 278.

153 Paciano Rizal (Calamba) to José Rizal, 27 May 1890, in ibid., p. 331. Paciano recognized the commercial potential of developing the natural mineral springs at Calamba and Los Banos, and urged Rizal to study this area of medicine.

154 Saturnina Hidalgo (Manila) to José Rizal, 2 June 1890, in ibid., p. 340.

155 Saturnina Hidalgo (Manila) to José Rizal, 6 September 1890, in ibid., p. 353.

156 The anaesthesia debate in relation to parturition is explored in Mary Poovey, "Scenes of an indelicate character: the medical 'treatment' of Victorian women," in *The Making of the Modern Body: sexuality and society in the nineteenth century*, ed. Catherine Gallagher, Thomas Laqueur, (Berkeley: University of California Press), pp. 137–68.

157 James Woycke, *Birth Control in Germany, 1871–1933* (London: Routledge, 1988), pp. 13–4.

158 Ibid., pp. 38–9.

159 Ibid., pp. 41–3.

160 Pride of place in hydriatic establishments was accorded the high-pressure shower, widely used in women's disorders as a local stimulant to the pelvic region. After a high-pressure cold water douche, the French physician Henri Scoutetten noted in 1843, the patient "dries herself off, refastens her corset and returns with a brisk step to her room." Rachel P. Maines, *The Technology of Orgasm: "hysteria," the vibrator, and women's sexual satisfaction* (Baltimore: Johns Hopkins University Press, 1998), p. 42.

161 Ibid., pp. 2–3.

162 Woycke, *Birth Control in Germany*, p. 41.

163 Rizal, listed in Clínica Medica as "Bed No. 6 – Women – (May 22) Double cyst of the ovary and uterus," in *Miscellaneous writings of Dr José Rizal*, p. 245.

[164] José Rizal (Heidelberg) to María Rizal, 7 February 1886, in *Cartas entre Rizal y los miembros de la familia*, vol. 1, pp. 218–9.
[165] Ibid.
[166] Asunción López Bantug, *Lolo José: an intimate portrait of Rizal* (Manila: Intramuros Administration, Ministry of Human Settlements, 1982), p. 197.
[167] Patricia B. Arinto, "Reading correspondences: a critical analysis of the letters between Rizal and his sisters," in Thelma B. Kintanar, ed., *Review of Women's Studies*, 5: 2 and 6: 1(1996). The writings on Rizal and women's citizenship in the national polity is voluminous. See for example: Encarnación Alzona, *Rizal's Legacy to the Filipino Woman* (Pasay City: Taft Publishing, 1953), pp. 1–20; Severina Luna-Orosa, ed., *Rizal and the Filipino Woman: Rizal's Liga Filipina* (Quezon City: Vibal Print, 1963).
[168] José Rizal (Germany) to Trinidad Rizal, 11 March 1886, in *Letters between Rizal and Family Members 1876–1896*, p. 223.
[169] Ibid.
[170] Ibid., pp. 223–4.
[171] Concha Leyba to José Rizal, 20 April 1890, Manila, in ibid., p. 325.
[172] Trinidad to Rizal, 30 May 1890, Calamba, in ibid., p. 338; Narcisa to Rizal, 2 June 1890, Manila, in ibid., p. 342.
[173] Manuel Hidalgo (Manila) to José Rizal, 31 December 1889, in ibid., p. 316. José Rizal (Brussels) to Soledad Quintero, 6 June 1890, in ibid., p. 344.
[174] Ibid., p. 345.
[175] Ibid.
[176] Ibid., p. 346.
[177] Ibid., p. 311.
[178] Ibid., p. 307.
[179] Ibid., p. 309.
[180] Thomas Laqueur, *Making Sex: body and gender from the Greeks to Freud* (Cambridge, Mass. and London: Harvard University Press, 1990), p. 189.
[181] Ibid.

Conclusion

Loving the Nation

Filósofo Tasio, the learned old man who represents the voice of reason and wisdom in Rizal's *Noli*, knows very well the failings of his own people. "Our young men," he laments, "think of nothing but loves and pleasures. They spend more time and effort in seducing and dishonoring a young woman than thinking of the good of their country. Our men are energetic only in vices and heroic only in shame." And women, he observes sadly, neglect their own households in order to attend assiduously to their Catholic devotions. Such behavior, he feels, demonstrates the culpable complicity of Filipinos in their own oppression.[1] When young men have only selfish, carnal and dishonorable desires in their hearts and lack the anchor and vision of ideals; when women, blinded by religious superstition, fail to care for their families; when the old are dissolute and serve only as models of corruption, only the darkness of servitude, cowardice and ignorance can be expected to prevail in the Philippines. "I am glad to die," concludes the disheartened Tasio, "lower the curtain."[2]

The debasement of the Filipino people that so dismayed Filósofo Tasio was the propagandistas' overriding concern; the transformation of Filipino bodies, sexualities and characters, this study has sought to show, was their overriding priority. All other reforms, they would have agreed with Tasio, were contingent on a collective moral regeneration. This entailed both a reaffirmation of the basic decencies that Spanish rule had destroyed and the acquisition of a new, more modern system of values in which the elemental forces of love and passion were harnessed to the higher moral virtues of selflessness and patriotism. Without this regeneration, they were convinced, the future could only hold either continued enslavement or anarchy.

As we saw, the ilustrados had been weaned since their childhoods in the 1860s and 1870s on the precepts of urbanidad and a bourgeois regime of polite etiquette, self-control and moderation. They understood and valued a system of personal discipline. Belonging to the most Hispanized strata of society, moreover, they deeply respected the Castilian codes of gentlemanly honor. These codes, they idealistically thought, should determine the actions and behavior of all honorable men. The young ilustrados strove to construct their social relations on the basis of urbanidad and honor. They also embodied these rules and codes in their social and sexual practices at a more unconscious level.[3] From the popular *manuales de urbanidad*, they had imbibed the idea that a man or woman's identity was rooted in the biological sex of his or her body.

Yet the everyday realities of colonial life constantly offended the ilustrados' sense of male honor and selfhood. They bitterly observed how the Hispanic codes they revered, whose virtues they prized as indistinguishable from manliness, were violated and betrayed by the insults, injustices and humiliations heaped upon themselves, their families, friends and neighbors by Spaniards who professed to be men of honor. Wealth and a privileged upbringing had nourished ilustrado idealism and pride, and the currents of liberalism had encouraged them to challenge racial prejudice and discrimination. It was only when the propaganda movement gathered momentum in Europe in the 1880s, however, that the indignation occasioned by Spanish affronts was channeled into the patriotic cause and the affirmation of Filipino honor and bourgeois worth was transformed into a patriotic duty. Spanish apologists for colonial rule used the columns of the Madrid newspapers to excoriate the sexual mores of Filipinos, to make invidious comparisons between Spanish and Filipino bodies, and to deny the manliness of Filipino men. In countering these insults, the propagandistas sought to subvert a colonial discourse that equated Spaniards with civilization, morality, health and cleanliness and Filipinos with animality, depravity, degeneration and filth. In this process, physical exercise, personal comportment, sartorial style and gentlemanly etiquette came to be translated into a language of patriotic desire whose rhetoric stipulated that the country's material and spiritual progress had to begin with industrious efforts at self-improvement.

Regimes of exercise, for the propagandistas, promoted more than physical fitness and health. Regenerating the enervated Filipino body was only part of the goal: the skilful and disciplined handling of weapons, especially pistols and the foil, proclaimed the virtues of mental and moral courage, and refuted colonial accusations of Filipino puerility, cowardice and dissipation. The gentlemanly courtesies, grace and sportsmanship inherent in fencing were valued as a means of building good character, discipline and gallantry. The physical disciplines and exertions of fencing promoted fitness, poise and courage, trained the expatriates in the gentlemanly art of revenge and prepared them psychologically to fight for the *patria*.

At a quotidian level, male sexuality was asserted through the adoption of stylish clothing and fastidious personal grooming. With the singular exception of Graciano López Jaena, who cultivated his own style of soiled, bohemian shabbiness, the propagandistas took great pride and care in their male toilette. Clothed in the same costume as their bourgeois European contemporaries, the Filipino expatriates wore dark, well-cut suits and coats, sported stiff black top hats and carried polished canes in their gloved hands. Those who were able to grow moustaches kept them manicured with the aid of curling tongs into a majestic upward sweep. Style manifested class and breeding, sobriety and high purpose. Racial and moral equality, even superiority, was affirmed in a sartorial code, expressed in a manly bearing and refined taste.

The fashions and tastes adopted by the propagandistas in Europe as declarations of self-worth, probity and sobriety were taken back home. Galicano Apacible continued to dress impeccably in a European suit long after he returned from temperate climes; he continued to savor French cuisine; and he retained his penchant for perfuming his body with violet water, a fragrance that evoked for him idyllic memories of French meadows.[4] Apacible was no male aesthete. His sprinkling of cologne intimated not delicacy or effeteness but distinction, social refinement and cosmopolitanism. Rizal himself strode out to his death by firing squad in 1896 immaculately attired to the last, wearing a dark suit, a shirt with cuffs fastened together with pearl and amethyst cufflinks, a tie neatly held in place by a small silver pin decorated with a tiny gold bee, and a derby hat.

The ilustrado determination to assert Filipino equality, or to buttress their own sense of moral worth by displays of courage, honor, integrity and style — qualities that were thought of as crucial components of their sex — was matched by their fervor to reform their compatriots. Men like themselves, they presumed, enlightened by the virtues of travel and an overseas European education, had a duty to bring modernity, progress and the ethos of good citizenship to their home country. Drawing upon his favorite metaphor of medicine, Rizal believed it to be the duty of the enlightened ilustrado man to heal his ailing country by bringing to it the knowledge he had acquired from Europe; by his ardent patriotism, his social, personal and political ideals. Yet, it is important to stress once again that they did not directly address those beneath them, the *pobres y ignorantes*. Rather, the main targets of their concern were women, particularly bourgeois women.

Filipino women, in the propagandistas' view, were ignorant and over-pious, and their mental atrophy and chronic religiosity could only be rectified by education. Under the direction of men like themselves, the theocratic darkness that engulfed women would be dispelled by the shining light of reason. The nature and purpose of women's education, however, was to have definite limits. The propagandistas did not exhort women to join them in European universities, to enter the professions, to engage in high commerce, or to participate equally with men in politics and public affairs.[5] Women's education would benefit society by promoting the intellect and demoting fleshly desires. The familiar ideology of woman's role in the family remained a recurring motif in propagandista discourse: women were society's bearers of honor and virtue; they acted as a "balm" to soothe the rigors of men's lives, and most importantly they had a special duty to the nation as the mothers who would raise future generations of patriotic sons.

Women's education needed to be secularized, to be taken out of the hands of friars, priests and nuns. But the rational and scientific discourses favored by the propagandistas did not radically challenge the traditional Catholic constructions of female sexuality. Ilustrado statements about the nature of their female compatriots were rife with contradictions. Publicly, it was claimed that Filipino women possessed the ideal feminine virtues of shame, modesty and passivity; that their laudable sense of sexual honor made them the equal of their European sisters. But at the same time the propagandistas found themselves grappling with historical and contemporary evidence of the Filipina's sexual freedom and sexual licentiousness. It was a rare ilustrado intellectual who admitted the unconstrained sexual nature of the pre-conquest native woman, and the native man's propensity to satisfy this female lustfulness.

The propagandistas' advice to their female compatriots to emulate the intellectual diligence and plain austerity of German and English (but certainly not French) women discloses how modernity was for them a double-edged sword. The modern woman was to be admired for having thrown off the shackles of superstition. But the modern woman's newfound independence of thought and action engendered deep anxieties. The *chulas* of Madrid, the prostitutes of Paris, the cultured bourgeois women they met in Europe and the daughters of the landlords with whom they lodged, the propagandistas perceived, all possessed a forceful sexuality that was at once exciting, desirable and repulsive. This ambivalence, as we saw, provoked for Juan Luna a crisis of masculinity that resulted in a tragedy of the most horrific proportions.

The homage the propagandistas paid to heroic passions, the emphasis they placed on the altruism of individual sacrifice stemmed partly from the conviction that their country could only be saved by a reform of their peoples' character that was moral in nature. But more importantly it arose from anger and embarrassment at the pusillanimity engendered by colonialism. They saw honor and noble desires as indispensable qualities that Filipino men and women must possess if the Philippines was to enjoy her liberty and progress. A man's very identity depended on courage and personal bravery and they saw themselves in chivalric terms, as avengers of their country's honor or, as Rizal imagined, in the mould of Dumas's *Three Musketeers*, men bound by ancient codes of honor. The recognition of duty to one's country, and the sacrificial demands and heroic efforts that duty elicited from a man, his life and fleshly love, was envisioned and celebrated as the highest form of Love.

Ultimately, this ideal of transcendent Love with its idiom of sacrifice, justified the relegation of women to domestic life and eschewal of domesticity for men; it spared men from the everyday problems of home and family. Patriotism, however genuine, could be variously used to justify physical and sensual privation, the avoidance of marital commitment and the abnegation of quotidian responsibilities, obligations and labors. It allowed the ilustrado patriots to evade responsibility for their carnal desires and to dodge the constraints of convention. The discourse of patriotic love therefore affirmed the separation of the public and the private spheres. Domestic life, sensual pleasures, sexual intimacies were to be set apart. Correspondingly, patriotism was exalted above all else; it was man's highest calling. That this rhetoric was taken utterly seriously is shown in a letter addressed to the Filipinos written by Rizal when he believed he was returning home to certain death:

I wish to show those who deny our patriotism that we know how to die for our duty and our convictions. What matters death if one dies for what one loves, for native land and adored beings? I have always loved my poor country and I am sure that I shall love her until my last moment.... I shall die happy, satisfied with the thought that all I have suffered, my past, my present, and my future, my life, my loves, my joys, everything, I have sacrificed for love of her. Whatever my fate may be, I shall die blessing her and wishing her the dawn of her redemption.[6]

Notes

[1] José Rizal, *Noli me tangere*, trans. Soledad Lacson-Locsin, ed. Raul L. Locsin (Honolulu: University of Hawai'i Press, 1997), p. 352.
[2] Ibid.
[3] Pierre Bourdieu, *The Logic of Practice*, trans. Richard Nice (Stanford: Stanford University Press, 1990), pp. 68–73.
[4] Encarnación Alzona, *Galicano Apacible: profile of a Filipino patriot* (Manila: National Historical Institute, 1971), p. 227.
[5] Many years later, the one-time propagandista Galicano Apacible had a long-running disagreement with his wife over their only daughter, who wanted to train to be either a doctor or a lawyer. Her mother supported her ambitions, but her father stubbornly opposed them, deciding on her behalf that she was best suited to being a "happy wife and mother" and living a "life without care." Alzona, *Galicano Apacible*, pp. 223–6.
[6] José Rizal (Hong Kong) "To the Filipinos," 20 June 1892, in *Cartas entre Rizal y sus colegas de la propaganda, 1889–1896* (Manila: Comisión Nacional del Centenario de Jose Rizal, 1961), p. 832.

Biographical Appendix

José Alejandrino (1870–1951)

Engineer. Born in the Manila district of Binondo to wealthy parents from the town of Arayat in Pampanga. Educated at the Ateneo Municipal and the University of Santo Tomas (UST). In 1889 he went to Barcelona, where he joined the predominantly Filipino lodge Revolución. In Madrid he joined the exclusively Filipino lodge Solidaridad No. 53. He later studied chemical engineering at the University of Ghent, and stayed for a time with José Rizal in Brussels. He arranged for Rizal's second novel *El filibusterismo* to be published in Ghent.

Galicano Apacible (1864–1949)

Physician, writer. Born in Balayan, Batangas, the son of a *hacendero*. Distant cousin of José Rizal, with whom he lodged whilst a student at boarding houses on Anda and Santo Tomas streets. Educated at the Colegio de San Juan de Letran and the University of Santo Tomas, where he took up medicine. In 1888 he went to continue his studies in Spain, graduating first as a Bachelor of Arts at the Instituto de Tarragona, then as a Licentiate in Medicine and Surgery at the University of Barcelona and finally as a Doctor of Medicine at the University of Madrid. Served as President of Solidaridad, the organization that launched the journal of the same name in February 1889. Whilst in Barcelona, he joined the predominantly Filipino lodge Revolución, taking the name "Lanatan" after a place in his home province of Batangas. Attended the 1889 Paris Exposition. In Madrid he joined the exclusively Filipino lodge Solidaridad No. 53. He returned to the Philippines in 1893 to practise his profession.

Ariston Bautista Lin (1863–1928)

Physician. Born in Santa Cruz, Manila, the son of an affluent Chinese mestizo couple. Obtained his bachelor's degree from the Ateneo Municipal in 1879 and a licentiate in medicine from the University of Santo Tomas in 1885. In 1889 he joined the predominantly Filipino lodge Revolución in Barcelona, taking the name "Balagtas" after the renowned eighteenth-century Tagalog poet. In Madrid he joined the exclusively Filipino lodge Solidaridad No. 53. Trained in hospitals in Berlin, Brussels and Paris. In Paris he formed a Masonic triangle with Antonio Luna and Trinidad H. Pardo de Tavera. Graduated as a doctor of medicine from Madrid University in 1891, writing his dissertation on the treatment of abscesses of the liver in the Philippines.

Fernando Canon (1860–1938)

Engineer. Born in Binan, Laguna, the son of a watchmaker and inventor. Classmate and close friend of José Rizal at the Ateneo Municipal. After obtaining his bachelor's degree in 1876 he went to Spain with Maximino Paterno and studied medicine at the University of Madrid for some years before switching careers and moving to the Royal School of Electrical Engineers in Barcelona. Canon is credited with despatching the first copies of Rizal's *Noli me tangere* to the Philippines, hidden in boxes containing dry goods and addressed to his Spanish sweetheart, Sra. Teresita Batle, who later became his wife.

Rafael del Pan (1863–1915)

Lawyer. Born in Manila. Educated at the Ateneo Municipal, Letran and the University of Santo Tomas. He went to Spain to study law at the University of Madrid and obtained his doctorate in 1887. A well-known Filipinologist, he collaborated with foreign writers in their studies of Philippine languages, particularly in the literary qualities of the local Spanish contact dialects. He also produced literary works and articles that were published in periodicals both in Europe and the Philippines.

Marcelo H. del Pilar (1850–96)

Lawyer, editor and a key figure in the propaganda movement. Born in Bulacan, the son of Don Julian, the wealthy owner of farmland, fishponds and a sugar mill who served three terms as the town *gobernadorcillo* (mayor). Marcelo's eldest brother Toribio was a priest who became active in the campaign for the advancement of native clergy and was deported to the Guam in the wake of the 1872 Cavite Mutiny. Marcelo graduated from the University of Santo Tomas as a Bachelor of Philosophy in 1871 and as a Licentiate in Jurisprudence in 1881. In 1878 he married his cousin, Marciana H. del Pilar ("Chanay"), with whom he was to have seven children, only two of whom survived. He founded and edited the first Tagalog daily newspaper, the short-lived *Diariong Tagalog*, in 1882. Whilst practising as a lawyer in the 1880s he came into conflict with the friars both in Manila and his home province, and in 1888 the Augustinians persuaded the Civil Governor of Bulacan that he was a *filibustero* who deserved to be formally "estranged," a euphemism for exiled. Forewarned of this action, Marcelo slipped away to Spain. Before his departure he co-authored a series of anti-friar pamphlets such as the mock catechism and prayer book entitled *Dasalan at Toksohan*, and during his voyage he wrote the poem "*Sagot nang España sa hibik nang Filipinas*"(Spain's response to the lament of Filipinas), which attacked the friars as the "source of all misery."

Upon his arrival in Barcelona he published an extended essay on the same theme, *La soberañia monacal en Filipinas*. In early 1889 del Pilar helped found the Masonic lodge "Revolución," which soon attracted most of the Filipinos living in the Catalan capital. Thereafter he played a very active role, from a distance, in promoting the spread of Masonry back in the Philippines. In late 1889 Del Pilar moved from Barcelona to Madrid to become the editor of the main organ of the propaganda movement, *La Solidaridad*, and he continued to publish the bi-weekly until its demise in 1895. In November 1889 he became head of the executive committee and the Seccion politica of the Asociación Hispano-Filipina. Founder member in 1889–90 of the exclusively Filipino lodge Solidaridad No. 53, which most of the leading propagandistas living in Madrid subsequently joined. In 1890 he succeeded Julio Llorente as master of the Lodge. Weakened by impoverishment, he died of tuberculosis in Barcelona without ever returning home.

Rafael Enriquez (1850–1937)

Artist. Born in Naga, Camarines Sur to Spanish parents. Educated at the Ateneo Municipal, the Academia de Dibujo y Pintura and the University of Santo Tomas. Went to Spain around 1868 to study law, but after obtaining his licentiate in 1871 he enrolled at the Academia de Bellas Artes de San Fernando and became a full-time painter. He lived and worked in Paris in the early 1880s and then moved to London, where he is said to have stayed for a time with Antonio Ma. Regidor. He married a Spanish woman from an aristocratic Andalusian family.

Dominador Gómez (1868–1929)

Physician. Born in Intramuros, Manila; largely Spanish by blood. Nephew of Padre Mariano Gomez, one of the three secular priests garrotted following the Cavite Mutiny of 1872. Received his bachelor's degree from the Ateneo Municipal in 1881; then studied medicine at UST until 1887 when he left for Spain for further studies. He finished his Licentiate in Medicine at the University of Barcelona around 1889 and then transferred to Madrid to pursue his doctorate. Completed his thesis only in 1895 due to his propaganda activities. He was a leading member of the Asociación Hispano-Filipina and a regular contributor to *La Solidaridad* under the pen name Ramiro Franco. In Madrid joined the exclusively Filipino lodge Solidaridad No. 53, taking the name "Marte," the god of war. He married a Spanish woman, Juana Pavon, in 1898.

Joaquín Gonzalez (1853–1900)

Physician. Born in Baliuag, Bulacan, the son of a Spanish friar. After obtaining his bachelor's degree from San Juan de Letran in 1872 he sailed for Spain, and there studied medicine first at the University of Valladolid and then at the University of Madrid, from where he received his doctorate in 1878. After his graduation he went to Paris where he specialized in ophthalmology at the clinic of Dr. Louis de Weckert. After returning to the Philippines he opened his own clinic on the Plaza de Binondo.

Juliana Gorricho [Pardo de Tavera] (?–1892)

Daughter of a Mexican Basque, a wealthy property owner in Manila. Married Felix Pardo de Tavera; mother of Felix Jr., Paz and Trinidad Pardo de Tavera. Widowed early. Her sister, Gertrudes Gorricho, was married to her late husband's brother, Joaquin Pardo de Tavera, and he became the legal guardian of the three children. He went to Paris in 1874 after being released from exile in the Marianas exile, where he had been banished together with other leading liberals in the wake of the 1872 Cavite Mutiny. Doña Juliana was killed together with her daughter Paz by Juan Luna in September 1892.

Felix Resurreccíon Hidalgo (1853–1913)

Artist. Born in Binondo, Manila, the son of wealthy lawyer and property owner. Educated at the Ateneo Municipal and UST (Bachelor of Civil Law 1871), and was enrolled simultaneously at the Escuela de Dibujo y Pintura. Had paintings exhibited at the Centennial Exposition in Philadelphia in 1876. In 1879 he traveled as a *pensionado* (scholarship student) of the city government of Manila to the Real Academia de Bellas Artes de San Fernando in Madrid. Later he spent time in Italy, Galicia and Normandy. His painting *Las virgenes christianas expuestos al populacho* was awarded ninth silver medal at the 1884 Madrid Exposición de Bellas Artes. He moved to Paris that same year. His many other prizes included a gold medal at the 1887 Exposición for *La Barca de Aqueronte*, which also won a silver medal at the Exposition Universelle in Paris in 1889. He did not return to the Philippines until 1912.

Julio Llorente (1863–?)

Lawyer. Born in Cebu, the son of a Spanish merchant. Classmate and close friend of José Rizal at the Ateneo Municipal. In 1881 he went to Spain, where he obtained his Doctorate of Laws from the Universidad Central de Madrid in 1885. Then practised law in the Spanish capital. He shared a house with Rizal in Madrid, attended the 1889 Paris Exposition with him and reportedly paid the fee for his licentiate in medicine. In 1889–90 he served as Worshipful Master of the exclusively Filipino lodge Solidaridad No. 53, which most of the leading propagandists living in Madrid subsequently joined. He married a Spanish woman and returned to the Philippines in 1891.

Graciano López Jaena (1856–96)

Writer, orator. Born in Jaro, Iloilo to poor parents, but had rich relatives, notably Claudio López, an honorary Vice Consul of Portugal. After a period as a seminarian in his hometown, López Jaena went to Manila to study medicine. Unable to gain admission to the University of Santo Tomas, he briefly trained instead at the Hospicio de San Juan de Dios before returning to his native province. There he reportedly gained a reputation as an anti-friar *filibustero*, and in 1880 he decided it was prudent to leave the Islands and resume his medical education in Spain, at the University of Valencia. Politics, journalism and masonry soon took him away from his studies, however, and he became a member of the Progressive Republican Party led by Manuel Ruiz Zorrilla. In Barcelona he joined the Masonic Lodge Porvenir No. 2, taking the name "Bolivar," after the liberator of South America. Contributed to the radical republican daily *El Progreso* and other Spanish papers; also to the *Revista Economica de la Camara de Comercio en España* (published in London). Vice-president of Solidaridad, the organization that launched the journal of the same name in February 1889; editor of *La Solidaridad* from its foundation in February 1889 until October 1889. Worshipful Master of the Lodge Revolución, founded in Barcelona in April 1889. Remained in Barcelona when Marcelo H. del Pilar and other leading propagandistas transferred the journal *La Solidaridad* to Madrid in the latter part of 1889. He returned to the Philippines briefly in 1891, but left again after being warned that he was in imminent danger of arrest. Weakened by impoverishment, he like Del Pilar died of tuberculosis in Barcelona.

Antonio Luna (1866–96)

Pharmacist. Born in Binondo, Manila to parents from the Ilocos region. He obtained his bachelor's degree from the Ateneo Municipal in 1883 and then studied pharmacy at the University of Santo Tomas. Went to Europe in 1886, stopping first in Paris to visit his brother Juan. He then proceeded to Barcelona, where he finished the Licentiate in Pharmacy, and later went on to pursue a doctoral course at the University of Madrid. Thereafter he worked in pharmaceutical laboratories in Ghent and Paris. He published a brief monograph on malaria, *El hematozoario del paludismo*, in Madrid in 1893 and contributed articles to a number of Spanish and French scientific journals. Under the pen name Taga-Ilog, he contributed regularly to the "Artes y Letras" section to *La Solidaridad*, many of his columns later being published under the title *Impresiones* in 1891. In Madrid he joined the exclusively Filipino lodge Solidaridad

No. 53, taking the name "Gay-Lussac," after an eminent French chemist. In Paris he formed a Masonic triangle with Ariston Bautista Lin and Trinidad H. Pardo de Tavera. He returned to the Philippines in 1894. He was assassinated by disaffected subordinates in 1899, when he was the Philippine Republic's Director of War, in charge of military operations against the occupation forces of the United States.

Juan Luna (1857–99)

Artist. Born in Badoc, Ilocos Norte. Family moved to Manila in 1861. Obtained his bachelor's degree from the Ateneo Municipal in 1874, but between 1869 and 1874 he also attended the Escuela Nautica, and qualified as a ship's pilot. Then took classes at the Academia de Dibujo y Pintura. He went to Spain in 1877 and enrolled at the Academia de San Fernando in Madrid, but did not stay long. Apprenticed himself instead to one of the professors at the school, Alejo Vera, and travelled with him in 1879 to Rome, where he remained until 1884. Won first prize with the *Spoliarium*, a massive canvas depicting slain Roman gladiators, at the National Exposition of Fine Arts in Madrid in 1884. That same year transferred to Paris. He gained many other awards, including diploma of honour at the 1887 Exposición de Filipinas for *Mestiza en su tocador*. In Paris he joined the Masonic club established by his brother Antonio, Trinidad H. Pardo de Tavera and others. He visited London and painted scenes in Richmond and Margate. In 1891 he joined the Société Nationale des Beaux Arts. In September 1892 he shot dead his wife and mother-in-law at his home in Paris. After receiving only a non-custodial sentence from the French court, he moved to Madrid and later Bilbao before returning to the Philippines in 1894. He died of a heart attack in Hong Kong.

José Maria Panganiban (1863–90)

Medical student. Born in Mambulao, Camarines Norte, the son of a clerk of court from Bulacan. Studied first at a Paulist seminary in Nueva Caceres and then with assistance from a priest went to Manila. Studied for a bachelor's degree at San Juan de Letran and for a licentiate in medicine at the University of Santo Tomas. Three essays he wrote on pathology, therapeutics and operations were deemed to have sufficient merit to be published by the University under the title "*Memorias escritas por el aventajado alumno del 3er año de la Facultad de Medicina D. José Maria Panganiban y Enverga para obtener los premios de fin de curso"* and exhibited at the 1887 Madrid Exposition. He went to Spain in 1888 to continue his medical studies at the University of Barcelona. In Barcelona he met López Jaena, who became his best friend. He joined the Asociación Hispano-Filipina and became auditor of the organization "La Solidaridad," formed in Barcelona in December 1888. Member of the Lodge Revolución, founded in Barcelona in April 1889. He contributed to *La Solidaridad* under the *noms de plumes* Jomapa and JMP and reportedly wrote two books or booklets, *El gobierno entre dos tendencias* and *El pensamiento*. He also is said to have translated some of Karl Julius Weber's writings on religion from German to Spanish. After he stopped receiving an allowance from home he was obliged to live in cheap boarding houses and eat very frugally, and he succumbed to tuberculosis aged just 27.

Felix Pardo de Tavera (1859–1932)

Physician, sculptor. Born in Manila, the son of a Spanish lawyer and government official and Doña Juliana Gorricho. After his father died in 1864 he, his brother Trinidad and sister Paz became the wards of their uncle, Joaquin Pardo de Tavera, counsellor of the Spanish administration, Professor of Law at the University of Santo Tomas and member of the Assembly of Reformers who was exiled in 1872. Felix obtained his bachelor's degree from the Ateneo Municipal in 1876, simultaneously taking art lessons at the Academia de Dibujo y Pintura. Left in 1877 to join his older brother in Paris. Like the latter, he enrolled at the Sorbonne and graduated with the degrees of Licentiate in Medicine around 1883 and Doctor of Medicine the following year. He then worked for a time at the Lariboisière Hospital in Paris. Specialized in paediatric surgery. In Paris joined the Masonic club established by his brother Trinidad and other Filipinos. Accomplished sculptor, winning a silver medal at the Exposición de Filipinas in Madrid in 1887 and a bronze medal at the Exposition Universelle held in Paris in 1889.

Trinidad H. Pardo de Tavera (1857–1925)

Physician, linguist, scholar. Born in Manila, the son of a Spanish lawyer and government official and Doña Juliana Gorricho, a Creole. His uncle and legal guardian was Joaquín Pardo de Tavera, member of the Assembly of Reformers who was exiled in 1872. Educated at the Ateneo Municipal, Letran and then studied medicine, philosophy and letters at the University of Santo Tomas. Went to Paris to complete his medical studies at the Sorbonne and later studied linguistics at the École Nationale des Langues Orientales. Returned to Manila to practise medicine in 1887, and in the same year married a Spanish mestiza, Doña Concepción Cembrano y Calderón. Returned to Paris in 1888, where he served for a time as secretary to the Legation of the Dominican Republic. Whilst in the French capital he formed a Masonic triangle with Antonio Luna and Ariston Bautista Lin. His publications include: *Contribución para el estudio de los antiguos alfabetos Filipinos* (Lausanne, 1884); *La medicine a l'île de Lucon* (Paris, 1884); *Contribution a l'étude de la périarthrite du genou* (Paris 1886); *El Sanscrito en la lengua Tagalog* (Paris, 1887); *Consideraciones sobre el origin del nombre de los numeros en Tagalog* (Manila 1889); *Las costumbres de los tagalos de Filipinas, segun el Pedro Plasencia* (Madrid, 1892); *Plantas medicinales de Filipinas* (Madrid, 1892); *Noticias sobre la imprenta y el grabado en Filipinas* (Madrid, 1893); *El mapa de Filipinas del P. Murillo Velarde* (Manila, 1894); and *Arte de cuidar enfermos* (Manila, 1895).

Pedro Paterno (1857–1911)

Lawyer, writer. Born in Manila, the son of Maximo Paterno, a wealthy businessman. Educated at the Ateneo Municipal. Pedro Paterno went to Spain before the other leading propagandistas, arriving in his mid-teens in 1871 to study philosophy and theology at the University of Salamanca. The following year his father was deported to the Marianas as a suspected liberal. Pedro Paterno later continued his studies at the University of Madrid and obtained a doctorate in law in 1880. His home in Madrid became a gathering place for Spanish literary figures and liberal politicians and for the steadily growing community of expatriate Filipinos. His contributions towards the organization of the Exposición de las Islas Filipinas held in Madrid in 1887 were reportedly later honored with the award of the Grand Cross of the Order of Isabela la Católica. Among his published writings are a collection of verses entitled *Sampaguitas* (1880), a work recognized as the "first Filipino novel" called *Ninay: costumbres filipinas* (1885) and a series of "ethnographic" studies of slight scholarly merit: *Influencia social del Cristianismo* (Madrid, 1876); *La antigua civilizacion tagalog* (Madrid, 1887). *Los Itas* (Madrid, 1890); *El Cristianismo en la antigua civilización tagalog* (Madrid, 1892); *El barangay* (Madrid, 1892); *La familia tagalog en la Historia Universal* (Madrid, 1892); *El individuo tagalog y su arte en la Exposición historico-americana* (Madrid, 1893); *El Regimen municipal en las Islas Filipinas* (Manila, 1893); and *Los Tagalog* (Madrid, 1894). In 1890 he married Luisa Pineyro, who came from an aristocratic Spanish family.

Mariano Ponce (1863–1918)

Physician, journalist, historian and bibliographer. Born in Baliuag, Bulacan. Obtained his bachelor's degree from San Juan de Letran in 1885. Friend of Marcelo H del Pilar. Contributed a section on Bulacan customs to Isabelo de los Reyes' *El Folk-Lore Filipino*, which won a prize at the 1887 Exposición de las Islas Filipinas. Went to Spain in 1887. In 1888 he took over responsibility of sending copies of Rizal's *Noli* to the Philippines. Secretary of the Asociación Hispano-Filipina. Treasurer of Solidaridad, the organization that launched the journal of the same name in February 1889. Managing editor of *La Solidaridad* and regular contributor under the pseudonym "Naning." Founder member of the Lodge Revolución, founded in Barcelona in April 1889, taking the name "Kalipulako" after the sixteenth-century chieftain (also known as Lapu-Lapu) whose men killed Ferdinand Magellan. Obtained his doctorate from the Universidad Central de Madrid in medicine in 1889. In Madrid he joined the exclusively Filipino lodge Solidaridad No. 53. His works include *Una excursión* (recounting his travels in Catalonia) (1889); *José Ma. Panganiban* (1890); *America en al descubrimiento de Filipinas* (1892); *Efemerides Filipinas* (1893), *Siam* (1893) and *Cronologia de los Ministros de Ultramar* (c.1894).

José A. Ramos (1856–1921)

Businessman. Born in San Roque, Cavite, the son of a wealthy property owner. Educated at the Ateneo Municipal and the University of Santo Tomas. In 1877 he went to study in England, taking classes in engraving and printing at a school of arts and trades in South Kensington. He married an Englishwoman, Agnes Gastrell. Whilst in London he was initiated into masonry through the invitation of Antonio Ma Regidor. From the time of his return to the Philippines in 1884 until 1890 he seems to have been the only active non-western mason in Manila, rising to be venerable master of the otherwise Spanish lodge Luz de Oriente. He worked together with Del Pilar in organising the anti friar demonstration of March 1888. In 1891 he became venerable master of "Nilad," the first purely Filipino lodge to be constituted in the Philippines. He imported manufactured goods from Britain, Europe and America and established a press that clandestinely printed liberal and anti-friar leaflets and broadsides. His bazaar, "La Gran Bretaña" in Binondo, became a meeting place for patriotic reformists.

Antonio Ma. Regidor (1845–1910)

Lawyer. Born in Manila to Spanish parents. Educated at San Juan de Letran and the University of Santo Tomas. Went to Spain c. 1863 and obtained a doctorate in canon and civil law from the University of Madrid. He then returned to Manila and held a number of important government positions during the liberal Governor-Generalship of the Carlos de la Torre — Recorder of the City of Manila; Chief Inspector of Municipal Schools, and Secretary of the Real Audiencia (Supreme Court). Leading member of the reformist Comision de Filipinos. Arrested after the Cavite Mutiny of January 1872, he was sentenced to be banished for eight years to the Marianas. From there he managed to escape in an American ship, and after residing for a while in France he settled in London. Contributed from there to several Spanish newspapers, among them *El Liberal*, *El Porvenir* and *El Pais*. Practised law from an office located in the same building in Billiter Street at the Spanish Consulate. Helped fund the main organ of the propaganda campaign, *La Solidaridad*. Regidor's substantial terraced house in the London district of Dalston became a gathering place for the handful of young Filipino professionals then living in London, including his brother Manuel Regidor; Pedro Ramos, a member of staff of the Spanish consulate; and Nicholas Montero, a Spanish mestizo who became secretary of the Royal Spanish naval commission in London. He married his Irish housekeeper, Julia Stanton, and they had five children. His household also included an Irish niece, an English governess and a Filipino male servant. Regidor is buried in a Catholic cemetery in the east London district of Leytonstone.

Manuel Regidor (1843–91)

Journalist. Born in Manila to Spanish parents. Went to Spain around 1868, and was appointed by the Overseas Minister Segismundo Moret as vocal of the Junta Consultiva de Reformas de Filipinas. Worked on a number of republican and anti-clerical Madrid newspapers around 1868–71, notably *El Correo de Espana* and *La Discusión*. The latter published a number of letters from the leading Filipino secular priest Fr. José Burgos. After the repression of 1872 he campaigned for the release of the many liberals banished to the Marianas, among them his brother Antonio. In the 1870s he also campaigned together with Rafael M. Labra, the autonomist deputy for Cuba in the Spanish Cortes. Though he denied it, he is assumed to be the author of *Islas Filipinas: Reseña de su organización social y administrativa y breves indicaciones de las principales reformas que reclaman*, published in Madrid in 1869 under the pseudonym Raimundo Geler — an exact anagram of his own name. Collaborated on the paper *España y Filipinas* (1887).

José Rizal (1861–96)

Physician, ophthalmologist, writer. Born in Calamba, Laguna, the son of a wealthy landowner and lessee of Dominican-owned sugar lands. Obtained his bachelor's degree from the Ateneo Municipal in 1877, then studied medicine at the University of Santo Tomas. Went to Spain in 1882, and obtained his Licentiate in Medicine from the University of Madrid in 1884. The following year he obtained a Licentiate in Philosophy and Letters from the same university. In 1885–86 he specialized in ophthalmology in Paris and Heidelberg. In 1886–87 he travelled and lived in Germany and Austria (where he briefly visited his scholarly correspondent Ferdinand Blumentritt), and published his first novel, *Noli me tangere*, in Berlin. He then returned to the Philippines for a few months, but felt it prudent for his own safety to leave again in February 1888. He then journeyed via the United States to London, where he undertook research on Philippine history in the British Museum until early 1889, work that resulted in his annotated edition of Antonio de Morga's *Sucesos de las Islas Filipinas* (1890). Thereafter he based himself successively in Paris and Brussels, contributing a number of major articles to *La Solidaridad*, the main organ of the propaganda movement.

In the latter part of 1890 he lived again in Madrid, and then in 1891 returned to France and Belgium. In 1891 he published his second novel, *El filibusterismo* in Ghent. In Madrid he joined the Masonic Lodge Acacia No. 9, taking the name "Dimasalang" ("Touch me Not"), the Tagalog equivalent of *Noli me tangere*. Disheartened by the disunity and lack of progress of the propaganda campaign in Europe, he left for Hong Kong in 1891. He was executed by firing squad in December 1896, convicted of instigating an uprising against Spain he in fact condemned as disastrous.

Paciano Rizal (1851–1930)

Farm manager. Elder and only brother of José Rizal. Born in Calamba, Laguna. Went to Manila to study at the Colegio de San José. Lived and worked with Fr. José Burgos, one of the three priests garrotted in 1872. Played a crucial role in arranging Rizal's departure for Europe and supporting him financially, sending him at first fifty and later thirty pesos a month. In 1890–91 he was exiled to the island of Mindoro for his role in the land conflict between Calamba residents and the Dominicans.

Felix Roxas (1864–1936)

Engineer. Born in the San Miguel district of Manila, the son of an architect. Educated at the Ateneo Municipal and then went to Spain to study civil engineering at the Escuela Especial de Inginieros de Caminos in Madrid. Returned to the Philippines due to the death of his father, and obtained a Licentiate in Law from the University of Santo Tomas.

Moises Salvador (1868–97)

Physician. Born in Quiapo, the son of a wealthy Spanish architect. Educated at the Ateneo Municipal and the University of Santo Tomas, then went to study medicine at the University of Madrid. Active propagandista and mason, taking the name "*Araw*," or sun. Returned to the Philippines in 1891, bringing with him the resolutions of the Filipino masons in Madrid regarding the founding of lodges in the Philippines. It is also said that he carried with him the instructions of Marcelo H. del Pilar about the founding of the Katipunan, the patriotic secret society that launched the 1896 revolution against Spain. Thereafter, played an active role in sending and receiving information to and from the propagandistas abroad.

Teodoro Sandiko (1860–1939)

Teacher, law student. Born in Pandacan. Educated at the Ateneo and started a law course at the University of Santo Tomas, but was reportedly obliged to abandon his studies due to quarrels with his Dominican professors. Then went to teach Latin in the town of Malolos, Bulacan, where his liberal ideas again aroused the ire of the friars. Suspected of being a *filibustero*, he departed for Hong Kong in 1888 and later made his way to Spain. In 1889 he was in Barcelona, where he joined the predominantly Filipino lodge Revolución and became treasurer of the Asociación Hispano-Filipina. Manager of *La Solidaridad*. He resumed his law studies at University of Madrid. In Madrid he joined the exclusively Filipino lodge Solidaridad No. 53, taking the name "Libertad." Also visited England, Germany, France and Belgium, where he ran a bicycle shop for a time in the town of Leige.

Pedro Serrano Laktaw (1853–1928)

Teacher, lexicographer. Born in Kupang, the same barrio in the municipality of Bulacan as Marcelo H. del Pilar. Educated at the Escuela Normal and taught for a while in San Luis, Pampanga. Contributed a section on Pampangan customs to Isabelo de los Reyes' *El Folk-Lore Filipino*, which won a prize at the 1887 Philippine Exposición in Madrid. Compiled the *Diccionario Hispano-Tagalog* (1889; 1914). Went to Spain in 1888, reportedly on a government scholarship, studying first in Salamanca and then at the Escuela Normal in Madrid. He was for a time employed as a private tutor to the Prince of Asturias, later King Alfonso XIII. Whilst in Madrid he joined the exclusively Filipino lodge Solidaridad No. 53, taking the name "Panday Pira," after a supposed sixteenth-century *indio* cannon maker. He returned to Manila around 1890 and there played a leading role in establishing the first Filipino Masonic lodges in Manila and the surrounding provinces. He also reportedly headed the Comité de Propaganda, which raised and remitted funds to support Marcelo H. del Pilar and the campaign in Spain, and distributed pamphlets and newspapers sent from Spain. Aside from Del Pilar, he is the only propagandista known to have got married before he left for Europe, and he eventually had 11 children.

Valentin Ventura (1860–1935)

From a wealthy family in Bacolor, Pampanga. Lived for a time in Paris, where he joined the Masonic club established by Trinidad H. Pardo de Tavera, Antonio Luna and others. Rizal stayed with him when visiting Paris, and he helped finance the publication of Rizal's second novel *El Filbusterismo*. In Madrid in the early 1890s he worked with Marcelo H. del Pilar in the office of *La Solidaridad*. Married a Spanish mestiza and settled in Barcelona.

Maximo Viola (1864–1933)

Physician. Born in San Miguel, Bulacan. Educated at Letran and the University of Santo Tomas. Went to Spain in 1882 and obtained a doctoral degree in medicine from the University of Barcelona in 1886. In 1887 he travelled with Rizal in Germany, Switzerland, Austria and Hungary, and that same year he helped finance the publication and despatch to the Philippines of Rizal's first novel, *Noli me tangere*. Also contributed to the support of Marcelo H. del Pilar. He returned to the Philippines in 1887.

Felipe Zamora (1854–1919)

Physician. Born in Capiz on the Visayan island of Panay, Zamora went to college in Manila and was among the first batch of students to enrol at the newly created Faculty of Medicine at the University of Santo Tomas, where he obtained his Licentiate in 1877. Two years later he travelled to Europe for further studies, working for a time in the Paris clinic of the eminent Étienne Stephane Tarnier, the obstetrician who first used incubators to care for babies born prematurely. Zamora returned to the Philippines in 1883 and quickly established a reputation in Manila society as a specialist in obstetrics. Among the women who went to his clinic on Calle Malinta in Binondo was Rizal's sister Saturnina.

Bibliography

Published Works

Abella, V.M. de Abella. *Vade-mecum Filipino, o manual de la conversación familiar español-tagalog seguido de un curioso vocabulario de modismos manileños* (Manila: C. Miralles, 1874).

Agoncillo, Teodoro A. *Malolos: the crisis of the Republic* (Quezon City: University of the Philippines Press, 1960).

———. "General Antonio Luna Reconsidered," *Solidarity* 10: 2 (March–April 1976): 58–80.

Aguilar Jr, Filomeno V. *Clash of Spirits: the history of power and sugar planter hegemony on a Visayan Island* (Quezon City: Ateneo de Manila University Press, 1998).

Aguilar Cruz, E. *Luna* (Manila: Bureau of National and Foreign Information, 1975).

Alejandrino, José. *La senda del sacrificio: episodios y anécdotas de nuestras luchas por la libertad* (Manila: Loyal Press, 1933).

———. *The Price of Freedom: episodes and anecdotes of our struggles for freedom*, trans. José M. Alejandrino (Manila: M. Colcol, 1949).

Alzona, Encarnación. *The Filipino Woman: her social, economic and political status 1565–1937* (Manila: Benipayo Press, 1938).

———. *Rizal's Legacy to the Filipino Woman* (Pasay City: Taft Publishing, 1953).

———. *Galicano Apacible: profile of a Filipino patriot* (Manila: Heirs of Galicano Apacible, 1971).

Andaya, Barbara Watson. "Thinking about the Philippine Revolution in a Gendered Southeast Asian Environment," in *1898: España y el Pacifico, interpretación del pasado, realidad del presente*, ed. Miguel Luque Talavan, Juan Pacheco Onrubia, and Fernando José y Pananco Aguado (Madrid: Asociación Espanola de estudios del Pacifico, 1999), pp. 249–65.

———, ed. *Other Pasts: women, gender and history in early modern Southeast Asia* (Honolulu: Center for Southeast Asian Studies, University of Hawai'i Press, 2000).

———. *The Flaming Womb: repositioning women in early modern Southeast Asia* (Honolulu: University of Hawai'i Press, 2006).

Anderson, Benedict. *Imagined Communities* (London: Verso, 1991).

———. *The Spectre of Comparisons: nationalism, Southeast Asia and the world* (London: Verso, 1998).

———. *Under Three Flags: Anarchism and the Anti-Colonial Imagination* (London and New York: Verso, 2005).

———. "The Rooster's Egg: pioneering world folklore in the Philippines," *New Left Review* 2 (March–April 2000): 47–62.

Arcilla, José. "Ateneo de Manila: problems and policies, 1859–1939," in *Jesuit Educational Tradition: the Philippine experience*, ed. Raul J. Bonoan and James A. O'Donell (Quezon City: Ateneo de Manila University Press, 1988).

Arinto, Patricia B. "Reading Correspondences: a critical analysis of the letters between Rizal and his sisters," in Thelma B. Kintanar, ed., *Review of Women's Studies* 5:2 and 6:1 (1996): 181–90.

Artigas y Cuerva, Manuel. *Glorias naciónales: Antonio Luna y Novicio, reseña bio–bibliográfía* (Manila: Imp. de La Vanguardia, 1910).

Atkinson, Jane Monnig and Shelly Errington, eds. *Power and Difference: gender in island Southeast Asia* (Stanford: Stanford University Press, 1990).

Bago, Eduardo López. *El cura, caso de incesto* (Madrid: Juan Munoz Sanchez, 1889).

———. *El confesionario (satiriasis)* (Madrid: Juan Munoz y Compania, 1890).

Baltazar, Francisco. "*La Filipina elegante y el Negrito amante*," trans. José T. Enriquez, Ignacio Manlapaz and A.V.H. Hartendorp, *Philippine Magazine* 29:6 (November 1932): 237–40.

Bankoff, Greg. "Households of Ill-repute: rape, prostitution and marriage in the 19th century Philippines," *Pilipinas* 17 (1991): 35–49.

———. "Servant-master Conflicts in Manila in the Late Nineteenth century," *Philippine Studies* 40 (1992): 281–301.

———. *Crime, Society and the State in the 19th Century Philippines* (Manila: Ateneo de Manila University Press, 1995).

Bantug, Asunción López. *Lolo José: an intimate portrait of José Rizal* (Intramuros Administration, 1982).

Bantug, José P., ed. *Epistolario del Pintor Juan Luna* (Madrid: Circulo Filipino, 1955).

Bantug, José P. "Rizal, the Physician," *Journal of History* 5: 1–2 (1957): 41–4.

Barrot, Georgiana M. *Account of a Voyage to Manilla, in a series of letters from the lady of the Consul-General of France to all India, M. Adolphe Barrot, to her uncle, Captain George W. Manby* (Yarmouth: Charles Sloman, 1842).

Barthes, Roland. *The Lover's Discourse: fragments*, trans. Richard Howard (London: Penguin, 1978).

Bartholow, Roberts. *Spermatorrhea: its causes, symptoms, results and treatment* (New York: William Wood, Co, 1879).

Baudelaire, Charles. "Le peintre de la vie moderne," [1863], reprinted in *Curiosités esthétiques, l"art romantique, et autres oeuvres critiques* (Paris: Editions Garnier Frères, 1962).

Bazaco, Evergisto. *History of Education in the Philippines* (Manila: University of Santo Tomas, 1953).

Beckman, Linda Hunt. *Amy Levy: her life and letters* (Athens: Ohio University Press, 2000).

Benjamin, Walter. *Illuminations*. With an introduction by Hannah Arendt, trans. Harry Zohn (London: Fontana Press, 1992).

Bennassar, Bartolome. *The Spanish Character: attitudes and mentalities from the sixteenth to the nineteenth century*, translated and with a preface by Benjamin Keen (Berkeley: University of California Press, 1975).

Bernad, Miguel, SJ. *The Christianization of the Philippines: problems and perspectives* (Manila: Filipiniana Book Guild, 1972).

———. *Rizal and Spain: an essay in biographical context* (Manila: Navotas Press, 1986).

Blair, Emma H. and James A. Robertson, eds., *The Philippine Islands, 1493–1898*, 52 vols. (Cleveland, Ohio: A.H. Clark, 1903–9).

Bloch, Iwan. *Beitrage zur Aetiologie der Psychopathia Sexualis* (Dresden: H.R. Dorn, 1902).

Blumentritt, Ferdinand. *An Attempt at Writing a Philippine Ethnography* [*Versuch einer ethnographie der Philippinen*] [1882]. Translated from the original German text by Marcelino N. Maceda (Marawi City: University Research Center, Mindanao State University, 1980).

———. "Der Ahnenkultus in die Religiosen Anschauungen der Malayen des Philippinen-Archipel," *Mittheilungen. d.k.k. Geographie Gesellschaft in Wien*, 2–3 (1882).

———. "La moralidad del indio salvaje," *La Solidaridad* 2: 46 (31 December 1890): 598–604.

———. "Lo que escribieron los extranjeros sobre Filipinas: apuntes bibliográficos," *La Solidaridad* 5: 107 (15 July 1893): 328–34.

Bonoan, Raul J., S.J. "Rizal's Record at the Ateneo," *Philippine Studies* 27 (1979): 53–79.

———. *The Rizal-Pastells correspondence: the hitherto unpublished letters of José Rizal and portions of Fr. Pablo Pastell's fourth letter and translation of the correspondence together with a historical background and theological critique* (Quezon City: Ateneo de Manila University Press, 1994).

———. "José Rizal: revolution of the mind," in Lorna Kalaw-Tirol, ed., *The World of 1896* (Manila: Ateneo de Manila University Press, 1998), pp. 213–35.

Bowring, Sir John, LLD, FRS. *A Visit to the Philippine Islands* (London: Smith, Elder & Co., 1859).

Boxer, Charles. *Mary and Misogyny: women in Iberian expansion overseas 1415–1815: some facts, fancies and personalities* (London: Duckworth, 1975).

The "Boxer Codex," trans. Carlos Quirino and Mauro Garcia, *Philippine Journal of Science* 87: 4 (December 1958): 325–453.

Bradbury, Malcolm and James McFarlane, eds. *Modernism: A guide to European literature, 1890–1930* (Harmondsworth: Penguin, 1991).

Brewer, Carolyn and Ann-Marie Medcalf, eds. *Researching the Fragments: histories of women in the Asian context* (Quezon City: New Day Publishers, 1999).

Brown, Donald, James W. Edwards and Ruth Moore, *The Penis Inserts of Southeast Asia: an annotated bibliography with an overview and comparative perspectives* (Berkeley: Center for South and Southeast Asian Studies, University of California Berkeley, 1988).

Brown, Donald. "The Penis Pin: an unsolved problem in the relations between the sexes in Borneo," in *Female and Male in Borneo: contributions and challenges to gender studies*, ed. Vinson H. Sutlive, Jnr. (Borneo Research Council Monograph Series, Ashley Press, n.d.), pp. 435–54.

Bryce, David (C.B.). *The Confessional Unmasked: showing the depravity of the priesthood, immorality of the confessional, being the questions put to females in confession, etc., etc., extracted from the theological works now used by Cardinal Wiseman, his bishops and priest*. With notes by C.B. (London: Thomas Johnston, 1851).

Bulatao, Jaime, S.J. "When Roman Theology meets an Animistic Culture: mysticism in present-day Philippines," *Kinaadman* 6: 1 (1984): 102–11.

Busto, Andrés del. *Título memorial razonado para la reforma de la enseñanza clínica de la especialidad de ginecología y paidología* (Madrid: Imprenta de Enrique Rubiños, 1881).

Butler, Judith. *Subjects of Desire: Hegelian reflections in twentieth century France* (New York: Columbia University Press, 1987).

Calvert, Albert F. *Madrid: an historical description and handbook of the Spanish capital* (London: John Lane, The Bodley Head, 1909).

Camagay, Ma. Luisa. *Working Women of Manila in the 19th century* (Quezon City: University of the Philippines Press and the University Center for Women's Studies, 1995).

Canamaque, Francisco. *Recuerdos de Filipinas: cosas, casos y usos de aquellas islas: vistos, ordos, tocados y contados*, 2 vols. (Madrid: Librería de Anllo y Rodriguez: 1877; Librería de Simon y Osler, 1879).

Caplan, Pat, ed. *The Cultural Construction of Sexuality* (London: Tavistock, 1987).

Carta itineraria de las isla de Luzon, 1 January 1882 (Madrid: Deposito de la Guerra, 1882).

Carter, Robert Brudnell. "On the Pathology and Treatment of Hysteria," in *Three hundred years of psychiatry 1535–1860: A history presented in selected English texts*, ed. Richard Hunter and Ida Macalpine (London: Oxford University Press, 1963).

Carvajal, Luis E. Otero and Angel Bahamonde, eds. *Madrid en la sociedad del siglo XIX*, 2 vols. (Madrid: Comunidad de Madrid, Consejeria de Cultura, 1986).

Casteras, Susan P. "Excluding Women: the cult of the male genius in Victorian painting," in *Rewriting the Victorians: theory, history and the politics of gender*, ed. Linda M. Shires (New York: Routledge, 1992).

Causing, Juan. *Freemasonry in the Philippines* (Cebu City: G.T. Printers, 1969).

Chung, Lilia Hernandez. *Facts in Fiction: a study of peninsular prose fiction, 1859–1897* (Manila: De La Salle University Press, 1998).

Clark, T.J. *The Painting of Modern Life: Paris in the art of Manet and his followers*, revised edition (Princeton, NJ: Princeton University Press, 1999).

Clayson, Hollis. *Painted Love: prostitution in French art of the Impressionist era* (New Haven: Yale University Press, 1991).

Coates, Austin. *Rizal: Filipino nationalist and martyr* (Manila: Solidaridad Publishing House, 1992).

Corbin, Alain. *Les Filles de Noce: misère sexuelle et prostitution aux XIXe–XXe siècles* (Paris: Aubier, 1978).

———. "Commercial Sexuality in Nineteenth Century France: a system of images and regulations," in *The Making of the Modern Body: sexuality and society in the nineteenth century*, ed. Catherine Gallagher and Thomas Laquer (Berkeley: University of California Press, 1987), pp. 209–19.

———. *Women for Hire: prostitution and sexuality in France after 1850*, trans. Alan Sheridan. (Cambridge, Mass: Harvard University Press, 1990).

Craig, Austin. *Lineage, Life and Labours of José Rizal* (Manila: Philippine Education Company, 1913).

D'Almeida, Anna. *A Lady's Visit to Manilla and Japan* (London: Hurst and Blackett, 1863).

De Bevoise, Ken. *Agents of Apocalypse: epidemic disease in colonial Philippines* (Princeton: Princeton University Press, 1995).

De Castro, Modesto. *Pagsusulatan nang dalauang binibini na si Urbana at ni Feliza*, Romulo P. Baquiran, Jr., ed. (Manila: Sentro ng Wikang Filipino, Sistemang Unibersidad ng Pilipinas at National Commission for Culture and the Arts, 1996).

De la Costa, Horacio, S.J. *Readings in Philippine History* (Manila: Bookmark, 1965).

De la Rosa, O.P. Rolando. *Beginnings of the Filipino Dominicans: history of the Filipinization of the Religious Orders in the Philippines* (Manila: University of Santo Tomas, 1990).

De los Reyes, Isabelo. *Filipinas* (Manila: J.A. Ramos, 1887).

—————. *Expedición de Li-mahong contra Filipinas en 1574* (Manila: n.p., 1888).

—————. *Triunfos del rosario, o los Holandeses en Filipinas* (Manila: n.p., 1888).

—————. *Artículos varios sobre etnográfia, historia y costumbres de Filipinas* (Manila: n.p., 1888).

—————. *Historia de Filipinas* (Manila: Imp. de D.E. Balbas, 1889).

—————. *Las islas Visayas en la epoca de la conquista* (Manila: Tipo-litografia de Chofre y Cia., 1889).

—————. *Historia de Ilocos* (Manila: Establecimiento tipográfico La Opinion, 1890).

—————. *El Folklore Filipino* (Manila: Imprenta Santa Cruz, 1890).

—————. *El Folklore Filipino* [1890]. Published with an English translation by Salud C. Dizon and María Elinora P. Imson (Quezon City: University of the Philippines Press, 1994).

De los Santos Cristobal, Epifanio. "Marcelo H. del Pilar." Photocopy taken from mimeograph copy in the library of Dr. Domingo Abella. This article was published in *Philippine Review* 3 (1918): 775–803, 861–85 and 947–75.

De Ocampo, Esteban. "Rizal as a Bibliophile," in *The Bibliographical Society of the Philippines*, Occasional Papers No. 2 (Manila: Unesco National Commission of the Philippines, 1960), pp. 27–52.

De Ocampo, Geminiano. "Our Foremost Ophthalmologist," *Historical Bulletin, Philippine Historical Association* 5:1–4 (December 1961): 298–308.

Del Pilar, Marcelo H. *Epistolario de Marcelo H. del Pilar*, 2 vols. (Manila: Imprenta del Gobierno, 1955; 1958).

—————. *Escritos de Marcelo H. del Pilar*, 2 vols. (Manila: La Biblioteca Nacional de Filipinas, 1970).

Dickens's Dictionary of London, 1888, An Unconventional handbook [1888] (Old House Books Facsimile edition, 1993).

Dionisio, Eleanor. "Sex and Gender," in *Sex and Gender in Philippine society: a discussion of issues on the relations between women and men*, ed.

Elizabeth Eviota, (Manila: National Commission on the Role of Filipino Women, 1994).
Dizon, Alma Jill. "Felipinas Caliban: colonialism as marriage of Spaniard and Filipina," *Philippine Studies* 46 (First Quarter, 1998): 24–45.
Doeppers, Daniel. *Manila 1900–1941: social change in a late colonial metropolis* (Manila: Ateneo de Manila University Press, 1984).
———. "The Development of Philippine Cities before 1900," *Journal of Asian Studies* 31 (August 1972): 769–92.
———. "Migration to Manila: changing gender representation, migration field and urban structure," in *Population and History: the demographic origins of the modern Philippines*, ed. Daniel F. Doeppers and Peter Xenos (Metro Manila: Ateneo de Manila University Press, 1998), pp. 139–79.
Doran, Christine. "Spanish and Mestizo Women of Manila," *Philippine Studies*, 41: 3 (1993): 269–86.
Ellis, Henry T., RN. *Hongkong to Manilla and the Lakes of Luzon, in the Philippine Islands, in the year 1856* (London: Smith, Elder and Co., 1859).
Eugenio, Damiana L. *Awit and Corrido: Philippine metrical romances* (Quezon City: University of the Philippines Press, 1987).
Eugenio, Damiana, ed., *The Folk Songs* (Philippine Folk Literature series, vol. 3) (Manila: De la Salle University Press, 1996).
Fajardo, Reynold S. *The Brethren: Masons in the struggle for Philippine Independence* (Manila: Enrique L. Locsin, 1998).
Fanon, Frantz. *Black Skin, White Masks* (New York: Grove, 1967).
Fast, Jonathan and Jim Richardson. *Roots of Dependency: political and economic revolution in 19th century Philippines* (Quezon City: Foundation for Nationalist Studies, 1979).
Feced, Pablo. *Esbozos y pinceladas por Quioquiap* (Manila: Ramirez y Cia, 1888).
Fernando, Gilda Cordero. *Turn of the Century* (Manila: GCF Books, 1978).
Flores, Hermenegildo. *Hibik ng Filipinas sa Inang España* ("Filipinas' Lament to Mother Spain") ([Manila]: n.p., c.1888).
Foreman, John. *The Philippine Islands: A Political, geographical, ethnographical, social and commercial history of the Philippine archipelago and its political dependencies embracing the whole period of Spanish rule* (London: Samson Low, Marston and Co., 1899).
———. *The Philippine Islands* (Shanghai: Kelly and Walsh Ltd, 1899).
Foucault, Michel. *The History of Sexuality*, vol. 1. *Introduction* (London: Penguin, 1990).
Fraxi, Pisanus. (Henry Spencer Ashbee), *Bibliography of Prohibited Books* (New York: Jack Brussel, 1962).

Gaite, Carmen Martin. *Love Customs in Eighteenth Century Spain*, trans. María G. Tomsich (Berkeley: University of California Press, 1991).

Gallagher, Catherine and Thomas Laqueur, eds. *The Making of the Modern Body: sexuality and society in the nineteenth century* (Berkeley: University of California Press, 1987).

Garb, Tamar. *Bodies of Modernity: figure and flesh in fin-de-siècle France* (New York: Thames and Hudson, 1998).

Garber, Marjorie. *Vested Interests: cross-dressing and cultural anxiety* (London: Routledge, 1997).

Gatmaitan, Magno S. *Marcelo H. del Pilar, 1850–1896* (Quezon City: Munoz Press, 1966).

Geler, Raimundo. *Islas Filipinas: Reseña de su organización social y administrativa y breves indicaciónes de las principales reformas que reclaman* (Madrid: Cargo de J.E. Morete, 1869), extract in *Documentary Sources of Philippine History*, compiled, edited and annotated by Gregorio F. Zaide, additional notes by Sonia M. Zaide, vol. 7 (Manila: National Book Store, 1990), pp. 228–9.

Gibson, Ian. *The Erotomaniac: the secret life of Henry Spencer Ashbee* (London: Faber and Faber, 2001).

Gonzalez, Carlos and Montse Marti. *Spanish Painters in Paris (1850–1900)* (London: Sammer, 1989).

Goncharov, Ivan. "The Voyage of the Frigate 'Pallada'," in *Travel Accounts of the Islands* (Manila: Filipiniana Book Guild, 1974), pp. 156–213.

Grifol y Aliaga, Daniel. *La instrucción primaria en Filipinas* (Manila: Tipo-Litografía de Chofre y Comp., 1894).

Guerrero, Leon Ma. *The First Filipino: a biography of José Rizal* (Manila: Guerrero Publishing House, 1961).

Haliczer, Stephen. *Sexuality in the Confessional: a sacrament profaned* (Oxford: Oxford University Press, 1996).

Haller, J.S. "Therapeutic Mule: the use of arsenic in the nineteenth century Materia Medica," *Pharmacy in History* 17 (1975): 87–100.

Harrison, Charles and Paul Wood with Jason Gaiger, eds. *Art in Theory, 1815–1900: an anthology of changing ideas* (Oxford: Blackwell, 1998).

Harrisson, Tom. "The 'Palang:' its history and proto-history in West Borneo and the Philippines," *Journal of the Malaysian Branch of the Royal Asiatic Society*, 37: 2 (1964): 162–74.

Hau, Caroline. *Necessary Fictions: Philippine literature and the nation, 1946–1980* (Manila: Ateneo de Manila University Press, 2000).

―――――. "Philippine Literary Nationalism and the Engendering of the Revolutionary Body," in *Body Politics: cultural representations of women's bodies*, ed. Odine de Guzman (Quezon City: UP Center for Women's Studies and The Ford Foundation, 2002).

Hauser, Renate. "Krafft-Ebing's Psychological Understanding of Sexual Behaviour," in *Sexual Knowledge, Sexual Science: the history of attitudes to sexuality*, ed. Roy Porter and Mikulas Teich (Cambridge: Cambridge University Press, 1994), pp. 210-7.
Heidegger, Martin. *Being and Time*, trans. John Macquarrie and Edward Robinson (New York: Harper and Row, 1962).
Highet, Gilbert. *Juvenal the Satirist* (Oxford: Clarendon Press, 1954).
Huetz de Lemps, Xavier. "Shifts in the Meaning of 'Manila' in the Nineteenth Century," in *Old Ties and New Solidarities: studies on Filipino communities*, ed. Charles J.H. MacDonald and Guillermo M. Pesigan (Metro Manila: Ateneo de Manila University Press, 2000), pp. 219-33.
Hufton, Olwen H. *Women and the Limits of Citizenship in the French Revolution* (Toronto: University of Toronto, 1992).
Hunt, Lynn. *Politics, Culture and Class in the French Revolution* (Berkeley: University of California Press, 1984).
Ileto, Reynaldo. *Pasyon and Revolution: popular movements in the Philippines, 1840-1910* (Quezon City: Ateneo de Manila University Press, 1979).
―――. *Filipinos and their Revolution: event, discourse, and historiography* (Quezon City: Ateneo de Manila University Press, 1998).
Illo, Jeanne. "Fair Skin and Sexy Body: imprints of colonialism and capitalism on the Filipina," *Australian Feminist Studies* 11: 24 (1996): 219-25.
Jacobs, Michael. *Madrid Observed* (London: Pallas Athene, 1992).
Jacolliot, Louis. *Les Moeurs et les Femmes de l'Extrême Orient: voyage au pays des bayadères* (Paris: E. Dentu, 1873).
Jagor, F. *Reisen in den Philippinen* (Berlin, 1873).
―――. *Travels in the Philippines* (London: Chapman and Hall, 1875).
―――. "Sexuelle Abnormitäten bei den Bisayern, Philippinen," *Verhandlungen der Berliner Gesellschaft fur Anthropologie, Ethnologie und Urgeschichte* 12 (1880): pp. 90-1.
Joaquin, Nick. *Almanac for Manileños* (Manila: Mr & Ms Publications, 1979).
―――. *A Question of Heroes* (Metro Manila: National Book Store, 1981).
Joll, James. *The Anarchists* (London: Eyre & Spottiswoode, 1964).
Jordanova, Ludmilla. *Sexual Visions: images of gender in science and medicine between the eighteenth and twentieth centuries* (Madison: University of Wisconsin Press, 1989).
José, Vivencio. *The Rise and Fall of Antonio Luna* (Metro Manila: Solar, 1986; Renato Constantino Filipiniana Reprint Series).
Junco, José Alvarez. "History, Politics and Culture, 1875-1936," in David T. Gies, *The Cambridge Companion to Modern Spanish Culture* (Cambridge: Cambridge University Press, 1999), pp. 67-85.
Kalaw, T.M. *La Masoneria Filipina: su origen, desarrollo y vicisitudes, hasta la epoca presente* (Manila: Bureau of Printing, 1920).

Kamen, Henry. *Spain's Road to Empire: the making of a world power, 1492–1763* (London: Allen Lane, Penguin Press, 2002).
Krafft-Ebing, Richard von. *Psychopathia sexualis: a medico-forensic study, with especial reference to the antipathic sexual instinct* [1887]. Translated from the twelfth German edition and with an introduction by Franklin S. Klaf (New York: Arcade Publishing, 1998).
Laconico-Buenaventura, Cristina. *The Theater in Manila, 1846–1946* (Manila: De La Salle University Press, 1994).
Laktaw, Pedro Serrano. *Dicciónario Tagalo-Hispano* (Manila: Estab. Tipografia "La Opinion," 1889).
Landes, Joan B. *Women in the Public Sphere in the Age of the French Revolution* (Ithaca, NY: Cornell University Press, 1988).
Laqueur, Thomas. *Making Sex: body and gender from the Greeks to Freud* (Cambridge, Mass. and London: Harvard University Press, 1990).
———. *Solitary Sex: the cultural history of masturbation* (New York: Zone Books, 2003).
Legarda, Benito J. Jr. *After the Galleons: foreign trade, economic change and entrepreneurship in the nineteenth century Philippines* (Manila: Ateneo de Manila University Press, 1999).
Le Gentil de la Galaisiere, Guillaume. *A Voyage to the Indian Seas* [1779] (Manila: Filipiniana Book Guild, 1964).
Legman, G. *The Horn Book: studies in erotic folklore and bibliography by G. Legman* (New York: University Books, 1964).
Loarca, Miguel de. "*Relación*," in *The Philippine Islands, 1493–1898*, ed. Emma H. Blair and James A. Robertson, vol. 5 (Cleveland, Ohio: A.H. Clark, 1909).
López Jaena, Graciano. *Discursos y artículos varios* [1891], Nueva edición revisada y adiciónada con escritos no incluido en la primera (Manila: Bureau of Printing, 1951).
———. *Speeches, Articles and Letters* (Manila: National Historical Institute, 1994).
López-Gonzaga, Violeta. "Images of Women and their Role in Society in José Rizal's Writings," in *José Rizal and the Asian Renaissance*, ed. M. Rajaretnam (Kuala Lumpur: Institut Kajian Dasar; Manila: Solidaridad Publishing House, 1996), pp. 171–89.
López-Pinero, José M.; Thomas F. Glick, Victor Navarro Brotons and Eugenio Portela Marco, eds. *Dicciónario histórico de la ciencia moderna en España* vol. I (Barcelona: Nova-Grafik, 1983).
Lumbera, Bienvenido. "Philippine Literature Old and New," in *Literaturen Abschnitt I.* ed. E.J. Brill (Leiden, 1976), pp. 273–315.
———. *Tagalog Poetry, 1570–1898: tradition and influences in its development* (Quezon City: Ateneo de Manila University Press, 1986).

Luna y Novicio, Antonio. *El hematozoario del paludismo: su estudio experimental* (Madrid: G. Pedraza, 1893).
Luna-Orosa, Severina, ed. *Rizal and the Filipino Woman: Rizal's Liga Filipina* (Quezon City: Vibal Print, 1963).
MacMicking, Robert. *Recollections of Manilla and the Philippines during 1848, 1849 and 1850*, edited and annotated by Morton J. Netzorg (Manila: Filipiniana Book Guild, 1967).
Mainardi, Patricia. *Husbands, Wives and Lovers: marriage and its discontents in 19th century France* (Yale: Yale University Press, 2003).
Maines, Rachel P. *The Technology of Orgasm: "hysteria," the vibrator, and women's sexual satisfaction* (Baltimore: Johns Hopkins University Press, 1998).
Majul, Cesar Adib. *Rizal's Concept of a Filipino Nation* (Quezon City: University of the Philippines Press, 1959).
———. "Principales, Ilustrados, Intellectuals and the Original Concept of a Filipino National Community," *Asian Studies* 15 (1977):1–20.
———. *The Political and Constitutional Ideas of the Philippine Revolution* (University of the Philippines Press, 1996).
Mallat, Jean. *The Philippines: history, geography, customs, agriculture, industry and commerce of the Spanish colonies in Oceania* [1846], trans. Pura Santillan-Castrence in collaboration with Lina S. Castrence (Manila: National Historical Institute, 1994).
Manuel, E. Arsenio, *Dictionary of Philippine Biography*, 4 vols. (Quezon City: Filipiniana Publications, 1955–86).
McClintock, Anne. *Imperial Leather: race, gender and sexuality in the colonial contest* (London: Routledge, 1995).
McCoy, Alfred W. "*Baylan*: animist religion and Philippine peasant ideology," *Philippine Quarterly of Culture and Society* 10: 3 (1982): 141–94.
McMillan, James. *Housewife or Harlot: the place of women in French society, 1870–1940* (New York: St. Martin's Press, 1981).
Meyer, A.B. "Ueber die Perforation des Penis bei den Malayen," *Mittheilungen anthropologischen gesselchaft in Wien* 7: 9 (1877): 242–4.
———. *Bilderschriften der Ostindischen Archipels und die Sudsee* (Leipzig: Verlag von A. Nauman und Schroeder, 1881)
Marche, Alfred. *Luzon and Palawan* [1879]. Translated from the French by Carmen Ojeda and Jovita Castro (Manila: The Filipiniana Book Guild, 1970).
Mojares, Resil B. *House of Memory* (Pasig City: Anvil, 1997).
———. *The Origins and Rise of the Filipino novel: a generic study of the novel until 1940* (Quezon City: University of the Philippines Press, 1998).
———. *Waiting for Mariang Makiling: essays in Philippine cultural history* (Quezon City: Ateneo de Manila University Press, 2002).

Molina, Antonio J. "The Sentiments of the Kundiman," in *Filipino Heritage: the making of a nation*, vol. 8 (Manila: Lahing Pilipino, 1978), p. 2026.

Montero y Vidal, José. *Historia General de Filipinas desde el descubrimiento de dichas islas hasta nuestros días*, 3 vols. (Madrid: Tello, 1887–95).

Morga, Antonio de. *Sucesos de las islas Philipinas* (Mexico: n.p., 1609).

———. *Sucesos de las islas Filipinas*. Obra publicada en Mejico el ano de 1609, nuevamente sacada a luz y anotada por José Rizal, y precedida de un prologo del Prof. Fernando Blumentritt (Paris: Librería de Garnier Hermanos, 1890).

———. *Sucesos de las islas Filipinas*. Nueva edición enriquecida con los escritos inéditos del mismo autor ilustrada con numerosas notas que amplíen el texto y prologada extensamente por W. E. Retana (Madrid: Librería General de Victoriana Suárez, 1909).

———. *Sucesos de las islas Filipinas*, trans. and ed. J.S. Cummins (Cambridge: Cambridge University Press, 1972).

Mrazek, Rudolf. *Engineers of Happy Land: Technology and nationalism in a colony* (Princeton and Oxford: Princeton University Press, 2002).

Nakpil, Carmen Guerrero. "María Clara" [1956], in *Woman Enough and Other Essays* (Manila: Ateneo de Manila University Press, 1999).

Noceda Juan de, y el P. Pedro de Sanlucar. *Vocabulario de la lengua Tagala compuesto por varios religiosos, doctos y graves* [1754] (Manila: Impr. de Ramirez y Giraudier, 1860).

Nochlin, Linda. *Women, Art and Power and other essays* (London: Thames and Hudson, 1994).

Nocturnal Paris and "Paris After Dark" (incorporated) An Indispensable Companion for the Stranger, The Only Genuine Night Guide for Gentlemen; Paris after dark containing a description of the fast women, their haunts, habits etc., to which is added a faithful description of the Night Amusements and Other Resorts. Also all particulars relative to the working of the Social Evil in the French Metropolis (London: n.p., 1877).

Nouveau Plan de Paris: nomenclature des rues du nouveau plan itinéraire des omnibus et tramways (Paris: Lanee, Editeur-Geograph, 1887).

Nuevo manual de urbanidad, cortesanía, decoro y etiqueta o el hombre fino contiene todas las reglas del arte de presentarse en el mundo según las practicas que la civilización ha introducido en todos los casos que occurren en la sociedad, como son visitas convites, reuniones, filarmónicas, matrimonies, duelos y lutos, & c., con un tratado sobre el arte cisoria (Madrid: s.n., 1880).

Nye, Robert. *Masculinity and Male Codes of Honor in Modern France* (Berkeley: University of California Press, 1998).

Ocampo, Ambeth. *Looking Back* (Manila: Anvil Publishing, 1990).

---. *Bonifacio's Bolo* (Pasig City: Anvil, 1995).
---. *Luna's Moustache* (Pasig City: Anvil, 1998).
---. *Rizal Without the Overcoat*, expanded edition (Pasig City: Anvil, 2000).
---. *Meaning and History: the Rizal lectures* (Pasig City: Anvil, 2001).
Ong, Aihwa and Michael G. Peletz, eds. *Bewitching Women, Pious Men: gender and body politics in Southeast Asia* (Berkeley: University of California Press, 1995).
Ovid, *Metamorphoses* (London: Penguin Classics, 1955).
Owen, Norman. "Masculinity and National Identity in the 19th Century Philippines," *Illes et Imperis* 2 (1999): 23–47.
Padgug, Robert A. "Sexual Matters: on conceptualising sexuality in history," *Radical History Review* 20 (Spring/Summer 1979): 3–23.
Palma, Rafael. *Biografía de Rizal* (Manila: Bureau of Printing, 1949).
Pardo de Tavera, Trinidad H. *Arte de cuidar enfermos* (Manila: Tipografía de Chofre y Comp., 1895).
---. *Biblioteca Filipina* (Washington: Government Printing Office, 1903).
Paredes, Ruby. "The Pardo de Taveras of Manila," in *An Anarchy of Families: state and family in the Philippines*, ed. Alfred W. McCoy (Quezon City: Ateneo de Manila University Press, 1994), pp. 347–427.
Paris and Environs with routes from London to Paris: handbook for travellers (London: Karl Baedeker, 1888).
Parker, Andrew, Mary Russo, Doris Sommer and Patricia Yaeger, eds. *Nationalisms and Sexualities* (London: Routledge, 1992).
Peakman, Julie. *Mighty Lewd Books: the development of pornography in eighteenth-century England* (Basingstoke: Palgrave MacMillan, 2003).
Pedrosa, Ramon. "Abortion and Infanticide in the Philippines during the Spanish contact," *Philippiniana Sacra* 18 (1983): 7–37.
Peratoner, Amancio. *Fisiología de la noche de bodas: misterios del lecho conyugal. Seguido de un estudio del Dr. A. Tardieu.* (Barcelona: Establecimiento tipográfico-editorial de José Miret, 1875).
---. *El mal de Venus estudio medico-popular sobre las enfermedades venéreas y sifilíticas tomado de las obras de los eminentes sifilógrafos Belhomme, Cullerier, Diday, Lancereaux, Martin, Mireur, Ricord, etc., etc.* (Madrid: Simon y Osler, 1881).
Perrot, Michelle, ed. *A History of Private Life: from the fires of revolution to the Great War*, trans. Arthur Goldhammer (Cambridge, Mass.: The Belknap Press of Harvard University Press, 1990).
Perrot, Michelle. "The New Eve and the Old Adam: changes in French Women's condition at the turn of the century," in *Behind the Lines: gender and the two World Wars*, ed. Margaret R. Higonnet et al. (New Haven: Yale University Press, 1989).

Pertierra, Raul. "Viscera-suckers and Female Sociality: the Philippine asuang," *Philippine Studies* 31 (1983): 319–37.

Pfeiffer, William R. *Music in the Philippines: indigenous, folk, modern — an introductory survey* (Dumaguete: Silliman Music Foundation, Inc., 1975).

Phelan, John Leddy. *The Hispanization of the Philippines: Spanish aims and Filipino responses 1565–1700* (Madison: University of Wisconsin Press, 1959).

Pigafetta, Antonio. *Magellan's Voyage around the World*, the original text of the Ambrosian MS, with English trans. notes, bibliography and index by James Alexander Robertson and Emma H. Blair (Cleveland: The Arthur H. Clark Company, 1906).

Pilar, Santiago A. "Letras y figuras: the charm of illustrated letters," *Archipelago*, A-30 (1976): 17–23.

Pilar, Santiago Albano. *Juan Luna: the Filipino as painter* (Manila: Eugenio López Foundation, 1980).

Plaridel, Mh. [Marcelo H. del Pilar]. *La soberanía monacal en Filipinas: apuntes sobre la funesta preponderancia del fraile en las islas, así en lo político como en lo económico y religioso* (Barcelona: F. Fossas, 1888).

——————. *La frailocracía Filipina* (Barcelona: Imprenta Ibérica de Francisco Fossas, 1889).

Ploss, H. *Das Weib in der Natur- und Volkerkunde: Anthropologische Studien* (Leipzig: Th. Grieben, 1884).

Ploss, Hermann Heinrich, Max Bartels and Paul Bartels. *Woman: an historical, gynaecological and anthropological compendium*, trans. and ed. Eric John Dingwall (London: William Heinemann Medical Books Ltd, 1935).

Poovey, Mary. "Scenes of an Indelicate Character: the medical 'treatment' of Victorian women," in *The Making of the Modern Body: sexuality and society in the nineteenth century*, ed. Catherine Gallagher, Thomas Laqueur (Berkeley: University of California Press), pp. 137–68.

Alfonso E. Perez Sanchez, Manuela Mena Marques, Juan J. Luna, Joaquin de la Puente and Matias Diaz Padron. *The Prado* (London: Scala Publishers, 2000).

Pratt, Mary Louise. *Imperial Eyes: travel writing and transculturation* (London: Routledge, 1992).

——————. "Women, Literature and National Brotherhood," *Nineteenth century contexts: an interdisciplinary journal* 18: 1 (1994): 27–47.

Pretty, Francis. "The admirable and prosperous voyage of the worshipfull Master Thomas Candish [Cavendish]," in *Hakluyt Voyages* (London: Everyman's Library, 1907).

Proceso: seguido contra el parricida Juan Luna San Pedro y Novicio, Natural de Badoc (Filipinas) Discurso Pronunciado en la audiencia del 18 Febrero de 1893 Par Maître Felix Decori — Abogado de la Corte de Apelation de Paris.

Quirino, Carlos. *The Great Malayan: the biography of Rizal* (Manila: Philippine Education Company, 1949).

———. "Manila's School of Painting," *Philippine Studies* 15 (1967): 348–53.

Radhakrishan, R. "Nationalism, Gender and the Narrative of Identity," in Parker *et al.*, *Nationalism and Sexualities*; and Nira Yuval-Davis and Floya Anthias, eds., *Woman-Nation-State* (London: Macmillan, 1989).

Rafael, Vicente, ed. *Discrepant Histories: translocal essays on Filipino cultures* (Pasig City: Anvil, 1995).

Rafael, Vicente L., "Language, Identity, and Gender in Rizal's *Noli*," *Review of Indonesian and Malaysian Affairs* 18 (Winter 1984): 110–40.

———. "Translation and Revenge: Castilian and the origins of Nationalism in the Philippines," in *The Places of History: regionalism revisited in Latin America*, ed. Doris Sommer (Durham, North Carolina; and London: Duke University Press, 1999), pp. 215–35.

———. *The Promise of the Foreign: Nationalism and the technics of translation in the Spanish Philippines* (Durham and London: Duke University Press, 2005).

Reed, Robert R. *Colonial Manila: the context of Hispanic urbanism and process of morphogenesis* (Berkeley: University of California Press, 1978).

———. "The Antipolo Pilgrimage: Hispanic origins, Filipino transformation and contemporary religious tourism," in *Converging Interests: traders, travelers and tourists in Southeast Asia*, ed. Jill Forshee with Christina Fink and Sandra Cate (Berkeley: University of California Press, 1999), pp. 151–206.

Reid, Anthony. *Southeast Asia in the Age of Commerce, 1450–1680.* vol. 1. *The lands below the winds* (New Haven: Yale University Press, 1988).

Retana, Wenceslao (Desengaños). *Apuntes para la historia (aniterías y solidaridades)* Folletos Filipinos II (Madrid: Manuel Minuesa de los Ríos, 1890).

———. *Sinapismos (bromitas y critiquillas)*, Folletos Filipinos III (Madrid: Libreria de Fernando Fe; Manila: Librería Amigos del País, 1890).

Retana, W.E. *Supersticiónes de los Indios Filipinos: un libro de aniterías* (Madrid: Vda de M. de los Rios, 1894).

———. *Archivo del bibliófilo filipino*, 5 vols. (Madrid: Imprenta de la Viuda de M. Minuesa de los Rios, 1895–1905).

———. *Aparato bibliográfico de la Historia General de Filipinas*, 3 vols. (Madrid: Imp. de la Sucesora de M. Minuesa de los Rios, 1906).

Retana, Wenceslao E. *Vida y escritos del Dr José Rizal* (Madrid: Victoriano Suarez, 1907).

Reyes, Soledad. "The Romance Mode in Philippine Popular Literature," *Philippine Studies* 32 (1984): 163–80.

———. "Urbana at Felisa," *Philippine Studies* 47 (1999): 3–29.

Reysio-Cruz, Emilia S. *Filipino Folksongs* (Manila: Community Publishers, 1950).

Rizal, José. *Epistolario Rizalino*, edited by Teodoro M. Kalaw. vols. [??] (Manila: Bureau of Printing, 1930–38).

———. "Juan Luna," in *La Ilustración-Revista Hispano-Americana* 7: 278 (28 February 1886).

———. *Noli me tangere* (Manila: Instituto Naciónal de Historia, 1978) [Facsimile of the first edition, published in Berlin by the Berliner Buchdruckerei-Actien-Gesellschaft in 1887].

———. *One Hundred Letters of José Rizal to his Parents, Brother, Sisters, Relatives* (Manila: Philippine National Historical Society, 1959).

———. *Cartas entre Rizal y sus colegas de la propaganda*, 2 vols. (Manila: Comisión Naciónal del Centenario de José Rizal, 1961).

———. *Cartas entre Rizal y otras personas, 1877–1896* (Manila: Comisión Naciónal del Centenario de José Rizal, 1961).

———. *Diarios y Memorias por José Rizal*, 2 vols. (Manila: José Rizal National Centennial Commission, 1961).

———. *Escritos Políticos y Históricos de José Rizal*.(Manila: National Centennial Commission, 1961).

———. *Reminiscences and Travels of José Rizal (1878–1896)* (Manila: José Rizal Centennial Commission, 1961).

———. *Rizal-Blumentritt Correspondence*, 3 vols. (Manila: José Rizal National Centennial Commission, 1961).

———. *Miscellaneous Correspondence* (Manila: National Heroes Commission, 1963).

———. *Rizal's Correspondence with Fellow Reformists, 1882–1896*, 3 vols. (Manila: National Heroes Commission, 1963).

———. *Letters between Rizal and Family Members*, 3 vols. (Manila: National Heroes Commission, 1964).

———. *Political and Historical Writings* (Manila: National Historical Commission, 1964).

———. *Letters between Rizal and Family Members, 1876–1896* (Manila: National Historical Institute, 1993).

———. *Noli me tangere* [1887], trans. Ma. Soledad Lacson-Locsin, ed. Raul L. Locsin (Manila: Bookmark, 1996).

———. *El filibusterismo* [1891], translated by Ma. Soledad Lacson-Locsin, edited by Raul L. Locsin (Manila: Bookmark Publishing, 1997).

———. *Rizal-Blumentritt Correspondence*, 2 vols. (Manila: National Historical Institute, 1999).

Roces, Alfredo R. "Philippine Art: Spanish period," in *Brown Heritage: essays on Philippine culture, tradition and literature*, ed. Antonio G. Manuud (Quezon City: Ateneo de Manila University Press, 1967).

———. *Felix Resurrección Hidalgo and the Generation of 1872* (Manila: Eugenio López Foundation, 1995).

Rodriguez de Ureta, Antonia. *Pacita, o la virtuosa Filipina: novella recreativa de costumbres orientales*, segunda edición (Barcelona: Herederos del V. Pla, 1892).

———. *El Difamador, novella originale* (Barcelona: Tip. de F Altes, 1894).

Roxas, Felix. *The World of Felix Roxas: anecdotes and reminiscences of a Manila newspaper columnist, 1926–36*, trans. Angel Estrada and Vicente del Carmen (Manila: Filipiniana Book Guild, 1970).

Rudd, Niall. *The Satires of Horace: a study* (Cambridge: Cambridge University Press, 1966).

Said, Edward. *Orientalism* (New York: Pantheon, 1978).

San Antonio, Francisco de, O.F.M. *Vocabulario Tagalo* [1624], ed. Antoon Postma (Quezon City: Ateneo de Manila University Press, 2000).

Sánchez Gómez, Luis Ángel, *Un imperio en la vitrina: el colonialismo español en el Pacífico y la Exposición de Filipinas de 1887* (Madrid: Consejo Superior de Investigaciones Científicas, Instituto de Historia, Departamento de Historia de América, 2003).

Santiago, Luciano P.R., MD. "The First Filipino Doctors of Pharmacy (1890–93)," *Philippine Quarterly of Culture and Society* 22 (1994): 90–102.

———. "The First Filipino Doctors of Medicine and Surgery (1878–97)," *Philippine Quarterly of Culture and Society* 22 (1994): 103–40.

———. "Centennial: the first psychiatric article in the Philippines (1895)," *Philippine Quarterly of Culture and Society* 23 (1995): 62–75.

Schadenberg, A. "Ueber die Negritos den Philippinen," *Zeitschrift fur Ethnologie* (1880).

Schumacher, John N., SJ. "Syncretism in Philippine Catholicism: its historical causes," *Philippine Studies* 32 (1984): 251–72.

———. *The Making of a Nation: essays on nineteenth century Filipino nationalism* (Quezon City: Ateneo de Manila University Press, 1991).

———. *The Propaganda Movement, 1880–1895: the creation of a Filipino consciousness, the making of the Revolution* (Quezon City: Ateneo de Manila University Press, 1997).

Scott, Joan W. *Gender and the Politics of History* (New York: Columbia University Press, 1988).

Scott, William Henry. "The Unión Obrera Democrática, first Filipino labor union," *Philippine Social Sciences and Humanities Review* 47:1–4 (January–December 1983): 131–92.

———. *Barangay: sixteenth century Philippine culture and society* (Quezon City: Ateneo de Manila University Press, 1995).

———. *Cracks in the Parchment Curtain and Other Essays in Philippine History* (Manila: New Day Publishers, 1996).

Serrano, Rosalio. *Nuevo diccionario manual Español — Tagalo para el uso de las escuelas de primera instrucción* (Manila: Establecimiento tipografico "Ciudad Condal" de Plana y ca., 1872).

Serrano Laktaw, Pedro. *Diccionario hispano-tagalog* (Manila: Estab. Tip "La Opinion" a cargo de G. Bautista, 1889).

———. *Diccionario hispano-tagalog* (Madrid: Ediciónes Cultura Hispanica, 1965).

Sheehan, Elizabeth A. "Victorian Clitoridectomy: Isaac Baker Brown and his harmless operative procedure," in *The Gender/Sexuality Reader: culture, history, political economy*, ed. Roger N. Lancaster and Micaela di Leonardo (London: Routledge, 1997), pp. 325–35.

Showalter, Elaine. *Sexual Anarchy: gender and culture at the fin de siècle* (London: Virago, 1995).

Siegel, James T. *Fetish, Recognition, Revolution* (Princeton: Princeton University Press, 1997).

Simon, J.M, S.I. Simon and G. Simon. "San Juan y La '*Noli me Tangere*'," *Archivos de la sociedad Española de oftalmología* 6 (Junio 2002).

La Solidaridad. Translated by Guadalupe Fores-Ganzon (Quezon City: University of Philippines Press, 1967; republished Pasig City: Fundación Santiago, 1995–96).

Sommer, Doris. *Foundational Fictions: the national romances of Latin America* (Berkeley: University of California Press, 1991).

Sta. María, Felice Prudente. *In excelsis: the mission of José P. Rizal* (Makati City: Studio Five Designs, 1996).

———. "Leisure Time in Old Manila," *Kasaysayan: The story of the Filipino people*, vol. 4 (Manila: Asia Publishing, 1998), pp. 12–3.

Stoler, Ann Laura. *Race and the Education of Desire: Foucault's History of Sexuality and the colonial order of things* (Durham: Duke University Press, 1995).

Szanton, Cristina Blanc. "Collision of Cultures: historical reformulations of gender in the lowland Visayas, Philippines," in *Power and Difference: gender in island Southeast Asia*, ed. Jane Monnig Atkinson and Shelly Errington (Stanford: Stanford University Press, 1990), pp. 346–83.

Taga-Ilog (Antonio Luna). *Impresiones* (Madrid: Imprenta de 'El Progreso de Tipográfico, 1891).

Taylor, John R.M. *The Philippine Insurrection against the United States: a compilation of documents*. With an introduction by Renato Constantino. 5 vols. (Pasay City: Eugenio López Foundation, 1971).

Terra, Jun. *Juan Luna Drawings: Paris period; from the collection of Dr. Eleuterio M. Pascual* (Makati City: Dr. Eleuterio M. Pascual Publishing House, 1998).
Terra, Perfecto Jr. "Villafranca's 'Desde Filipinas a Europa'," *Philippine Studies* 32 (1984): 197–224.
Tratadito de urbanidad, adaptado para los niños en Visaya-Cebuano. Cebuano translation by Carlos Arpon (Manila: Colegio de Santo Tomas, 1894).
United States, 56th Congress, 2nd Session. *Lands Held for Ecclesiastical or Religious Uses in the Philippine Islands, etc.* Senate Document No. 190 (Washington: Government Printing Office, 1901).
United States, War Department, Bureau of Insular Affairs. *A Pronouncing Gazeteer and Geographical Dictionary of the Philippine Islands* (Washington: Government Printing Office, 1902).
Valis, Noel. *The Culture of Cursilería: bad taste, kitsch, and class in modern Spain* (Durham: Duke University Press, 2002).
Varela, Miguel María. "Rizal's Studies in the University of Madrid," *Philippine Studies* 9: 2 (April 1961): 294–300.
Vasquez de Aldana, Antonio. "Viaje pintoresco al rededor de un tapis," *Trastos viejos*, vol. 1 (Manila: Ramirez y Giraudier, 1883).
Villamor, Juan. *General D. Antonio Luna y Novicio: vida hechos y trágica muerte* (Manila: Tipográfia "Dia Filipino," 1932).
Villanueva, Francisco Jr. *Reminiscences of Rizal's stay in Europe* (Manila: Loyal Press, 1936).
Villarroel, Fidel, OP. *Marcelo H. del Pilar at the University of Santo Tomas* (Manila: University of Santo Tomas, 1997).
―――――. *Marcelo H. del Pilar at the University of Santo Tomas* (Manila: University of Santo Tomas, 1997).
―――――. *The Dominicans and the Philippine Revolution, 1896–1903* (Manila: University of Santo Tomas, 1999).
Viola, Maximo. "Mis viajes con el Dr. Rizal," *The Journal of History Special Rizal Edition*, 5: 1–2 (Manila: Philippine National Historical Society, 1957), pp. 53–79.
Von Scherzer, Karl. *Narrative of the Circumnavigation of the Globe by the Austrian Frigate "Novara" in the years 1857, 1858 & 1859*, 2 vols. (London: Saunders, Otley and Co, 1862).
Waitz, Theodor, Georg Gerland. *Anthropologie der Naturvolker*, 6 vols. (Leipzig: F. Fleischer, 1859–72).
Walls y Merino, Manuel. *La música popular de Filipinas* (Madrid: Imp. de M.G. Hernandez, 1892).
Warner, Marina. *Monuments and Maidens: the allegory of the female form* (London: Wiedenfeld and Nicholson, c. 1985).

Warren, T. Robinson. *Dust and Foam, or three oceans and two continents* (New York: Charles Scribner, 1858).
Weeks, Jeffrey. *Sex, Politics and Society: the regulation of sexuality since 1800* (London: Longman, 1981).
Wendt, Reinhard. "Philippine Fiesta and Colonial Culture," *Philippine Studies* 46 (1998): 3–53.
Wickberg, Edgar. *The Chinese in Philippine Life, 1850–1898* (New Haven and London: Yale University Press, 1965).
Williams, Leonard. *Toledo and Madrid: their records and romances* (London: Cassell, 1903).
Wilson, Michael. *The Impressionists* (Oxford: Phaidon, 1983).
Worcester, Dean C. *The Philippine Islands and their people: A record of personal observation and experience, with a short summary of the more important facts in the history of the Archipelago* (New York: The Macmillan Co., 1898).
Woycke, James. *Birth Control in Germany, 1871–1933* (London: Routledge, 1988).
Zaide, Gregorio F. *Great Filipinos in History* (Manila: Verde Book Store, 1970).
Zialcita, Fernando and Martin Tinio, Jr. *Philippine Ancestral Houses, 1810–1930* (Manila: GCF Books, 1980).

Newspapers

Diario de Manila (Manila, 1869).
El Bello Sexo: semanario ilustrado del literatura, bellas artes, ciencias y conocimientos útiles, dedicado exclusivamente a la mujer (Manila, 1891).
El Porvenir Filipino (Manila, 1869).
Gazette des Tribunaux: journal de jurisprudence et des débats judiciaires (Paris, 1893).

Unpublished Sources

Aguilar, Filemon V. "Civilisation and Migration: 'Igorrotes' and 'Negritos' in the ilustrado national imagination." Paper read at the Fourth European Philippine Studies Conference, Alcala, Spain, September 2001.
Baltazar, Francisco. "La india elegante y el negrito amante." Sayneteng wikang tagalog na sinulat sa tula ni Francisco Baltazar at nilapatan ng tugtugin ni Gregorio San José. [Udyong, Bataan, 1855]. Unpublished manuscript, Philippine National Library.
British Museum, Signatures of Readers, 4 June 1887–11 October 1888. British Museum Reading Room Archive.

Camposano, Clement C. "Rethinking López Jaena's Struggle against Monastic Supremacy." M.A. dissertation, University of the Philippines, Diliman, 1992.

Carcel de Bilibid, Letras (Ayer Manuscript Collection, No.1393, Newberry Library).

O'Connor, D.J. "Racial Stereotyping of Filipinos in the Spanish Press and Popular Fiction, 1887–1898." Paper presented at "1848/1898-1998: Transhistoric Thresholds" Conference, Arizona State University, 8–12 December 1998.

Cour d'Appel de Paris Chambre des mises en accusation, No. 1750, Novembre, 1892.

Dizon, Alma Jill, "Beyond the Melodramatic Vision: national identity and the novels of José Rizal." PhD dissertation, Yale University, 1996.

Doña Juliana Gorricho's Kitchen Notebooks, unpaged blue notebook (Pardo de Tavera Room, Rizal Library, Ateneo de Manila University).

Guerrero, Milagros C. "Sources on Women's Role in Philippine History, 1590–1898; text and countertext."

Owen, Norman G. "Masculinity and National Identity in the 19th Century Philippines." Paper delivered at the 6th International Philippine Studies Conference, University of the Philippines, Diliman 10–14 July 2000.

Ragsdale, Jane Slichter. "Coping with the Yankees: the Filipino elite, 1898–1903." PhD thesis, University of Wisconsin, 1974.

Rizal, José. "[Impressions of Madrid]," written in French in his notebook: Clinica Medica, 1881–1887 (Ayer Manuscript Collection, Newberry Library).

———. Madrid Diary, 1884: Agenda Bufete (Ayer Manuscript Collection, Newberry Library).

Salazar, Wigan. "German Economic Involvement in the Philippines, 1871–1918." Unpublished PhD dissertation, School of Oriental and African Studies, University of London, 2000.

Thomas, Megan. "Orientalist Enlightenment: the emergence of nationalist thought in the Philippines, 1880–1890." PhD dissertation, Cornell University, 2002.

Wright, Ma. Teresa H. "Woman's Place as defined in ten Nineteenth century Books of Conduct." MA dissertation, Ateneo de Manila University, 1990.

Index

Academia de Dibujo y Pintura, 3, 51, 262, 266–7
Andaya, Barbara Watson, xxiv, xxxiii
Anderson, Benedict, xxii, xxxiii
aeta, 12–3, 205
Alejandrino, José, 185, 187–9, 228, 260
alta sociedad, 5
America/American, xx, 4, 19, 89, 134–5, 183, 185, 270
amor propio, xxx, 30, 73, 77, 84, 107–10
  manly pride, xxx, 73
Apacible, Galicano, 106, 233, 259–60
Arejola, Tomás, 105, 109, 115
Arellano, Deodato, 141, 152
arsenic, 231, 251
art, xx, xxv–xxvii, 37, 39–40, 46–8, 50–2, 65, 67, 70, 75, 82, 132, 158, 256, 267
Asia, 135
Ateneo Municipal, 3, 21, 260–9, 271–2
Augustinian, 118, 123–4, 137–8, 142, 145, 192, 262
awit, 15, 18, 128

Baltazar (Balagtas), Francisco, 12, 261
Barcelona, xi, xvii, xxvi, 50, 85, 92–5, 105, 109, 115, 122, 129, 143, 150, 188, 193, 260–2, 265, 267, 269, 273–4
Barrantes, Vicente, 87, 158–9

Barthes, Roland, 88, 109
Basa, José Maria, 100, 114, 150, 193
Baudelaire, Charles, 42, 60–1
Bautista, Ariston, 56, 233, 266, 268
bayaderas, 127–8
Beckett, Gertrude, 186, 197
belle époque, 39, 46
Benjamin, Walter, xxix, 42
Berlin, 160, 193–4, 202–3, 206, 244–5, 251, 261, 271
Bilibid, 85, 118
Binondo, 3, 6, 7–9, 18, 32, 36, 168, 260, 264–5, 274
Bloch, Iwan, 198–9
Blumentritt, Ferdinand, 86, 91, 104–5, 115, 142, 153, 159–61, 177, 181, 184, 193, 196, 200–7, 211, 233, 244–7, 251–2, 271
Bohemia, 142, 204, 256
botany, xxvi, 203
boticas, 7, see also pharmacies
bourgeois, xxx, 28, 31, 70–1, 103, 107, 139, 238
Boustead, Adelina, 108
Boustead, Nelly, 92, 108–9
Bowring, John, 5, 16
Bracken, Josephine, 155, 189
British, 4–5
British Museum, xxvii, 206, 271
Brussels, 185, 187–8, 190–1, 193, 196–7, 228, 239, 241, 253, 260–1, 271
Burgos, José, 2–3, 271–2

Cabangis, Tomás, 94
cafés, xi, xxvii, 39, 53–4, 56, 58–9, 95, 101
Calamba, 155, 158, 185, 190, 234, 237, 240, 251–2, 271–2
Calderon, Felipe, 117, 145
Cañamaque, Francisco, 85–6, 89, 91, 201
capitalism, 4, 148
Carlyle, Thomas, 157
Catholic, 14, 16, 18–9, 22, 31, 121–2, 131–3, 136–7, 142–4, 149, 170, 203–4, 218, 224, 228, 254, 257, 270
  Catholicism, 123–4, 128, 142–3, 145, 160, 200
Cavendish, Thomas, 208, 214
Cavite, 2–3, 82, 118, 262–4, 269–70, *see also* Mutiny
Cecilio, José M., 162–7, 194, *see also* Chengoy
Champs de Mars, 49
Charcot, Jean Martin, xxviii
Chenggoy, 162–7, 194, *see also* José M. Cecilio
China, 33, 89, 134, 213
Chinese, 7–9, 214, 224, 260
Chirino, Pedro, 208–9, 212, 217
Christian, 10, 14, 21, 23, 37, 126, 128–9, 131, 144, 179–80, 182, 199, 212–3
  Christianity, 141, 212
chula, 43, 45–6, 88, 90, 258
civilization, xxx, 93, 102, 177, 198–200, 220, 222, 238, 241–2, 255
Clara, María, 124–5, 162–3, 167–70, 172, 176
clinical history, 156
Colegio de San Juan de Letran, 21, 260–1, 263, 266, 268–70, 274

Colín, Francisco, 208
colonial, xxvi, 13, 85, 117–8, 154, 171–2, 199
  ideology, xxi, 159
Comisión de Filipinos, 1, 31, 270
commodification, 4
  labor, 4
  sexual, 4
concubine, 19, 117, 121, 132, 208
Corbin, Alain, 42, 54
Cordillera, 107, 201
Corpuz, O.D., 7
cosmopolitanism, xxvi, xxix, 5, 90, 256
Craig, Austin, 185
crime passionnel, 40

dandy, 11–2
  Filipino, 11
  Indonesian, 11
Danet, 71
Dapitan, 155, 189, 191, 231, 251
Decori, Felix, 65
Degas, Edgar, 50
De Castro, Modesto, 22–5
De la Torre, Carlos María, 1–2
De Mas, Sinibaldo, 9, 17
Del Pilar, Marcelo, xi, xv, 3–4, 21, 91, 95–7, 101, 118–9, 123, 129–32, 134, 137–44, 147, 150, 152, 190, 217, 221, 261–2, 265, 269–70, 272–4
Del Pilar, Marciana (also Chanay), 114, 139–41, 152, 262
Diderot, Denis, 121, 143
dilettante, xi
Doeppers, Daniel, 19, 33
domesticity, xxiii, xxviii, 24, 27, 42, 176, 258
Dominican, 32, 118, 120, 142, 144, 179, 268, 271–3

Dresden, 202
Dumas, Alexandre, 189
Dutch, 11, 202

East End, *see* London
El Filibusterismo, 114, 123–4, 272
El Pacto de Sangre, 41
El Sexo Masculino, xxviii
emporia, 9
England, xxvi–xxvii, 122–3, 134, 136, 183, 225, 250, 269, 273
English, xii, 7, 10, 19, 33–4, 66, 111, 186, 191, 194, 197, 199, 219, 221, 245, 248, 257, 270
Enlightened, 121, 157, 225
Escolta, 7, 9–10, 18, 236
European, xi, xxi, xxv–xxvii, xxix, 1, 5, 7–12, 16–9, 26–7, 51, 79, 85, 88, 90, 95–6, 106–7, 120–1, 131, 134, 143, 145, 155, 157, 165, 169, 172, 177, 189, 199, 205, 209, 214–5, 222, 225–6, 236–7, 239, 256–7
   bourgeoisie, 11, 16, 27, 67
   women, xvii–xviii, xxvii, xxix–xxx, 59, 108, 110, 151, 155, 191, 209–10, 235, 239
Exposición Nacional de Bellas Artes, 40, 50, 264

Feced, Pablo, 85–7, 112
Feminist, xxiii, 147, 230, 238–9
Ferrer y Guardia, Francisco, 43, 78
filibustero, 92, 118, 262, 265, 273
Filipino, xi, xvii–xviii, xix, xx–xxi, xxiv–xxvii, xxix–xxxii, 1–3, 5, 7, 11, 19, 22, 26, 31, 37, 39–41, 44, 48, 50–4, 56–7, 59–60, 65–7, 69–70, 77–80, 84–98, 100–1, 103–7, 109–10, 113, 115, 118–21, 126–9, 131, 133–7, 139–40, 143, 145–6, 148–9, 155, 160–1, 163, 167, 170, 173, 175, 186, 189–92, 199–210, 212–6, 218, 221, 224–5, 232, 238–9, 241, 243, 245, 249, 252, 254–8, 260–5, 267–73
Filipina, xxix, xxxi, 4, 11, 66, 105, 109–10, 125, 131, 135, 138–9, 166, 169–70, 172, 177, 203, 206, 209–10, 212, 216–7, 239, 241–2, 257, 262–3, 266–9, 271, 273
fin-de-siècle, 46, 71, 79, 97
flâneur, xi
Flaubert, Gustave, 124
folklore, xx, 205, 210
fornication, xviii, 19, 201, 206, 208
Foucault, Michel, xix
frailocracia, 119, 133
Franciscan, 118, 124, 135, 142, 145, 218
freemason, xxvi, 143, 183
friars, xxv, xxx, 88, 117–23, 128, 130–5, 138, 142, 144–5, 147, 158, 172, 201, 263, 273

Gaíte, Carmen Martín, 11, 34
Garb, Tamar, 46
Gatmaytan, Josefa, 138, 148, 151–3
Gauguin, Paul, 50
German, xii, xiv, xxvii, 7, 9, 104, 158, 191, 196, 198, 201–3, 205, 237–9, 243, 253, 257, 267
Germany, xxvi, 136, 155, 158, 199, 202–3, 206, 225, 230, 235, 237, 271, 273–4
Ghent, xi, 185, 260, 265, 272
Gil Celso, Mir Deas, 91–2, 109, 113

Gil y Montes de Sanchiz, María, 1–2, 31
Gómez, Dominador, 103, 105, 263
Gómez de la Serna, Javier, 49, 79, 82
Goncharov, Ivan, 9–10
Goncourt, Edmond de, 122
Gorricho, Juliana, 64, 65–6, 72–4, 76, 82, 108, 263–4, 267
gossip, xviii, 25, 27, 101, 105, 162, 194
Greek, 14, 155, 182
Guerrero, Lorenzo, 51

Haliczer, Stephen, 122
Haussmann (Baron), 54
    Haussmannization, 56
Heidelberg, 155, 160, 197, 253, 271
Hidalgo, Felix Resurreccion, 51, 79, 126, 148–9, 161, 264
Higiene del Matrimonio, xxviii
history, xi, xiii, xix–xxi, xxiii–xxiv, xxvi, xxxiii–xxxiv, 36, 39, 47, 49, 66, 112, 154–6, 160, 201, 203–7, 212, 243, 245, 271
Holland, xxvii, 237
homosexual, xxvii, 208
Hong Kong, 5, 33, 155, 193, 259, 266, 272–3
honor, xi–xix, xxi, xxv, xxxi, 4, 25–6, 30, 52, 86, 91–4, 100, 103, 109, 123, 134, 144, 171, 211–2, 240–1, 255–8
    patriotic, xviii, 98, 199
    sexual, 239–41, 257
hysteria, xxvii–xxviii, 162, 226–7

Ibarra, Crisostomo, 124–5, 136, 167–70, 176
Igorot, 90, 107, 126, 200–1, 205

imperialism, 12, 85
Impressionists, 47, 79, 84
indio, 17, 30, 51–3, 86–7, 95, 100, 158, 172, 207–8, 210–4, 216–7, 273
Indonesia, xix, xxxiii, 33
intellectual, xiii, xx–xxi, xxiv–xxvi, xxix, xxxiv, 9, 11, 65–6, 95, 121, 126, 156, 179–80, 199–200, 202–3, 205, 229–30, 239, 242, 257
ilustrado, xx, xxiv–xxvii, xxix, xxxiv, 9, 15, 18, 20, 28, 31, 39–40, 49–51, 58–60, 67, 77, 80, 85, 88, 92–6, 103–5, 108–10, 117–8, 120–1, 130, 139, 142, 145, 147, 154–5, 157, 189, 202, 204–5, 207, 217, 222, 224–5, 234, 243, 254–8, *see also* enlightened

Jacoby, Suzanne, 185–6, 197
Jacolliot, Louis, 70, 127–8
Jagor, Feodor, 200–3
Jesuit, 119, 133, 135–6, 138, 142, 179
Jordanova, Ludmilla, 179

Kipling, Rudyard, 206
Krafft-Ebing, Richard von, 175, 198–201, 242
Kropotkin, Peter, 206
kundiman, 13–4, 29

La Concordia, 29, 167
La Parisienne, 41–3, 45–7, 77
La Solidaridad, xxvii, 84, 87, 91, 103, 108, 190, 202, 222, 225, 262–3, 265, 267, 269–71, 273–4
laborantes, xx

Laktaw, Pedro Serrano, 217, 219–22, 249, 273
Landes, Joan, xxiii
Laqueur, Thomas, 242
Latin, 17, 21, 54, 129, 155, 169, 178, 182, 273
Lavater, Johann Kaspar, 47
law, xxvi, 3, 71, 76, 86, 118, 155, 212, 217, 246–7, 261–2, 264, 267–8, 270, 272–3
Lecour, Charles, 56
Leiden, 202
Leitmeritz, 160, 193, 196, 204, 244–5
lesbianism, 224, 226
Lete, Eduardo de, xv–xvi
Leyba, Concha, 239, 252–3
liberalism, xxi, 88, 255
  liberal reforms, xx, 122
libido, 217, 243
  libidinal, xii, xxvii, xxix–xxx, 4, 45, 65, 77, 108, 168, 180, 191, 218, 228
Loarca, Miguel de, 208, 214
London, xi–xiv, xxvi–xxviii, 9, 46, 143, 147, 157, 161, 177, 186, 206, 235, 244, 246–7, 263, 265–6, 269–71
López Bago, Eduardo, 122
López Jaena, Graciano, xi, xviii–xix, xxvi, 45, 50, 79, 86, 91, 118–9, 121, 125–8, 133–8, 143, 146, 148, 256, 264
Los Indios Bravos, 100–1, 114
Loyola, Ignatius, 122
Luna, Antonio, xi, xv–xvi, xxvi, xxx, 3–4, 21, 29, 73–4, 84–5, 87–93, 98, 101–4, 106–10, 118, 125, 143, 187, 261, 265, 268, 274, *see also* Taga-ilog
Luna, Juan, xi, xvi, xxvi, xxx, 3–4, 39–43, 44, 45, 47–54, 56, 57, 58–61, 62, 63, 64, 65–7, 68, 69–76, 79–80, 84–5, 91, 94–5, 98–100, 109, 118, 143, 148, 258, 264–6
Luling (San Pedro, Andres Luna de), 72–5

MacMicking, Robert, 117, 145
Madrid, xi–xii, 43, 50–2, 85–93, 95–6, 98, 101, 103–9, 119, 122, 143, 158, 160–1, 185, 192, 194, 206, 228, 232, 255, 258, 261–5, 267–8, 271–3
Malabon, 5
Malacañang Palace, 1, 31
Malay, 89–90, 198–200, 202, 245
Mallat, Jean, 17
Malolos, 138–9, 239, 241, 273
  young women of, 135, 137, 238
Manila, xi–xii, xxix, 1, 3–5, 7–8, 10–1, 18, 22, 29–30, 41, 50–2, 65, 73, 81, 85, 94, 98, 101, 105, 118–9, 129–30, 139–41, 143, 150, 161–2, 164, 193–4, 201, 213, 217, 219, 229, 233–4, 249, 260, 262–8, 270–2, 274
  Manileño, 10
manly, xxi, xxx, 77, 92, 95–6, 99–100, 106, 241, 256
  pride, xxx, 73, *see also amor propio*
Mapa y Belmonte, Cornelio, 18
Marche, Alfred, 7–8
Marx, Eleanor, xxvii, 206
masculinity, xxiv, xxviii, xxix, xxxi, xxxiii, 31, 75, 92–3, 95, 99, 114, 258
masonry, 143, 262, 265, 270
masturbation, xxvii, 225–9

McClintock, Anne, xxii
medicine, xvii, xxvii, 155–7, 179–80, 225, 227, 230–1, 233–4, 252, 256, 260–1, 263–9, 271–2, 274
Menangge, 12
mestizo, mestiza, 4–5, 9, 13, 26, 41, 51, 66, 89, 117, 125, 219, 260
Meyer, A.B., 201–2
Michelet, Jules, 122, 134, 136, 157–8, 250
miembro viril, 214, 218
Mis Impresiones, 84, 87, 91–3, 125, 265
modernity, xi, xix–xx, xxv, xxix, 4–5, 11, 40, 42–3, 46, 53, 58, 60, 77, 118, 161, 169, 225, 238, 256–7
    modern, xii, xix, xxii–xxiii, xxix–xxxi, 1, 11, 31, 40, 42, 46–9, 53–4, 58, 60, 65, 72, 74, 76–7, 93, 97, 107, 119, 135–6, 142, 170, 178–80, 220, 224–5, 230, 237, 254
    Modern Woman, 39–40, 43, 46–8
Mojares, Resil, xxvi, xxxiv, 22, 37, 207, 218
monastic supremacy, xxx, 119, 121
Monet, Claude, 50
Monlau, Felipe, xxviii, 199, 225
Montero y Vidal, José, 3, 31
Montmartre, 54, 59
moral authority, xxx, 139, 240
Morga, Antonio de, 203, 206, 246, 271
Mosse, George, xxiii
Mrazek, Rudolf, 11
Murillo, Bartoleme Esteban, 51
mutiny, 2–3, 82, 118, 262–4, 270, *see also* Cavite

Nakpil, Carmen Guerrero, 170
Napoleonic wars, 4
national identity, xi, xx, xxii, xxiv, xxxii, 95
New York, 183, 196
Nochlin, Linda, 67
Noli me Tangere, 118, 123–4, 129, 135, 150, 154–5, 158–61, 163, 167, 169, 171, 176–8, 192, 194, 254, 261, 269, 271, 274
novena, 22, 29, 120, 129, 133, 136–7

opium, 5, 7
orgasm, 71, 226, 236, 242
Orient, 8, 199
Ortiga, Consuelo y Rey, 108, 115
Owen, Norman, xxiv

Panganiban, José, xvii–xix, 266
Pardo de Tavera, Felix, xvi, 65, 76, 232, 263, 267
Pardo de Tavera, Paz, 41, 61, 62, 63, 64, 65–6, 71–4, 76, 99, 263–4, 267
Pardo de Tavera, Trinidad H., xiii, 41, 65–6, 73–4, 76, 205, 229–30, 237, 261, 263, 266–8, 274
Paris, xi–xii, xxvi, xxviii, xxx, 9, 39–41, 46–50, 53–4, 55, 56, 58–9, 61, 65, 71, 73, 76, 78, 80, 82, 85, 89–90, 92–3, 99, 101, 105, 109, 115, 143, 155, 185, 187, 206, 232, 237, 258, 263, 266–8, 271
Parisian, 7, 10, 41, 48, 56–9, 61, 199
    woman, 39, 42, 46–7, 60–1, 63, 77

womanhood, 47, 58
  chic, 59
  sophistication, 59
Pastells, Pablo, 154
pasyon, 22, 131
Paterno, Pedro, 161, 205, 268
patria, 177–81, 225, 256
patriotic love, xix, xxix, 258
patriotism, xviii, xxv, xxviii, xxxi, 99, 108, 176, 207, 211, 254, 258–9, *see also* patriotic love
Payo, Pedro, 158
Péladan, Adrien, 122
penis pins, 214–5, 248
Peratoner, Amancio, 225
Perrot, Michelle, 46, 69, 78
Petite Suzanne, 185–7, 197
pharmacies, 7, 236, *see also* bioticas
philology, xxvi
physician, xxvii–xxviii, 155–7, 164, 177–8, 188, 199, 222, 225, 227, 233–7, 242, 251–2, 260, 263, 267, 269, 271–2, 274
Pigafetta, Antonio, 208, 215
Pilar, Santiago Albano, xiii, 41, 44, 57, 69–70, 81
Pissarro, Camille, 50
Plaza de Cataluña, xvii
Ploss, Heinrich, 198, 200–1, 243–4
poetry, xx, xxiv, xxviii, 1, 7, 14, 16, 21, 131, 180
Ponce, Mariano, xv, xvii, 91, 93, 115, 130, 193, 269
Potenciana, Santa, 1
Pratt, Mary Louise, 87, 91, 115
principalia, 4
propaganda, xix–xx, 66, 91, 150, 200, 202, 211, 217, 255, 261–3, 270–3
propagandista, xi–xii, xx–xxii, xxiv–xxxiii, 40, 49, 52, 66, 71, 77–8, 84, 86–7, 89, 91–3, 100–1, 105, 108, 110, 112, 115, 118–9, 121, 125–6, 129–30, 133–40, 142, 144–5, 151–3, 177, 201, 204–5, 219, 222, 254–9, 265, 268, 272–3
prostitute, xxvii, 4, 5, 18–20, 40, 42–3, 46–7, 54, 56, 59, 76–7, 105, 127, 144, 175, 187, 189, 251, 258
prostitution, xxvii, 4, 18–20, 35, 54, 56, 61, 76–7, 175, 201, 212–3, 227

querida, 19, 71, *see also* concubine

Rafael, Vicente L., xiii, xxiv–xxvii, xxxii, 90, 95, 99, 120
Real Compañía de Filipinas, 4
Recollect, 31, 118, 142
Regidor, Antonio, 76, 161, 177, 270–1
Regidor Manuel (also Raimundo Geler), 177, 271
Renan, Ernst, 121, 143
Renoir, Auguste, 50
Republican, xxiii, 43, 97, 265, 271
Retana, Wenceslao, 10–1, 87, 112, 203, 205, 247
Reyes, Isabelo de los, 205, 207, 210–1, 216, 245, 269
Reyes, Soledad, 15, 36
Rivera, Leonor, 163–5, 167, 194, 240
Rizal, José, xi–xiii, xv–xvi, xvii–xviii, xxv–xxvii, xxx, xxxiii, 3–4, 15, 18, 21, 27–9, 40, 43, 48, 50–4, 56, 66, 75, 79–80, 84, 86, 91–8, 100–1, 105, 108–9, 113–5, 117–8, 120–1, 123–5,

128–9, 133–7, 139, 142–4,
147–8, 150, 153–68, 170–92,
194–5, 199–217, 219, 222,
224, 228, 230–40, 242–3, 245,
251–2, 254, 256, 258, 260–1,
264, 271, 274
Rizal, Josefa, 232, 240
Rizal, Lucia, 232–4
Rada, Martin de, 208
Rizal, María, 237–9, 253
Rizal, Narcisa, 233–4, 239, 252–3
Rizal, Olimpia, 233, 252
Rizal, Paciano, 272
Rizal, Saturnina, 231–4, 236–7,
251–2, 274
Rizal, Soledad, 233, 239–41, 253
Rizal, Teodora Alonso, 118, 153
Rizal, Trinidad, 232, 239–40, 253
Rocha, Lorenzo, 51
Rodriguez de Ureta, Antonia, 104–5
Roman, 14, 111, 266
Romance, 11, 14–6, 18, 28, 30,
106, 108, 128
Rome, 40, 50, 212, 227, 266
Rousseau, Henri, 50
Roxas, Baldomero, 106
Roxas, Felix, 94, 272

Saéz, Agustín, 51
Salpetrière, xxviii
San Agustin, Gaspar, 208
Sand, George, 122
Sanskrit, 202
Sartre, Jean-Paul, 70
Schreiner, Olive, xxvii
secular, xxx, 16, 22, 179–80, 263,
271
sex, xi, xix, xxi–xxiii, xxvii–xxviii,
5, 23, 26, 30, 42, 46, 56, 59,
66, 78, 110, 121, 131, 170,
184, 198, 202, 208, 211, 213,
217–8, 220, 224–8, 255–6
sexual anarchy, xxvii, 176
sexual desire, xix, xxx, 3–4, 54,
103, 107–8, 155, 162, 167,
169–70, 176–7, 191, 208,
217–23, 225, 242–3
sexual difference, xxi, xxiv,
xxviii, 106–8, 174
sexual pleasure, xxxi, 70, 128,
176, 198, 215, 225–6, 242
science, xxviii, xxxii, 21, 37, 134,
138, 157–8, 178–81, 199, 222,
224–5, 230–1
biomedical, xxvi, 157
Schumacher, John, xx
scientia, 181–3
Showalter, Elaine, 46
Siegel, James T., xix
sodomy, 212–5, 224
Spain, xi, xvii, xx, xxvi, xxxii, 1,
4, 9, 11, 32, 34, 40–1, 50, 66,
80, 85–8, 90–3, 104–5, 108,
117, 119, 129, 130–1, 134–5,
139–40, 143, 152, 169, 177,
219, 225, 227, 243, 260–74
Peninsula, xx, 87, 91, 120, 155,
172
Spanish, xii, xiv, xvii–xviii, xx,
xxiv–xxv, xxviii, xxx, 2–4,
9–10, 12–4, 17–22, 26, 28, 30,
33–4, 40–1, 43, 46, 50–2, 65–6,
76, 78–9, 82, 84–9, 91–2, 95,
97, 101, 103–12, 117–20,
126–7, 129, 134, 137–40, 142,
145, 147, 149–50, 155, 159,
161, 163, 172–4, 187, 190,
194, 197, 199–203, 205–9,
213, 216–22, 225, 230, 233,
247, 249–50, 254–5, 261–5,
267–72, 274

sperm, 42
   spermatic expenditure, xxviii, 226, 228
syphilis, 18

Taga-ilog, 84, 92, 265, *see also* Antonio Luna
Tagalog, xii, xiv, 2, 12–4, 17, 19–20, 22, 96, 101, 130, 139, 157, 161, 172, 200–2, 210, 213, 218, 220–2, 232, 245, 249–50
Teatro Tagalo, 14–5
tikbalang, 15–6
Toming (Kapitan), 12–4
Tondo, 5
Toulouse-Lautrec, Henri de, 50
tuberculosis, xi, xvii, xxvi, 262, 265, 267

Uban, 12
Universidad Central de Madrid, 155–6, 264, 269
Universidad de Santo Tomás, 3, 118, 158, 163, 260–2, 265–74
Urbana at Feliza, 22–6
urbanidad, xxix, 5, 11, 20–1, 23, 254–5
uterus, 226–7, 233–4, 236, 252

Valenzuela, Leonor, 165
van Gogh, Vincent, 50
Velázquez, Diego, 51
venereal disease, 18, 20, 225, 227
Ventura, Valentin, 71, 98, 181, 184–5, 187, 190–1, 274
Victory of Death, 181, 183–4
Viola, Maximo, 188–9, 274
virgin, 2, 10, 15, 123–4, 126, 132, 171–2, 175, 201, 211, 217, 222, 225
Virgin Mary, 10, 16, 29
virginity, 17, 30, 198, 201
virility, xxviii, xxxi, 71
Visayas, 200–2, 210–1, 214
Voltaire, François-Marie Arouet, 121, 143, 147

Wells, H.G., 206
Wendt, Reinhardt, 16

Zamora, Felipe, 232–4, 236, 274
Zeldin, Theodore, 60
Zola, Émile, 50, 76, 121–2, 157–8, 192
Zorrilla, Manuel Ruiz, 265

www.ingramcontent.com/pod-product-compliance
Lightning Source LLC
Chambersburg PA
CBHW030606230426
43661CB00053B/1860